Don't Be a Victim

DON'T BE A VICTIM

Fighting Back Against
America's Crime Wave

NANCY GRACE

WITH JOHN HASSAN

GRAND CENTRAL
PUBLISHING
New York Boston

Grand Central Publishing
Hachette Book Group
1290 Avenue of the Americas, New York, NY 10104
grandcentralpublishing.com
twitter.com/grandcentralpub

First published in hardcover and ebook by Grand Central Publishing in June 2020
First Trade Paperback Edition: September 2021

Grand Central Publishing is a division of Hachette Book Group, Inc. The Grand Central Publishing name and logo is a trademark of Hachette Book Group, Inc.

The publisher is not responsible for websites (or their content) that are not owned by the publisher.

The Hachette Speakers Bureau provides a wide range of authors for speaking events. To find out more, go to www.hachettespeakersbureau.com or call (866) 376-6591.

The Library of Congress has cataloged the hardcover as follows:
Names: Grace, Nancy, author. | Hassan, John, author.
Title: Don't be a victim : fighting back against America's crime wave / Nancy Grace and John Hassan.
Description: First edition. | New York : Grand Central Publishing, 2020. | Includes index.
Identifiers: LCCN 2019049269 | ISBN 9781538732298 (hardcover) | ISBN 9781538732274 (ebook)
Subjects: LCSH: Victims of crimes--United States. | Self-protective behavior--United States.
Classification: LCC HV6250.3.U5 G73 2020 | DDC 613.6--dc23
LC record available at https://lccn.loc.gov/2019049269

ISBNs: 978-1-5387-3228-1 (trade paperback), 978-1-5387-3227-4 (ebook)

Printed in the United States of America

LSC-C

Printing 1, 2021

To David
You changed my life

Contents

Introduction

Now it seems like another world, a world where I set out to follow my dream of teaching Shakespearean literature. When I studied all of his works in the silence of a library, everything else seemed to disappear. I couldn't think of anything I'd rather do, and I planned a lifetime of doing just that.

But that all changed. I remember pushing through the heavy doors of Mercer University's math building. I had just finished a statistics exam and after a few more classes, I was heading for a graduate program in Shakespearean studies. It was all right there within my reach, and I distinctly remember thinking as I stepped out of the darkened halls how the world looked so bright and shiny and new outside. I headed across campus to my job in the library, stopping to use a pay phone and let the librarians know I was en route. They gave me the message to call my fiancé's sister, Judy.

Right then, I knew.

I kept trying to dial the numbers, but my hand wouldn't cooperate. It was like a moth batting around an outdoor porch light, back and forth in erratic, darting movements. I couldn't quite get the numbers straight. But then, I did. I don't know how I knew, but I knew. I asked her one question: "Is Keith gone?"

She said yes.

I hung up the phone, and that was the beginning of a dark, hazy blur...a blur that ended up lasting for years.

Everything was fine, everything was perfect, and then, in a flash, it all changed. Just before our wedding, Keith's world ended. My world exploded.

I grew up in a world where there was nothing but tall pine trees and soybean fields as far as the eye could see, where violence was something unknown and very, very far away. We could ride our bikes anywhere we wanted after school. We could build forts between pine trees and only come home when we'd hear chimes in the church steeple telling us it was six o'clock and time for supper. I could explore rushing streams and pastures full of cows munching grass and edged with trees. I could swing from a long rope out in a circle over a deep gully full of water, crash-running once I hit the soil when the circle ended. Keith's murder changed all that.

I found out about an alternate universe, a world of violence and unnamed hate. I couldn't eat, couldn't sleep. I couldn't stand to hear music or the TV. My mom had to stop the clocks because I couldn't bear the *tick-tick-tick*ing. I dropped out of school.

Weeks, then months passed. I would sit for days on our front porch in the hot sun. I was fading away mentally and physically. Nothing mattered.

In a last-ditch effort, my parents sent me to visit my sister, who had made it to the Wharton School in Philadelphia. I remember sitting on a bench watching students pouring in and out of the bookstore. They were getting books and supplies to go back to school for fall semester. Back to school . . . I knew I could never be happy in a classroom, not anymore. I had to *do something*, but what? Sitting on that bench outdoors in the late afternoon, I had an inkling of an idea . . . an inkling that turned into a life's devotion. Heaven threw me a rope, and even though I didn't realize it at the time, I grabbed it.

Yes, I went back to school, but teaching literature was no longer an option for me. My one burning goal was to somehow get into law school and then fight crime with all my might.

I had only one reference to present to the law school admissions department, from my Sunday school teacher. I remember riding by the law school and seeing the lights burning in the library into the night and wondering if I could possibly get in, wondering if good grades and a letter from a Sunday school teacher could possibly be enough. And then, I got a letter. It was sitting in our black metal mailbox at the end of our driveway near the road, which had finally been paved over just a few years before. The pavement is important because when I opened the letter and read it, I remember the hard asphalt when I went down on my knees and thanked God. I got in.

Before my first day of law school, I actually had to look up the definitions of *plaintiff* and *defendant*. It took me seven years before I struck my first jury and tried my first jury trial in inner-city Atlanta, which was at the time one of the murder capitals of the country.

For the next ten years I had a life very different from the way it was before or after. For ten years, an ordinary person like me had an extraordinary opportunity to speak for those who could not speak for themselves and be their voice in courts of law.

Fighting crime is nothing like what you see on TV and in movies. Being on a real murder scene is something I wish on no one. The sight, the smell, the malice hanging in the air is something I never forget. It sticks with you.

Other cases stuck in my heart. I remember a little girl with a hundred pigtails on her head, just three feet tall. She was the victim of repeated rapes by Mommy's boyfriend. Turned out he had been molesting young girls for thirty years. I found seven of them and brought "similar transactions" before the jury when the little girls were too afraid to testify. But they did.

I remember Ms. Leola, the mom of a teen boy gunned down in cold blood over ten dollars, knitting during the trial when testimony was too raw or crime scene photos and bloody clothes were too unsettling for her to look up. But Ms. Leola wouldn't leave, not during witnesses, not during arguments, not during jury selection, not during graphic photos of her son on the autopsy table as the medical examiner testified to mortal wounds. Standing at the jury rail, I looked over at her sitting in the very first row behind me. Ms. Leola would look right back at me, smile and continue knitting, urging me on. She gave me strength, and even the recollection of her renews me.

I remember so many families of murder victims lining up to come into the courtroom and sitting on the hard wooden pews, numb. Standing before many a jury to deliver final closing arguments, I argued this: there are people in our society who are too weak, too poor, too afraid, or too intimidated to speak for themselves and be heard. It is our duty to speak for them and fight injustice in every way we can, in every place we can, whenever we can, as hard as we can, for as long as we can.

After well over twenty years, I still carried the same grief and the same burden, even in my personal life. I couldn't bring myself to risk it again, loving and losing and going back into a world of hurt. I accepted that after Keith's murder, being a wife and mother would never be for me. But just before my window closed, a miracle happened. I married David and had my miracle twins, John David and Lucy. I never thought I would have joy in my life again, but I do. With that joy comes an overpowering drive to protect them, to never allow violence or evil to destroy their lives the way it nearly destroyed mine.

So many times at night, I watch them sleep and I imagine the dream world they visit, where it is innocent, peaceful, safe. My mind plays back what I remember from the years I prosecuted, the thousands of cases I worked and covered. When all is said and done, my message is the same one I argued to every jury: do all you can to fight the fight, as long as you can and wherever you can.

I still hear my own words ringing in my head. I carried that message from juries of twelve to juries of hundreds of thousands per minute, whether on *Crime Stories*, Sirius XM, ABC, NBC, CBS, Oxygen— different juries, but always the same message. And now, I bring that message along with all the cases I tried and pled and investigated, every legal argument I've ever made, and every story I've ever covered, and pour them all into this book. For you.

Don't be a victim. Join me. Fight back.

PART ONE

How Do I Protect My Child?

CHAPTER ONE

Your Child Safe at School

I remember one night, sitting in the hair and makeup chair at CNN-HLN headquarters, just before airtime. That means it was about seven p.m. because I hadn't left yet to walk to the studio. I was on a conference call with staffers in New York, L.A., and Atlanta, talking about the lead story for that night. Just as we were finishing up, a phone buzzed. My longtime friend and makeup artist, Shayzon, got a call. Her face went ghost white as she listened to the voice on the other end.

When she hung up, she just stared at me blankly.

"Shay, what is it?"

I instinctively stood up, the long makeup cape still around my neck covering my clothes. She didn't speak. I repeated the same question, and she answered in two words.

"Arlie's gone."

Arlie is her son, Arlington.

"What do you mean, Arlie's gone?" I can still remember my words coming out harshly.

"He didn't get off the school bus. He's not answering his cell."

Instead of hugging her, I immediately started firing off questions as we hurriedly packed all her things to leave. Where was he last seen? Where was her younger daughter? Was she safe? When did they realize he was gone? A million questions. Then the big question: Is there any reason to think he was ever on the school bus to start with?

We all rushed her to the elevator to leave, and on the way she collapsed and crumpled into a ball with her back against the cement wall in the employee hallway. I tried to pull her up, but she wouldn't budge. I knelt down close to her face, and she said, "Nancy, I know what's happening. We cover it every night...he's gone!"

I will never forget the look on her face as long as I live...completely without hope. I hugged her and got her up and was saying all sorts of things like "We'll find him. Arlie's too smart to get into somebody's car. He's probably at some little friend's house playing video games right now. I'll be on my way there in one hour."

She got on the elevator, and as it closed, she looked me in the face and said, "He doesn't really play video games." The doors shut and she was gone.

School buses have been around forever in our country. The sight of a yellow school bus trundling down the road is familiar and comforting. Nearly all of us have been on them, including during our early formative years en route to elementary school. We grew up catching the school bus, climbing up its steps, settling into a shared seat, and ending up, every time, safe at school.

Believe it or not, over 25 million children ride the school bus every day in our country. My dear friend Marc Klaas founded KlaasKids after his daughter Polly was kidnapped. He tells me that the dark side of that stat is that nearly 40 percent of all attempted child kidnappings take place when a child is walking or riding a bike to or from school or walking to or from the school bus. A friend at the National Center for Missing and Exploited Children confirms those statistics and it took a while for me to grasp the numbers. Let that soak in: nearly 40 percent of all child kidnapping attempts are related to school, bus stops, and school routes.

Read on.

BEN OWNBY

Rural Missouri. A straight-A student and Boy Scout jumped the last step of his school bus, hit the ground, and ran toward home. Beaufort was sunny that January day in 2007 as he ran down the gravel road. Minutes later, the boy's friend spotted a white pickup with a camper top speeding away, but the Boy Scout, Ben Ownby, was no longer walking along the gravel road. He was gone.

Ownby's parents were beside themselves. Where was their boy? In hours, searchers by foot, by air, ATV, and horseback were scouring the hilly terrain sixty miles south of St. Louis. Even with that incredible effort, they turned up nothing.

Days passed and then, finally, there was a break in the case. Kirkwood police officers spotted a white truck with a cab attached. Franklin County Sheriff's Department, working off the truck's plates, determined who and where the owner of the truck was and then descended on the home of Michael Devlin. Up until that time, Devlin, a white male in his forties, had no known criminal history and remained under the radar. When cops swarmed his place, they found Ben Ownby, alive. To their shock, they found another boy who had disappeared at age eleven from his parents' home in Richwoods when he left to go ride his bike and never came back. Devlin had held the second boy, Shawn Hornbeck, for four long years.

Craig Akers, Shawn's stepdad, had quit his job in software design to devote his time to a foundation named after Shawn. He and Shawn's mom, Pam, drained their entire savings to search for Shawn, exploring all avenues, including psychics. At the time of his rescue, Shawn stated Devlin had ordered him to help "find" a younger boy to kidnap. Shawn feared Devlin was set to kill him once Devlin replaced him with a newer, younger victim. Since being found following four years of molestation in captivity, Hornbeck has disappeared from the public eye.

ALIANNA DEFREEZE

It was cold in Cleveland, Ohio, the morning of January 26, 2017, when fourteen-year-old Alianna left for a bus to school at seven a.m., but she was bright-eyed and eager to get to tutoring early, so off she went. She had quite a trek to get to special tutoring before school, but it was a route she'd traveled often. The day passed as usual, but by four thirty, Alianna wasn't home. Mom and Dad started an odyssey of frantic calls before, to their shock, they learned their girl never made it to school that morning.

But why? Her family had specifically signed up for text message alerts from the school to be notified if Alianna did not arrive or was ever absent. The school knew about Alianna's developmental disability and that she practically never missed school. But because no text came, ten hours were lost, precluding an immediate and potentially life-saving search for Alianna. Realizing late in the afternoon that their girl never made it to school, her parents called police.

Weighing heavy on her family was the knowledge that with each passing hour, the likelihood of finding Alianna alive dwindled drastically. The search was on, including wading through security footage from the buses she took to school and their pickup and drop-off points. The young girl with long dark hair was spotted, which normally would have been a huge victory, but the surveillance video continued. It showed her getting off her bus en route to school, on time, around seven a.m. that morning. In the video, Alianna is smiling and laughing.

She crosses the street at East 93rd, but then she's stopped outside a church by a man. She steps back away from him and continues on. As the video shows, he follows. Shortly after, the video shows the same man leading Alianna through a field toward Fuller Avenue.

Minutes, then hours, then three days passed by the time Cleveland police officer Willie Hodges and his partner were sent to check vacant houses. They found a house with the back door swinging wide open. When Hodges stepped through the doorway, he saw a trail of blood from the living room all the way to a closed door. Kicking the door open, he found the lifeless body of missing schoolgirl Alianna. Scattered through the abandoned home were Alianna's school clothes, a bloody drill, a hammer, and a box cutter.

Cuyahoga County's deputy medical examiner, David Dolinak, observed that Alianna's injuries were so numerous and severe that he couldn't positively say exactly which one caused her death. Police learned the man in the video, forty-five-year-old registered sex offender Christopher Whitaker, had followed her from her bus stop, forced her into the abandoned home, and then raped her, tortured her with a drill, and murdered her.

Alianna's parents say the school's negligence ensured that the last hours of their girl's life were nothing but excruciating, paralyzing, and debilitating physical and mental pain. They claim the school lied when they said they tried to text the parents and that their system failed. The school says they've tried to be supportive of Alianna's parents. I've listened as Alianna's dad told her story, and the pain he is still suffering is just beneath the surface of every word.

Alianna's twisted, heartless killer now sits on death row. In 2019, Alianna's Alert went into effect in Ohio, a law requiring all schools to contact parents and guardians of children who are unaccountably absent from school. But it comes too late for one family.

Alianna's parents still look out the window and imagine their girl walking up the path home.

JAYCEE DUGARD

It was bright and sunny on June 10, 1991, when eleven-year-old Jaycee Dugard headed out on her morning trek up a hill to her school bus stop in rural Lake Tahoe. Mom Terry had left for work and stepdad Carl watched from the garage as she walked by. Doing chores in the garage, he could still easily spot her about a third of a mile away.

But then, at a distance, he saw a gray sedan make a U-turn and head back up the hill toward Jaycee, cutting across the road to swing open the door. In a flash, he saw his daughter being dragged into the car, and he watched it take off. He heard Jaycee scream. He chased after the car on his mountain bike but to no avail. Jaycee was gone.

That horrific moment started mom Terry's descent into a chain-smoking alcohol-soaked hell, and even though husband Carl immediately called 911, she blamed him. But one day, Terry found her strength, making over a half million posters, collecting donations to search for her daughter, waking up when it was still dark outside to write hundreds of letters to the media, hospitals, and homeless shelters, begging them to be on the lookout for Jaycee and speaking with the press ceaselessly. She even went to casinos, rapping on car trunk after car trunk on car after car because a psychic "felt" Jaycee was imprisoned in a trunk.

The nightmare lasted for eighteen years. After several suspicious, unrelated incidents, feds raided the suburban home of Phillip Garrido, a sex offender on parole at the time Jaycee was snatched, and his wife, Nancy. The two lived just three hours away from the Dugard home. In a backyard shed, they found Jaycee, alive. With her were two other little girls. They were Jaycee's. Their father was her kidnapper and tormenter, Phillip Garrido.

The horrible day Jaycee vanished, the two Garridos stun-gunned Jaycee and abducted her. For the next eighteen years, she was held captive and raped by Garrido. Today, Garrido and his minion are both in prison, and Terry has her daughter back. They lost eighteen years together. But the miracle is that Jaycee lived to make it back to her mother's arms.

ETAN PATZ

On a sunny Friday morning, May 25, 1979, six-year-old Etan Patz sprinted out of his family's apartment in SoHo, headed for school. After much practice, that Friday would be his very first solo trip walking the two blocks to his school bus stop. Etan was dressed in his black "Future Flight Captain" pilot cap, blue jeans, blue tennis shoes with stripes, and a blue corduroy jacket.

But Etan did not come home after school. Mom Julie called the school and discovered that while his teacher had marked him absent, she never notified the principal. Julie called police. Nearly one hundred police plus bloodhounds combed the area for weeks. Neighbors and volunteers joined the effort to canvass the city, flooding it with missing posters. Etan was the first child ever to appear on a milk carton, and even though his photo was projected larger than life on screens in Times Square, Etan never came home.

Decades later, it was determined that Etan was kidnapped and murdered the same morning he walked out of the family apartment. Pedro Hernandez confessed to the murder, and after one basement excavation that yielded nothing, one mistrial, and twenty years of heartbreak, Hernandez was finally convicted for Etan's murder. One six-year-old little boy, Etan Patz, launched the missing children movement that lives to this day, major legislation, and the national milk-carton campaign. Etan's case led to President Ronald Reagan declaring an annual National Missing Children's Day, May 25. While all those accomplishments are irreplaceable, it is cold, cold comfort for Etan's parents.

True cases of children gone missing in and around schools and bus stops go on and on. Each one is a heartbreak, but what can we do to fight back?

SAFETY TIPS FOR BUS STOPS, BUS ROUTES, AND SCHOOL ARRIVALS

- Instruct your child's school to call and text you immediately if your child is absent, and insist that they follow through.
- Tell your child that, if confronted by a stranger, they should not worry about schoolbooks, backpacks, or belongings. Drop them and run.
- Put everything inside your child's backpack or school bag and keep it secure so that the child doesn't drop things on the way, causing them to bend over and be distracted. Don't give a predator an edge.
- Never have your child's belongings monogrammed or stylized with their name or initials. This makes it so much easier for a predator to get your child's attention by calling out their name, and in that one moment they attack. Being called by their name also lulls a child into the belief the predator knows them and their family.
- Get your child to the bus stop ten minutes early. You do not want them left stranded and alone at the bus stop (or running in the street after the bus that just left).
- Walk your child to the bus stop, if possible. Same for after school. Be there if you can.
- If you do walk your child to the bus stop, wait for the bus. It won't take long. Some of my happiest moments are getting the twins to school. We have so much fun, we get to talk and laugh and I hear about what they think will happen that day. I love it. It's not a chore.
- If you can't walk your child, try to have your child walk with another mom or dad that can or already does walk to the stop in the mornings. Same thing for after school.
- If there is no adult, have your child travel with a group. I walked to the school bus stop all through elementary school and also walked home after school. By the time I left for the bus in the mornings, both my parents were typically long gone for work. We were latchkey kids, so no one was there when I was walking home. I don't know if my mom or dad warned me to do this—they must have—but we always traveled in a pack. Any child is more vulnerable when alone.
- Long story short: if you or another adult can't walk your children to the bus, have them walk in a group with other children if possible. There is safety in numbers. Look at the animal world: there's a reason they travel in packs. An added safety bonus is that drivers can spot groups more easily.

- If groups don't form daily and naturally, join with other parents in the neighborhood to create a bus walk group.
- Walk the route with your child before they walk it alone. Use the most direct and the safest route. Avoid isolated shortcuts and abandoned structures, anything that is a spot where a potential predator could lie in wait. You won't know this until you walk the route yourself.
- Train your child to stop, look left, right, and left again before crossing. This isn't just to spot oncoming traffic. It's also to spot cars slowing down to approach your child as in the Jaycee Dugard and Ben Ownby kidnappings and to spot anyone loitering nearby.
- Instruct your child not to become engrossed with games or devices like smartphones, Switches, and Game Boys at the bus stop. They need to stay alert to what's happening around them. Also, horseplay can end up with someone being unintentionally shoved into the street.
- Teach your children to be especially careful in bad weather when they are focusing on an umbrella, a raincoat, and staying dry, and not on what's happening around them.
- Go to the bus stop yourself and show your child where to stand. They need to stay at least ten to fifteen feet from the road not only to be safe from traffic zooming by (even though it's a school bus stop zone) but also to make it more difficult to be snatched. If your child is five to ten feet from the street, a bad guy must get out of the car to get to your child. Jaycee was near the street.
- Move heaven and earth to get surveillance cameras at your child's stop.
- If your child's bus stop is on or near a neighbor's property, take it upon yourself to get to know them. Visit, introduce your child, and get their number to program into your child's phone if they have one. Don't necessarily program it in by name because your child may not remember the name. Use an identifier such as "School Bus Stop Lady." You never know when that number could make all the difference in the world.
- Teach your child to wait for the bus to come to a complete stop before crossing in front of it, not behind, and to try to make eye contact with the driver first. This way, the driver knows they are crossing, and you want the driver's complete attention on your child as people are jostling and moving to get onto that bus. A distracted driver can

provide a moment for a predator to act. There is a blind spot in the very back of a school bus that the driver can't see. It is a perfect spot for predators.

- Your child must never crawl under the bus to retrieve anything.
- Have your child look both ways when exiting the school bus. If an adult is loitering there that your child doesn't recognize, have your child alert the bus driver, get back on the bus, and call Mom or Dad immediately.
- Make sure your child doesn't have strings or straps hanging from coats, sweatshirts, jackets, or backpacks that are easy to grab by anyone, whether it's another child roughhousing or an adult.
- Teach your child to run away from danger and not toward it, including away from anyone getting too close to them. For instance, if a car approaches them at or near a bus stop, they are to run *away* from the direction the car is headed and to try to cross barriers that a car can't cross, like a street-side ditch, a yard, a gate, a flight of stairs. A criminal is not likely to leave his car to attempt a grab.
- Go over neighborhood escape routes with your child. Walk the route with them. For instance, whose home can they run to if you're not there? Is there a path or a backyard they can run through where a perp in a car likely wouldn't follow? Go from the bus stop to your home and identify the escape routes. Then, practice. To make it less scary, you be "it" and let your child chase you.
- Locate and identify homes of neighbors that are a safe place for your child to run to if they are approached going to or from the bus stop. Discuss the scenario with those particular neighbors. Think of neighbors who may be retired, work at home, or have hours that place them there at bus stop times. Then practice with your child. A known safe house is preferable, but tell them to bang on any neighbor's door if there is no other alternative. They should do anything they can to get to safety.
- Train your child to pretend they are going to a home if they are followed by a car and there are no other options, even if the home is unoccupied. It's highly unlikely a predator will exit his car and risk being seen or apprehended to chase your child around to the back of a home. This is not ideal, but is a choice when out of options.
- Your child must never go near a vehicle or get into one without your permission. Tell them that you will *never* ask someone to pull up to

the bus stop or along the way and drive them to or from school. Warn your child that someone else might claim you said to pick them up, but that will *never* be true. Instruct your child to never leave or get in a car under those circumstances

- Determine a family code word to use in situations when someone else must pick up your child. Only those you authorize to pick up your child will know the secret code word. Tell your child to practice.
- Remind your child that their safety is much more important than being polite to a stranger.
- Teach your child not to even engage in a conversation with a stranger at the bus stop, particularly one in a car. Once the attacker is close enough to have a conversation, forcing a child into their vehicle is easy.
- Your child must know that they can and must make a scene in public, even though normally that's exactly what they are not supposed to do. You must teach your child that if approached by a stranger or pulled toward a car, they must scream, kick, punch, and scratch as much and as loudly as possible. Throw books and belongings. *Anything!* I did it in the middle of a Toys "R" Us when I couldn't find John David. Throw inhibition to the wind—it could be a matter of life or death. Noise, and lots of it, could be your child's best defense.
- The National Center for Missing and Exploited Children tells me that 84 percent of the children who escape a kidnapping attempt do so by screaming, kicking, running, and generally calling attention to the kidnapper. The remaining 16 percent were rescued by either a Good Samaritan or a parent. The phrase for them to yell is "Help me! This is not my dad/mom!"
- Consider being a bus stop mom or dad and joining a core group of parents willing to rotate as volunteers at the school bus stop.
- It's your duty to know where your child is at all times, including what time they are getting on and off that bus and how long it will take them to get to and from their departure point and destination. Knowing drop-off and pick-up times is critical because they are perfect opportunities for predators. Kidnappers often watch bus stops in the mornings and afternoons, trolling to look for targets.
- Go to the bus stop with your child and act out what they are supposed to do in case of a threat. Don't leave it to your child to figure it out on their own. They can't. Then, practice.

- If your child has a cell phone, keep the tracker on and put Mom and Dad on speed dial.
- Know who is driving your child's bus. That's easy.
- Make sure there has been a security check on the bus driver.
- If you have home surveillance cameras, train them to follow your child as far down the street as possible and have other parents in the neighborhood do the same.
- Go to your child's school at least once for bus loading in the afternoon. Make sure your child understands which bus to board.
- Make it easy for your child to confide in you so they can freely tell you if there is something at or about the bus stop that scares them or makes them feel bad, uncomfortable, or confused.
- Teach your child to immediately tell the bus driver and their teacher if they are approached by an adult at the bus stop. Ensure that the driver and teacher know that they are to immediately call you if this happens.

For more information on how to help your kids play an active role in their own safety, visit revvedupkids.org. There is a ton of information and smart ideas. They offer a variety of workshops, too. Here is their advice on kids and self-defense: be **smart** (recognize dangerous people and avoid unsafe situations) and be **strong** (use voice and body with power and confidence to escape an attacker) so they can be **safe** from predators, sex abuse, and violence.

THE REST OF THE STORY

The night that Arlie disappeared, I raced off the set and jumped in the car to go help find him. Flying down the interstate as fast as I could, I called Shay, hoping she could pick up. She answered and said three words:

"I have him."

We both burst into tears and thanked God over the phone! Turns out Arlie took a different school bus with his older girl cousin. The two had gone all the way across town to a church youth singing event. In the excitement, Arlie left his cell phone, turned off, in a zippered compartment of his backpack. Of all things...it's kind of hard to reprimand your teen for going to a church sing-off. But Arlie did get a stern talking-to, in between hugs, tears, and kisses. In fact, Shay was so beside herself that Arlie's little sister, London, got the reprimand, too. It was the scariest—and the happiest—night of their lives.

Rest of the story? Today, Arlie is six foot four and wants to write music. I've listened to his work, and it's amazing. He has dark brown eyes and a beautiful, perfect smile. I look up at him now, he's so tall, but I remember when he was a little boy lost. But now, he's found.

Shay's happy ending.

MOM'S SCHOOL PICKUP NIGHTMARE

It was a gorgeous spring morning in Florida on March 10, 2017, when Port Orange mom Holly Smith showed up at Pathways Early Learning Center. Holly was there to pick up her four-year-old daughter, but when she approached the front desk, she got the shock of a lifetime: she was told her daughter was gone! Where? A Pathways staffer told Holly the girl's mom had already retrieved her. *Her daughter's mom? What?*

Needless to say, a very heated exchange ensued. Holly tried repeatedly to convince daycare staff she was the true mom. Holly got nowhere and she finally called police. Then, a parent's worst nightmare came true for the thirty-two-year-old mom. She learned her baby girl had been handed over to a complete stranger in what the daycare called a "mix-up." And the stranger had left with the toddler an hour before Holly arrived!

With tears streaming down her face, Holly told 911 that another woman had shown ID and told the daycare that she, Holly, approved the pickup. That's all it takes to take a baby out of a registered daycare? An ID and a story?

To make it worse, Holly then described the daycare staff telling her that her daughter didn't want to go with the woman and that someone on the phone claiming to be the mom actually ordered the little girl to leave with the stranger. In the 911 call, it's explained that the woman who showed up at Pathways claimed to be Holly's co-worker. She said she was babysitting that day and had never met the child, which would explain the tot's reaction. Then, to top it all off, the Pathways surveillance cameras weren't working, so there was no way to determine who took the child.

Part of the irony is that Holly chose Pathways because she thought it was super safe. She was impressed by its security measures, which included—or so she thought—a fingerprint identification system on a touch screen computer. She was also told that caregivers like babysitters and nannies had to present photo identification to pick up a child.

So, what went wrong and where was her little girl?

At some point, the staff realized they had an extra child on location and had "handed off" the wrong child. The woman finally came back with Holly's baby girl, claiming she didn't know she'd taken the wrong tot. Needless to say, Holly removed her child from Pathways Early Learning. No criminal charges were ever filed.

Holly's baby was safe and sound, but to this day, I remain agitated and upset about the case because...what if?

SUBSTITUTE TEACHER HANDS CHILD OVER TO STRANGER

Another little girl in another city didn't make it home when the school day ended. A substitute teacher at Philadelphia's Bryant Elementary gave a five-year-old girl to a complete stranger. A woman walked into the school, intentionally posing as the mom. She headed not to the office, but directly to the tot's class and told the sub she'd come early for her little girl.

The facts are clear. Five-year-old Nailla's mom dropped her off around eight forty-five in the morning. Only five minutes later, another woman entered Nailla's classroom, called her by name, and said she was Nailla's mom. She told the sub she wanted to take Nailla out to breakfast and that she'd already signed her daughter out at the office. Since the imposter knew Nailla by name, the sub let her walk out with the girl!

In a sickening twist, surveillance video shows the imposter-mom leading Nailla through the school hallways and out the door. This was wrong on so many levels. First, school policy was that all pick-ups must report to the school office, show ID, and get screened. But notwithstanding the rules, the sub handed the little girl over like she was handing over a loaf of bread at the grocery checkout. Imagine handing over a little child to someone who just "shows up"!

Six crucial hours had passed before anyone realized Nailla was missing, and it was only discovered when her daycare came to pick her up at the end of the school day. An intense search for the missing girl ensued, going all day and into the evening. Then, fate intervened.

A heroic Philadelphia sanitation worker just happened to be near a dark public playground at four thirty the following morning. It was there, under a set of bleachers, that he found little Nailla all alone, shivering, crying for help. She was naked except for a T-shirt. The rest of her clothes, including her pants and underwear, were gone. Nailla told police a stranger took her from her school, blindfolded her, and led her to a nearby house.

How could this happen? In my line of work, there are very few happy endings. While I'm so grateful the child is alive, I can't help but have a slow burn when I think of what this little girl endured.

SCHOOL PICK-UP TIPS*

- Make sure your child's school has a protocol for pick-ups.
- That protocol should require proper government-issued photo identification, not just a name on a library card or other similar non-government-issued ID.
- That ID must match a list of people allowed to take your child off school premises.
- The list must be renewed annually, at the very least.
- If someone other than those on that list is to pick up a child, written verification from a known source should be required, such as an email.
- Choose a facility, if possible, that has a main sign-in/sign-out location at which the adult must be seen and sign in before taking a child.
- Make sure the school doors are locked during the day and that visitors are allowed in only when they are buzzed in by school personnel.
- The school personnel should be in a position to see the children before they are taken off the premises.
- It is your duty to know the school personnel, including those in

---

* The following advice also applies to keeping your very little ones safe at daycare (see chapter five).

charge of signing your children in and out. That way, they *know* who is authorized to sign your child out!

- Check to see if security cameras are positioned at the sign-in/sign-out.

- On the rare occasions I or my husband, David, do not pick up the twins, I call and email both the school principal and their teacher and notify them of who is getting the twins and what they will be driving—every time, without fail.

- If I'm picking up another child along with the twins, I make sure the other child's parents do the same, even if it's simply responding to a group email to teachers, principals, and parents.

- Train your child that they are not to leave the school with anyone but you or the few designated friends or family you trust. Make sure your child knows who is authorized to pick them up and that they must use the family password.

- Drop in unannounced and observe drop-off and pick-up. Speak up or inquire if you see something amiss or policies being ignored. A few weeks ago, I had a TV shoot go long. David was out of town, and I had no one to call for help. I had to send another long-time makeup artist I've known since 1994 to the school to get the twins. He was driving his own sports car, not my old beat-up minivan. I shot off an email to several teachers, the principal, the receptionist, and my husband saying there would be a different face at carpool. It all went off without a hitch...but a week later a very nice mom approached me at the school band performance. She said she saw a strange man in a sports car, not David, getting the twins and that she was worried. I couldn't help but wonder...why didn't she text or call me? Even the most lovely people just assume nothing is amiss. Don't assume. *If you see something...say something!*

- Be involved at the school. By now, when staff at the twins' school see my cowboy boots in the distance, they know it's me.

- Get to know the teachers, so they will recognize if a stranger tries to pick up your child.

- Get to know other parents for the same reason.

- Listen to what's happening at pickup.

- Research the school history, including past police reports.

- Read blogs and social media postings and learn about any past incidents at your child's school. Be prepared.

STAYING SAFE AT SCHOOL

The school day itself can present dangers, too. It's another reason to stay close to your kids and know what's going on in their lives, day in and day out.

DROPPED AT SCHOOL AND NEVER SEEN AGAIN

Kyron Horman, a second grader at Skyline Elementary in rural northwest Portland, usually rode the bus to school. Skyline was just two miles from Kyron's home on Sheltered Nook Road. On June 4, 2010, stepmom Terri drove him because he had a science fair that day and needed to set up his display on the red-eyed tree frog. They arrived at eight a.m. and dropped his backpack and coat in his classroom. The stepmom said Kyron headed to the area where the fair was held in another part of the school. The school bell rang at eight forty-five a.m., and stepmom Terri left.

That afternoon, Kyron didn't bounce off the school bus as he always did. As a matter of fact, upon frantic questioning, no one could state they had seen him at school at all after the eight forty-five bell rang. His teacher marked him absent at ten a.m. but explains she assumed he had a doctor's appointment. Thus ensued one of the largest searches the region had ever seen. Kyron Horman has never been seen alive again.

Less than two weeks after Kyron's disappearance, police stopped the search and announced they had upgraded his case from a missing child case to a criminal investigation. Even though his disappearance led to the single largest criminal investigation in Oregon history, Kyron's case remains unsolved. Despite spending over $1.4 million and fielding over four thousand tips, police have been unable to recover his body, and no one has ever been charged. Kyron's natural parents say they hold out hope he is still alive.

TEACHER ABUSE

Loving mom Amber Pack, from Martinsburg, West Virginia, told me she kept noticing her seven-year-old girl, Adri, would come home from school agitated and upset. Adri had begun to cry when it was time to get out of the car and head into Berkeley Heights Elementary School in the morning, but Amber couldn't figure out why. Adri is developmentally disabled and couldn't tell Mommy what was wrong.

After trying repeatedly to figure it all out, even questioning her teachers and teacher's aides, Amber resorted to technology. Amber explained to me in detail how she went online and found just what she was looking for: a "secret" recording device that she hid in Adri's hair, squirreled away in a bow. What she heard was upsetting and shocking, and it changed her life forever. We listened to the audio together. The secret audio purports to reveal horrible verbal abuse and possibly physical abuse as well. I couldn't believe my ears when I heard the cruel threats, taunts, and name calling—all inflicted by the teaching staff!

And this was just eight hours of one day. Amber broke down in tears as we talked. She told me when she would simply look at Adri, she'd begin to cry all over again because of what her little girl, unable to communicate to Mommy, had been through.

The next day, Amber alerted the school district and Martinsburg police. The school seemingly did not respond, and it was only when Amber posted the incident on social media that the school finally placed two employees on administrative leave. I later discovered they were placed on leave *with* pay.

The team representing Adri's mom says the insults and threats are just the tip of the iceberg. They believe they've managed to match the sound of verbal abuse and loud smacks followed by children crying to bruises little Adri had on her body when she got home. Now physical abuse is alleged as well, and other families have come forward with complaints.

The Office for Civil Rights of the US Department of Education has launched its own investigation into possible disability discrimination at the Berkeley school. But even with recordings and bruises, local prosecutors claimed there was not enough evidence for a criminal case, stating: "The verbal treatment of Ms. Pack and Ms. Murphy's children is shocking and disturbing. However, under West Virginia law, verbal abuse of children is not a criminal act."

Allegations that these special needs children are being mistreated every day at school are so upsetting. During a special meeting, the Berkeley County Board of Education accepted the resignations of two

Berkeley Heights special ed aides connected with the tape. Amazingly, the two aides now insist their resignations be annulled and they be placed back on administrative leave with pay and back pay!

In a stunning twist, Amber Pack's lawyer, Ben Salango, confirms the Berkeley County Board of Education is actually suing mom Amber Pack for recording the alleged abuse! They contend Amber was wrong for recording the alleged abuse without the teacher's or aides' consent. And as of this writing, three staffers have been arrested. There is still hope for justice, but at what price?

TEACHER MOLESTATION LEADS TO SUICIDE OF STUDENT ATHLETE

The parents of a teen boy voted "senior prince" in high school are devastated, left with nothing but photos, souvenirs, and memories of their boy. Corbin Madison was one of four students sexually molested by Tennille Whitaker, a married mom and teacher at his Elko, Nevada, school. His parents say that following her conviction and jail sentencing, Corbin was so humiliated when the facts were made public, he killed himself on August 23, 2018.

Investigation showed that Whitaker abused students in a private reading area she set up in her classroom. The reading area couldn't be seen from either windows or the school hallway. Whitaker assigned the victims jobs as student aides and kept them after school to molest them. Claims allege that the Elko County School District never addressed or prevented the molestations even though the Wells High School principal was warned six times that Whitaker was having "unlawful sexual relations with minor students." The warnings came from several ranks: a school district director, a custodial worker, two teachers, and one parent.

Whitaker became brazen, giving the students gifts and alcohol and even driving them to hotels to molest them. A school employee described finding Whitaker with a boy student in a locked classroom with all the lights off. For reasons unknown, nothing was done, and now it's too late.

TIPS FOR KEEPING CHILDREN SAFE DURING THE SCHOOL DAY

- Drop in unannounced. Visit the class. Use a pretext if you have to. I've gone many times to check on the twins unannounced, to give them "medicine" (a gummy vitamin), to take an assignment "left behind" (a note from me to them), drop off supplies (a Hershey's Kiss), bring a jacket. Use your imagination.
- Be involved at the school. You don't have to be president of the PTA. Just be around. I love the twins' school and the people there. If the school and the teachers don't welcome parent involvement, there is something very wrong. Find out what it is.
- Know the teachers. Your child's future is partially in their hands.
- Know other parents in your child's class. Parents often have their ears to the ground.
- Listen to what's happening. Translation: eavesdrop and find out what's going on in your child's classes.
- Arrive at events early and talk to other moms and dads. It's hard to get to extracurricular events on time or at all when you're juggling family and work, but I've learned it's worth it.
- Research the school history as well as particular teachers.
- Check out your child's teacher on Facebook, Instagram, Twitter, and other social media. You might get a surprise.
- If you get bad vibes, ask that your child be transferred to a different teacher.
- If your child is singled out for any special treatment or asked to stay after school, investigate immediately.
- If a teacher shows special interest in your child, that's wonderful! John David had an awesome teacher who gave him extra books and fun assignments, and he loved it! Lucy had a teacher who took extra time to rehearse piano with her. It was incredible. But if the attention is inappropriate, you must report it immediately. I'm not talking about your child getting student of the month or making honor roll. I'm talking about meetings after school for dinner, movies, trips alone of any nature, or visits to the teacher's home—all red flags.
- Don't be shy. Ask questions, and if you don't get answers, approach the school principal and superintendent. If you think this is heli-copter parenting, think again. Protecting your child is your main

job, and you must get answers and action when you think something is off.

SCHOOL SHOOTINGS

The name *Columbine* sends a chill down my spine and brings with
it a sense of dread. But even though the Columbine school massacre
took place in 1999, sending a chilling and deadly message to us all,
school shootings are still plaguing America. They are so memorable
and powerful that they can all be rendered in one or two words: Virginia
Tech, Sandy Hook, Paducah, Santa Fe, Roseburg—the list goes on.
Then came the deadliest school shooting in US history: Parkland.

On Valentine's Day 2018, the morning school bells rang as usual
at Marjory Stoneman Douglas High School in Parkland, Florida. By
that afternoon, the school's name would be known around the world.
Stoneman Douglas sits in an upscale suburb thirty minutes from tourist
town Fort Lauderdale. Teen boy Nikolas Cruz made his way by Uber
to the school that afternoon just before dismissal. With him, he carried
a backpack and a rifle bag. When a Stoneman staff member, knowing
Cruz had been expelled for violent behavior, spotted Cruz heading
toward the school, he simply radioed another staffer. He later claimed
his training required him only to "report" a threat. His colleagues hid
in a closet as Cruz kept walking.

Cruz entered the three-story structure housing thirty classrooms and
about nine hundred students. In his bag, he had an AR-15 semi-
automatic rifle and dozens of ammo clips. Cruz pulled a fire alarm to
create chaos and started firing as students and teachers flooded from
their classes.

When the same staffer heard gunfire, he launched a code red
lockdown.

The shooting itself lasted just minutes. Seventeen people, mostly
young teen students, lay dead. Seventeen more were left in critical
condition. After the shooting, Cruz went to a mall and had a soda,
loitered at the food court, left on foot, and was spotted in a nearby
neighborhood and arrested.

The Parkland shooting massacre reigns in infamy as the single deadliest high school shooting in US history, even worse than the Columbine

High School shooting, which ended with thirteen dead. Most shocking is that there were numerous forewarnings. For years, the local sheriffs were inundated with tips about Cruz's threats to carry out a school shooting. A YouTuber with the name "nikolas cruz" posted about being a school shooter, and the FBI even got a direct tip in the weeks leading up to the Parkland shooting that Cruz had made a death threat.

The Broward County police department came under fire for its poor response and for ignoring so many red flags leading up to the fateful day. We learned of loopholes that allowed Cruz to purchase a weapon even with a history of violence and threats. It was also revealed that at least one deputy stayed outside and hid during the shooting, never trying to stop Cruz.

What do we know about Cruz? He was a member of the school's varsity air rifle team and in Junior ROTC training. He earned honors for good grades, but it was well understood that he'd had behavioral issues for years, starting in middle school. Cruz transferred schools six times in three years, leaving Stoneman Douglas in 2014 for a school for students with emotional or learning disabilities to address the problems. Reports indicate he threatened other students.

Two years later, he returned to Stoneman Douglas. The school emailed the teachers to specifically warn them Cruz was again making threats against other students. Then, he was forbidden to wear a backpack anywhere on campus. Cruz was eventually expelled in 2017 for disciplinary reasons.

Even the sheriffs knew about online profiles with photos of him with all sorts of guns and knives, posts about his extremist and hateful grudges and about wanting to kill a "sh*t ton" of people. The sheriff's office had gotten more than twenty calls about Cruz in the past, including a tipster afraid Cruz would become a school shooter. The stories, reports, and red flags go on and on, but even more upsetting is that nothing was done.

Just after the first anniversary of the shooting, two Parkland survivors committed suicide: a former student who graduated the year before and a current student. Reportedly the suicides were a result of "survivor's guilt" and the lasting, long-term effects of the trauma. And in March 2019, the father of a child slain at Sandy Hook took his own life.

The aftereffects of these mass shootings reverberate for years.

SCHOOL SHOOTING TIPS

Safety is often based in common sense, and there are general rules that apply to many situations, so these tips are similar to the ones I offer on pages 222–225 if a shooting takes place at a concert or when you are out in public. Please, take heed. I know it seems trite and superficial to give tips for the moment you are face-to-face with a school shooter, but after speaking with victims who survived mass shootings, this is what I and other experts have learned. Teach your children the following strategies.

- You must force yourself to react immediately. Many people freeze in the moment. You can't. You also do not have time to ponder what to do. Seconds count in a school shooting scenario.
- Obviously, if possible, run. Most of the Parkland students who survived—and there were many—knew the closest exits and ran to save their own lives. The only way you don't run is if your only escape route is blocked by the shooter, in which case you hide as best you can.
- That leads me to the next point: always know a way out, the closest exit (think fire escapes, back stairs, service entrances, stairs, windows). Do not immediately conclude that the main entry or hallway is the best or closest escape.
- Try to have two escapes in the back of your mind wherever you may be—a classroom or school auditorium, movie theater, concert hall, sporting event—in case the shooter is blocking one.
- Don't immediately dismiss the idea of jumping out of a second-floor window as an escape route. Do it if you have to. Survivors of the Virginia Tech shooting escaped through second-story windows. A broken bone is better than a gunshot.
- Understand how to break glass in a window to escape without dangerous cuts. Use a jacket or shirt to cover your hands or, better, use an object to break a window such as a chair. The main thing is to get out.
- Get out of the area immediately if you hear screams or loud voices, running, or "firecracker" sounds. You should not try to find out what's happening and should just get away. Better to be wrong later.

- If something resembles, looks like, or sounds like a gun, you must run away as quickly as possible.
- Know that most school shooters and mass shooters in general act alone.
- Go in the opposite direction from the gunfire.
- If gunfire is in the distance, you likely have time to get out. Don't wait.
- Take off shoes that make noise or slow you down.
- Go straight for the exit. Don't waste time ducking and diving or hiding along the way unless you make visual contact with the shooter.
- Don't try evasive maneuvers like zigzagging or hunching over, unless you are in direct contact with a shooter. If you can see the shooter or are that close, look for cover, preferably a hard surface that could stop or deflect a bullet: a locker, filing cabinet, concrete or brick wall or partition, cement pillar, lab sink, tree, steel beam, metal door, teacher's or student's metal desk.
- If you spot someone too scared to move, grab them and take them with you, but do not slow down. If it doesn't slow you down, grab anything you can to use as a weapon. Remember: only if it doesn't slow you down. Think stapler, scissors, or anything sharp or heavy. Fire extinguishers are a good choice because they are heavy, can be used to spray the gunman at a distance, and are found all over the school.
- *But remember: your best option is to get out, not fight back.*
- Hide or build a barricade only if there is absolutely no way to run or escape.
- Hiding is the second option because it traps you in one area. While hiding does limit your escape, if you can manage to hide for fifteen to twenty minutes, your survival likelihood rises immensely, as most school shootings are over within fifteen minutes.
- Of course, call 911.
- If you are stuck in a room, turn off the lights. This may dissuade the shooter from entering that room.
- Lock the door immediately, use a standard-issue school doorstop, and then try to barricade the door. The shooter is trying to target as many people as possible before the police arrive, not dismantle a barricade.
- Stay away from windows and doors.
- If you can get to a landline, use it so police can trace the call immediately.

- If you can't get to a phone and don't have a mobile phone, try to trigger the sprinkler system to get the fire department there. Do not pull the fire alarm—that's how Cruz confused victims at Parkland. Pulling the alarm could cause other students to pour out into the halls, the likely location of the shooter.
- Crouch as low as possible and stay close to the ground. Shooters usually aim at torso level or above. Have you seen in movies or on TV when a gun is pulled and everybody hits the ground? That's what I'm talking about.
- When hiding, never open a locked door to anyone, regardless of how sweetly they ask.
- Know and understand the school emergency protocol.
- If there's nothing solid to hide behind, at least get out of sight. Even hide behind curtains, which certainly won't stop a bullet but at least will get you out of the shooter's eyesight.
- If hiding, stay on hands and knees to protect vital organs from ricochets.
- Do not run to the bathroom to hide, because you end up boxed in with nowhere to go, often not even a window.
- In that same vein, avoid all closed-in areas, such as conference rooms and similar spaces.
- Do not count on interior walls for any protection other than concealment. They are likely just drywall and won't stop a bullet.
- If you are in direct contact with a shooter and there is no escape route, hiding place, or cover, then employ evasive maneuvers such as running in an erratic path. Experts say your chance to survive increases if you are a moving target.
- Turn off any electronic device that could make a noise, including cell phones (after calling 911).
- Do not in any way draw attention to yourself.
- You must remain completely silent and motion to others to do the same. It is of the utmost importance.
- As a last resort, if you can't run, escape, protect, barricade, or hide, play dead. Animals in the wild do it because it can work. People have managed to live through mass shootings by playing dead, not by choice, but because there was no other choice.
- Do not engage the shooter, reason with him, talk him down, threaten him—nothing.

- Do not confront the shooter. That is a final option.
- When police arrive at the scene, they will likely have no way to know exactly who the shooter is. You must put your hands in the air or behind your head.
- Don't rush the cops and start talking or grabbing them. If you are in a hiding place, stay there and don't move, even if you hear what you think are cops or a siren.
- Once you can move, get as far away from the building as you can. There is no guarantee the shooter has been disabled.
- Make sure your child's school has an active shooter protocol and that it is practiced routinely.
- Consider a school that offers livestream to parents.
- Consider a school that maintains trained security guards during school hours.
- Consider a school that has an enclosure around the grounds such as a fence and gates. Can they be scaled? Of course they can. But fences or gates offer one more hurdle a killer has to literally get over. They also buy a little more time and could provide a warning, if the perpetrator is spotted climbing over or slipping through a gate. That's certainly not the same as walking to the front entrance and ringing the buzzer. It immediately stands out and will get noticed quickly.
- If possible, choose a school that remains locked once classes start except for a single buzz-in point, usually near the school's office. Other entries to the school are to remain locked during the day. Test it. Can you get in? After trying three different entry points at random at the twins' school, I couldn't get in. I was so happy.
- Listen to hallway chatter. When there was a major bully at the twins' school who had extremely violent and aggressive tendencies, I sat up and listened. Don't worry, he's gone now. But sadly, he's somewhere else.
- School shooters don't warn their future victims they plan to kill them, but they do often brag to others, be it online or around them.
- Caution your child to tell you promptly if she/he hears another student make threats to harm themselves or others. The twins know of a classmate in another grade who keeps drawing death pictures and talking about death. Believe me, the school is on it.
- You must play Solomon and make the wise decision as to when you speak to the teacher, principal, or administrator about something

you've seen or heard. I believe most issues are all talk. That's "most," not "all." Better safe than sorry.

- You must be the calm and understanding one so your child will come to you with these and other matters. Otherwise, they will keep the secret. That's not good. You want them to feel comfortable opening up to you.

- Teach your children this lesson and apply it in your own life: If you see something, say something.

- I learned about a group of moms that joined together to safeguard classrooms as best they could. I was impressed. They raised money and bought safety kits and devices for the classrooms at their children's school. One item in particular struck me as innovative for schools, a device by Fighting Chance Solutions in Muscatine, Iowa. It is a device that fits over the classroom's door that secures it from inside and prevents it from opening from the outside. If children are trapped in a classroom, this device is so easy to use they could quickly barricade a door if there was an active shooter in play. Nothing is a 100% deterrent, but this device could buy time for innocent students. The Fighting Chance Solution door security device was reportedly used in a California shooting and stayed firm when there was a breach attempt.

- Bring up the ALICE (alert, lockdown, inform, counter, evacuate) method to your school administrator. It helps students systematically escape a shooting scene instead of hiding and waiting to hear gunshots.

I believe the single most common mistake we all make is not being aware of what's happening around us or not noticing when something abnormal is occurring. The clue may be slight, but there are clues. In Parkland, there was a mountain of clues and red flags and warnings galore.

SCHOOL BULLIES

There are so many stories of bullying, I hardly know where to start. But here is the case of Toledo, Ohio, sixth grader Aaron Fuller. I spoke at length with Aaron's parents, and what they told me broke my heart.

I still think about what they said, that "they," the school bullies, told Aaron to do "it"—kill himself.

And it worked. On January 11, 2019, Aaron's brother, Joseph, found him dead with a belt around his neck. But how did it all start, and why did it have to end this way?

I spoke with Aaron's mom and dad for a long time. Dad Steven outlined to me, in detail, how he reported all the bullying to the Lake Local School District, but says they told him there was "nothing they could do" because his son had "responded" to the bullies. Now Aaron's parents blame the school because they refused to help and let the ceaseless bullying go on. No classmates would come to Aaron's aid over fear they'd be the next one tortured if they did.

His family says Aaron was bullied in the worst way, over and over, at Lake Middle School. At first, he defended himself, but it never worked and, in fact, trying to defend himself only made the bullying worse. Finally, Aaron gave up. At the end, he would sit quietly in the school cafeteria when attacked and teased over everything from forgetting his lunch to the clothes he wore. The bullying ultimately escalated to urging Aaron to kill himself.

On the night Aaron died, his family had left him alone for just forty-five minutes to go pick up dinner, and when they got back home, Aaron was dead. In the end, the bullies won, and Aaron's gone. Who's their next target? Believe me, there will be one.

COUNTERING SCHOOL BULLYING

First, determine if your child is being bullied. Sometimes, they'll outright tell you the truth. A mom-friend of mine knew something was wrong when her first grader would start crying in the back seat on the way home from school. When she asked, Suzie would confide in her mom, actually openly referring to two other girls as "my bullies." She called it like it was. Mom went to the teachers, but somehow, it never got fixed. They worked through it, but it took a while, working on how to respond, how to deflect, how to stay strong every single day...strong to the finish. They did the whole nine yards. At the end of that year, Mom made sure Suzie was never in the bullies' class again. They may pass in the halls or meet on the playground, but now, she's ready for them.

Her son, however, didn't mention a thing. It took months before his sister recounted how a much older boy who had been held back and landed in their grade would trip her brother in the hallways at school, then laugh. Brother Nicholas is a gentle giant, easygoing and always ready to smile. He always seemed to brush it off and pretended every incident was an accident. It was another year before the bully punched Nicholas in the gut, knocked him down on the playground, and spit on him in front of the other boys. Nicholas never cried and never told. Suzie did.

In the school pickup line the next day, three mothers asked about Nicholas, and by the time Mom met with the principal, another mother had spoken out, and another and another. Turned out the same bully had choked another boy on the playground until he went dizzy the year before. He punched another boy in the stomach, pulled one kid's pants and underwear down in front of students, and bullied multiple girls as well. All in all, twelve other children had been his victims. The parents managed to finally fix it—for the moment, anyway, and for that year, anyway. The bully left for another school, and I don't know where the bully is now. But I do know this: bullies change lives of children, sometimes forever. How do we change that?

TIPS TO STOP BULLIES

- If intuition tells you your child has a problem, proceed with caution. Sometimes they are too proud or embarrassed to admit it's happening to them.
- Your child may think you will be disappointed in them for being bullied. Don't let them think that.
- Let your child know they are not alone. You are on their side.
- Encourage your child to speak out when they see someone else being bullied.
- Document the bullying your child is enduring. Include every incident and the details.
- If the bullying is taking place at school or on school grounds, contact the school. You have to remain cool and be the calm one. Keep the focus on protecting your child, not ranting about the bully (which is very tempting).

- Support your child every day and talk openly about bullies at the breakfast and supper table. When the "accidental" tripping and shoving was happening, my friend promised her son she would say nothing, because that was his wish. The punch in the stomach, however, was another thing. At that point, my friend explained she had to intervene.
- First, help your child learn how to be proactive and, perhaps, resolve the bullying. Role-play what your child should say. It works. When they practice ahead of time, they don't have to come up with something on the fly.
- If your child needs a counselor, get one. Most schools provide one for free.
- Talk to your child's teacher and let them know immediately what's happening. If there is a school protocol for reporting a bully, find out what it is and follow it.
- Have your facts straight and speak coherently. Don't be the crazy one in the room, or your message will be lost in your behavior.
- Contact the bully's parents if the bullying does not dissipate. Make it *nonconfrontational*. You won't get anywhere being angry at a parent who may or may not know what's going on with their child. For instance: "I'm calling because my girl has cried every day after school this week. She's upset because she tells me Donna calls her names and pushed her down. I'd really like the two of them to get along. What do you think?" Hope for the best, but remember, bullies learn their behavior from somewhere.
- Fighting back usually is not the answer.
- Teach them to walk away at first.
- If walking away doesn't work and the bully pursues them, instruct them to get help from a teacher.
- On the school bus, have them sit with a friend to avoid being bullied. Again, there is always strength in numbers.
- If problems on the bus continue, have the school seek help from the bus driver or do it yourself.
- Encourage positive behavior in your child. Teach by example. Teach your child to always look people, including the bully, in the face, directly in the eyes. Some experts tell children to focus on getting the color of the eyes of people they are talking to in order to train them to look people in the eyes. This is a nonverbal

sign that your child is not affected by the bully. It also keeps their head up.

- Practice a script for what they should say and the tone in which they will say it. Practice makes perfect. For instance: "Stop bothering me!" "Leave me alone!" "Stop bullying me!"
- Stress that tone is important. Bullies love nothing more than a victim's crying or whining, which will only encourage them. They need to respond with strength and toughness. Praise progress.
- When your child comes home and tells you how they handled a bully, give praise, clap, and cheer!
- Bullies often pick on children who are shy or lack social skills. Work with your child on how to join in with others on the playground and how to make friends and introduce themselves. Lead by example. Let them see you do it.
- Teach your child about bully avoidance. Bullies attack when no adult is near. Your child should avoid isolated bathrooms, empty hallways, empty spots on the playground, and the back of the school bus.
- Have your child seek out adults. Sit near the bus driver while on the bus, play near a teacher on the playground, sit near a teacher in the lunchroom.
- You are the parent. It is your duty to protect your child, including intervening in the most effective way possible.
- Bullies love knowing they've upset their victim, so ignoring a bully is a great tactic. Tell your child to repeatedly walk away without looking at the bully. After a while, the bully will realize it's no fun picking on your child.
- Don't reward a bully with tears.
- There are other fish in the sea. Your child doesn't need the bully as their friend.
- Help your child identify and hang out with other children who are positive friends.
- Encourage those positive friendships and help them along.
- If the bullying escalates and you can't get help, call the police. They can help you file a restraining order.
- Take legal action, before it's too late.
- It's a last resort, but teach your child how to throw a punch. I don't want it to come to that, but it may be necessary.

Is your child being bullied? Look for these signs.

- Does your child seem less confident?
- Is your child irritable?
- Does your child have unexplained anxiety?
- Does your child have unexplained tears?
- Is your child depressed?
- Have your child's grades nosedived?
- Has your child started having ailments at school time?
- Is your child suddenly having trouble sleeping?
- Has your child suddenly lost interest in going to school events or activities?
- Does your child suddenly want to skip the school bus?
- Does your child keep missing the same class?
- Is your child coming home with injuries?
- Have your child's belongings been damaged or "lost"?
- Does your child exhibit a personality change or mood swing on Sunday nights before school on Monday morning?

The signs of bullying can be subtle, but the effects can be devastating and last your child a lifetime. You have to be on the lookout and then act!

CYBERBULLYING

Bullying doesn't just happen on the playground or in class behind the teacher's back. It sneaks into your children's lives without you ever even knowing it...online. I discuss this more in chapter 6, but if your child is being cyberbullied, here is some guidance for starters. Look for these signs:

- Your child is upset after being on their device.
- Seeming upset or nervous when their device pings or they get an email, text, or IM.
- Your child is avoiding their devices.
- Your child is avoiding any talk of their devices or online games, or changing the subject or withdrawing when you bring up the topics.
- Your child is trying to keep their online life a secret.

- Your child's grades begin to drop and you don't know why.
- Your child begins to withdraw from real life, including family, friends, and activities they once loved.
- There is unexplained anger at home.
- Your child is prone to outbursts.
- There are changes in your child's behavior, including appetite and sleep habits.

TIPS FOR WHEN YOU SUSPECT YOUR CHILD IS BEING CYBERBULLIED

- *Never* take talk of suicide lightly.
- Listen closely to what your child is saying.
- Watch carefully for signs of depression.
- Assure your child you love them no matter what and you are there for them.
- Learn the signs of depression.
- Watch your child's behavior to determine if there has been a significant change.
- Many children, teens, and tweens who are being cyberbullied don't want anyone, including you, to know because they are ashamed. They think it's their fault. You must convince them otherwise. Sometimes children don't tell parents about cyberbullying because they are afraid the parent will take away all their devices to stop the bullying. That sends the message that it *is* your child's fault, which is not true. You must convince your child of the truth: the cyberbullying is not their fault. It's all about the bully feeling powerful, not about your child.
- Make sure you praise your child for telling you.
- Tell your child a bullying story from your youth or about someone they know who was bullied and how it was successfully handled.
- Let them know that a lot of people get made fun of and bullied, even into adulthood. Your child, like many other people of all ages, can and will learn to deal with a hateful bully.
- Convince your child of the truth, that you are in this together and you *will* figure it out.
- Tell someone at school, be it the principal, a teacher, or a counselor,

about the bullying. Most schools have a protocol for bullying, including cyberbullying. Advise your child first, and get a plan that is comfortable for your child.

- Keep threatening messages, texts, and photos in case you need them as evidence for the school, the bully's parents, or police.
- Take screenshots of the bullying and print them. Or take a picture of the bullying message with another phone in case the app in question alerts the sender of a screenshot.
- Obviously, block the bully. This can be done electronically for emails, texts, or instant messages.
- Don't be too proud or the least bit ashamed to get your child to a counselor pronto.
- Teach your child they are not to respond to hateful or upsetting messages or behavior. It adds fuel to the fire and keeps the bully dialogue going. Cut it off. Instead, your child is to tell you or a teacher and let adults handle it.
- If you have reason to think your child is being cyberbullied, be completely supportive and contact a professional to help you, whether from the school or police.
- Social media and the internet are today's playgrounds, and your children are out there. Be there to catch them when they fall, then dust them off and help them keep going.

The rest of the story? Suzie's bully had bullied so many people, not just Suzie, that she has only a few sidekicks left, and most of the other girls, including Suzie, are free of her. Nicholas's bully was ultimately kicked to another school. Word is that he immediately got a suspension for punching a kid on the playground at the new school.

Both Suzie and Nicholas are making their way through middle school now. Elementary school is behind them. But the sixth-grade suicide victim, Aaron, weighs on my mind. There are so many more like him, I couldn't bear to report more of them here. Wonderful children, forever gone, because of bullying. How do we know it won't be our child? If not this year, then next year or the one after that?

We can end it. We have the power. We can make a difference in the lives of our children. We can be heard at schools all across our country. We must stand up for our children so they won't live the rest of their lives in the shadow of the schoolyard bully.

CHAPTER TWO

Safe at Parks, Playgrounds, Amusement Parks, and Malls

EVIL INCARNATE

When I heard about the testimony of a twenty-two-year-old Coldwater, Michigan, woman, Brittany Raymond, I physically recoiled. On the stand in November 2018, she was as cool as a cucumber, which made me realize just how cold-blooded child sex predators really are. Raymond described in detail how she and four others actually sat around a table together scheming to kidnap a little girl, any little girl or, as they called them, "little pretties." Their plan was to kidnap a little girl from a playground or park or from the Jackson County Fairgrounds "to torture this child, sexually assault her, kill her [and] dispose of her." Testifying with full immunity against her ex, thirty-seven-year-old David Bailey, Brittany Raymond detailed how she, Bailey, Jayme LaPointe, Matthew Toole, and Talia Furman hoped to kidnap and then transport the child victim to a remote cabin miles away in Alpena, Michigan, for the torture and rape to begin.

In the cabin, the child victim "would be tied to a chair," because the predators believed "fear was going to…make this child obedient." They decided that LaPointe looked youngest and therefore was best suited to target a "young, frail, helpless child who couldn't defend herself." LaPointe was to appear upset, then ask the little girl to use her phone and call for help. Once LaPointe had lured the child, she was to throw the phone into a car to get the child to go after it, then all five of these villains would grab the child and destroy her phone so she couldn't be tracked. The child was to be "beaten, cut, tortured brutally.

She would be a mess as wounds go. If she wasn't dead, she was going to die." The child was to be raped until she died.

This group of five evil predators planned to then put the child in a burn barrel and set it on fire, even if the child was still alive, in order to get rid of the body. Raymond testified that Bailey's love of porn focused on incest themes and little girls. Again, the plan was to snatch a little girl from a Walmart or Meijer parking lot, a fairground, or a playground. They were looking in public places for any little girl.

And it wasn't all talk. LaPointe was charged in a separate case with sex abuse of a baby girl less than two years old while in her care. When her cell phone was seized, cops found videos of a woman digitally penetrating the baby. The woman told investigators she and Bailey made videos of sex acts with the child. A digital expert testified the phone he examined revealed texts about "hunting... for a pretty."

I repeat: their plan was to go out into the world and take a child. The random, wide-open nature of it is terrifying. They had the devil's to-do list, and any child they saw could have been taken, tortured, and killed. Any child at all. They were not specific. They were simply hunting. For a child.

Imagining a world that doesn't include people like Raymond, Bailey, LaPointe, Toole, or Furman is tempting and soothing. The world would be a more wonderful place if that fantasy were true. But it's not true. These five are like characters out of your worst nightmare, and I wish they were. But they're not. They are real. And there are many, many more just like them and even worse. They are out there. They are at the same fairgrounds, water parks, and ballfields as your children.

But guess what? I'm ready for them and you can be, too.

I'll share a few more stories to illustrate just how potent and prevalent a danger kidnapping is in the world around you.

AMUSEMENT PARKS AND FAIRGROUNDS

In the Brittany Raymond story, the demons that intricately planned the kidnapping of a little child considered many venues, but largely agreed that a local fair would be ideal. I remember, growing up, we would very often talk about it being "fair weather." That meant it was the fall and the Georgia State Fair was coming to town. The fair came every

October and we would all go together unless my dad was working at night, and if he was, my mom would take us. We would always stop at the exhibits first to see if we had won ribbons for 4-H projects like crafts and canning. And yes, we looked at the livestock, enormous pigs and precious calves with shiny coats. And then came the real fun: Ferris wheels and big barrels to walk through at the Crazy House (my mom got stuck once), cotton candy, cinnamon elephant ears, treats, and drinks—next to Christmas and Easter, the Georgia State Fair was the highlight of the year.

Why can't it still be like that? Maybe in the minds of children, it still is.

Fast-forward to today. I've read every single Harry Potter book to my children (editing out parts that were too scary). At this point, they've seen all the movies and naturally, we all wanted to go to the Wizarding World of Harry Potter theme park. We call it Potter Land. Now, I admit, we've been four times. We love it and I want to go back. But I must tell you about a recent scare.

On December 30, 2018, a nine-year-old girl and her family were at Wizarding World, which is part of Universal Parks and Resorts in Orlando. It was about three forty-five in the afternoon, broad daylight, near lockers at the Forbidden Journey ride. The girl was loving the ginger beer and the magical ice cream and the Bertie Bott's Every Flavour Beans, I'm sure. Then a man in the crowd approached her. He waited for the right moment and then grabbed the nine-year-old by the shoulders and ordered her to go outside to her mother. A witness heard him tell the little girl that "Mommy's over here . . ."

Later, her mother told police she had only lost sight of her daughter for a brief moment. That moment was long enough for a predator to make his move. Imagine: one brief moment and your child is grabbed in plain sight at a packed amusement park.

The man, now identified as twenty-three-year-old Jason Mikel, had traveled to Wizarding World in Orlando all the way from Minooka, Illinois. The bystander who heard what was happening spotted Mikel heading toward the Hogwarts Express train ride, which would take him to another section of the park. The witness immediately alerted park employees. The little girl managed to struggle free of the stranger's grasp and run. Universal, at the ready, has police within the park, and Mikel was nabbed by a police sergeant.

Mikel was charged with battery, attempted kidnapping, and marijuana possession. A judge, however, told prosecutors they had twenty-four hours to file another report in response to a defense attorney arguing insufficient evidence for a kidnapping charge. In a surprise twist, Mikel was released from custody when the judge ruled there was not enough probable cause to keep him behind bars without bail on a kidnapping charge. He did get a trespass warning barring him indefinitely from all Universal properties. His family says he is very loving and wouldn't hurt a soul.

EVIL IN DISGUISE

In 2012, police in Fishers, Indiana, issued warnings for parents to not only watch their children but to also watch the sitters watching their children. It all came about when nine-year-old Kendall Groninger went to her softball game at the Olio Fields sports complex near a local high school. Kendall was taken there by the family's trusted babysitter.

While sitting in the stands, a blond woman in her mid-thirties came up to the babysitter. She's described as tall, thin, with her hair pulled back in a ponytail, like many of the women there that day with their girls. After going straight to the babysitter out of all the people in the stands, she stated she'd just gotten off the phone with Kendall's mom and that she'd take Kendall home that day.

The woman had all the right details, so the babysitter agreed and left the field, and Kendall, behind. At first when Erin Groninger called the babysitter and was told she didn't have Kendall, she thought it was a joke. All too soon, she realized it was no joke. The babysitter recalled seeing the mystery blonde hanging around the bleachers within earshot as she told the other moms that Erin Groninger couldn't be at the game that night. She was described as looking like all the other moms there to see their girls play that night.

Talk about a needle-in-a-haystack moment. But this is one story that has a happy ending. When Kendall couldn't find her real babysitter after the game, she got a ride home with another mom she knew. But if this seeming soccer mom could convince a babysitter, don't you know she could convince a little child playing by themselves on a playground or at a park or ball field?

Take a listen to a similar story to Kendall's. It's a reminder that sometimes we have to be on the lookout for the safety of other people's children.

At Orchard Hill Park near the quiet town of Griffin, Georgia, on the outskirts of Atlanta, a mom spotted a woman talking to a little boy, and something just didn't seem right. The mom, Nora Jean, approached the little boy and took his hand. The tot turned to her and said, "I was just trying to help her find her puppy." Nora Jean immediately knew this was all wrong. She turned to go after the woman, but she saw her leaving hastily. She was so concerned about the woman, she got a good description of the car: a late '90s white Aerostar van with a piece of chrome missing from the side door. She described the woman as thin, tall at about five foot eight with blond hair to her shoulders.

After investigators met with Nora Jean to create a composite sketch, an eerie realization set in. The woman in Orchard Park was strikingly similar to a woman who had been knocking on doors in the same area pretending to be a Department of Family and Children's Service worker. The Spalding County sheriff also reported that the blonde in Orchard Hill Park may be connected to yet another child abduction attempt in nearby Milner, Georgia, that Friday night.

There was a time when people thought they could tell their children what the bad guy looks like; that's not true anymore. Maybe it never was.

TAKEN IN PLAIN SIGHT

On the night of Saturday November 14, 2015, Gabriella Doolin, just seven years old, was watching her brother play in an all-star football game at Allen County-Scottsville High School in Scottsville, Kentucky. This was Gabbi's first year cheerleading for her brother's team. At 7:40 p.m., Gabriella got separated from her parents and lost in the crowd. Her parents immediately called police and had a stadium official call out her name over loudspeakers. In just minutes, the school was put on lockdown. The game came to an abrupt halt, and parents poured from their seats to look for Gabriella. Within twenty-five minutes of her being lost, it was all over. Her tiny body was found four hundred yards away, submerged in a creek behind the school.

Within a week, Timothy Madden, a thirty-eight-year-old Scottsville father of five, was booked on charges of kidnapping, rape, sodomy, and first-degree murder. He says he knew Gabriella's dad in school, and that Madden's daughter and Gabriella went to cheerleading classes together.

Madden has consistently maintained his innocence but, in a twist, pled guilty to kidnapping and murder charges rather than face a jury trial...and the death penalty. He was sentenced to life without parole, but even that won't mend the hearts of Gabriella's grieving family.

ABDUCTION AT A LITTLE LEAGUE BALLFIELD

On June 9, 1995, six-year-old Morgan Nick was, at first, too shy to go catch fireflies at the local baseball field. But the other kids persuaded her. After asking her mom, she kissed her and ran from their seats in the bleachers to the other children about fifty yards away. Dressed in her green Girl Scout T-shirt, denim shorts, and white tennis shoes, Morgan was easy to spot, and her mom, Colleen Nick, could see her bobbing and weaving, catching and releasing. When all the children trooped back to their moms fifteen minutes later, Morgan Nick wasn't with them. She was nowhere to be found. Morgan Nick has never been seen again. The case took over the police HQ and an entire room was filled with files, documents, and thousands of tips, but they never brought Morgan home. Her disappearance, still unsolved, has hung over the Alma, Arkansas, police department ever since, and the tiny town of about five thousand has never been quite the same.

"HE STOLE ME"

On July 4, 2017, when an eight-year-old girl in Prince Albert, Saskatchewan, went with her grandmother to a local playground around three p.m., everything seemed fine. After playing a while, the grandma went to get water for her granddaughter. It was confirmed she was only gone a matter of minutes, just enough time to retrieve the water and walk back to the spot where they were playing. But by the time she walked back, the girl was gone. Completely gone.

The grandma searched the area as quickly as she could, then raised the alarm. Immediately, an AMBER Alert was issued and police began to scour the area. Cops pulled the area surveillance video, and what they saw left them sick in the pits of their stomachs.

A shaggy-haired man was seen, at first alone, in the video. As soon as he saw the grandma leave, he got out of a black car and started following the girl as she played. He tried to talk to her, but she moved away. He followed. As soon as he was close enough, he grabbed the girl, picked her up, carried her to his car, and put her in the back, driving away. The video shows the grandma returning literally just seconds later.

With that visual, the criminal probation department confirmed that the man caught on camera was Jared John Charles, already on probation for "sexually touching a minor" and, in a third incident, accused of taking two boys, ages eight and ten, to "play video games and eat junk food," also triggering an AMBER Alert. Charles was under court order not to have unsupervised contact with any minor or to be in a place where children play, yet there he was at three thirty in the afternoon at a school playground where an eight-year-old girl and her grandmother were playing.

Armed with a name and a face plus a make and model of the car, police went on the hunt. They identified the car belonging to Charles's roommate and discovered that Charles and the roommate were out smoking hookah. They found Charles and, disturbingly, the search of his home turned up a huge stash of girls' clothing. He was arrested and booked around eleven fifteen that night, and although cops found Charles and his supply of little girls' clothes, there was no little girl.

Miles away, on a rural property east of Prince Albert, locals spy a little girl coming up their walk. Recognizing her face from the AMBER Alert, they call police. It's the missing eight-year-old. She's alive but has been sexually assaulted by Charles. The brave little girl said she didn't answer when Charles approached her on the playground and that "He stole me." Charles told the girl he was taking her to a place where she wouldn't be found. It was an abandoned house, and though she fought as hard as she could, the sex attack on her lasted three hours. After, Charles dumped her in a remote portion of the Nisbet Forest. She walked over three hours to get help.

Charles told police he picked that girl in particular because "she looked small and weak," that "I wasn't worried about her," and "I'm one step closer to hell. I don't care what I did." When asked if he had anything to say to her family, he simply said, "See you in hell."

DANGER ON A HIKING TRAIL

Bridle Trails State Park in Kirkland, Washington, is breathtaking. Long trails have towering trees on either side that let the sun peek down on the paths as you walk. It's about five hundred acres of nature that welcomes hikers, horses, and dogs with their humans, including children. And that is where this story starts.

Just before noon on March 1, 2018, a grandma was walking an easy path with her two-year-old grandson while the boy's mom was in their car with her baby. Imagine Mommy's shock when she saw her tot coming out of the woods and down the path without his grandma but with an unknown woman pulling him by the hand! Mommy took off after her son and had to physically take the son back. Enter Grandma, who emerged from the woods after taking a blow to the head from the female kidnapper. The two managed to get the tot and run from the woman. Kirkland PD arrived and were able to apprehend the kidnapper and take her into custody. She was booked into the King County jail on assault and attempted kidnapping of the little boy.

PARKS TURNED PLAYGROUNDS FOR PEDOPHILES

In suburban Florida near ritzy Naples, on a December late afternoon, a six-year-old boy was playing at the Golden Gate Community Park. The boy was riding a friend's scooter around the park while his mom kept score at a game nearby. His sisters and others were watching him, too. But in the few moments no eyes were on him, a dark-haired man approached and asked if the boy wanted a scooter of his own. What six-year-old boy wouldn't?

But they had to go to the dark-haired man's truck to get it. He carried the tot to his truck and put the seats down, ordering him to lie down so cops wouldn't see him. After a stop at a Circle K for water and candy, the dark-haired man drove him to a wooded area, removed the boy's clothes, took his own pants off, molested him in the truck, and then told the boy he'd take him home if he would just stop crying. He dumped the boy at an unknown home, where the boy called his mommy.

(If you or your child find yourself in this situation, a stop along the way after being kidnapped, the best move is to risk everything to alert others to your situation. Scream, yell, kick. Break things. Call attention to yourself however you can.)

Fast-forward four months: the dark-haired man, becoming even more brazen, lured another six-year-old boy from his own front yard, keeping him for hours and molesting him, too.

Through modern science, the dark-haired man's saliva DNA was found on both boys' underwear and then, through the national DNA data bank, was matched up to thirty-seven-year-old William Salisbury. At the time of both the December and April child kidnappings, Salisbury was already on probation for trafficking stolen goods. One year or so before that, he was released early on two ten-year prison terms for molesting two more little boys in Pinellas County.

A man who should have been in jail reverted immediately to his predatory ways and ended up in a park scoping a kindergartener and in a nearby neighborhood entering a family's yard to take their son.

And who knows where else?

The trial on the front-yard snatching included testimony of the little boy, his dad, DNA experts, and deputy sheriffs. The little boy was too traumatized and had either blocked details of his attack or didn't want to tell them out loud in a courtroom of strangers. He did, however, tell of a man who took him to a truck and told him to take off his pants. Salisbury received a life sentence for this crime, the second one he has received for crimes of this nature.

THE DELPHI MURDERS

February 13, 2017, thirteen-year-old Abby Williams and fourteen-year-old Libby German were dropped off by Libby's sister at a trailhead near the Monon High Bridge over Deer Creek in the Historic Trails in Delphi, Indiana. When they didn't arrive at the arranged pick-up site a few hours later, they were reported as missing. Their bodies were discovered around noon the next day, about fifty feet from the north bank of Deer Creek and about a half mile from the bridge. The case remains unsolved but has held national attention because it was reported that German's cell phone contained a photo and a voice recording of the man believed to have committed the murders. I've spoken at length with the girls' families, and they are trying their best to compartmentalize their pain to focus on catching the killer. Sometimes, when we are talking, they describe the girls as if they are still alive. I think about them so much, trying their best to soldier on in a new and lonely world without their girls.

Parents, grandparents, and even great-grandparents have warned their children: "Don't talk to strangers." Those warnings aren't working. How many child abductions and murders do we have to read about before the message sticks?

Now is the time to be proactive and protect our children.

Child predators come from all walks of life and cross all socio-economic divisions. All ages, races, religions, backgrounds, and sexes are represented in this sorry lot. There is no specific mold. They can range from rich to poor, unemployed to CEOs, day laborers to priests, sixth-grade dropouts to PhDs. In fact, many child molesters are married, have children of their own, and hold down jobs. You'd never suspect they have a sinister and destructive double life.

Often, a predator is someone the family trusts, a layperson at your church, a pillar of your community, the longtime janitor at the elementary school, a dentist, a doctor, a daycare worker, or a swim instructor. It happens.

Molesters act with no remorse or guilt. They are focused on the commission of their evil deed. They'll use anything as a lure: candy, a puppy, a kitten, a ride, a motor scooter, an Xbox, a modeling contract, an A on a report card. You name it and someone has tried it. Devastated parents are left full of rage and self-blame.

But it doesn't have to be this way. Your child's safety starts here.

SAFETY TIPS TO PREVENT KIDNAPPINGS

- Tell your children very clearly that Mommy or Daddy do not need help outside the family. Should a stranger approach them to suggest, under any scenario, that they've been sent to collect them because Mommy or Daddy needs help, make sure they know immediately that *It's not true!* That's where use of a code word comes into play.

- Create and practice a code word. We have one in our family, and we all talked about it a long time and came up with one we'd all remember. I know for a fact that code words work. Here's proof. An eleven-year-old girl was walking with her little friend in an Arizona park just southeast of Phoenix in the San Tan Valley. It was about four p.m. when a man driving a white SUV pulled up beside the girl and told her that there was an emergency. He said her brother had been in an accident and that it was serious. He insisted she needed to come with him immediately. But this little girl and her parents had come up with a code word, and when she asked the driver of the SUV to say it, he floored the gas and took off. The Pinal County sheriff and family insist that the little girl's demand that her would-be abductor use the code word stopped her from being kidnapped, molested, or worse.

- Don't talk to or "help" strangers. Explain to your child that adults do not need children to help them and that adults will ask other adults for help. It's a trick, and it takes many forms. You must instruct your children to never, ever "help" anyone, adult or child, go look for their lost pet, child, toy, or laptop. They should not get close enough to look at a picture or be within arm's reach of the person. They must leave immediately and, if followed, scream. Ditto for an adult or unfamiliar child asking for directions.

- Instruct your child to never, ever get close to a car. They should stay at least twenty feet from any car except their family's car. It only takes seconds for the driver or an accomplice to leap out, grab the child, put the child into the car, and be gone—literally seconds. It's key to instruct your child that when they run from a car, they should run in the opposite direction from which the car is headed.

- Further instruct your child that if an adult asks them to get help for any other reason, they should run toward the concession stands, the bathroom, the trailhead, the gift shop, or *anywhere else* other people are. Run. And scream.

- Teach your child to *scream, run, fight, claw, kick* if anyone ever grabs them. But they should *not* get in the car!

Out and About

- Predators at playgrounds, games, and parks listen and watch carefully. If they hear someone call out your child's name, they will use that information to approach your child and act like they know you or your child. Warn your children that just because someone says their name, they are still a stranger and therefore a danger.
- Have photos of your child on your phone that you can give to cops or mall, park, or playground security.
- When out as a family, have a plan in place in case you get separated.
- If separated in public, tell your children they should never leave to go outside to look for you. If in a store or public place, they are to go up front and get help from a security guard or cashier, preferably a woman or an employee in uniform.
- It's always better to have a friend along with your child and instruct them to never split up, even in the bathroom. They should wait for each other.
- In big crowds, we all four hold hands or on to each other's shirts. If someone breaks the chain, we all stop.
- When taking your child to a park or playground, try to select one with a single entry/exit if possible. You can more easily watch to see if your child leaves.
- If possible, select playgrounds, parks, and play spaces that are fenced in or contained.
- Never let the sightline between you and your child be obstructed.
- If you can't see your child, do not think twice about yelling out their name at the park, playground, parking lot, or store. Keep calling until they answer and you get to them.
- Try to select play areas where you can easily see who is approaching or nearby.
- Instruct your child that it's not being rude to an adult if they scream, run, or reject.
- Avoid shortcuts when you are walking from one place to another. Stay on the beaten path.

Strangers at the Door

Some strangers will come to your home. You and your children must be ready.

- If someone knocks on the door, tell your child not to open it under any circumstances. In a recent study, children opened the door time and time again to "a neighbor" needing help. Some even said "I'm not supposed to open the door" while doing so.
- Instruct your child that they are not to believe a stranger even if that person is wearing a uniform or displays a badge or an ID.
- Tell your children that they should never go with anyone or to any place without asking Mom or Dad. They should never move from where they are without checking in with you.
- If your kids are ever home without you for some reason, they must never open the door unless it is someone *you* agreed to.
- Show your children which home or apartment they can go to if there is an emergency.
- Doors are to be kept locked while you are gone.
- The home alarm is to remain on while you are gone.
- If your child goes missing, know that, statistically, they will turn up safe. But please do not wait to call 911. Minutes count.
- You should know what your child is wearing each day.
- Get your child a cell phone. (I know, I didn't want to either, and there have been a lot of issues we've had to deal with surrounding cell phone usage and texting. But I felt it was the right thing to do. See page 108 for how our family made this decision.)
- Teach your child how to call 911 and also how to give identifying information such as location, cross street, and situation.
- When they get their first phone, the only numbers programmed in should be those of family members.
- Make sure your child's cell phone tracker is always turned on.

CHAPTER THREE

Safe While Shopping

Malls, department stores, superstores, grocery stores. They all feel so safe with everyone shopping, smells in the air from the food courts and restaurants, and lovely displays, but it's simply not true. While you let your guard down in front of Macy's or Foot Locker or Forever 21, someone else is thinking about shoving you or your child into the back of an unmarked SUV. For many people, trips to the mall don't have happy endings.

I once got a tiny glimpse of that feeling. I remember like it was yesterday. I had been totally shamed by a mom at the community pool. She went on and on about how she made, at home by hand, her children's sunscreen. I looked at the twins, covered head to toe with streaks of white, sticky sunscreen all over them. I thought I had done a good job greasing them up and then choking them with sunblock spray for an extra layer of sun protection out in the parking lot. I accepted I was a failure, but ever the optimist, I vowed to find them natural, organic sunscreen.

The next morning, with the twins in tow, realizing I had to be at the set for air in a few hours and did not have time to create homemade sunscreen in a kitchen mixing bowl, I headed to a baby superstore, Babies "R" Us. I loved that place when the twins were toddlers. We got out of the car and into the store, and after pulling them away from their stuffies and toys, we got to the lotions and potions section. The shelves were tall and started at the floor level. We circled several aisles until I spotted sunscreens. The bottom shelf, as I mentioned, was literally on the floor, so there I was bent down trying to read the ingredients of various sunscreen products.

I couldn't find anything organic or even remotely "natural." Had the evil mom in the frilly swimsuit at the pool actually won? That thought only egged me on, so I kept looking, determined. Finally, unsuccessful, I stood up and turned to Lucy and told her we'd head back to the toys and look somewhere else for the elusive natural sunscreen.

That was the problem: I told *Lucy*...just Lucy...John David wasn't there. I felt a tingle go over my whole body. I looked both ways and called his name, quickly calculating I had been searching intently for sunscreen for five to eight minutes between the two aisles. No answer from John David.

I called out louder, grabbing Lucy by her little hand, and started walking, quickly, down a main aisle. Nothing. I turned and went in the opposite direction, scanning aisles on either side as I went. Nothing. Another minute had passed.

I know a car can travel at sixty miles an hour or more. I know that a child kidnapping victim is usually dead in the first three hours. One picture kept crowding into my vision of John David. It was the face of little Adam Walsh wearing his Little League cap, abducted from a Sears and never seen alive again.

All these thoughts were colliding in my brain, bouncing off my skull like it was a pinball machine, and I screamed. Not muffled, not subdued, but like there was a siren in my throat: *"My baby's missing! Lock the doors now!"*

I kept saying it over and over and over. No, not saying it...screaming it! I have a vague recollection of people standing behind their shopping carts staring at me. By this point, since she couldn't run fast enough, I had Lucy under my right arm, carrying her like a running back with a football.

I made it to the front of the store, which had an all-glass wall with doors in the center. I scanned the parking lot. Nothing. I whipped out my cell phone and started one last loop of the store, looking down every aisle as I ran. I remember the sound of my worn-out tennis shoes on the tile floor, with Lucy so quiet in my arm.

And then, there he was. In the middle of the aisle smiling at me, wearing his little blue Crocs with socks. Even typing this now, my eyes still fill up with tears. The thought of losing him or Lucy washes over me like a riptide.

This is how it went down.

As I was digging through sunscreen, John David, silent as Santa in those Crocs, snuck off to look for toy action figures. Piecing it together, as I ran through the toy aisles, he was circling the end of an aisle. We were like the Keystone Kops.

I remember four moments most vividly: realizing he was gone and screaming, running with Lucy with a panic rising up my chest into my throat and eyes, then turning to see my sweet boy standing in the center of the big aisle looking at me, and dropping to my knees to hug him tight. I held him so close and tried to explain, without scaring him, that it wasn't safe to wander away from Mommy. As months passed, I explained as best as I could the dangers that literally lurked around the corner of the next aisle at the grocery store or the mall or even the library. I didn't want to destroy their innocence, but what was my alternative? To leave them unarmed?

But for right now, I want to remember the moment when I was kneeling there on the floor of Babies "R" Us with the twins in my arms, other moms and store employees all crowding around us, happy in that moment. My throat tightens up remembering it. I wish dearly that so many other moms and dads had the same happy ending.

EASTER HORROR

In 1975, the daughters of a famous radio star, sisters Sheila and Katherine Lyon, just twelve and ten, headed to an upscale suburban mall in Maryland, Wheaton Plaza, to shop during Easter vacation week. Although the girls, then about the age of my twins, were seen by several people at the mall, they later seemingly disappeared into thin air. A massive search was launched, with police combing through woods, hills, ponds, storm sewers, and abandoned houses, and hundreds of witnesses were interviewed, but neither the girls nor their remains were ever found.

In 2013, however, came a twist in the case. A convicted child sex predator, Lloyd Lee Welch, came under suspicion after one of his relatives told the police he helped Welch burn two bloody "army-style" duffel bags in Virginia's Bedford County. Each bag weighed sixty to seventy pounds and "smelled like death." In 2017, Welch was sentenced to two forty-eight-year prison terms after admitting to abducting the girls while never acknowledging his role in their deaths.

FOOD COURT FEARS

On March 31, 2016, a young Pennsylvania mom of two, Malika Hunter, took her two-year-old boy and her newborn boy to King of Prussia Mall for a day out of the house. She was befriended by another woman about her age, Cherie Amoore. The two chummed around, and after they were seated in the food court chatting away, Mommy's attention was diverted. Her new friend, Cherie, seized the moment and, in the blink of an eye, kidnapped baby Ahsir.

I've watched the mall video over and over of that precise moment when Mommy, tending to her two-year-old, isn't looking and Cherie takes the baby. Police immediately sifted through the very same video to identify the kidnapper and locate her. Family and friends told police that thirty-two-year-old Amoore had recently been given a baby shower and that she had created several baby registries for herself. She told police she had been pregnant and gave birth and that the baby boy died after a few hours. She claimed she did not give birth in a hospital and that she never told anyone the infant had died. Police could never confirm whether she had ever actually been pregnant or given birth recently.

I wonder if the registries were not part of a pregnancy ruse capped off by kidnapping an infant. With all the comings and goings and distractions of a mall food court, Cherie Amoore thought it would be the perfect place to steal a baby, and she was right.

Baby Ahsir was found by police before he was harmed by his kidnapper or could be whisked far away. Amoore got seven years in jail for the kidnapping, and baby Ahsir was returned to his mom. I wish all parents of abducted children could be so lucky.

HUMAN TRAFFICKING AT THE MALL

What teen girl wouldn't head straight for a self-described "family-oriented mall" featuring her dream stores, like Aeropostale, Claire's, Bath and Body Works, MAC Cosmetics, and Foot Locker and treats like Cinnabon and Auntie Anne's? In California in March 2015, a teen girl was walking into the Moreno Valley Mall, and instead of browsing Macy's, she was abducted by two adults, a male and a female, and spirited away to Palm Desert. They forced the girl to pose for photos, which they then used for online "ads." But they didn't kidnap her just to take photos of her; they then forced her into a horrible life, sex-trafficking her for two months in and around San Bernardino County and the Coachella Valley, giving her a daily "John" quota. A third evil-doer is accused of sexually assaulting her when she failed to bring in enough money. After escaping in May of that year, the teenager reported the ordeal to police and, after counseling and therapy, was able to provide descriptions. The two thugs were arrested first, and the third one eventually turned himself in to police.

MALL ATTACK

On March 13, 2013, just six short weeks after making bond on charges of possessing child porn, David Renz ditched his court-ordered ankle monitor and headed straight for...the mall. After considering several options, Renz chose the Great Northern Mall in Clay, New York, as his hunting ground. Almost immediately after he arrived, he spotted librarian Lori Ann Bresnahan and her daughter near their car after just leaving an exercise class. Without a pause, Renz forced his way into Lori Ann's car by brandishing a fake pistol. He bound both and sex-ually assaulted the ten-year-old daughter. Lori Ann put up a fight and screamed for her daughter to run, which she did. Mom Lori Ann, who distracted her attacker so her daughter could get away, was not so lucky. Renz, who should have been behind bars at the time, stabbed Lori Ann to death as her little girl ran for help. The ten-year-old later required surgery following the sexual attack. Renz was apprehended within hours and was later sentenced to life in prison for first-degree murder.

The above are a small sampling of cases I've covered or investigated in some form or fashion. My heart goes out to all people affected by these or similar crimes. Two particular cases, however, are etched onto my heart. They have changed me and the way I parent forever. They are the cases of eight-year-old Cherish Perrywinkle and six-year-old Adam Walsh. To this day, I call their parents my friends.

CHERISH PERRYWINKLE

Eight-year-old Cherish Perrywinkle was just like the poem: "sugar and spice and everything nice." On a hot June 22, 2013, in Jacksonville, Florida, mom Rayne Perrywinkle took her three girls shopping for clothes. Mom Rayne explained to me that they were looking for bargains and started at Dollar General. Rayne knew she had to hold back about fifty dollars in cash to get Cherish to the airport the next day to fly west to visit her dad, so, at the counter at Dollar General, she was working out how to pay for the clothes. It was then she noticed a guy standing nearby watching her. When she left the store, he was still there, waiting. She also told me she'd spotted him briefly earlier, watching them shop inside Dollar General, and then he was gone. His name was Donald Smith.

Outside, he approached them and stated he was meeting his wife at a nearby Walmart and knew they were short on money. He offered up a $150 gift card they could use at Walmart. It took convincing Rayne, but in her desire to get the girls their clothes, she agreed. They all piled into Smith's white van and headed to Walmart. They took their time shopping and waiting for Smith's wife to show and when ten p.m. came, Rayne noticed the girls were antsy because they hadn't eaten. Smith volunteered to walk up to the front of the store with Cherish for cheeseburgers at the in-store McDonald's.

About twenty minutes later, Rayne headed up front to the checkout area, but couldn't find either Cherish or Smith. She began calling out for her daughter. Fear set in when she realized the in-store McDonald's was closed. Her cell phone wouldn't work, and she says no one at the store would help. Rayne tells me that it was about forty minutes after her daughter went missing that an employee finally handed over her own phone for Rayne to call 911.

I've listened to the call over and over. At first police were slow to act because they thought Cherish's disappearance was some sort of custody battle ruse. It wasn't, and police wasted crucial time questioning Rayne over and over as her desperation grew.

When police arrived, Rayne begged them to pull up store surveillance video. Watching it is awful. You see Cherish and Smith strolling along...then *passing* the McDonald's, heading through the front doors and into the parking lot, where they disappear. It took police six long hours before they notified media of a possible abduction, and then it took FDLE another hour to get out an AMBER Alert. Seven hours...wasted.

Once the AMBER Alert was issued and went public, a television viewer quickly recognized Smith's van. Only twelve hours after she walked through the Walmart's doors, Cherish's body was found wedged under a log, submerged in a creek.

She had been raped, sodomized, and beaten. She sustained a horrific blow to the back of her head, but Cherish died of asphyxiation. One of her eyes had started to bleed. At trial, the medical examiner had to stop mid-testimony in tears as she described the many severe injuries that occurred during the attack and strangulation with a piece of cloth. Cherish sustained bruises and cuts on her knees and thighs, and a "totally distorted" female anatomy, both vagina and rectum. She suffered "busted" blood vessels and skin abrasions to her neck. The ME says it would have taken three to five minutes for Cherish to die in this manner.

Semen was found in her mouth, vagina, and rectum. Tapes were later played in court of Smith bragging about Cherish's body: "She had a lot for a white girl" was how he described the little girl's rear end.

As it turned out, Smith was a longtime sex offender. I managed to locate and speak with one of his earlier victims and her mother. On that occasion, he called the family pretending to be a social worker and tried to take the girl from a fast-food restaurant in that same white van. That time, the mother got wise earlier and physically tried to block him and, in so doing, saved her daughter. Smith's rap sheet goes back to the 1970s, and he's been a registered sex offender since the 1990s. Yet he was out that June day, hunting for prey at Dollar General.

In 2018, Smith received the death penalty after being found guilty of first-degree murder and several sexual battery charges. I don't think I will ever get over the kidnapping and murder of Cherish Perrywinkle, and the toll her death has taken on Rayne is indescribable.

ADAM WALSH

On July 27, 1981, Revé Walsh and her six-year-old son, Adam, went to the Hollywood Mall Sears in Hollywood, Florida, to look at a lamp for their home. Adam was intrigued by an Atari video game on display and joined several other boys who were all taking turns playing. Revé finished her lamp search a few aisles away, and when she went to find Adam, he wasn't around. She looked and looked with no success. When she located a Sears security guard, she learned the older boys had "gotten rowdy" and the guard had made them leave the store. The older boys told the guard their parents weren't there, but Adam, being much younger and likely too shy to talk to the guard, was likely left alone and unattended outside the Sears entrance they were escorted to, a different one than he had entered with his mom.

Revé tried everything. A frantic search ensued, and she had him paged over and over on the store's loudspeaker. After ninety minutes of panic, she called police. Adam was never seen alive again. On August 10, his head was found in a drainage canal 130 miles away off the Florida Turnpike in Vero Beach. He died of asphyxiation. A man named Ottis Toole is believed to have taken him from the store that day and is thought to be Adam's killer.

The name John Walsh must surely ring a bell. Losing Adam changed his life forever. He has tried through the years to channel his and Revé's pain into a crusade for justice. God bless Revé. God bless John. God bless Adam.

Now, what, if anything, can we learn?

Many of the tips offered here echo tips in other sections. But a big part of learning how to be safe is repetition and stressing of important ideas, plans, and procedures. I'm very happy to repeat this information where it's needed because, quite simply, it can save lives.

SAFETY TIPS FOR SHOPPING WITH CHILDREN

- Safe shopping starts with paying attention to what's around you: the people, the cars, the situation in which you are placing yourself and your children.
- Watch out for people paying a particular interest in you or your child.
- Always keep your child in your sight. It's just that simple.
- Keep your child occupied. Take along snacks like Cheerios in a sandwich bag, books, crayons, or small toys to entertain them while you shop. A bored child is more likely to wander off or get lost.

- One great way to keep your children safe and happy is to let them participate in the shopping. Allow them to help you find items on the shelf or pick sizes or colors for you. Play I Spy as you move through the store. People-watch, count carts... anything to keep them with you.

- You must help your child memorize your and your partner's cell phone number, home phone number, and basic family information, including names, ages, and address. If they have a problem, set it to music. They can do it. Mine had it down by three years old.

- In addition to your child knowing important numbers and info, make sure your child has your cell number in physical form. I put it in the twins' pockets. I have written it on their arms when we've been in large crowds, just in case.

- Some experts even advise a temporary tattoo or a wristband emblazoned with their name, your name, and contact info. I found the customizable temporary tattoos on Etsy, and they're ingenious. The ones I found have an outline of Mickey Mouse. They are, of course, nontoxic and last one or two days. You can remove them whenever you're ready with soap, Purell, and a little scrubbing.

- A further tip is writing your numbers and information on your child's wrist or arm and then painting over that with liquid bandage in case you get separated. The liquid bandage stops the ink from rubbing off.

- Many parents place ID tags somewhere on their child's body or clothing as opposed to a card with numbers or a temporary tattoo or wristband. Do what feels right for you and your family.

- When you arrive at the store or mall, approach an employee and ask them in front of your child: "Do you work here? Who else works here? Is this your uniform? Your tag? Your ID? Your walkie-talkie?" This helps your child know who works there by identifying their shirt or nametag. That way, if you do get separated, they can sort out who is a go-to person.

- Have a plan in case you are separated, and make sure your children know the plan, whether you're at the grocery store, mall, or superstore. Each has its own peculiarities. Explain carefully to your child what to do if you are separated: stay where they are and call out your name *loudly*, alert a store employee identified by uniforms and tags, and then, as a last resort, ask another mommy or grandmommy for help.

- If you become separated from your child, immediately alert store employees and mall security. They have procedures in place (such as Code Adam) to find your child.
- Remember, contrary to what many people believe, there is no longer a waiting period needed to report your child missing to police.
- Go back to the last place you saw your child, calling their name *loudly* as you go. My children are as tall as me, but I have no problem calling out their names loudly in any store at any time because one thing I know is that minutes count.
- Some parents give their child a whistle on a necklace to use if they are afraid or get separated.
- Snap a quick cell phone photo of your child that day before you head to the mall, store, or event so you have their exact clothes, shoes, jewelry, hairstyle.
- Make sure the photo is full-length, including shoes. If you do get separated, it will help those searching for your child to find them.
- Lots of mall play areas (also parks, theme parks, and other venues) offer paper bracelets at security. Use them or something like them and write your name and numbers on them when you go shopping as well.
- Repetition, repetition, repetition. Every time you go shopping, remind your children about staying together, the plan in case you are separated, the rundown of what to do just in case.
- If you decide to go to a movie at the mall or you are at an event with assigned seating, put their ticket into their pocket so the ushers can reconnect you in case they get away.
- Some moms match the family's clothes when they go to crowded places.
- Always choose a home base. It can be the entrance or a bench in front of the candy store or a particular booth at the food court or the cashiers up front. This goes for amusement parks and other venues as well. If they get lost, they know where to go. Reinforce the home base and pick it out with them whenever you are out and about. Have them repeat back to you where home base is whenever you enter a store, mall, superstore, or grocery store.
- Talk to the child about what's happening. Tell them that the area will be crowded and you want them to stay safe.
- You can also turn some of these ideas into a game. Give your child

rules; for instance, stay within sight of your parent. If they can see you, you can see them.

- If you are weaving through a crowd, say during Christmas shopping or Black Friday, physically hold hands. If the chain is broken, stop. Make it clear that if rules are not followed, you will have to leave.
- When the rules are broken, follow through and leave. This is a good reinforcement that these rules are mandatory, not optional.
- Make sure that everyone who owns a cell phone has it with them and that it's charged.
- All family cell phones need to be placed on both ring and vibrate.
- All family cell phones need to have the volume turned up all the way.
- All family cell phones need to have the "find my phone" feature or its equivalent activated.
- All family cell phones need the geotagging and tracker features on.
- Carry a portable charger. Mophie has good options.
- Speaking of phones, stay off your phone while you're shopping, walking through a mall, down aisles, or in parking lots or parking decks.
- If you must be on the phone, stop what you're doing and keep your children close to you until you can get off the phone and focus.
- A family locator app makes locating and contacting family members easy, and it's very simple to use, even for non-techies. You just download an app on your smartphone and then log in. The app allows you to know instantly where every member is 24/7/365. It also provides location history so you know where your child has been, and most offer a geofence that alerts you when your child arrives at a location that you designate. These apps also give your child a super-quick way to let you know when to pick them up, and they allow you to message each other one on one or as a family. You can watch over your child no matter what devices you all are using. They're brilliant and really deliver peace of mind.
- Consider GPS tracking devices. They are easy and fairly inexpensive. Some of the most highly rated are AngelSense Guardian, PocketFinder+ Personal Tracker, Trax G+, Amber Alert GPS Smart Locator, and the LG GizmoPal 2.
- Once your child is old enough to understand, teach them the phrase and meaning of "Stranger danger. If it's a stranger, it's a danger."
- Some parents use safety harnesses to stop tots from straying.
- For children who will tire easily or can't walk steadily in a crowd,

take a stroller or wagon. Many venues offer them. I've used them several times at Disney and Universal.

- Brightly colored, vibrant clothing is easier to spot in a crowd. I take a neon orange baseball hat for John David to wear.
- Use glow sticks, glow-in-the-dark bracelets, or light-up shoes to spot your children in dimly lit areas or in the evening.
- If you are worried about taking packages to your car and keeping your children in tow, ask for someone from the store to escort you. You may be surprised at how willing they are to help.
- Another alternative is to ask the cashier or help desk to hold your items while you take the children to the car, then circle back, park at the edge, turn on your emergency lights and go in with your children to retrieve the bags.
- Keep your vehicle locked, especially when your child is in the car.
- Don't use your car to store whatever you buy. Criminals are there on the scene, watching shoppers come and go from their cars. If you have a lot of bags you don't want to carry, try a cart. If you absolutely must load them into your car and go back and forth into the mall or store (which I do *not* advise), try this: take your bags to your car, store them in the trunk and out of sight, then drive to a different parking lot or distant location in that lot. Act like you're leaving.
- Use a blanket or cargo cover to conceal purchases you stash in your car. You don't want to get hurt by someone trying to get your stuff.
- Make pricey, expensive purchases at the end of your shopping. Don't carry them out and leave them sitting in your car. Someone will either break into your car to get them or, worse, wait for you to get back and open the car yourself.
- Instruct your child to *never* leave the store or area with anyone.
- Warn your child against anyone who tells them they saw you leave or that you are in another aisle or in the parking lot or bathroom and need them.
- I know it's scary, but teach your child how to get out of a stranger's car. Of kidnapped children who are murdered, most are killed within the first three hours. Do not be passive about this potential danger. Remember: all parents of kidnapped children thought it would never happen to their kids.
- Have your child practice reaching for the car door and trying to get out the minute they get in.

- If your child is in a four-door car, teach them to jump to the back seat and try the door immediately upon being put in the car.
- Tell your child that if they are in a trunk, don't panic. Instead, look for a wall panel inside the trunk that comes out when you pull on it. This could possibly tear out the wires to the tail-lights and brakes. There's a chance cops may pull over the kidnapper.
- Never allow or ask a stranger to hold your child. Even for a moment.
- Explain to your child that bad guys often look just like regular people and sometimes are women.
- *Never* label backpacks, clothing, lunch bags, pencil holders, or jewelry. Predators use this information to strike up conversations with your child as if they know them.
- In addition to knowing how to call 911, instruct your child how to make collect calls or use a pay phone to call an operator, just in case.
- Practice, practice, practice! Practice reactions with your children so, God forbid, if the time comes, they can act quickly.
- Do not leave your child unattended, even for a moment, in a stroller.
- *Never* leave your child alone in a car.
- Never let your child go alone to a mall or store bathroom.
- Tell your children to never ask for or accept offers of rides with anyone unless you have agreed to it or arranged the ride. This goes for when they are at malls, stores, playgrounds, schools, bus stops, ball parks, or playgrounds or just around the neighborhood.
- Your child may be shy in front of others at stores or malls, but you must teach them that in addition to screaming "This is not my dad/ mommy!" they should kick, scream, bite, flail, and hit in order to get away.
- Teach your child to always ask your permission to leave one area and go to the next (house to yard, fellowship hall to bathroom or playground, swing sets to nature path). Explain that if they don't ask permission, you will all have to leave. This ritual will come in handy when you are shopping and the kids want to check something out.
- Children should always use the buddy system and never go anywhere alone.
- Teach your child that if anyone approaches them at a store or mall who wants to take them somewhere, they must run and try to get back to you, a store employee, or another mom with children.

CHAPTER FOUR

Bathroom Attacks

In 2018, I tracked down a mom I'd heard about because I wanted to hear the story for myself. Her words really touched a nerve with me, and I had her tell her story on our SiriusXM radio program and our *Crime Stories* podcast.

Misty McDavid's voice, going out across the airwaves, got higher and higher as she told the listeners and me what happened to her son in the local Michael's craft store in Tennessee. Who doesn't love Michael's? I go there and to Hobby Lobby with the twins every time they get assigned another school project.

Misty told me that her "baby," ten-year-old Luke, was with her and they lingered and shopped so long that finally, he just had to "go." She told me, "It was Michael's. I thought it was fine."

It wasn't.

When Luke came out of the bathroom, he had a look of sheer terror on his face and, very shaken, told his mom he had just been scared "the worst I have ever been."

Of course, Mom was distraught and asked what happened.

Luke said that a man tried over and over to force his way into Luke's bathroom stall while Luke was inside. The stranger, jerking repeatedly on the door and trying to force it open, peered at Luke from between the crack in the metal doors. While the perv kept kicking at the door and shaking it, Luke stood inside, completely frozen in fear.

Mom Misty was absolutely horrified and asked if Luke could identify the man who had tried to hurt him. The only thing Luke could say was the guy was wearing muddy black work boots.

Misty searched the whole store until she spotted the shoes of the guy who tried to get to her son. She said, tearfully, that in that moment on the floor of Michael's, she too, froze. She "looked him dead in the eyes" and he just "smirked and kind of laughed at me, ran his fingers through his black greasy hair, and walked off."

She alerted Michael's and went on Facebook soon after to warn other moms in a widely circulated post, but looking back, she replays it over and over in her mind. She thinks of all the times she rehearsed with her son what they would do in a situation like that, but they both ended up frozen and silent when the danger was real.

Who are we to say we wouldn't do the same no matter how much we rehearse or plan our big reaction?

Misty said she always believed she'd know exactly what to say in a situation like that, but not a word would come that day, only shock and fear. But when the moment arrived, she said, "Luke couldn't remember [my] advice. [He was] dead silent. He was scared to death and stayed as quiet as he could."

Even though Misty and Luke may have "frozen" at the time, she has taken to the airwaves and social media to warn other moms of the danger Luke encountered. And Misty taught me something very important: no matter what we teach our children, they may not be able to act in that terrifying moment.

What does that mean?

It means it's on us parents. We must protect our children when they can't protect themselves.

In addition to planning self-defense classes, Misty said, "I will not ever let him go to the bathroom alone again and [even if] it's awkward to take a ten-year-old to the ladies' room, I don't care."

I learned a lot from Misty McDavid, and her courage in telling this story to help others is admirable. I now understand that no matter how much we work with them, they are still only children in a world of predators. Unfortunately, there is an endless supply of stories to remind us that we must be ever vigilant when out in public with our little ones. Here are a few from which we can learn.

A laid-back family evening at the food court at Town Center Mall near Atlanta turned into a nightmare. As Dad waited outside the food court ladies' bathroom for his eleven-year-old daughter, he heard a scream. He immediately recognized it... it was his daughter inside the bathroom. Cobb County cops say when she came out of the privacy stall, thinking she was all alone in the bathroom and heading toward the sinks to wash her hands, a twenty-six-year-old male jumped out. Brandishing a knife at the girl, he rushed out from his hiding place in a different stall and grabbed her. When she let loose with a piercing scream, other adults came running to the bathroom, attacked the attacker, and held him on the ground until police arrived.

Early in the evening in Jacksonville, Florida, a six-year-old boy and his seven-year-old brother went into a McDonald's bathroom together. When just the seven-year-old came out of the bathroom, Dad went in to check on his six-year-old. Dad spotted a strange man coming out of the same stall his little boy was still in. According to police, the dad saw his six-year-old little boy, still in the stall, trying to adjust his pants. The dad took off after the man, chasing him out of the McDonald's and down the street before the perp got away. The next day, the Jacksonville sheriff's office director announced they arrested a grown man on charges of capital sexual battery. This turned out to be the man's second sexual attack on a child in just one week.

In Orlando, a Chick-fil-A customer says that he caught a glimpse of a reflection of a little child "bouncing" in the lap of a grown man inside one of the bathroom stalls. Both the adult male and the baby girl were naked from the waist down. When the customer flushed his commode, the perpetrator realized he was not alone with the baby and quickly tried to get dressed. To make it worse, the perp then pulled out a stun gun and tried to stop the customer from leaving the bathroom. The attacker first denied wrongdoing but later said he may have "accidentally" had sexual contact with the two-year-old.

Police eventually charged the man with sex battery, raping a two-year-old in the Chick-fil-A bathroom just as the witness described. To make matters worse, I later learned the perp had a job...at a daycare.

In Centennial, Colorado, Arapahoe County sheriffs reported that a Denver man followed a little girl into the women's restroom at a Marshall's department store and actually crawled under her locked stall door to get to her. Once in the stall, he exposed himself to her and then assaulted her. Investigators suspect the little girl in Marshall's is not the man's only child assault victim in that area and that he has been very "active." They publicized a tip line to locate his other alleged sexual assault victims. There's no telling how many public bathrooms, and children, this one guy alone has targeted.

MATTHEW CECCHI

I am often asked which case out of all that I have tried or covered stands out the most. I normally don't pick a single case, because no victim is more or less important than any other. But one case in particular haunts me and, I must say, changed my life. It's the case of nine-year-old Matthew Cecchi.

Let me tell you about him. Matthew loved Legos. He was just saying goodbye to all his baby teeth. He hit his first (and only) homerun for his Little League team. He made all A's.

He was murdered.

As I write this, the tapping of the keys conjures up the image in my mind of Matthew Cecchi, dressed in his Little League uniform and smiling at the camera.

Matthew went to a big family reunion picnic on the beach at Oceanside Harbor, California. Everyone was there. When he asked to go to the public bathrooms beside the beach, his aunt said she'd go with him to keep him safe. She waited outside the men's restroom, just at the door. When he didn't emerge, she called his name and then went in to check on him. She was the one who found Matthew lying on the floor bleeding to death. His throat was slashed, and he had been stabbed seven times in the back as he stood at the urinal.

She saw a drifter, Brandon Wilson, run from the bathroom, and later, she positively identified him. She had to be carried out of Matthew's funeral, wailing in grief. The day of his funeral at St. Thomas the Apostle Catholic Church, the killer's name was never mentioned. I covered the trial live at my first TV home, Court TV. Later, as I sat in a darkened studio day in and day out, watching the testimony, my heart broke. Wilson was convicted of first-degree murder. He committed suicide by hanging on November 4, 2011, while on death row.

Matthew's death affected me in a way I couldn't really name. I never met him or his family, but the random nature of the attack on an innocent child, when his family was trying to protect him, truly not letting him far from their sight, shook me. I felt then, and often have afterward, that there was no way, no matter how much we try, to fight back.

Let me tell you now, there is.

PUBLIC BATHROOM SAFETY TIPS

- I don't care what the naysayers and the parents of "free-range" children may say to me or about me. Never, ever allow your child to go into a public restroom alone.
- If possible, use a family restroom. You can all go in together with no issue. It's usually a stand-alone bathroom and typically found near the usual men's and ladies' rooms. They have a locking door as well, so your children are safe with you in there even if your back is turned to the door.
- As an alternative, use the stall closest to the main entrance.
- Without fail, glance under the door first to see if the stall is already occupied.
- Look under the doors to stalls on either side. You can tell if you see men's feet in a ladies' restroom.
- Push the stall door open and look before you go in.
- Never allow a stranger, no matter their age or sex and no matter how friendly or well-intentioned they seem, to help. They might help you right into making a missing poster for your child.
- Make sure your stall door locks.
- If possible, bring both or all your children into the same stall.
- If they won't all fit, secure the oldest one in the stall next to you and have them lock that door.
- I always to this day play a game with whichever twin is in the stall next to me. I put my foot just into their stall and say "Hi!" and then they put a foot on top of mine and say "Hi!" I know they are there next to me and safe. Someone could snatch one of them in the moments it takes me to get the other twin's clothes straight and get out of the stall.
- Don't use the purse hook situated up high on the stall door. Keep your backpack or purse on your person. This way, a crook can't reach over and steal it. If that happens, when you leave to get the purse back, your child is unattended.

- If there is no family restroom, your children won't fit with you in one stall, and the stall next to you isn't free, then do what I did: I had one child stand in front of my stall, leaning on the door, so I could see their legs while I took care of the other child. It's not ideal, but I didn't have a choice then.
- If you are in an isolated or remote location, listen carefully in case someone else enters while you or your children are in a stall. Is it a woman? (Less likely to offend but still a potential danger.) Is she alone? Did she actually go into a stall, or is she loitering around doing nothing? That's a sign you need to get your child and leave.
- Teach your son that if he is ever alone, he is to use a private stall rather than a urinal with the grown men.
- You must teach your children to never, ever talk to a stranger in a public bathroom, no matter how friendly they seem or if they insist they know your child or the family. They don't.
- Teach your child that if they find themselves alone in a public bathroom, maybe while on a school field trip, and they are spoken to in that public bathroom, they are to say they are not allowed to speak to strangers. *Practice this and reinforce it regularly.*
- Avoid bathrooms that have more than one entry/exit.
- Make eye contact with anyone going into the bathroom where your child is.
- Even though my son is no longer a little boy and is taller than me, I still stand near the door and talk to him during his entire time in the bathroom.
- I call out, "I'm right here, son." "Wash your hands!" "Are you okay?" "Is anybody in there with you?" Yes, your child may claim he's embarrassed. That's a discussion you can have when he's thirty years old and is taking his own child to the bathroom. (I'm not mentioning my daughter here because I go into the ladies' room with her.)
- Remind your child that a public bathroom is not a social opportunity for them. They are not there to make friends, play games, or do anything but use the bathroom, wash their hands, and leave.
- If you and your children must split up because of gender bathroom issues, do not under any circumstance leave the door of the bathroom where your child entered alone. One child will have to wait while the other goes so you can be there to guard the door.

*   *   *

After Matthew Cecchi was murdered, there was an outcry for better protection for children in public places. The Matthew Cecchi Public Safety Act was passed allowing for unisex family bathrooms in public campgrounds and parks in San Diego. All new parks and facilities in San Diego County now have these restrooms in their plans. Nothing will ever bring little Matthew back, but it's a start.

CHAPTER FIVE

Nannies and Babysitters from Hell: Daycare Dangers— Not on My Watch!

As a felony prosecutor, I investigated literally hundreds of cases of child abuse and neglect. The facts of those cases range from horrible cigarette burns on children whose photos made me cry (not in front of a jury, of course) to children brutally beaten into vegetative states, sexually molested, or starved to near death. Each case took its toll on me, and I can still see the victims in my mind's eye.

I remember the first such case I covered that gained national attention... I analyzed it live day in and day out, gavel to gavel. It was known as the "Au Pair Murder Trial," the trial of British nanny Louise Woodward.

At the time, I couldn't stop listening as the evidence poured from the witness stand. It was very hard for me to process, as I'm sure it was for the jury, that this young girl could do such a horrible thing. I remember the first time I saw her blank face, eyes either blinking rapidly or fixed in a vacant stare.

But for me, it was and will always be about baby boy Matthew Eappen. May he rest in peace.

LOUISE WOODWARD, THE BOSTON AU PAIR

Dr. Deborah Eappen, an ophthalmologist from Newton, Massachusetts, was thrilled when she and her husband, Sunil, also a doctor, learned she was pregnant. It was on May 24, 1996, that their dream came true in the form of baby Matthew. Baby Matty was a joy, and Deborah cut her workload to just three days a week to be with him. Even on the days she had to leave for work, Deborah rushed home during the day to breastfeed her little love.

Enter Louise Woodward, an eighteen-year-old girl from Great Britain with a beautiful accent, a seemingly sweet demeanor, an obsession with Broadway (she traveled to New York to see one musical, the stage production of *Rent*, nearly thirty times), and a penchant for staying out late. Her outward appearance would prove to be misleading. She landed in the US and hit the nanny market thanks to the EF au pair agency. After leaving her first placement, she made her way to the Eappen family at the end of 1996.

After a few months on the job, the Eappens talked to Louise about having a curfew, as her social life was limiting her ability to be the nanny they wanted. It came out in trial that Louise Woodward was angry—very angry—that the Eappens had reprimanded her about partying late and wished to curtail her social life. A crying baby is all it took for that anger to boil over.

Woodward admitted that eight-month-old Matty was cranky and crying the morning of February 4, 1997, and she had been "rough" with the baby, shaking him and "throwing him onto a pile of towels." Just imagining someone "throwing" John David or Lucy onto a stack of towels makes my blood boil...*throwing* a tiny baby? Those are her words, not mine!

When Matty "became unresponsive," Woodward called 911. The medical evidence is undisputed that Matty had a fractured skull with a brain so swollen from bleeding that a clot of blood spontaneously shot out onto the floor while he was undergoing an operation to save his life. He also had a fractured wrist that appeared to be two weeks old. Doctors who treated Matty were adamant that this was child abuse and that his brain injuries were caused by violent shaking back and forth, known as "shaken baby syndrome." This was proven by the many tiny hemorrhages in Matty's eyes, only seen when a baby's eyes have bounced back and forth so much that the retina rips and bleeding in the eye vessels occurs, like bruises elsewhere in the body. Matty passed away on February 9.

After Woodward was convicted of second-degree murder, the trial judge, who felt Woodward's action lacked malice, felt sympathy for her, not the baby, and reduced the charge to involuntary manslaughter and cut her sentence to *time served*.

Two hundred seventy-nine days in jail for actions leading to the death of a baby! She walked free. But grieving mother Deborah was the target of a huge backlash, including letters trashing her and her choice to practice medicine and not stay home full-time. Matty's dad noted that everyone focused on Woodward and forgot the most important piece of the puzzle: baby Matty. I never forgot what the trial was all about and I never will...it was about baby Matty.

LEO AND LULU KRIM

I have tried so many cases of atrocities upon children that I actually try to block them from my memory. I ache over the betrayal parents must feel after they trust someone with their child, pay that someone to come into their home and be part of their family, and have it all end in heartbreak of the worst sort.

In 2012, I was so distraught about the so-called Manhattan nanny case that I wouldn't even report on it for several nights. Only when viewers began asking why we weren't covering it did I break down and report on it. The words tasted like dirt in my mouth. I cried during commercial breaks and actually felt nauseous just reporting the facts.

On October 24, 2012, at about 5:30 p.m., working mom Marina Krim came rushing home to her family's apartment. When Marina opened the apartment door, she had no idea her life would change forever.

Before she opened the door, she already had a sense something was off, because when she went to pick up her six-year-old daughter, Lucia, at ballet earlier, the instructor said Lulu never made it there. That was wrong, and Mommy knew it immediately.

"Where are you?" she texted the babysitter. No response.

As Marina headed home, panic rising, she stopped to pick up her middle child, Nessie, from swimming.

When she got up to her apartment, everything was dead quiet, which in itself was way wrong. She immediately spotted two-year-old Leo's stroller and Lulu's backpack in the living room. She called out and went to each room, pulling Nessie along with her. But no one answered Marina when she called.

Heading to the back of the apartment, Marina was about to see the worst thing imaginable for a parent. Her babies, Leo and Lulu, were in the tub, stabbed with a kitchen knife. Babysitter Yoselyn Ortega was standing over them, and as soon as Marina opened the door and made eye contact, Ortega made a stabbing motion at her own neck, resulting in a superficial wound.

Motive? Ortega had recently mentioned she was short on money, and Marina, hoping to help, offered extra hours of light housekeeping work. At the time of the murders, Ortega was making $500 a week helping to pick up and drop off the children. She was furious that it would take a little extra work to earn another $100. Instead of giving the money back or finding another job, she lashed out, brutally stabbing the little children.

During opening statements, it came out that Ortega deeply resented Marina Krim for the good life she tried to give her three children, the life Ortega never gave her own son. Ortega had met the Krims through her sister and promptly given them a fake reference.

Videotape of police interviews establish Ortega's bitterness over her own money problems and anger about her work schedule. She also had family problems; one sister had ordered her out of the apartment they shared, and the other sister insisted Ortega take her own son back. (Ortega left her son when he was just four years old.)

With no medical history of mental illness, the state argued that Ortega conveniently made up all her stories of devilish commands. Yet the very same interview tapes show Ortega consistently denying that any "voices" ordered her to kill the two children. She couldn't have it both ways, arguing that the devil made her do it and also that no he didn't.

A difficult trial ensued with mom Marina breaking down while detailing the horrific scene she saw in her own home, her two children stabbed dead in a bloody bathtub. Their dad revealed a deep anger that Ortega and her family had lied about her background and qualifications. Finally, on May 14, 2018, Ortega was sentenced to life in prison with no possibility of parole.

An hour after the verdict, mom Marina posted a shot from the top of the Empire State Building near their apartment, a spot her little Leo had loved. She wrote, "You two never made it to the top, but I'm up here now for the first time, in peace, on top of the world, remembering another lifetime and thinking of you." Oh my stars, I hurt just writing this.

These painful stories reveal the dangers and risks of letting people you really don't know into your homes and lives, the nannies from hell. But there are also risks to recognize when you drop your children off at a daycare center, as the following examples demonstrate. Read on.

CHRISTOPHER GARDNER JR.

June 12, 2017, 6:40 a.m. sharp. Five-year-old Christopher Gardner Jr., who had learning disabilities, was picked up in a van by two employees of Ascent Children's Health Services in West Memphis, Arkansas, and headed to their daycare facility.

Eight hours later, little boy Christopher was dead. His lifeless body was found in the Ascent van he'd been picked up in.

The temperature inside the van climbed to 141 degrees that day. Can you even imagine the heat? Evidence shows Christopher managed to get free from the car seat and to take off his shirt and one shoe. When he was finally found, he was sitting upright in a seat directly across the aisle from where he had first been placed. While the daycare workers laughed and talked and had their morning coffee and their lunches and sodas, Christopher was just a few yards away and dying of heatstroke.

His body was discovered only when staff went out to load children for their trips back home. Four daycare workers were charged with manslaughter: Felicia Phillips, the driver; Pamela Robinson, who assisted with the pick-ups; Wanda Taylor, who signed little Christopher into daycare even though he never got out of the van; and Kendra Washington, who was specifically entrusted with making sure all children got out of the van. Facing a multimillion-dollar lawsuit from Christopher's family, Ascent Children's Health Services closed their facilities throughout the state of Arkansas.

EVIL COMES TO ELYRIA, OHIO

In September 2013, when sheriffs made a routine check on a registered sex offender, James Osborne, they found an unregistered laptop. On the laptop, in addition to explicit photos of a teen girl, they found a very disturbing video. The video depicted a female performing sex acts with tiny children as young as one year old. That woman was twenty-five-year-old Heather Koon. Heather Koon was not only Osborne's "girlfriend" but also a daycare worker at ABC Kidz Child Center in Elyria, Ohio, and at the Country Day School in Amherst.

Brace yourself. Koon was "dating" the sex offender, Osborne, and according to a lengthy and painful investigation, he convinced her to rape the children, among other things, and videotape the attacks. At least four children that we know of were molested.

I don't like thinking about this. I don't like writing this. I'd like to delete this whole chapter. But I can't because this is the truth, and I share it with you now so we are all armed with facts. We can use facts and knowledge to protect our children. Because of that, I will continue.

Koon would molest the children and then send videos and photos of the molestations to Osborne.

Some of the children are too young to remember what she did to them, but I've learned others are still extremely traumatized. Some of the children still wake up screaming with nightmares, and others have a deep fear of adults.

During the trial, multiple text messages between Osborne and Koon were read out loud as court watchers cringed, gasped, and cried. The court heard the defendants, in their own words, as Osborne gave Koon specific instructions on how to molest the babies. He egged her on to groom the children for future sex abuse and convinced her to nab babysitting gigs so he could get to the children himself.

Of course, Koon apologized in court. *Blah-blah.* I don't even want to hear her talk. She claims Osborne convinced her to do these things. But how much convincing did it take? Also, he wasn't even there! They both bought a one-way coach ticket to hell, and that's where they belong. I'm sure they'll be welcomed with open arms there.

Oh yes, Koon got life in prison without parole. Osborne got four consecutive life sentences. They each deserve so much more.

SYSTEMIC FAILURE

According to a story by Jenifer B. McKim in the *Boston Globe*, dad Kevin (last name withheld for privacy reasons) made the shocking and life-changing discovery that his middle son had been molested by a trusted babysitter. Kevin immediately wanted to storm out the door to hunt down and kill the man, but his wife stopped him, convincing him he had to call police. Soon, the twenty-five-year-old babysitter, John Burbine, was in custody.

The police eventually determined that Burbine had molested all three little boys, and he was convicted of three counts of indecent assault and battery. In a stunning injustice, Burbine got only a slap on the wrist for sexually molesting *three little boys*: a suspended sentence of six months followed by two years of probation. While disappointed beyond belief, the boys' parents accepted the outcome because they believed that as a registered sex offender, this real-life demon, John Burbine, would never be allowed near children again.

Wrong.

Burbine and his enabler-wife went on to open an unlicensed daycare center in 2010 called the Waterfall Education Center. They brazenly advertised online. You know the rest. Pedophile John Burbine was eventually caught and convicted for raping another thirteen children, ages eight months to three years old. His wife received a five-year prison sentence for her involvement in her husband's crimes. How could they continue molesting children day in and day out after Burbine was already convicted?

Facing life behind bars, Burbine committed suicide in 2014. Now the devil can decide what to do with him and spare a jury from hearing the horrible details and also spare the child victims from having to recount what happened at the hands of this fiend. His death also spared his future victims the pain that both he and the legal system would heap on them.

KIDDIE FIGHT CLUBS

One of the worst examples of child abuse in a daycare setting that I know of took place at the Minnieland Academy at the Glen in Woodbridge, Virginia, in 2013. I'm sure Walt Disney is rolling over in his grave over this unfortunate naming and would want me to point out immediately there is no relation between the lovely Minnie Mouse of Disney fame and the infamous Minnieland Academy daycare center in Virginia.

As social workers headed over to Minnieland, they likely had no idea what they'd find. Claims of stomping on tots' naked toes, dunking children underwater, hosing them with water in their faces, and forcing them to eat spicy foods were just the tips of the icebergs. What they found was even worse: a "tot fight club," where children were forced to fight each other hand to hand so teachers could stand by and laugh. The two teachers seemingly enjoyed snapping rubber bands on the tots' wrists to hurt them, forcing them to chew Flamin' Hot Cheetos, and making them hit and kick each other. It all went down in what Minnieland called the "monkey room."

Can you imagine the stories the tots were trying to communicate to Mom and Dad, but couldn't? Now the angry parents say their tots are afraid, fearful, and overly aggressive after being forced into these "monkey room" fights. While Minnieland denies it, several other teachers stated on the record that they reported the abuse months before Minnieland acted. I'm sure it will all get sorted out during the $12 million lawsuit against Minnieland. (Minnieland Academy was back in the news in 2018 when a former employee was charged with sexually assaulting four young children.)

The two women behind the tot fight club were fired and found guilty on child cruelty–related charges, both going to prison for two years. You'd think jailtime for both would be the end of "tot fight clubs," right?

Sadly, think again. I later covered a similar incident. Seems like child predators never learn from history. On December 7, 2016, when the heater broke down at Adventure Learning Center in St. Louis, the teachers got bored.

To amuse themselves, they decided to start their own tot fight club. What happened to finger-painting?

What they didn't count on was one boy's older brother playing in the next room and secretly taping the incident on his iPad after seeing his little brother cry from getting beaten in the "ring" for three fights. The children in the video are crying and begging not to have to hit and punch their little friends. And what did the teachers do? They pushed them back into the "ring"! The tot fights only stopped when the boy texted the video to his mom, Nicole Merseal, who called the center immediately and then filed a lawsuit, as she should have.

The teachers had clean records. But in the video, you see one of the teachers in her Ugg boots cheering, making kicking motions to one boy to kick another little boy already down. One teacher is so excited, she's cheering and jumping up and down in glee as the children cry at one tot pounding another tot's head into the ground.

The only one who tried to intervene was another little boy who ran in and tried without success to stop the fighting. The "teachers" took no notice.

Ultimately, I learned that the center's own cameras caught fight after fight on video that could be easily monitored by the staff. When I watched and listened to the raw audio of the tot fight club from the brother's iPad, it made me sick. I took to the airwaves to expose it. The center says both teachers were fired, and that the center called a child abuse hotline. But even after all that, the St. Louis Circuit Attorney's Office declined to prosecute, claiming there was "insufficient evidence." Didn't they see the same iPad video I did? Even though state regulators substantiated the tot fight club complaint, Adventure Learning Center continued operating, business as usual. Public outcry led police to reopen the case in late 2018.

But the initial finding is chilling. With all that evidence, no charges were filed.

How safe are our children at daycare centers?

KIDDIE OD AT DAYCARE

On March 22, 2016, when four-month-old Adam Seagull suddenly died in daycare after being there just eleven days, the healthy baby's passing was chalked up to sudden infant death syndrome (SIDS). In other words, it was labeled an unexplained death at a daycare facility in the upscale suburbs near Bridgeport, Connecticut. Adam's parents were heartbroken and dumbfounded. Adam was healthy.

It was only after months of investigation and toxicology studies that the local medical examiner returned a stunning report: Adam overdosed on diphenhydramine, the main ingredient in over-the-counter Benadryl. But you can bet your bottom dollar the infant didn't chug it on his own.

At first, the daycare owner/operator Carol Cardillo insisted she never dosed Adam with Benadryl, knowing full well infants should never get this medicine at all. But the postmortem showed Adam had 41,000 nanograms per milliliter of Benadryl in his system, nearly ten times the reportable limit. Cardillo indignantly denied even having Benadryl in her home, but pharmacy receipts from over two and a half years show she'd purchased *ninety bottles* of Benadryl, including just days before Adam died. That's nearly three gallons of Benadryl! Cardillo claimed she used the drug for a "skin condition."

At sentencing on manslaughter, the lying persisted as Cardillo souped up her act. She never admitted guilt and instead whined that the "incident" (Adam's death) caused "havoc" within her own family. She only got thirty months.

Wow. Just thirty months behind bars? Baby Adam was with Cardillo for eleven short days, but she robbed the Seagull family of a lifetime together. She's pure evil. She didn't want to take the time necessary to get Adam to nod off naturally, so she got Adam to sleep with drugs. Her laziness killed him.

HARPER ROSE BRIAR

Marissa Colburn thought long and hard before she decided to go back to school, but she wanted so badly to make a great living and give her daughter, Harper Rose Briar, everything she could ever need as she grew up. Out of love and devotion to Harper Rose, she made the tough decision to put her daughter into daycare while she attended classes. Three days in, on January 24, 2019, Mommy got a text from EMTs saying that Harper was in very bad condition and she should rush to the hospital immediately. Wondering why Stacey Vaillancourt, the fifty-three-year-old Rutland, Vermont, mom keeping Harper, hadn't called her, she raced to the hospital.

As much as EMTs and others tried, they could not revive baby Harper. Mommy couldn't understand what had happened. Harper had been perfectly fine just that morning. The final autopsy report states that Harper was found "unresponsive." The medical examiner discovered extremely high concentrations of diphenhydramine, the main ingredient in Benadryl, in Harper's system. The autopsy report went on to say that diphenhydramine is never to be used on infants unless a doctor has specifically ordered it. There was no such doctor's order for Harper, say Vermont State Police.

Prosecutors now allege that Vaillancourt "sedated an otherwise beautiful, happy, healthy 6-month-old to the point where that baby could not lift her head and died." While Vaillancourt's legal team says she is not guilty in court, forty supporters of Harper sat and watched the proceedings in court, all of them wearing pink T-shirts saying "Justice for Harper Rose."

As I go about my days and nights, taking care of the twins, cooking for them, sitting around the table with them, watching movies, playing with the pets, driving them home from school, and listening to them chatter about what happened that day, I think of Harper's mom and dad. They are making T-shirts, planning for the next court date, and remembering their little girl.

KIDS UNATTENDED WHILE TEACHER GOES TO TARGET

When I drop my twins at school, it never crosses my mind their teacher would leave them alone for any reason at all, much less to make a Target run. But that's exactly what happened in Houston, Texas, on February 24, 2011. A twenty-four-year-old woman, Jessica Tata, decided it was a good idea to go shop at Target despite having seven children in her care, all under the age of three. She actually left them to go shopping at Target.

To make matters worse—if you can imagine this story getting worse—Tata left a pan of cooking oil on the stovetop, and it ignited a blaze that ripped through the daycare. Four of these abandoned children died, and the other three were seriously injured.

Salt in the wound? There's a lot to go around.

First, Target video surveillance shows Tata wasn't even in a hurry. She browsed! A Target manager testified that Tata wasn't even slightly ruffled even after she realized she had left the stove on. Second, anguished neighbors said they could hear the tots crying during the fire as they tried to rescue them. Third, distraught parents say they trusted Tata and had been convinced she was qualified to take care of their babies.

Finally, this wasn't the first time she'd left the infants alone to shop and run errands, as older children who had previously been under Tata's care testified. She did it often, but, of course, none of the little children could verbalize it to their moms and dads.

Six-month-old Elias Castillo died in the blaze, and it was for his death that Tata was finally held accountable legally. She got eighty years behind bars, but the parents of those children got a lifetime of regret. Tata still faces three more counts of felony murder, three counts of abandoning a child, and two counts of reckless injury to a child.

GUNS AND CHILDREN DON'T MIX

Timothy and Samantha Eubanks owned and operated a daycare business out of their Dearborn, Michigan, home. In late September 2017, when their three-year-old son wanted to play, he got Daddy's gun from an unlocked gun safe and took it over to the other children. In the end, two other three-year-olds were rushed to the hospital, one shot in the shoulder and the other in the face. The second child lost an eye. The other children waited at the police station until parents could come to bring them home. The Eubankses were charged with firearms violations and child abuse. Timothy Eubanks pled guilty to six counts of second-degree child abuse and was placed on two years' probation in February 2019. It's a miracle the two three-year-olds lived, but there are plenty of nightmares to torture these children for the rest of their lives.

ALLERGIC TO DAIRY, NUTS ... AND DAYCARE

Elijah Silvera's parents did everything they could to keep him safe. The Seventh Avenue Center for Family Services in New York City was given all his medical records, which clearly emphasized a deadly allergy to dairy products. Elijah's mom went over and over it with staff at Seventh Avenue. She gave them his meds and even an EpiPen. Even so, a few days later, on November 3, 2017, one of the staff members served little Elijah a grilled cheese sandwich, and instead of calling 911 or using the EpiPen when the tot's airway began to constrict and close, they called his mom as Elijah died of anaphylactic shock. The city closed the Seventh Avenue Center after little Elijah passed away.

AUTUMN ELGERSMA

It was only nine a.m. on October 29, 2013, when Jennifer Elgersma got a call at her desk in Range City, Iowa, from her daycare center to report that her three-year-old daughter, Autumn, had taken a fall down the stairs. Jennifer quickly gathered her things and was out the door in a flash. Jennifer picked up Autumn and took her straight to a nearby emergency room. It was there she first learned Autumn had an acute head injury. Autumn was promptly airlifted to specialists at the Sanford Children's Hospital in Sioux Falls, South Dakota. At Sanford, Jennifer got a clearer picture of Autumn's injuries: the tot had a fractured skull and brain trauma.

After a two-day bedside vigil, Jennifer and her husband, Phillip, were present when Autumn went on to heaven. To add to their heartache, they later learned the daycare worker who first said that Autumn had simply fallen down the stairs had confessed to police what really happened. Rochelle Sapp says she *threw* baby Autumn down the stairs when little Autumn didn't want to take off her coat as Sapp ordered. The tot simply didn't want to take off her coat, and now she's dead, thrown down the stairs with such force that her skull was fractured.

Autumn's parents say, "Autumn was a joy in our lives, and we are blessed to have called her ours. We take comfort in the fact that she is now with her Savior, Jesus Christ."

That statement shows that Autumn's parents are stronger than I am. They will never see Autumn grow up, but they found comfort in their faith to help them cope with this unspeakable tragedy. Sapp got fifty years in jail, but it doesn't seem like enough to me. I can't stop thinking about little Autumn at the top of the stairs, wearing the little coat Mommy buttoned for her that morning. I can't stand the thought of her on an autopsy table.

"MAGICAL" KARL TOWNDROW

On a hot July day in 2015, Amber Scorah dropped Karl, her fifteen-week-old son, at SoHo Child Care in New York City for the very first time. Amber didn't feel ready to rejoin the workforce, but she reasoned she was just a few blocks away and she could go breastfeed and visit Karl on her lunch break. It seemed like the perfect setup for a working mom. But when Amber got there for her first check-in on her baby, she discovered Karl unconscious, lying on a changing table. Karl's lips were blue. The daycare's owner was trying her best to resuscitate him. Karl died less than three hours after Amber left him for the first time. The facility was shut down the next day after it was discovered that the workers were never trained in CPR and that the facility was not licensed, but that's cold comfort for Karl's mom. The baby's cause of death is unknown. Amber described Karl as "magical." When I've studied photos of her with baby Karl, I see what she means. How do you get beyond a loss like that? I don't know the answer.

SHEPARD DODD

Just like Amber Scorah, Ali Dodd dropped her baby, eleven-week-old Shepard, at daycare on April 6, 2015, in Edmond, Oklahoma. But in just a few hours, she got the call every parent dreads: her son wasn't breathing. Ali was told over the phone that EMTs were performing CPR on Shepard at that moment and to come quickly. She did.

When Ali and her husband, Derek, arrived at the hospital, Shepard had passed on. She kissed his face and wanted to die herself. She and Derek both believe Shepard's death was completely avoidable, because the police report reveals Shepard was placed to nap in a car seat for two full hours. While he was sleeping, his chin rested on his chest, and the little baby died of what is known as positional asphyxiation. He lacked air because of the dangerous body position that no one corrected. Worse, the care provider had already been warned about unsafe sleep practices by the Department of Human Services, but no one ever told Ali.

Ali and Derek now campaign to protect other children and seek to educate care providers. They founded Shepard's Watch to help other babies live by spreading awareness of safe infant sleep habits. God bless them.

BENSON XIONG

Heather Gardner of Wausau, Wisconsin, was looking hard to find the right babysitter for her two-month old son, Benson Xiong. A working mother, Heather got a recommendation from a friend at work. This babysitter was from Heather's hometown, so it felt right. Benson loved to smile, and he was smiling when his mom dropped him off at the home of Marissa Tietsort.

A few weeks in, Heather noticed Benson had a scratch in his mouth and immediately took the baby to the ER. She voiced a fear that something—she didn't know what, exactly—had happened to Benson while at the babysitter's house. The ER doctors told Heather not to worry, and so the baby boy was handed over again to Tietsort.

When Heather picked up Benson the following day, the sweet baby was dressed in his snowsuit, buckled in his car seat, and fast asleep with his little hat pulled over his eyes. After a long day at work, Mom still had to stop by the laundromat. Heather took Benson in, and when she started unpacking him from his car seat, she noticed that the baby's lips seemed stuck together. The young mom unzipped his snowsuit, and it was then she realized something was very wrong: her baby was rock hard.

The criminal complaint, as told by the policeman who raced to the laundromat to help, reveals that when he arrived, he found Heather frantically performing chest compressions on Benson. But baby Benson was motionless, his mouth clenched shut. His body was cold and his legs were rigidly stuck in the car seat sitting position. Heather told the officer it had only been minutes since she picked up Benson, already snapped in his car seat and asleep. Then, just minutes later, Benson was dead? It couldn't be.

And it wasn't. Later, Tietsort confessed she noticed baby Benson was cold to the touch. She knew he was dead but didn't know why and did not check for a pulse or try to get help or perform CPR. Instead, she says she put the baby's dead body on the floor in her hall, dressed him in his snowsuit, and strapped him into his car seat bundled with blankets, pulling his cap down over his eyes. When Tietsort's boyfriend got home, Tietsort didn't mention a word, and they went on a date to eat at McDonald's with Benson's dead body in the car. When Heather arrived, she handed him over to his mom and pretended he was sleeping.

But the autopsy proved a very different and much more violent scenario. Benson sustained at least three separate blunt force injuries to his head, and his tailbone was broken off, which requires a huge amount of force. Rigor mortis showed that Benson was killed at least two hours before Heather called police.

That's not all. The babysitter who got a glowing recommendation from Heather's co-worker had multiple incidents with police and child services. Just weeks before Benson was killed, Tietsort said an eleven-month-old she was keeping fell off a sofa and injured her face, but doctors said the baby's injuries didn't come from a simple fall. One year earlier, a three-month-old child suffered a skull fracture in Tietsort's care. Tietsort wasn't charged. Before that, her then-boyfriend got a temporary restraining order against her, claiming she abused their two sons. Social workers took four of her children away, unaware she had a fifth and a sixth was on the way.

When I think of baby Benson in his little snowsuit and his mom in the laundromat working frantically to bring her baby back to life, it's almost too much to take. Although she was charged with Benson's murder, and despite all the other evidence to the contrary, Tietsort still insists she's a great mom. She was charged with first-degree intentional homicide and was awaiting trial at the time of this writing.

RYLAN KOOPMEINERS—CARE.COM NIGHTMARE

I investigated when I learned a Kenosha County, Wisconsin, couple filed a wrongful death lawsuit against the highly popular caregiver website Care.com. I had used the site twice myself when I was working out of town and had the twins with me. Like me, Reggan and Nathan Koopmeiners used Care.com to hire a nanny, thirty-five-year-old Sarah Gumm, to sit with their baby girl, Rylan Koopmeiners.

They accused Care.com of failing to reveal that Gumm had drunken driving citations and a battery incident. This, the Koopmeinerses say, was after they paid extra for the very highest level of background check possible on the Care.com website.

The wrongful death lawsuit goes further, stating Gumm was drunk when Rylan's skull was fractured. The autopsy revealed no doubt: Rylan died of brutal blunt force trauma.

Evidence in court showed Gumm was changing baby Rylan's diaper on July 27, 2012, and, angry when the infant wriggled and squirmed, she struck the baby's head on the changing table with such force that she fractured Rylan's skull, causing bleeding to the brain. At four thirty that afternoon, Gumm called police to report Rylan wasn't breathing, and by five, three-month-old Rylan was pronounced dead.

Gumm first claimed Rylan was sleeping, made "gurgling noises," and seemed to be in distress. She stated she'd been home with Rylan all day, but neighbors spotted her leaving alone in a taxi that same afternoon. In fact, receipts show Gumm used her credit card twice that day at the drugstore to buy wine, the second trip just before calling police. She left the injured baby all alone. Finally, she admitted she slammed the baby down on the changing table out of frustration. She was hired just six weeks before she killed baby Rylan. Gumm was sentenced to twenty-three years in prison for Rylan's death, the lawsuit against Care.com goes on, and Rylan's parents mourn her death to this day.

Care.com issued a statement: "While we remain deeply saddened by these events, we cannot comment on matters of ongoing litigation."

I know the cases I highlighted are upsetting to read, but I chose each one for a specific reason: to underline various dangers and reinforce how horrific scenarios manifest in the most seemingly innocent, everyday settings. Most important, what can we learn from them?

HOW TO KEEP YOUR CHILD SAFE FROM HELLISH CHILD CARE PROVIDERS

- Inspect the center with your own eyes. I repeat: inspect the facility in person. If the facility looks dated, that's a warning. Is there mold? Do windows or blinds present a health hazard? You want equipment and products that meet the most recent safety standards.
- Avoid facilities that have cords dangling from drapes or blinds (see chapter 7).
- Avoid facilities with cribs featuring spindle sides.
- How often is it cleaned and how? Not just the floors but the surfaces, changing tables, toys, sheets, and rugs—everything.
- Licensed daycare facilities must have the most recent inspections posted in writing (like you see on elevators and mammogram machines). Ask to see it.

- Is there livestreaming at the facility? Even daycare for cats and dogs has livestreaming. If dog owners get livestreaming, shouldn't the parents of human babies have it, too?
- Check playground equipment for the latest in safety standards including a spongey or earth foundation as opposed to asphalt or cement.
- No pool or pond should be in the play area. Period.
- Make sure there is an appropriate staff-to-child ratio. Even with qualifying credentials, the provider can still fall short when there are too many kids per adult. At the very least, aim for one adult for every three babies, one adult for every four to six tots, and one adult for every six or seven preschoolers.
- Make sure the provider does not include anyone underqualified. Daycare providers are constantly on the lookout for loopholes to cut costs. *All staffers* need to have qualifying credentials, not just the owner/operator. The owner may not be the one caring for your child day to day.
- Double-check that all staff are CPR and first aid trained. I had to be certified to be a camp counselor—it should be a given for a daycare.
- Ask to see the background checks on every person working there. There is a state-by-state resource map that will tell you your state's legal requirements for child care providers and whether your daycare center is regulated. There are also child care resource agencies online to help. If your child care is not regulated or licensed, ask to see the full background checks. If they haven't been done, ask that they be done immediately.
- Who should be checked? Anyone involved in your child's care or supervision, anyone who could have unsupervised access to your child (bus/van drivers, service, repair, groundskeepers, kitchen staff, janitors, and clerks), family members who live in a home child care center and are eighteen or older, and volunteers at the facility.
- A background check is essential,* as are several references, and

---

* Note: federal statute requires many care providers to submit requests for background checks for all staff. The background check, by law, must be renewed every five years at a minimum.

should include state and federal (NCIC) rap sheets for felonies, misdemeanors, and ordinance violations; state and federal sex offender registries; state child abuse/neglect registry, and an FBI fingerprint check.

- Run vehicle checks for accident history.
- Do a credit check. You may be surprised, and it may change your child care decision. Rats will do anything if they are on a sinking financial ship.
- Look for low staff turnover. Children, whether infants, toddlers, or preschoolers, need stable relationships, whether they can articulate it or not. Low turnover ensures your child's likes and dislikes and any special care instructions are known and not forgotten when a particular staff member leaves. Also, if there's a rapid turnover, you must ask why. Investigate.
- If you are going to leave your child at a daycare center, you must become an authority on that facility and its staff and its policies.
- Are there brothers, husbands, male friends or relatives that visit the center?
- Are there male repairmen or service providers that frequent the premises? What's the policy as to whether these visitors are supervised? Do they have unfettered access to children there? Of course female visitors must be screened as well, but statistically, males commit many, many more predatory crimes.
- When other parents visit, would they ever be alone with your child?
- Are all areas of the daycare visible through glass walls or doors with glass panes? Or are there secret areas not visible to you, the parent?
- Are the children's bathroom doors kept open so they can be heard inside?
- There should be clear policy requirements for moving children from room to room, to the bathroom, to the van or bus, and to different locations. Find out what they are.
- Can the daycare center provide references from other parents? They should.
- What is their discipline policy?
- Are there car seats, boosters, and seat belts? Are they up to date, and what is their use policy?
- Does transport include one bus driver, or do chaperones ride along?

- Does the provider have written policies on medication? Transportation? Outdoor play? Meals and nutrition? Nap time? Bathroom visits? Illness?
- Is there a qualified health professional for the provider? National standards call for monthly visits from a health care pro such as a nurse or doctor.
- What is the pick-up policy? How does the provider ensure children are not sent home with an imposter?
- Are children supervised at all times, even if they are sleeping?
- Is there a daily schedule for activities, meals, naps?

Ask these questions. It's your right to know, as a parent and a potential customer, who will be near your child. Vague answers are a gigantic red flag. From tummy time to sunscreen and bug spray, nail down the rules. The provider must have clear guidelines the employees understand. It won't hurt for you to reinforce with notes or calls.

Neglect?

Look for signs your child is being left alone or neglected at daycare. Some of those signs could be:

- Medical problems, like a cut that has become infected because it wasn't bandaged.
- Ripped or dirty clothes at the end of the day.
- Wet or soiled diapers, pull-ups, or pants.
- Complaints from your child that they are cold or hot at daycare. This could signal long periods outdoors, lack of heat or AC, or going outside without a coat.
- Poor hygiene at the end of the day. Dirty faces, crusty noses or eyes, dirty nails, and lice are all clues.
- Crying when you drop them off.
- Bad dreams.
- Bed wetting.
- Biting nails.
- Changes in behavior.
- Lack of energy or exuberance.
- Clinginess.
- Withdrawal.

- Unusual fatigue.
- Stealing or hoarding food from the fridge, classmates, or siblings.
- Fear of abandonment. If your child is left alone on the playground or in a room at daycare, they will manifest this anxiety.

You know your child. Get to the bottom of any changes you notice in their mood or disposition.

Your Child's Meds

Daycares often are responsible for dosing your children. You must ensure your request is followed with specific written consent and directions. Then double- and triple-check to make sure it happens exactly as you request. Call immediately if you suspect the dosage is not administered correctly. Your child's life could depend on it.

- If your child is constantly sick after starting daycare, check again. Are they mismanaging sanitation?
- What are the handwashing practices for children and employees?
- Are the other children immunized? And for what?

Food

- What type of food is served, and how is it prepped?
- Is food handled correctly? Are containers left out? What about milk? How often are snacks and drinks purchased?
- Label your child's food.
- Ask about how food is stored and served. Foodborne illnesses have special consequences for children because their still-developing immune systems have trouble warding off infections.
- How are babies bottle-fed? Is there policy against bottle propping?
- Does the provider document food and formula intake?
- Make sure food allergies are noted and respected.
- Find out if the provider can accommodate a child with allergies. My IILN executive producer saved his own son's life in the nick of time when the boy was unwittingly served a dish made with cashew milk. If Dean hadn't known how to use an EpiPen, his son wouldn't have survived. Without that knowledge, a child with severe allergies could die in minutes.

More Guidelines

- Make sure your facility practices "Back to Sleep." This means all caregivers know your infant must sleep on their back to avoid SIDS.
- Make sure the center is gated and fenced.
- Make sure the center is not near a body of water to which the children have access.
- Leave multiple emergency numbers with your care provider.
- Make sure your daycare calls each number they have when your child doesn't show up.
- Make sure the center is locked down, that no one can just walk in, and the doors remain locked to outsiders.
- Make sure parents can drop in unannounced. A responsible baby-sitter or daycare person will understand your request and go one step further, giving you full access to your child 24/7/365. I go spy on the twins, unannounced, whenever I can. No one has ever suggested that it is unusual.
- Let your child know you are not spying on them for the fun of it, but that it's your duty to protect them. If that calls for watching or monitoring, then so be it.
- All drugs, cleaning supplies, and anything potentially hazardous (dishwashing or detergent pods) must be kept locked away.

Friendliness is not a good indication of daycare safety. To ensure your child's safety, you have the right to ask all the above.

In-Home Nannies and Babysitters

- When hiring a nanny, you must do a background check. They are easy to do, and you can do them online. Make no bones about it: tell the candidate you need their full name and date of birth to run a background check. If they object, there's a problem.
- Same thing goes for a credit check as mentioned above.
- Don't judge a book by its cover. All the nannies from hell discussed above were "friendly," and many came with strong recommendations from trusted sources.
- Look him or her up on social media. See if your prospective nanny boozes, drugs up, or parties way too much. You can also gauge their personality.

- Ask friends, neighbors, or co-workers for recommendations.
- You can do initial screenings over the phone. Candidates who clear that hurdle then sit for a full, in-person interview.
- Have the first meet-up at a neutral location, like a diner or coffee shop. You don't want a kook to know your address.
- Smell them. Don't laugh! I interviewed three sisters who swore they didn't smoke, but they stunk to high heaven of cigarettes. It oozed out of them. My twins were extremely premature, and being around smoke or nicotine, even slightly, is very bad for them. To be sure I was right and they hadn't just been somewhere smoky, I interviewed them twice. Both times, they stunk! And what if they smell like alcohol or pot? Trust me. You're not so precious that you can't take a whiff of someone you are contemplating for such an important job.
- If possible, interview with a husband, partner, or friend. They may catch things you don't.
- Do a test run. Introduce the candidate to your children and let them play. Watch awhile and then leave them. After the candidate leaves, ask your child what they thought or if they'd like to play again.
- Before you formally hire the nanny or sitter, get a background check as explained above. Again, don't be embarrassed. If the sitter objects, there is a problem. She should want you to check her background.
- For Pete's sake, get a nanny cam. I *love* mine and watch the twins from all over the country when I travel. Even though I never worry about our babysitter, Ms. Michell, I get peace of mind knowing they are okay. Plus, with all the cases I've covered where parents spot nannies from hell abusing their child, I'd be irresponsible if I didn't use a nanny cam. I access mine from my smartphone. I have it handy every time I'm on the air so I can work with my mind clear, knowing the twins are safe. Also, I tell babysitters up front I have nanny cams all over. If they object, there's a problem.
- Try out the nanny for a short time, a week or so. Make it clear it's a test run. Be vigilant and truly assess how it all goes and how your children are reacting to this new person.
- Make sure your nanny knows CPR and first aid.
- Check your nanny's driving history if she has to shuttle your children. Go for a few drives with her and watch how she handles herself behind the wheel. If possible, use your car, not hers, because you know it's safe.

- Get references and *call them*. When asking for references, a rule of thumb is to have the candidate supply names and numbers for employers for the last five years, dates of employment, and three references, two of which are former employers. (If there are jobs listed without a contact or reference, you can still call and verify she worked there and ask why she left.)
- Keep the first runner-up nanny's info, just in case. Use her when number one has a day off.
- Make sure your babysitter has a cell phone, but enforce strict limits on the babysitter's cell phone usage. Then verify over the nanny cam. If she has a problem with that, she *is* the problem.
- Always leave a note for the babysitter and your children with your whereabouts, contact numbers (more than one), the time you'll be home, and emergency numbers.
- Always leave instructions about answering doors, locking up, lights to be left on, fire emergency rules, and activating the burglar alarm.
- Try to schedule deliveries when you are home, not the nanny.
- If something must arrive at the door when you're not there, leave money or a credit card for the babysitter for deliveries so they don't go searching for funds while a guy you don't know is standing at the door.
- Instruct the babysitter to never acknowledge on the phone or at the door that you are not home.
- Leave numbers for police, fire, ambulance, and the poison control hotline (1-800-222-1222) in addition to 911, in case 911 is busy or not working.
- Review the location of exits, fire extinguisher, flashlights, medicine, and first aid supplies.
- Tell your child the babysitter or nanny is coming and carefully watch how they react.
- Make sure your sitter acknowledges and understands instructions.
- If your sitter is always late or cancels more than once, there is a problem. Get rid of her.
- If your child has frequent "accidents" while in the babysitter's or nanny's care, there is a problem.
- If your sitter or nanny invites someone over without permission, there is a problem. First, they could be a danger, and second, with a guest over, your child is getting less attention.

- If your sitter or nanny is exhausted, there is a problem. You need full attention from an alert sitter.
- Tell the nanny or sitter that there is *no* posting of photos or videos of your child on social media.
- We all do a lot of research on restaurants, vacation spots, appliances, and gadgets before making decisions. Do the same for your child. The internet makes it easier than it ever was before to verify and evaluate people you are considering to care for your child.

YOUR CHILDREN AND OTHER ADULTS

Do not let your child be alone with any other adult outside of friends and family, no matter who they are and no matter the circumstance. There should always be others around at church, youth group, choir, school, music lessons, and similar situations. I just got back from dragging my husband along on a week-long Scout camping trip with John David and Lucy. It rained through the tents, and I had to trudge up a steep hill just to get a cup of coffee, but I was thrilled to see strict rules in place keeping adults away from children. I couldn't even sleep in one of the twins' tents—not that I wanted to! On one occasion, a little Scout was crying, and I reached out to hug him instinctively. When a troop leader made a stern face at me, I backed off. He later explained the absolutely-no-touching rule, not even a comforting hug…and he was right!

At our little Methodist church, that is the standard operating procedure. It should be everywhere, and it should be in your family. No other adults around? Then you need to change your child's plans, especially if you have a gut feeling about a figure of authority such as at daycare, or a babysitter, camp counselor, troop leader, teacher, or church volunteer. Don't leave your child alone with that person. *It's not worth it.*

When your child says they don't want to be alone with an adult, *listen.* And follow up with questions. If your child acts oddly after being alone with an adult or older child/teen, investigate.

As I've noted, it's always your responsibility to investigate whoever is around your children. Use trusted recommendations and pay the money for a background check. There are now plenty of websites where you can run a background check. Make no bones about it: ask the person for their full name and ID. Blame your spouse or your insurance company if you feel uncomfortable asking. (I don't feel uncomfortable at all. Everyone should understand that my twins come first in my life and I will do anything to protect them—and I know your children come first, too.)

Look up the sex offender registry in your zip code and in the zip codes surrounding your area.

Don't forget to find out who else will be around when your children are being taken care of. Older brothers, uncles, and grandpas may be wolves in sheep's clothing. Check them out.

If your child is out with another family, ask your child or, in a friendly way, the other parents to send photos.

If your child gets an odd babysitting offer or some other job offer out of the blue, pass on it. If it feels off, just say no.

Instruct your child that teens can also harm them. They must stay away from unknown teens or the teen brothers of friends.

Investigate anyone who takes a special interest in your child. After I had the twins, a home nurse told me about a dynamic local pastor who offered to buy her teen son a car. Right then, from my sickbed, I told her to get her son away from the pastor. She didn't believe me. Two years passed before I read in the paper about the pastor's multiple molestation charges.

I hate sleepovers. I've covered so many cases where molestations or worse befell children at sleepovers. I much prefer having the sleepover at our house, but that can't always be the case. I advise you to limit them. Wait until your child is at least ten years old unless you truly know and trust the family. Many psychologists say ten years old with the belief that by that age, children have overcome not only bedwetting but separation anxieties that come with a night away from Mom and Dad.

Give your child a cell phone for the night, if they don't already have one, with your number programmed in, or write your cell number in ink on their wrist. I've had John David call me at midnight to pick him up and, luckily, I had my cell right beside me. As it turns out, he was just feeling sick to his stomach after too much pizza and birthday cake. I thought about that later. Children often won't tell you what happened. John David just said, "Bring me home." No details. So, if they don't want to go to a certain place, that's fine. If they want to come home, go pick them up. You may never really know why; just trust them and get them out—pronto.

BODY SAFETY

You have to speak to your children about potential predators. You don't have to be explicit, but speak on their level about how no one should ever rearrange their pants or shirt or dress or skirt and how no one should ever touch them when Mommy isn't around.

Tell them the *very short* list of people who can give them a bath or see them without their clothes on. You don't have to scare them, just let them know no one should see their naked booty but Mommy, Daddy and Grandmommy (or words to that effect). Reinforce it at bath time or whenever you can. And if anyone touches them or tries to touch them in places that make them feel ashamed or uncomfortable, they can tell Mom or Dad.

They must also be told that if anyone does try to touch their private parts, they are to run. They are to tell Mommy or Daddy immediately. Tell them that nothing at all is wrong with their privates. Something is wrong with the weirdo who tries to touch them.

Most of all, follow your instincts and intuition. They are the result of thousands of years of evolution. Bad vibes exist for a reason. Pay attention to them.

CHAPTER SIX

Cyberthreats

Not too long ago, my ten-year-old son, John David, woke up early and came into the den where I was working. It was a Saturday morning and I was up super early, sitting alone in my chair tapping away on my laptop. I was surprised that my number one sleepyhead was up so early. And I was happy to have a few moments alone with him, as I am with his sister, since we always travel in a pack.

I made him his favorite breakfast—sliced bananas with Nutella and some cold milk—and we settled back in. He begged for his iPad, so I agreed. I had been working at least twenty minutes, chatting back and forth with him, when he jumped up and ran into another room.

Something had happened on his iPad.

Of course, I tiptoed behind him and spied onto his iPad.

I saw the name "NicholasOfOz" appear in the chat box.

Who was up chatting with my son at seven thirty in the morning? What total perv was trying to lure him out of the safe little bubble we've created for him and his twin sister? For Pete's sake, they'd just turned ten. They were still babies who love Santa and the Tooth Fairy. My chest actually hurt.

Some freak was capitalizing on *The Wizard of Oz* and using the classic book and movie I've played for the twins a dozen times to trap my son. And to make it worse, NicholasOfOz was inviting my sweet child to his home...to play.

Then came the moment of truth. After all, I had given my twins all the warnings, all the edited, airbrushed versions of what could happen to them if they ever went away with a stranger or someone they really didn't know online. What would John David do?

My chest got tighter when he wrote back, "Sure! That sounds fun! I can't wait to come play at your house!"

NICOLE LOVELL

If only little Nicole Lovell's parents had the same opportunity I did to look over her shoulder at her iPad screen at that one crucial moment. The seventh-grade girl lived at home with her mom and stepdad and had already, in her short life, overcome so much.

Shortly after she was born, Nicole was diagnosed with a deadly tumor in her liver. The tot underwent a dangerous liver transplant, leaving permanent scars along her neck and stomach. This little survivor fought for her life and won, returning home with her parents to start life all over again.

But the joy was cut short when shortly after coming home, Nicole was diagnosed with non-Hodgkin's lymphoma. This time, Nicole slipped into a coma after respiratory distress and developing MRSA. By age five, this miraculous little girl had battled a lifetime's worth of health issues. With a 1 percent chance of survival, Nicole battled back from her hospital bed and beat the odds. Nicole Lovell not only survived, she thrived.

When I look back at it, now I see it, even though it pains me: this little girl who loved pandas, religiously kept a schoolgirl diary, and wanted desperately to be on *American Idol* never had a chance.

By the tender age of twelve, she was already being bullied. Mean girls called her fat and made fun of the tracheotomy scar across her throat, a leftover from the surgery that saved her life. Almost every day, little Nicole would cry and beg to stay home from school. Her mom, Tammy Weeks-Dowdy, cried herself when she admitted the bullying was so bad that often she would just keep Nicole home to spare her feelings for that one day.

But even when Nicole did stay home from school, the bullying continued on social media. It was online that the little girl tried to be accepted and to find the friends and fun she didn't get at school. In doing so, Nicole posted a selfie. Keep in mind she's as cute as a button in this photo, but that single photo she posted got over three hundred replies. You know the rest...so many of the replies were horrible, vicious, mean, and hurtful.

How awful for this sweet girl. How she must have cried over every single hateful reply she read.

I imagine my little girl Lucy getting her feelings hurt, and it just breaks my heart. I can still remember when some horrible three-year-old boy with a runny nose made fun of her ballet outfit one day at a birthday party. She never would wear it again and wanted to quit ballet. I tried the whole "sticks and stones" lecture, but she was sobbing. I was very torn, but felt I couldn't let her just stop something she was good at because of hurtful words that poured out of some terribly mannered child's mouth. But his hateful words really stuck with her...and me every week as I marched her into ballet and tap class.

On the cold morning of January 16, 2016, Nicole went sledding with two neighbor girls, eight-year-old twins, and then to the mall with her bestie to scour the shops for matching necklaces. After she came home, she played some more, ate, took a shower, and went to play in her own room as usual. Tammy thought Nicole had gone to her room to play dress-up like she often did. When Tammy was going to sleep, she thought about knocking on the wall to signal Nicole to get in bed with her as usual, but she decided not to. She let Nicole sleep in her own room.

The following morning, when she went to give Nicole her liver meds, she couldn't get the door open. At first she didn't worry, because sometimes Nicole pushed a nightstand to the door when she played dress-up. In that moment, when Tammy couldn't open Nicole's door, everything changed forever. When she finally entered the room, she saw that Nicole's bedroom window was open.

Nicole had vanished. Her bedroom was normal, and everything was in its place, except Nicole was gone. Tammy did notice something else odd: also missing were a few water bottles and Nicole's favorite Minion blanket. Looking out the bedroom window that January morning, she could see no sign of thirteen-year-old Nicole.

Tammy immediately called Nicole's cell over and over, and each time it went straight to voice mail. As the hours passed, police canvassed the neighborhood, and slowly a lead emerged.

On Nicole's bedroom wall was a handwritten list of passwords and user names, all keys to the tween's online life. One was for Kik, a chat app. Tweens love it, because they can communicate anonymously and any parents snooping over their shoulders can't really tell what's happening. Even though Tammy had spotted the app and ordered Nicole to delete it, the tween would simply reinstall it afterward, convinced her mom was wrong about being on Kik.

But when the FBI sifted through Nicole's Kik account, they realized Tammy may have been right. One name kept popping up, and it's not one I would want to see flicker across either of my twins' screen.

The name was Dr. Tombstone.

Police and family were going haywire, canvassing the neighborhood, going door to door knocking, looking at parks, playgrounds, and trails. During these frantic hours, Nicole's girlfriends revealed a chilling development: Nicole had an online "boyfriend," who convinced the tween they'd run away together. He'd convinced a girl who still drew panda bears in her school notebooks that they would get married and have children.

Let that sink in for just a moment. That very day she was sledding down a hill on her belly and looking for plastic necklaces at the mall. Twenty-four hours later we find out some guy online wants to "marry her" and get her pregnant? Have a family? With a thirteen-year-old girl?

I remember reporting on the search for Nicole night after night and, during that search, managed to locate a little friend of Nicole's, Natasha Bryant. To my dismay, I learned Nicole truly believed she and her online "boyfriend" would run away together, get married, and start a family—a seventh grader!

Here is a small part of what the friend told me:

BRYANT: She said that he was really nice and that they would have a family one day and then get married and a bunch of stuff like that . . . I mean, she said that he was the perfect guy for her, and they would then have a family, get married, and I mean— what the fairy tale would be—they would have a perfect life.

Nicole's loneliness and heartache made her vulnerable to attention and "affection" of any kind, even from a stranger online. Her youth prevented her from being cautious and careful.

In fact, Nicole's "boyfriend" and Dr. Tombstone were one and the same. Bringing in computer forensic specialists, the feds identified Dr. Tombstone's IP address. That address led straight to David Eisenhauer, who was a Virginia Tech University track star and had been featured on the local news as a student athlete of the week. Using his "relationship" with Nicole, established through love notes and fake promises, he lured a trusting seventh-grade girl from the safety of her bedroom, where she still played dress-up and shared a wall with her mom, out into the night.

As I write this, my twins are sound asleep, and I can't help imagining going into their room and finding one of them gone. The thought of their window wide open and no trace of them is excruciating. Imagine Tammy standing there in that bedroom doorway.

It would be three long days of searches on foot, horseback, helicopter, boat, and ATV before Nicole was found. Or should I say, before her body was found. This child's remains were finally discovered ninety miles away in Surry County, North Carolina, just over the Virginia border. Nicole's little body was covered in abrasions, and she had been stabbed fourteen times. Her throat was slit. Her body had been stripped and wiped down with cleaning solution and bleach. This sweet little girl was thrown away like trash on the side of a country road, facedown and naked.

Just days later, "Dr. Tombstone" was charged with kidnapping and murder.

Motive? Prosecutors say Eisenhauer murdered Lovell because he was afraid people would find out about his relationship with the underaged girl.

But that wasn't the end of the story. In a bizarre twist a few days later, another Virginia Tech student, Natalie Keepers, was booked and fingerprinted on charges of murder before the fact, concealing a body, and accessory to murder after the fact. Before that night, Keepers was studying engineering and had already snagged a prestigious NASA internship. Why would a lovely young coed become involved in the kidnapping and murder of a little girl? It turns out Keepers and Eisenhauer went to high school just five miles apart.

Hometown friendships aside, horrific details began to emerge as to how Keepers and Eisenhauer meticulously planned Nicole's kidnapping and murder. They agreed Eisenhauer would lure Nicole out of her home at night, take her to a remote location, and use a knife to cut her throat. Keepers said she was excited to be part of something "secretive and special."

Then comes the icing on the cake: when the two monsters appeared in court, Natalie Keepers, instead of showing any remorse at all, demanded a hypoallergenic mattress and a gluten-free diet in jail.

When evidence began to unfold in open court, Eisenhauer cracked and pled no contest to first-degree murder, abduction, and concealing Nicole's body. Prosecutors asked the court to sentence Eisenhauer to life behind bars, but instead, the judge reduced that to a fifty-year sentence. Keepers was sentenced to forty years in prison.

Nicole's dad, David Lovell, revealed his battle with severe depression and post-traumatic stress disorder since Nicole was murdered. Her mom, Tammy, sees a grief counselor and to this day can't sleep at night. Tammy recently celebrated what would have been her daughter's sixteenth birthday . . . at her gravesite.

Nicole Lovell had a difficult thirteen years on this planet. Her early health problems led to physical problems that led to bullying. She sought comfort on social media, but what she found was the horrifying evil of "Dr. Tombstone" David Eisenhauer and his devilish minion, Natalie Keepers.

ALICIA KOZAKIEWICZ

When I met Alicia "Kozak" Kozakiewicz, I was immediately struck by not only her beauty, but her poise. Alicia has a story like Nicole's but with a different ending. She escaped her hell. Today, at thirty, Alicia is a television personality and advocate for internet safety and missing persons. She is the founder of the Alicia Project, a group whose mission is to raise awareness of online predators, abduction, and child sexual exploitation. She is also the namesake of Alicia's Law, which seeks to provide dependable, dedicated revenue in states to fund the Internet Crimes Against Children Task Force program and is now active in twelve states.

It was hard to reconcile that this young woman was the same thirteen-year-old girl that had been lured from her family's home after a beautiful holiday dinner, just after Christmas, kidnapped on the street as the snow fell gently around her, driven five hours, repeatedly molested and forced to wear a choke collar. I couldn't help but look at her in wonderment. How had she survived? Not only did she survive, but she lived to tell her story over and over to bring about change.

How did it happen? And how did she survive?

It all started in 2001, when Alicia, extremely shy, struck up an online friendship with a sweet-natured fourteen-year-old girl much like herself. "Christine" described herself as a redheaded teen girl. After months of online chats about school crushes, grades, worries, and woes, she became Alicia's "best friend." When Christine revealed she was really a young man named John, Alicia first balked but, later, decided to keep Christine-now-John as an online friend. Eventually, John introduced her to Scott Tyree in a Yahoo chat room. She then began an online correspondence with Tyree, who became a trusted "friend."

Over the next six months, he was always there for Alicia. If she made a bad grade, he convinced her it wasn't her fault and reminded her she was brilliant. If she had a problem, he helped solve it. When she was lonely, he was there to talk any time of the day or night. So, it is no surprise that when there came a suggestion that she should leave her family inside and come outside on the night of January 1, 2002, it seemed like a wonderful idea to Alicia. (See sidebar below.)

GROOMING

To most of us, befriending a stranger online would seem like a *horrible* idea, but not to an insecure and vulnerable girl like Alicia. In fact, for months, she had been groomed for this very moment. *Grooming* is the term used for essentially brainwashing a child, tween, or teen, lulling the victim into a false sense of security and complacency with the predator. As weeks turn to months, the victim begins to trust and even cooperate with the predator. Very often, but not always, the predator will, bit by bit, introduce a sexual component into the online or phone relationship. Over time, as with nearly everything else, the child victim becomes desensitized to the predator's inappropriate behavior.

Before the internet, grooming took place in the form of buying a child ice cream, candy, or treats, or taking them to a movie or the mall and buying them gifts.

I distinctly recall the first time I encountered a child that had been groomed and then repeatedly molested and sodomized. When I got the police file, I couldn't understand why the boy victim had not been interviewed by anyone. The report only included statements made by the boy's mom, a single parent. When I drove to their apartment to meet the young victim myself, I understood why. The boy was mentally handicapped and had a difficult time communicating. Often, the only person who could understand him was his mother. I immediately wondered how he could ever tell his story to a jury in open court.

I worked and worked and worked with him. Bit by bit, I began to understand him, and over time, I knew a jury would, too. I learned that the perpetrator, an outwardly normal young man with a good job, had met the boy victim at an arcade. This made sense because the boy's mom told me he loved arcades and would lose himself in the games for hours while she sat there with him. On one occasion, the eleven-year-old took cans he had collected to the local recycling plant to trade for quarters to use at the arcade.

The man at the arcade offered quarters in exchange for "helping with chores" around his house. Hungry for quarters, the boy agreed. The molester began to give the boy, unable to communicate, rolls and rolls of quarters and would take the boy to his place and the molestation would occur. This took place over and over and over. The rolls of quarters, the candy and Slurpees at the arcade—it's all grooming. His mom became concerned when she found a ten-dollar bill in her son's pocket.

I took the case to trial. The victim stopped talking after just a few minutes on the stand. I remember the moment it went sideways. The courtroom went quiet and I had a vision flash across my mind of a mistrial being declared, the case being dropped, and the guy walking free. He would be free to find his next victim.

I approached the stand. The victim's mom sat behind me in the first row, and I could feel her heart racing and her eyes on my back. The boy held his sweet head up and looked at me. I took his hand and he smiled. He looked back at his mom and, somehow, everything evened out. It wasn't sideways anymore. He kept looking at his mom. The jury convicted. The streets are safe from this guy...this one guy, at least...for a long, long time.

That's how it goes. Grooming can be nearly anything a child

> would want. With barriers eroded, inappropriate behavior that once would have alerted or alarmed the child no longer does.

Alicia's grooming online over a period of many months culminated on that night of her kidnapping when she was snatched from her neighborhood with her family sitting inside, having no idea she was gone. Even now, there are chunks of time and events she can no longer remember, a common result of extreme trauma. Alicia cannot recall now just exactly how she ended up inside the car of Scott Tyree. But very quickly, she knew she had a great deal to fear. After he told her he had made room for her in the trunk, her worst fears came true.

Alicia told me how she was kidnapped, driven hours away from home through the night, beaten, stripped, bound, gagged, and repeatedly raped. She was chained to the floor in a homemade basement torture chamber with a shock collar around her neck. For days and days, the abuse went on until the day Alicia became convinced Tyree planned to do away with the evidence of his crimes... *her*.

In the early morning hours of January 4, as usual, the thirteen-year-old was cowering, chained to the floor with the collar around her neck. But that morning, before Tyree left for his day job at Computer Associates International, he said the words "Alicia, I'm beginning to like you too much. Tonight, we're going to go for a ride." That "ride" meant only one thing. After Tyree came home from work that night, she would be murdered, and her remains would be hidden or destroyed.

But Tyree had made one mistake. True, he had lured Alicia from her family home and made off with her. True, he had traveled hundreds of miles away without detection, eluding her family and police and even tricking his own neighbors, who had no idea he was holding a child hostage and repeatedly abusing her. But to stoke his own sadistic pleasure, he sent an online post using his webcam. The post, sent to *another child predator*, was a video of Alicia, naked, crying, her arms bound above her head. The text accompanying the chilling post read simply "I got one."

At first thinking the video was a fake, the "friend" discounted the image. But after reading about Alicia's disappearance online, he called the FBI from a pay phone. After much finagling, he gave up Tyree's screen name, masterforteenslavegirls. Armed with that info, the feds contacted a Yahoo VP for the corresponding IP address. From there, investigators got Verizon on the phone and learned the identity masked by his screen name: Scott William Tyree.

Just minutes before Tyree was due home, Alicia describes cringing when she heard pounding at the door. Not realizing she could ever be rescued, she hid under the bed. She tells me that when she saw the letters *FBI*, she knew that finally she was safe. It didn't sink in completely until she saw her dad and he held her tightly in a bear hug she will never forget.

That day, Tyree was arrested at work. He was sentenced to nineteen years behind bars and is still there today. Alicia has gone on to become one of the foremost experts in child online safety, and I am proud to have gotten to know her and to have had the opportunity to learn from her, and I am also very proud of her wonderful website, aliciakozak.com.

Tyree, Eisenhauer, and Keepers, on the other hand, are not only killers but also prime examples of a brand-new kind of predator. We are conditioned to imagine a pervy guy in a raincoat stalking the playground for child victims, and yes, those predators exist. Sometimes, however, the predator is the one we don't expect, like a family "friend," neighbor, or teacher. Sometimes, the predator hides behind a fake profile and a computer or phone. Apps like Kik are a predators' dream because minors spend a lot of time there. Millions of teens use Kik to talk 24/7. It's perfect for pedophiles who go online pretending to be a thirteen- or fourteen-year-old. They can present themselves in any way they want. The anonymity of these chat apps and rooms is why they use them to meet innocent children like Nicole and Alicia. Or your child.

The lures used by predators are almost irresistible to children, tweens, and teens. Like Alicia and Nicole, many cybervictims are simply shy children or teens looking for friends online. Many of them feel like outsiders at school. Many have home problems or struggle with depression or loneliness. That friendly person online who always "understands" can seem like the perfect answer and a new friend. And these cons are good. They can fool even the sharpest kids, not just the vulnerable and weak ones.

A PREDATOR'S STANDARD OPERATING PROCEDURE

It's disconcerting, but you have to get inside the minds of predators. To defend your family against them, you have to be familiar with their methods.

A predator will hang out in chat rooms where kids of the age he is targeting also hang out. This can be JusTalk, Houseparty, or any number of chat apps and websites.

A predator will pretend to be a child of a similar age to your child.

A predator will take on a very believable child identity, complete with name, description, school, family, likes, and dislikes.

A predator will, over time, create a rapport with your child. He will "like" what they like, especially your child's online posts and yak about all their "shared" interests, be it American Girl, makeovers, Fortnite, Roblox, Minecraft, or fifth-grade soccer. (The recent Fortnite craze attracted a lot of predators, and the UK's National Crime Agency issued an official warning about it in 2018. Pedophiles use conversation about the game to lure and groom victims.)

A predator will push your child to exchange personal information. The predator seeks your child's address and phone number.

A predator will try to talk to your child by phone in real time. Even if your child knows not to hand out a phone number, a predator will try to entice your child to call him under some ruse. Once your child is lured and tricked into making that call, the predator then sees your child's number on caller ID. With the number, the predator can get your address.

A predator begins sex talk and role playing. Make no mistake, that's merely a method of grooming; their goal is not the sex chitchat.

A predator will ask for photos of your child, then work up to explicit photos. And get them. A part of their evil is their endless patience. They don't give up.

A predator will send photos claiming to be of him but likely not genuine.

All the above techniques are tried-and-true tricks in a predator's bag. Alicia survived. Nicole did not.

In the back of my mind, I keep thinking of my own twins. I'd like to think this could never happen to them...to us...but I know that it could. I have learned the hard way over the course of many years of crimefighting that no one is special...no one has a magic incantation that can protect them from other people who mean to do them harm.

SIGNS A PREDATOR IS TARGETING YOUR CHILD

Your child begins spending a noticeably long time online.

Your child begins going online late at night.

Your child gets calls from people you don't know. (I always ask casually, "Hey, who's that you're talking to?" or "Who are you playing with?")

Your child gets gifts in the mail from someone you don't know. You better get to know them and quickly find out if they are trouble. If it's already at the gift stage, there's a serious problem. The gift may be something as simple as McDonald's gift cards or crazy-colored shoelaces or a T-shirt. Be on the alert!

When you walk into the room, your child suddenly stops playing whatever they were playing, hangs up the phone abruptly, hides the screen, closes a page, or turns off the computer.

Your child is beginning to distance themselves from family life or no longer seems interested in things that they were previously interested in.

Your child doesn't want to talk about what they are doing online.

Be proactive. Go to missingkids.org, complete the child ID Kit, and keep it safe at home. It's like insurance. You don't want to imagine having to use it, but you'll be glad it's there if you need it.

The internet can be a dangerous place for children, tweens, and teens. From social media posts that can follow them forever, to evil trolls, to cyberbullies, to innocently playing games with online predators or unintentionally handing over bank accounts and sensitive data to cybercriminals via malware, the internet is a wolf in sheep's clothing. Our little ones are the most vulnerable.

So, with all this in mind, how can we fight back and protect our children?

TIPS: ONLINE SAFETY STARTS AT HOME

Every family is wildly different: fast food or home-cooked meals; apartment or house; car or bus; church, synagogue, or neither; single parent, both parents, grandparents, adopted parents; lizards, turtles, cats, dogs, or guinea pigs. I could fill up so many pages with how many differences there can be among families. But certain internet safety rules are universal.

Talk to them.

Learn about their world. Educate yourself about your child's internet life to get a bead on potential predators. Find out what games they play, whom they talk to, why they like different apps. Surf the internet with them and have them show you what they do when they're online. Remember: if you want to catch a varmint, you gotta think like a varmint.

CELL PHONE OR NO CELL PHONE?

It's your duty to figure out which device or devices are best for your child: laptop, desktop, tablet, gaming device, phone...there's a lot to choose from. We went through a real dilemma when trying to decide if the twins would get phones. Of course, as with the dog, cat, guinea pigs, Razor scooters, iPads, and trampoline, the begging was nonstop. That, of course, did not enter into the decision except for the nag factor. For a good while, my simple answer was that a cell phone was how the bad guys find you. While that remains true, I did eventually realize that they would need them, despite the danger.

This is how it happened. I planned for them to get cell phones at age fourteen, although "all their friends had them." I held firm because I know that cell phones are avenues for predators to get straight to your child. With laptops and iPads, with their big screens and mostly home use, I could monitor them so much more easily, but not so with cell phones, which are small and private and often with the child all day long.

Then one weekend we went to a local high school football game to watch our friends' son in the marching band. I never knew he had a rhythmic bone in his body, but there he was on the field dancing and weaving while playing a trombone. That part was great. But every five minutes, one of the twins would want to run off to the concession stand or the bathroom or to get their face painted or one of a million things.

I looked out at that sea of people. I hardly knew any of them. Lucy had been gone with her little friends longer than her allotted fifteen minutes. I waded into the crowd calling her name. Being short, I couldn't see over anyone's head. I went back to the bleachers and climbed up to the highest spot. I still couldn't find her, so I dove back into the crowd. I asked David to stay in our seats in case she came back.

All I could think about was Gabbi Doolin (page 40). Directly behind the field, lots of parents were tailgating (at a high school ball game!). I wandered through their tailgate village, calling out for Lucy. I couldn't help but notice a lot of them were drinking (to put it mildly). I'm certainly not the church lady, but I do know that when adults are under the influence of alcohol or drugs, they do things, awful things, that they may not do when sober.

By this time, my chest was hurting. A good twenty minutes had passed. Gabbi was only gone a few minutes, too.

Out of nowhere, Lucy came up behind me and put both arms around me. She had a sparkly butterfly on her face, just to the right of a big grin. She had been back at the face painting booth and gone to the bathroom and gotten a bottle of water with all her friends. I hugged her back, and I'm pretty sure she didn't see that my eyes were full of tears once I found her. I knew right then that I was getting them cell phones. There are risks and benefits, but I've decided to take the good with the bad.

My twins got their cell phones just a few weeks after that football game, on their eleventh birthday, but we put a lot of rules in place.

There is very little social media use, and all of their profiles are private.

Only use social media or play games with kids they already know in real life.

No posting of photos.

All geotagging is disabled.

And at the end of each day, right in front of them, I review their web history and look at the content on the apps they used. They have their phones and the independence and social status it gives them, and I have peace of mind.

MORE ONLINE SAFETY TIPS

- Keep computers in family living areas. Position your computer in a common, high-traffic area like a living room or kitchen where you can watch and monitor when your children are using it. I think it's best not to have kids alone in their room when online. But Alicia Kozakiewicz's family computer was in their living room. So, you must do more.

- Know who they are talking to or playing with online. Make sure they are people you or your children know in real life.

- Again, there's nothing wrong with peeking over their shoulder. I sneak up on the twins and do ambush-style peeking, and we end up laughing, but I see what they're doing. If their computer is in their room, just go in the bedroom with them and work on your phone or laptop. There are many, many parental monitoring options, so select the one that works for your family.

- Never feel you are "spying." Just as you'd watch your child on the playground, you must watch your child on the internet. You are the parent, and it is your responsibility to keep your child safe. Word to the wise: while you are monitoring their computer use, know that they have devised abbreviations you need to learn. You can find many different lists of these shorthand communications online. Here is a list of the more deceptive and sneaky ones:

8: Oral sex
143/459: I love you.
303: Mom.
53X: Sex
1174: Nude club.
ASL: Age, sex, location.
CD9: Code 9, parents are around.
GNOC: Get naked on cam.
GYPO: Get your pants off.
H/8: Hate. (Can be used in a scale too; i.e., H/1 up to H/10.)
IWSN: I want sex now.
KPC: Keeping parents clueless.
LMIRL: Let's meet in real life.
NIFOC: Nude in front of computer.

PAL: Parents are listening. (There are many variations on this idea; all begin with P.)
RUH: Are you horny?
Pornado: Large amounts of pornographic content.
Sugarpic: Erotic picture of self.

I had to drastically cut down the list of abbreviated codes and signals specifically designed to avoid detection. Look online, find them, and familiarize yourself with them. Pray you will never have to decipher them on your child's or teen's devices.

- Don't be afraid to set time limits on your child's overall internet use. Set reasonable limits for which online sites your child can visit and how long they can stay there or play that specific game.
- Setting arbitrary limits or banning internet use will backfire.

Review These Ideas Often with Your Child

- Teach your child what personal information is and why it should be private.
- Teach your child to never give out personal data online. Ever.
- Explain to your child why they should not fill in answers on a profile that asks for name, address, phone, school name, sports teams they play on, school uniform, or other critical data.
- Talk about what "safe online" means.
- Instruct your child not to talk to strangers on the internet.
- Remind your child that just because someone is talking to them online does not mean they have to talk back. Just don't answer or blame Mom and say, "I am not allowed to speak to strangers or share information." That might even tip off a creep that this child's parents are closely involved.
- Ask your child what they would do if anyone asked to meet them and if that has ever happened.
- Remind your child to not share email addresses.
- Remind your child to not share personal information via email even from sources that appear legitimate.
- Instruct your child to not reveal or share passwords, even with friends, "boyfriends," or "girlfriends."

- Speaking of emails, remind your child to never respond to hurtful or upsetting emails.
- Explain to your child that they should never open email from someone they don't know.
- In that same vein, remind your child that they should not answer the cell phone unless they recognize the person from caller ID.
- Ask your child if they have ever been afraid or bullied. Have they ever seen anyone else bullied or mistreated online? What do they think is the right thing to do? Besides Mom or Dad, who could they tell if something is going wrong online?
- Instruct your child not to stay online if they see or hear something they think you won't like. A condition of having internet privileges is reporting to you anything disturbing or suspicious.
- Make your children feel safe if they report bullying or other scary or troubling things they see online to you.
- If your child describes something that makes them feel bad, angry, afraid, or threatened online, *listen*! And act.
- If you discover anyone sending or viewing child porn online or if your child has been solicited in any way, you must call police immediately and make sure you ask for the cybercrimes division to get in touch with the internet provider and app company. I would also advise calling the National Center for Missing and Exploited Children at 800-843-5678. I trust them.
- If your child gets a threatening text, post, or message, *do not respond*. Call the police and follow the same instructions above for encountering child porn.
- Instruct your child not to download anything without asking first.
- Don't forget that internet technology is not limited to a desktop computer. Be aware you need to check out your child's gaming devices, cell phones, tablets, and laptops, too.
- Parents must be "friended." That means you can see your child's social media activity. I advise you stay friended through your child's teen years, at least through high school if you can manage it.
- You must know your child's passwords. Secret passwords are not allowed.
- Your child should never share a password unless it's with you. My son's school has shared passwords for their grade, and we just found out another kid copied a whole book report John David turned in

several months ago. That's a rather benign example, but imagine how a predator could use that password.

- Speaking of passwords, make sure you explain to your child that if they use a public access computer, they should log out completely to ensure no one gets their password.
- All new apps must be reviewed and approved by a parent. Instruct your children they are not to visit chat rooms or use apps without your okay. Before your child joins a new social network like TikTok, Facebook, Houseparty, Snapchat, or WhatsApp, you, the parent, must approve it first. Go online and learn about the various apps. I just went through it myself with TikTok and WhatsApp. We let them use and make TikToks, which I review each day. We let them have WhatsApp for a while but quickly deleted it because the chat history was difficult to discern.
- Do not allow your child to "check in." Many apps for kids, tweens, and teens encourage them to share their current location in real time on social media sites. *Don't do that!* It's like putting out an APB to predators: "Look! I'm at Disney! Come and find me! I'm the one in the green T-shirt and blue shorts at Epcot!" Tell your child they can share all those photos with specific friends later.
- Do not allow geotagging on your child's devices. Geotagging immediately pinpoints your child's exact location. Find geotagging in settings and disable it.
- Go into your child's privacy settings on each social networking site and app and make sure they are all strong. Make sure they are not by default public. After routine and systematic updates, check and update the privacy settings again.
- Speaking of settings, block sites with explicit materials. You can usually find this in your preferences settings for your computer, mobile devices, browsers, and apps. Also, Internet Explorer has Content Advisor. You can find it at Tools/Internet/Options/Content. This feature filters out violence, nudity, sex, and curse words on a scale of zero to four.
- Children and teens must play online games or online chat only with people they know in real life.
- Instruct your child not to buy anything online without your okay. Lots of ads try to trick your child into thinking they are buying something or by offering something free or some sort of a prize. Your child ends

up with nothing and the crook ends up with all your child's personal data and maybe even your credit card info. Eek.

- Instruct your child not to lie about their age when going to websites or games. There's a reason for minimum age requirements— a good one.
- Never allow your child to delete browsing histories. If you find that your child never has a history to display, something's very wrong. If your child is online, there should be a browser history, and if there's not, that means there is something they don't want you or anyone else to see. It's your job to find out what. Some experts believe it's important to make a home internet rule that browsing histories are never to be deleted. In the same vein, do not allow private browsing modes or incognito browsing.
- Set Facebook and other social media privacy settings along with all other of your children's apps. The world doesn't need to see what your children are doing online.
- We use an app called Bark. It alerts me to all sorts of potential problems that may appear on the twins' devices, including cyberbullying, curse words, and more.

Consequences

At some point, the rules will be broken. It's just human nature. It may not be a serious breach but, if you don't follow the rules and enforce loss of privileges for violations, your children certainly won't follow the rules, either. You have to follow through, or the family internet rules will mean nothing and will not be respected.

Play a good defense. And for more bang for your buck with less hassle, look at Net Nanny, Bark, Screen Time, Qustodio, FamilyTime, Circle, TeenSafe, WebSafety, ESET, or Norton. Many of these programs block sites on a huge list of inappropriate addresses while constantly patrolling for smut and offensive words and content. Some can customize what's allowed or disallowed and block your own choices of sites and categories. Some software allows parents to configure the software to "pre-read" the site a child is attempting to load and block access to a site if the content contains prohibited material. At the same time, software can capture the screen image of the site and save it to a password-protected file so parents can see the sites their kids have tried to visit.

If you want to know exactly what your child is viewing, try Veriato Cerebral or PCTattletale. These programs snap screenshots at various intervals and record keystrokes, websites visited, photos, webcam activity, the works. It's not discernable and you can play it forward and back like a video. You can have it on stealth mode or not. Stealth mode makes it completely invisible. Using this program is a big step, as it amounts to spying on your child. But if your child has broken rules, this step could be the natural consequence of the infraction and a way of showing that you are serious about internet safety and behavior. I tell my children point blank I watch what they do online. When Bark red flags an issue, I show them the notice and we figure out what it is. So far, it's been pretty mild stuff, like a naughty word contained in a YouTube video or a song, but I'm bracing myself. At some point I may need to use a more robust monitoring program.

Always, always talk to your children with love. Let them know you are on their side and that the rules must be followed because they are created for only one reason: to protect them.

Internet Safety Laws

A federal law, the Children's Online Privacy Protection Act (COPPA) helps protect children younger than thirteen online. It's designed to keep a criminal from getting a child's personal information without a parent agreeing to it first.

COPPA demands that websites explain privacy policies and get parental consent before collecting or using a child's information like name, address, phone number, or Social Security number. The law also prohibits a site from getting more personal information from a child than needed in order to play a game or enter a contest.

Find and use all online protection tools. These tools help stop adult content from making its way to your child's device. By doing this, you also shield them from cyber predators. Internet service providers offer parental control filters. As I mentioned above, find these options in your preferences.

Practically all internet service providers have free parental controls that limit a child's ability to access email, chats, instant messaging, and websites by age, time, content, and more. There is also software that disallows any personal information being sent out into cyberspace.

Be Involved

Keeping your children safe on the internet calls for a two-pronged attack. Educate yourself, and then share what you have learned with your children. In addition to blocking dangerous or inappropriate content, you must also teach your children about dangers online. Ignorance could cost them their lives.

- No photo trading. Make sure your child never posts or trades their personal pictures online.
- Be smart about screen names. Make sure your child never uses their real name. They should only use a made-up screen name when online.
- Also ensure your child's screenname doesn't give away identity, school, or location. Much can be inferred from how children depict themselves online. The screen name alone could prompt a predator's first contact with your child. That's certainly food for thought.
- No meet-ups. Period.
- Never, ever should your child discuss or agree to meet someone they have met online unless you, the parent, are there.
- Review credit card statements and phone bills. I would get odd PayPal charges, and when I investigated, they were all for additional storage space online. It was simply to accommodate all the twins' games and apps, but if you don't review your charges, all sorts of activity can take place.
- Determine online safety protections outside your home.
- Investigate what online protections are in place at your child's school and after-school programs. I recently spent time with parents of a young girl who met her predator in an anorexia chat room he was trolling. She got access to the internet at school on her school-issued Chromebook. I was shocked. Needless to say, find out if every area of the school is monitoring students' online activity, including in classrooms, the library, study halls, free time areas, and any place within the school that your child could get computer access.
- Find out if the parents of your child's friends supervise time online when your child is over. You don't have to be accusatory; just have a casual conversation about what you do to protect your child and ask what they do or if they have any ideas. It doesn't have to be threatening.

OTHER CYBER CONCERNS: SAFE ZONES

There are lots of kid-friendly zones for beginners online. You can start with reliable sources like Disney and websites for kid TV shows on PBS like *Sesame Street*, or programming on other networks like *Paw Patrol*, *Star Wars Rebels*, *SpongeBob SquarePants*, and *Horrible Histories*. If you like the show, the website will likely be good for your children, too.

Education-oriented sites are also good places to start. You can look for trivia sites and science sites like BrainPop. The American Library Association has an up-to-date list of great web sites for kids. There are also fun online game sites. Check all these options out with your kids. It's fun!

We also love to download age-appropriate books from Kindle, and we Google and look at the school library website to find other books online.

One caution: be on the lookout for redirecting. Double-entendre phrases or word games can lead you astray. For instance, your child may look up "pirates booty" and end up getting a very unexpected booty...pirate-themed porn.

OTHER ONLINE DANGERS FACING YOUR CHILD: CYBERBULLIES

Cyberbullying is when a person uses technology such as texts, emails, online games, or social media in order to threaten, torture, harass, embarrass, or hurt their target. (Remember: if an adult harasses or stalks, that's a crime.)

Some cyberbullying, like outright insults, is obvious. Sometimes, cyberbullies are more devious and do things like post personal information about the target, post upsetting photos or videos about the target, or impersonate them in a hateful way, even creating fake accounts strictly for the purpose of bullying. Cyberbullies' "jokes" aren't funny at all.

GABRIELLA GREEN

When I searched for "children who commit suicide after cyberbullying" on the internet, the resulting list was long and heartbreaking. One case I studied was that of Gabriella Green.

On January 10, 2018, Gabbie's parents found her hanging in her closet, unresponsive. She was pronounced dead at the hospital shortly after.

In this case, police ended up charging two twelve-year-old middle-schoolers with cyberstalking after friends and family told police Gabbie had been cyberbullied.

Gabbie's phone and social media led police straight to two children she knew well. One of the two, a girl, admitted to starting horrible rumors that twelve-year-old Gabbie had an STD, disgusting name-calling, and threats to spread some of Gabbie's sensitive, personal life details. As soon as the child found out about the suicide, she deleted all the messages from her devices. That didn't work, because this information is easily retrievable and the messages were on Gabbie's phone as well.

The other, a boy, allegedly admitted Gabbie texted him to say she tried to hang herself but failed. The boy responded, "If you're going to do it, just do it," and hung up. Well, she heard him loud and clear, and now Gabbie's gone.

CONRAD ROY

The list of other such suicides won't get out of my head. I remember very well covering the Michelle Carter case from beginning to end. It was awful. Michelle Carter is a girl who, according to prosecutors and a Fairhaven, Massachusetts, judge, drove Conrad Roy, her extremely shy and sensitive teen boyfriend, to commit suicide on July 13, 2014.

Don't believe it?

Evidence shows she egged him on over and over in texts, calls, and emails, even detailing to him how to pump carbon monoxide into the cab of his truck and where to park it and not get caught. This evil cyberbully even explained how Roy could rig a mini generator so that no matter what, his suicide mission wouldn't fail. She even listened in on the phone during his last moments as he did the deed in a lonely parking lot. She listened in...and did nothing.

Here are just a few of the over one thousand texts Carter sent to convince Conrad he had to park his pickup in a lonely Kmart parking lot, turn on the ignition, and inhale deeply until he died.

"The time is right and you are ready... just do it babe," Carter wrote in a text the day Roy committed suicide.

Carter: So are you sure you don't wanna [kill yourself] tonight?
Roy: What do you mean am I sure?
Carter: Like, are you definitely not doing it tonight?
Roy: Idk yet I'll let you know
Carter: Because I'll stay up with you if you wanna do it tonight
Roy: Another day wouldn't hurt
Carter: You can't keep pushing it off, tho, that's all you keep doing
Carter: You're gonna have to prove me wrong because I just don't think you really want this. You just keep pushing it off to another night and say you'll do it but you never do

Later she texts:

Carter: SEE THAT'S WHAT I MEAN. YOU KEEP PUSHING IT OFF! You just said you were gonna do it tonight and now you're saying eventually...
Carter: But I bet you're gonna be like "oh, it didn't work because I didn't tape the tube right or something like that"... I bet you're gonna say an excuse like that

Later she texts:

Carter: Do you have the generator?
Roy: not yet lol
Carter: WELL WHEN ARE YOU GETTING IT
Carter: You better not be bulls***ing me and saying you're gonna do this and then purposely get caught

These were some of their earlier texts, from July 11–12, 2014:

Roy: I'm just too sensitive. I want my family to know there was nothing they could do. I am entrapped in my own thoughts
Carter: I think your parents know you're in a really bad place. Im not saying they want you to do it, but I honestly feel like they can

accept it. They know there's nothing they can do, they've tried helping, everyone's tried. But there's a point that comes where there isn't anything anyone can do to save you, not even yourself, and you've hit that point and I think your parents know you've hit that point. You said your mom saw a suicide thing on your computer and she didn't say anything. I think she knows it's on your mind and she's prepared for it

Carter: Everyone will be sad for a while, but they will get over it and move on. They won't be in depression I won't let that happen. They know how sad you are and they know that you're doing this to be happy, and I think they will understand and accept it. They'll always carry u in their hearts

A bit later.

Roy: i don't want anyone hurt in the process though

Roy: I meant when they open the door, all the carbon monoxide is gonna come out they can't see it or smell it. whoever opens the door

Carter: They will see the generator and know that you died of CO...

Later

Roy: hey can you do me a favor

Carter: Yes of course

Roy: just be there for my family:)

Carter: Conrad, of course I will be there for your family. I will help them as much as I can to get thru this, I'll tell them about how amazing their son/brother truly was

Later she texts:

Carter: I thought you wanted to do this. The time is right and you're ready, you just need to do it! You can't keep living this way. You just need to do it like you did last time and not think about it and just do it babe. You can't keep doing this every day

Roy: I do want to. but like I'm freaking for my family. I guess

Roy: idkkk

Carter: Conrad. I told you I'll take care of them. Everyone will take care of them to make sure they won't be alone and people will help them get thru it. We talked about this, they will be okay and accept it. People who commit suicide don't think this much and they just do it.

Reading these texts is heartbreaking. This case, combined with the growing list of young children committing suicide because of cyberbullies, is enough to make any parent sick with concern.

Carter, who was a minor and had problems of her own, was convicted of involuntary manslaughter and was sentenced to fifteen months in prison, but Conrad Roy's family got a life sentence.

IF YOU SUSPECT YOUR CHILD IS BEING CYBERBULLIED

Never take talk of suicide lightly.

Listen closely to what your child is saying.

Watch carefully for signs of depression.

Assure your child you love them no matter what and you are there for them.

Learn the signs of depression.

Watch your child's behavior to determine if there has been a significant change.

Many children, teens, and tweens who are being cyberbullied don't want anyone, including you, to know because they are ashamed. They think it's their fault. You must convince them otherwise.

Sometimes children don't tell parents about cyberbullying because they are afraid the parent will take away all their devices to stop the bullying. That sends the message that it *is* your child's fault, which is not true. Best to discuss the issue openly and deal with the bully appropriately. See below.

Look for These Signs

Your child is upset after being on their device.

Your child seems upset or nervous when their device pings or they get an email, text, or IM.

They avoid their devices.

They avoid any talk of their devices or online games, changing the subject or withdrawing when you bring up the topics.

Your child tries to keep their online life a secret.

Your child's grades begin to drop and you don't know why.

Your child begins to withdraw from real life, including family, friends, and activities they once loved.

Your child experiences unexplained anger at home.

They have unusual outbursts.

There are changes in behavior, including appetite and sleep habits.

If Your Child Is Being Cyberbullied

You must convince your child of the truth: the cyberbullying is not their fault. It's all about the bully feeling powerful, not about your child.

Make sure you praise your child for telling you.

Tell your child a bully story from your youth or about someone they know who was bullied and how it was successfully handled.

Let them know that a *lot* of people get made fun of and bullied, even into adulthood. Your child, like many other people of all ages, can and will learn to deal with a hateful bully.

Convince your child that you are in this together and you *will* figure it out.

Tell someone at school, be it the teacher, principal, or counselor, about the bullying. Most schools have a protocol for bullying, including cyberbullying. Advise your child first and get a plan that is comfortable for your child. If you do not get action from the teacher, principal, or counselor, you must go to the principal's superior, such as the superintendent or school board. It sounds daunting, but it starts with a simple call, letter, and email. Set your frustration to the side and communicate calmly and with facts.

Keep threatening messages, texts, and photos in case you need them as evidence for the school, the bully's parents, or police.

Take screenshots of the bullying and print them. Obviously, block the bully. This can be done electronically for emails, texts, or instant messages.

Don't be too proud or the least bit ashamed to get your child to a counselor pronto.

Teach your child they are not to respond to hateful or upsetting messages or behavior. It adds fuel to the fire and keeps the bully dialogue going. Cut it off.

Instead, your child is to tell you or a teacher and let adults handle it.

If you have reason to think your child is being cyberbullied, be completely supportive and contact a professional to help you, be it from the school or police.

Social media and the internet are today's playgrounds, and your children are out there. Be there to catch them when they fall, dust them off, and help them keep going.

PHISHING

Like adults, children can be phished. This is when a con artist uses emails to trick your child into clicking on a malware link. If by text, it's called smishing. Phishing can start with an email that says something like "Hey! Want to try something new?" or "Fun for you!"

It could say anything—just don't click. We just took John David's laptop to the Geek Squad because of several red flags and found out it was loaded with unintentionally downloaded malware. I couldn't believe it! But it was true!

Phishing can happen anytime to anyone, but there is a niche of cyberperps who watch kid sites for a living. Don't picture some lonely dude in his parents' garage or basement. People make money by gathering all the data they can, like names, emails, addresses, to scam you and your family out of money.

In a nutshell, instruct your child to never click on a text or email from someone they don't know. Stay away from messages from friends that have nothing attached except a weird address and no personal message at all. This situation simply means the friend has been hacked or the perp is mimicking a friend's email address. When in doubt, don't click.

MALWARE

As devious as it is, criminals target children to get their malware onto your family computer system. As you may already know, malware (from the Latin root *mal*, or bad, as in *malevolent*) is software that installs itself without your permission or knowledge. It steals your personal and critical data and can even hijack your computer to do things like send all your contacts emails or texts that spread the virus or malware to them, too. Malware can delete, destroy, infect, block, copy, or modify your data. It also disrupts your computer or device's performance.

Sometimes kid malware comes in the form of game offerings, and all your child has to do to get the "awesome game" is download it.

Answer? Antivirus! The solution is using antivirus software, the security protections highlighted above, and parental controls and talking to your child about malware.

HAUNTING POSTS

Your child will, God willing, mature as time goes by. But internet posts are forever. That one "fun" picture will haunt you. Future bosses, potential dates, colleges, organizations offering internships...they can all look back at what your teen has posted. Ugh. It may be funny today, but unfortunate tomorrow. Instruct your child to think twice about what they post. There are endless examples of athletes, actors, singers, politicians, and celebrities who have had to defend a regrettable post. Often, these digital misfires cost people money, opportunities, and relationships. The problem is real. The solution is to think first. A good rule of thumb is, would I be okay if everyone I know saw this post? If the answer is no, don't post it.

THE DARK SIDE OF THE INTERNET

Alicia Kozakiewicz and her story affected me profoundly. As you know, other child victims like Alicia are taken far from home, trafficked, and used as sex slaves or prostitutes. Furthering the misery, images are taken of these innocent children, teens, and tweens and shared thousands of times online.

Long before I met Alicia, I met another little girl.

MASHA ALLEN

I'll always remember a special little girl who went with me before a congressional committee to share her heartbreaking story. Masha Allen was adopted at five years old from a Russian orphanage straight into the hands of an American pedophile. Horrible and twisted photos of this little child were taken of her doing unspeakable acts in many, many places. She was saved after years of abuse when certain photos of her, traded freely on the internet and confiscated in many separate cases, were determined to have been taken at a Disney World property. The setting, the wallpaper, the bedspread, and so much more in the background of the photo helped police narrow down the location until they were literally on her doorstep. When they found her, they also found a virtual clearinghouse of child porn that had been sold and traded online for years. Her adoptive "father" was sentenced to so many long prison terms in Pennsylvania and Florida that he hopefully will never again see the light of day or be able to prey on another little child.

Because of Masha, I took the fight against child victimization on the internet to the Capitol and testified before members of Congress. I gave them an earful about internet child predators. But it had nothing to do with me; it was all about Masha.

Even though Masha and Alicia escaped their predators, the images of them taken by those predators still live on the web today. And now Masha has a meaningful law named after her just like Alicia does. Masha's Law is a federal civil remedy that provides statutory damages of $150,000 for anyone convicted of dealing in child pornography. The victims can sue their abusers as well as anyone who did anything with the images.

I pray that the fight against child predators is won and that other innocents will never go through what these brave girls, Alicia and Masha, miraculously survived.

THE INTERNET IS NOT YOUR BABYSITTER

First and foremost, your children are watching you. How they act for the rest of their lives depends largely on how *you* behave. So set a good example.

Limit your own media use. I recall that before I had the twins, I took in a starving solid-black stray cat, and I was not yet a cat person. I had Coco for eighteen years. He stayed with me until I found happiness when the twins were born, and then he passed on to cat heaven. But I recall that every time I would get on my BlackBerry, the cat would just get up and leave. This cat resented bad online manners, so how do you think your child feels?

Bottom line? Exhibit good manners online, they will follow. And learn from Coco as I did. Your children will be happier with conversation and lots of hugs versus you staring at your iPhone.

Yes, sometimes it may be easier to let your children get on their devices every once in a while when you have your hands full. But lots of parents are guilty of using the internet as a free babysitter. If that's you, you're falling down on your job and you may not like what the "babysitter" is teaching your child.

Enforce tech time-outs. Mealtimes, family get-togethers, at social gatherings—none of these is the time or place for your child to be glued to a device. They need to interact normally in social settings and put family time before tech time. But this applies to you as well. No devices at the dinner table.

No devices while your child should be sleeping. This includes under-the-covers sneaking. You can tell by the eerie glow coming from under their blanket when that's going on. Some parents let their children play online until they fall asleep. Don't do that.

Online activity stimulates their brains and makes it more difficult to get to sleep. And think about it—who do you think is trolling online late at night? As I used to tell juries, nothing good happens after midnight.

Research shows that active face-to-face conversation increases language skills. Just listening and watching a screen doesn't cut it. Have those conversations every day with your child. Their screen, be it a smartphone, laptop, or tablet, is not their role model. You are.

Screen time doesn't mean alone time. Engage with your children. Play a game or watch them play and comment. Stream a program or watch crazy TikToks with them or, even better, help them make TikToks. Do what you need to do to relate to and with them online. Don't just be the probation officer, monitoring their screen activity. Be part of it. Get in there.

Balance online play with offline play to jump-start their imaginations. Make sure your child has plenty of playtime, including outdoor time.

If this all seems like overkill, think again. These are my tips, and the stories I share here are just the tips of the icebergs. Believe me, I could write and write and write about the dangers lurking online, but I will end this chapter with a happy note.

My sweet boy, John David, went to the home of his online "friend," none other than NicolasOfOz. Afterward, I took the two of them for frozen yogurt. The "predator" I feared was a boy at John David's school who was in another class.

And yes, Lucy did quit ballet, with my blessings. No more pale pink tights, leotards, or tutus. Instead, she's my little soccer star. In fact, my baby girl made the final kick in a sudden-death match and helped her team win the league's "World Cup." Her nickname is Goldenfoot. She also plays piano like an angel and clarinet like a maniac. She's on a mission. In other words, she's perfect, with or without a tutu.

My little loves.

CHAPTER SEVEN

"Accidental" Deaths

HOT CAR DEATHS

Digest this: There are children alive right now who will be dead in a matter of months, baked to death inside their parents' and sitters' cars. Child deaths in hot cars have been taking place for decades, but they came to the national forefront recently with the very upsetting case of a twenty-two-month-old baby boy named Cooper.

COOPER HARRIS

On the morning of June 14, 2014, Justin Ross Harris left home in his silver Hyundai Tucson SUV and headed to work at Home Depot corporate offices in Vinings, Georgia. Baby Cooper was in his car seat, strapped in behind him. The two made a pit stop at a Smyrna, Georgia, Chick-fil-A en route, and restaurant employees later described baby Cooper as happy and alert. But just minutes later, when the married dad got out of his SUV, "sexting" various "girlfriends" all the while, he inexplicably left Cooper in the car.

We know the tot wasn't asleep, as he was laughing and perky just minutes before. I've driven the route myself, and it could not have been more than five minutes from the Chick-fil-A to the Home Depot offices. It's hard to comprehend that the little boy was so quiet that he became invisible to his dad over the course of such a short drive.

Harris walked into work and later went out to lunch with

colleagues, walking back by his SUV with his child still baking to death inside. After lunch, Harris asked to stop at a Home Depot to purchase light bulbs, which he dropped off in his SUV before going back to his office. He later claimed that he did not notice his son was in the car.

With temperatures in the Atlanta metro area soaring to near 100 degrees that day, inside the car, where Cooper was still strapped into his seat, the temperature climbed to a stifling 125 degrees. No human can endure that heat for very long. Harris, meanwhile, sat in his air-conditioned office working but also texting X-rated messages and photos to girlfriends and even talking about his son. Evidence showed that Harris messaged at least six different women the day Cooper died, telling one, "I love my son and all but we both need escapes." Yet nothing seemed to ring an alarm in his mind that his son was dying a grisly death over the course of seven long hours in the parking lot outside his building.

At the end of the workday, Harris sauntered out to his car, drove a short distance, and then leaped out of the car, shouting. Witnesses say he briefly tried CPR, then walked away, his son's body left lying there on the asphalt. His lawyers later claimed he was "too overwhelmed and couldn't concentrate" to perform CPR.

The baby's legs were bent, stiff from rigor mortis, frozen in the sitting position from being in the car seat for so long. Cooper's little face was covered in scratches from trying to claw out of his seat and clawing his own face in pain. Baby Cooper was cooked alive.

While it first appeared to be an awful accident, once it came to light that Harris researched child deaths in hot cars just before Cooper died, that initial perception quickly changed, and a jury agreed. Justin Ross Harris was convicted of murder one and is currently serving life behind bars. He's still in solitary confinement because the general population loathes him so much that even the prison staff is worried he'd be beaten dead in the yard if he was mixed in with the other inmates.

After baby Cooper's excruciating death, a similar scenario in Tennessee, another hot car death, played out quite differently.

KATERA BARKER

An East Nashville, Tennessee, dad, Matt Barker, had a plane to catch. The father of two was racing to the airport to catch a plane for an important business trip. Around seven a.m. on the morning of May 23, 2018, Barker walked out of the house. He had to take his newly adopted one-year-old daughter, Katera, and his five-year-old biological son to daycare. He came back home and left for the airport via rideshare. His wife, Jenny, had already left for work. That afternoon, Jenny went to daycare to get the two children and was told by daycare workers that Katera had never come in. Panic set in. Soon after, Katera was discovered still strapped in her dad's pickup, parked in the driveway. Mom called 911 and performed CPR until medics transported Katera to Vanderbilt Children's Hospital. The baby died upon arrival. Temperatures had soared near ninety degrees that day in Nashville. Barker flew home to Nashville later that night, and the couple reportedly was fully cooperative with police. There was much confusion surrounding the question of how one child was taken in to daycare and the other was not. Charges were never filed. It was determined that Matt Barker had no criminal intent and this tragedy was the result of a horrific mistake.

SAMARIA MOTYKA

On the morning of July 22, 2016, thirty-year-old Brittany Borgess dropped her two-year-old son, Isaac, at his Williamsport, Pennsylvania, daycare and then continued on to work. She parked her SUV outside her building and went in. Six and a half hours later, Borgess returned to the truck, she says, to discover her boyfriend's four-year-old daughter, Samaria Motyka, in the car. The tot had climbed out of her booster seat and made it to the front seat. She was found there on the floor. Outside it was 97 degrees; inside the car, the temperature rose to 120. When Samaria was taken to the hospital, her internal temperature was still 110 degrees. Samaria sweltered to death in a locked SUV parked in a downtown parking lot with no trees or shade at all. Borgess had been taking Samaria to daycare regularly, so it's a mystery why she forgot the little girl on this fateful day. Her defense suggested a memory lapse due to sleep deprivation and stress due to her upcoming marriage.

At trial, Borgess was found not guilty of involuntary manslaughter, endangering the welfare of a child, and reckless endangerment. She was sentenced to simply paying a fine of just twenty-five dollars for leaving a child unattended in a car. Four-year-old Samaria was found dead as her "caregiver" left her to bake for nearly seven hours, never giving her a thought...or did she?

A twenty-five-dollar fine!

Still, whether by forgetfulness, negligence, or malicious intent, far too many kids die in this horrifying way. According to the National Safety Commission, vehicular heatstroke (hyperthermia) is the leading cause of non-crash vehicle deaths among children. These deaths occur when children enter unlocked vehicles or are left alone in vehicles. These child deaths are 100 percent preventable. What can we do to avoid these tragedies?

HOT CAR SAFETY TIPS

- Stick to a routine. After a while, muscle memory takes over.
- Avoid distractions when getting out of the car.
- As you exit your car, make sure everyone's out before you lock it and walk away. One would think this is obvious, but I've learned that almost nothing is. So, I'm comfortable offering this fundamental reminder.
- Lock your car doors *every* time. Why? Some estimates say at least thirty percent of hot car deaths in America happen when a tot climbs into an unlocked vehicle.
- After you lock the car doors, keep them locked. That way, your child can't get into the car at will and therefore can't be locked in and trapped.
- Teach your child not to play alone in the car.
- Many parents advise they keep something they need in the back seat. They put a purse, briefcase, shoe, or even cell phone or laptop in the back seat. This forces you to look back or even open the back door before you leave that car.
- Keep a written note or stickie near your steering wheel to remind you to check your back seat.
- Some parents always place a stuffed animal in their child's car seat.

When they put the child in the seat, they take the stuffy and place it beside the parent up front. The stuffy is a visual reminder your child is in the back.

- Routinely hide your keys away from your children and, at the very least, out of their reach. Keeping them out of a child's reach will help reduce the risk of them climbing into the car without you knowing.
- Always ask your daycare provider to notify you promptly if your child is not present, out of the car, or checked in on time. Both Katera and Samaria would have been found much sooner if their absence from daycare had been communicated. This needs to be a routine text, call, or email. Put a plan in place by asking the daycare to call you in the event your child does not arrive on time when you have not contacted them about an absence or tardy arrival.
- Always act when you see a child alone in a car. Do not delay. Minutes count. Call 911. You have to.
- Discuss car rules with sitters and caregivers.
- Take advantage of technology.
- General Motors' Rear Seat Reminder has been shown to work. It does not detect the presence of a rear seat passenger, but it does, however, remind drivers to take a look inside the vehicle. If a rear door is opened and then closed within ten minutes before the vehicle is cranked, or if a door is opened and closed while the car is running, five chimes sound and a message pops up on the instrument panel every time the car shuts off, reminding the driver to check the back seats.
- New car seat technology now exists as well. Tones are activated through a smart chest clip and a wireless receiver. The beeps remind the driver that there's a child still in the rear seat within two minutes of the ignition turning off.
- A good app for child car security is Kars4Kids Safety. An alarm goes off every time you and your phone leave the car to remind you your child is in the car seat. All you need is a Bluetooth-enabled Android phone, a car...and a baby!
- More devices that work: ibabyseat, Driver's Little Helper sensor system, a new Waze setting that reminds drivers to check the back seat once they make it to the entered destination, and Baby Alert International's ChildMinder SoftClip, a digital shoulder harness clip.

It syncs to a smartphone app or key fob and alarms when you walk more than fifteen feet from the clip.
- Look for cars like Hyundai's Santa Fe. It comes with a built-in alert to tell the driver if there's a passenger in the rear seat.
- Go online and check out all of these helpful tools.

Make it your habit to open the back door before locking. I always do. Some people remember by always flipping their rearview or side-view mirror out of place before they walk away. When they get back into the car, it serves as a reminder that their baby's on board. It's similar to the routine some people have about leaving the house in the morning: turn off the coffee maker and the kitchen lights and lock the door. Practice makes perfect. Practice always opening that door and looking in back, and pretty soon, it will be your habit.

And don't count on your rearview mirror. When your child is in a rear-facing car seat, it always looks the same, whether the baby is in it or not. That was one of Justin Ross Harris's planned defenses, that he didn't notice Cooper in back because the baby seat was rear-facing and he didn't see his child's face in the rearview mirror. It didn't work at trial, and a glance in your rearview mirror won't save your baby's life.

The stresses and pressures of modern life can be massive, especially for working parents. There are so many things to do each day, and it can take a cognitive toll. We can have memory lapses concerning the most basic and important things in our lives. Take advantage of technology and develop good habits to make sure you and your child don't fall victim to one of these terrible accidents.

BATH TIME TRAGEDIES

Giving a small child or infant a bath can be a lovely, soothing bonding experience. Yet the simplest act of selfishness or negligence on the part of the parent during a bath can lead to the baby's death. It happens in a flash.

ZAYLA STUCKEY

On June 13, 2017, when mom of four Cheyenne Stuckey sat down to surf the internet and talk to her friends on Facebook, there was only one problem. Her eight-month-old girl, Zayla, was drowning. Stuckey said she left her daughter alone in the tub with the water still running for only two minutes. But according to police who reviewed computer records, it was closer to twenty minutes—eighteen to be exact. She also claimed she was "distracted" by another child and then got on Facebook Messenger, with the TV blaring. She chatted idly with two people while Zayla was alone in the tub. Eventually, Stuckey found Zayla floating facedown and tried to revive the little girl, but didn't know how. Zayla died alone, forgotten, unattended, and helpless.

Stuckey's three other children, four-year-old twins and a two-year-old son, were placed in a foster home. Does anyone even remember Zayla? I do.

CECILIA BODEM

Katherine Bodem loved shopping online for shoes. In fact, she admits she left her eleven-month old daughter, Cecilia, upstairs in a bathtub with her two-year-old son "supervising." Bodem then went downstairs to surf the internet and shop for shoes. No, that's not a typo. *She left the baby in the bathtub upstairs while she surfed the internet* and shopped for shoes for about twenty minutes.

When the thirty-eight-year-old mom finally went back upstairs, she found water overflowing from the tub. The baby had drowned. In court, Bodem called her daughter's death a "tragic accident." She pled guilty to second-degree manslaughter.

VIRTUAL PLAY, REAL DEATH

Thirty-year-old Colorado mom Shannon Johnson was obsessed with running her own "restaurant" in the virtual reality game Café World on Facebook. In this game, the player runs a pretend restaurant and chooses from numerous imaginary dishes to cook. They then pretend to cook and bake themselves through an imaginary culinary hierarchy. Shannon could decorate her imaginary café, take a break from all the pretend work in the pretend café, and visit pretend friends' restaurants and taste-test their imaginary daily specials.

My head hurts just writing that, because while Johnson was pretending to run a café online, her thirteen-month-old son was left alone to drown on March 11, 2011. The Fort Lupton woman said perhaps the bathwater was a little higher than usual. That was her excuse: the bathwater was a little higher than usual. She left out the fact that the baby drowned all alone while his mommy played online in a virtual café. Johnson says she found her baby slumped facedown in the bath making gurgling sounds. She also says she left him alone because she didn't want him to be known as a mama's boy. Johnson pled guilty to child abuse and negligently causing a death and was sentenced to ten years in prison.

These grim stories have one thing in common: extreme neglect and irresponsibility on the part of the parent. But they also show us how quickly babies and infants can drown. The facts couldn't be clearer: drowning is the leading cause of accidental death of children five and younger. So, while vigilance is your main defense, there are other things to consider to keep your little ones safe at bath time.

SAFETY TIPS FOR BATH TIME

Rule number one: *never* leave an infant or tot alone in the bathtub for even one second. Don't even step out quickly to get a towel or to get the phone. Don't. It is so easy for an infant or tot to die in a bathtub, and it can happen in one to two minutes. Babies are unstable and can't manage their own body weight. This is especially true for infants. If they slip under the bathwater, they die without a sound, and there is nothing they can do to save themselves.

- Baby bath seats or rings do not change rule number one. Rings and tub seats for children are intended to serve as child-bathing aids; they do not prevent a child from drowning.
- *Never* leave the water running. Sit there until it is right for your baby. You should be thinking about how deep it is and if the temperature is right. Only then do you place your baby in the tub.

- Gather whatever you will need for bath time within arm's reach before starting the bath or putting the baby in the water. This includes soap, towel, shampoo, moisturizer, and clothes or PJs. Everything should be right there to keep you from leaving baby in the tub to go get it.
- Don't fill the tub too high. Children can drown in just two inches of water.
- Block your child from getting into the bathroom unsupervised. Bathrooms are risky because of scalding or drowning dangers. Keep the bathroom door closed at all times. The easiest way to avoid bathroom injuries is to keep the bathroom off-limits to your child unless you or another adult are with them.
- Use a safety latch or lock on your bathroom door that your child cannot reach.
- Make sure any lock or latch can be unlocked or unlatched from the outside, just in case your child locks the door.
- Doorknob covers work well to keep bathrooms closed when you're not using them.
- Go the extra mile and install latches on toilet seat lids, too.
- Remove and hide the bathtub drain plug when you're not using it.
- Your child needs constant supervision in the tub. Keep one hand on them during tub time.
- Avoid doing things that keep you from staying focused, like talking on the phone, checking email or texts, doing chores, drinking, or going outside for a smoke.
- If you can't ignore a distraction like the phone, a text, email, or the doorbell, wrap your infant or tot in a towel and take her with you.
- Child and infant bathtub drownings in the home usually occur during a lapse in supervision. Be there.
- Don't leave water in the tub; it's so easy for a child to fall in and drown. A child can tip in and drown in an instant. (This also applies to buckets. Approximately twenty children die in the US each year by drowning in buckets.)
- Place a soft protector over the faucet to avoid your tot getting a head injury. Ours looked like a frog.
- Install no-slip strips on the bottom of the tub to keep tots from falling.
- Speaking of the bathroom, keep meds in containers with safety caps, high up and out of reach. It's even better to have them in a locked

cabinet, not with all the toothpaste and other items you share or use frequently.

IN HOT WATER

On January 17, 2018, a Homestead, Florida, mom thought nothing of it when she sent her brood back for baths, but that one moment changed all their lives forever. Her ten-year-old drew a bath for the baby, but apparently the four-year-old brother added extremely hot water. Baby Ethan Coley suffered excruciating burns all the way from his toes to his chest, caused by the blistering hot water. But things actually got worse.

Mom Christina Marie Hurt, who had a history with child abuse investigations, was worried what authorities would think. Hoping Ethan would recover, she did not take him to the hospital. Instead, she took him to a friend's house after dropping her other children at school. A woman saw Hurt place Ethan on a mattress outside a house in the neighborhood and called police, who took Ethan to the hospital, where he died as a result of the scalding and the lack of care.

Christina Hurt was charged with second-degree murder and aggravated child abuse for refusing to hospitalize him. Her other five children have been fostered out. She was awaiting trial at the time of this writing.

The cases go on and on. I've investigated, reported on, and researched similar cases, from Atlanta's disabled Bradley Downing to Milwaukee's little Zayanna Simmons to four-year-old Austin Cooper's death in Dayton, Ohio. There is a common chain. My question is, how can that chain be broken?

HOT WATER SAFETY

Once a child is exposed to extremely hot water, whether by incorrectly drawing the water or because of an overheated water heater, in under five seconds, the child suffers serious third-degree burns. Less than five seconds.

Children under age five are at the greatest risk of hot water burns leading to death. Some estimates say a full 25 percent of all burns involving children stem from hot tap water.

The Consumer Product Safety Commission advises that hot water tanks should be set no higher than 120 degrees Fahrenheit (49 degrees Celsius). Even then, a child could still suffer second-degree burns, though it would take a longer time. A longer time period allows a child to get out of the water. But what if it's a baby that can't get out on their own? You must supervise!

Hot water heaters have adjustable thermostats right on the outside of the tank, either out in the open or behind the cover plate. Just turn the temperature down to 120 degrees. That temperature is so much safer for children and for anyone in the shower when a sudden change occurs. For instance, we all know that flushing a commode can immediately cause a surge of hot water in the shower.

One problem, however, is that homes with older dishwashers without their own heater call for water temperatures higher than 120 degrees to thoroughly sanitize the dishes. Most current dishwashers have heaters to heat the interior, so 120 degrees is fine for those machines. If your dishwasher is older, check the specs. If you have an older model that is still working well, you can use cold-water detergent that works at practically any temperature, so you can keep your water heater at a safe setting.

With babies, pay very special attention to water temperatures. Bath-water for infants should be lukewarm, not hot. It's so easy to scald or overheat an infant.

Never leave the water running in the tub if you leave the room. The water can heat up considerably more than you want.

Home hot water valves should be switched to anti-scald devices. It's an easy fix for you or your plumber to make. The anti-scald devices will interrupt your water flow when temperatures reach a certain degree.

Always test your child's water before putting them in the tub.

As you test the bathwater for your child, remember that when you first start the tap, the water in your pipes is cool. The temperature will rise dramatically once the water from the tank reaches the tub faucet.

When your child is old enough to understand how to turn faucets, teach him or her to start the cold water first, then the hot.

WINDOW CORD DANGERS

People often believe that only certain subsets of the population suffer tragedy. After all of my years prosecuting felony crimes, I know this isn't true. Victims' families ran the entire gamut from white to Hispanic to African American to Asian, rich to poor, and well educated to grade-school dropouts.

Ask NFL football star and Philadelphia Eagles running back Reno Mahe. I imagine he'd give up every achievement he has ever attained to replay a single day of his family's life. On Tuesday, November 22, 2016, the Mahes were at their lovely Utah home. Friends were over and his three-year-old girl, Elsie, was playing with a friend. No one knows exactly how it happened, but Elsie got tangled in the cords from miniblinds, and they twisted around her neck.

Mom Sunny rushed into the room and started CPR even before EMTs arrived. Elsie was raced to the Primary Children's Hospital in Salt Lake City. That night, Reno and Sunny posted a heartbreaking Instagram message: "Our Elsie girl has officially been released to heaven—at least from a worldly, paperwork stand point. Her second neurological death exam was also positive for brain death...We feel peace and we are again so grateful for the privilege of being Elsie's parents."

Now Elsie's parents are suing window blinds manufacturers, installers, distributors, and marketers, alleging that they manufactured, assembled, marketed, distributed, installed, and sold the window coverings involved in Elsie's death. The suit says that the window coverings were unreasonably dangerous and defective and were sold without proper warnings and safety mechanisms. Hopefully, their voices will be heard and their fight will result in lasting changes for the better.

Before I prosecuted violent crimes, I was with the Federal Trade Commission, and we often worked very closely with the Consumer Product Safety Commission (CPSC). Our friends at the CPSC say windows and window blinds are among the top five hidden hazards in American homes. Cords present the greatest danger to children under nine years of age.

The reality is that nearly seventeen thousand children were hurt by window blinds between 1990 and 2015. Most of the accidents were minor cuts and scrapes, but almost three hundred children died. Window treatments such as drape and blind cords have been in homes for many years, and we have come to accept that as normal. But now our eyes have been opened: cords kill children. In the US, one child per month dies in this manner. The two most common ways cords kill children are when a window with a cord is next to a crib and the cord falls into the crib. Then, the child gets tangled while sleeping or playing. Cords also kill when a child plays near a cord and accidentally gets tangled up and asphyxiated. Children lose consciousness in seconds. In one minute, a child can be brain-dead from lack of oxygen.

The problem is so bad that there is a movement afoot to ban all forms of blinds and drapes that have cords. Until that day comes, be smart and heed these suggestions.

WINDOW CORD SAFETY TIPS

I admit it: we had dangling window cords in our house. I didn't give it much thought until I learned so much about the dangers of window cord strangling. The cords are gone now and the lesson is simple: cords and children don't mix—#GoCordless.

- All cords are bad, whether they are on the side, back, or front.
- There is something known in safety circles as the six-inch rule. Never allow a length of string, cord, floss—you name it—longer than six inches around your children. It can get wrapped around their necks. So make sure to keep *all cords of any kind*, not just window treatment cords, out of the reach of children.
- Look for stops in the internal cords (or "ladders) so they can't be pulled through the slats and looped around a tot's neck.
- Look for cordless shades that push up and down with no cord.
- Consider motorized shades that use a remote control.
- Retrofit your blinds. Seek out kits for existing blinds in order to go cordless. They can be found through the CPSC. Up-to-date blind systems are not perfect but are safer than older models.
- At the very least, childproof blinds by shortening dangling cords and securing them tightly to the wall high up out of your child's reach. Move all furniture away from the window so the cords can't be reached from a bed, chair, table, or crib. Remember, children climb and jump, making their reach higher than you think.

- Eliminate all looped blind or drape cords. Cut those loops.
- Buy cordless window treatments. You can find them many places. The majority of the stock at SelectBlinds.com is available with no cords. Ikea and Target have changed their stocks to cordless, too. Lowe's, Home Depot, and Walmart have pledged to do the same.

TIP-OVER DANGERS

Some family stories are told so many times, they become part of the family lore. As a child, I would always chop off all my hair and cover my arms and legs with lipstick. My sister would shut herself in her room with books and peanut butter. My brother would lock us out of the house in the afternoons after school, and we would climb in through the bathroom window. (We were latchkey kids.) One story still gives me the chills.

My big brother, Macky (Walter Malcolm Grace Jr.), was a toddler at the time. We all lived in a tiny, tiny house in rural middle Georgia. My big sister, Ginny (Elizabeth Virginia), under two years old at the time, was with him playing in a narrow hallway. My brother was climbing up the side of a big china cabinet that displayed my mom's prize collection, her Apple Blossom patterned fine china by Haviland. It must have been really beautiful.

Back to Macky climbing up the side of a cabinet full of china and crystal given as treasured wedding presents. Baby Ginny was sitting on the floor beside him. Suddenly: *crash!* The huge cabinet fell forward as he climbed and crashed downward. Rest easy, they both lived.

The hallway was so tiny that the cabinet's path was blocked, and it ended up wedged into the wall in front of it, forming a sort of lean-to over my sister and brother. How the two of them survived all that china and crystal raining down around them without so much as a scratch I will never know. It was a miracle.

Others have not been so lucky.

TED MCGEE

On Valentine's Day, 2016, on a lazy Sunday after church, Apple Valley, Minnesota, mom Janet McGee was checking her baby boy Ted, just twenty-two months old, every fifteen minutes to be there when he woke up from his afternoon nap. I remember doing the same thing, sneaking down the hall and barely breathing as I cracked open the door to peer into a darkened room to check on the twins.

All was fine with baby Ted until the last time Janet checked in. She saw, to her shock, that the clothes dresser had tipped over. Immediately, she knew, even though she couldn't see him: Ted was under the dresser. Mother's intuition. I hate to write these words, but she was right. She used all her strength and speed to lift the chest and found him under it. She screamed and her other son called 911 as Mommy started CPR.

EMTs raced the tot to the emergency room, but when Mommy held his hand, it was cold.

Ted was suffocated by the weight of the furniture on top of him. They thought Ted's death was just an anomaly, a bizarre accident. It wasn't. They soon learned that Ikea furniture had already been linked to other tot deaths. By June 2016, Ikea announced a recall of the Malm dressers because poor Ted was the third child killed by one.

Fast-forward to November 2018. Ikea relaunched the same recall of nearly 30 million chests and dressers. That's not a typo: *30 million.* Ikea did this second massive recall after an eighth child died.

The first recall did not raise awareness enough to save little Jozef Dudek's life. On May 24, 2017, Jozef was discovered trapped between drawers of a three-drawer Ikea dresser in his Buena Park, California, bedroom. He had been put down for a nap that May afternoon, and no one heard the crash. Jozef was the eighth child that we know of to die because of an Ikea dresser fall. The dressers do not meet voluntary safety standards that make sure the dresser will stand upright even if a child plays on it. Jozef's parents say they never got a recall notice, even though they are sure Ikea had their contact information via the Ikea customer loyalty program.

Ikea has paid out more than $50 million for four of these tip-over accidents, and there are other lawsuits piling up and a lot of finger pointing. Most important, eight tots lost their lives.

There are allegations that Ikea had known of the tipping danger for years, with fourteen known Malm tip-overs reported between 1989 and 2015 related to four injuries and five deaths. The company had offered kits to secure the dressers and ran awareness campaigns to warn customers. Then came the unprecedented recall of Malm, one of their bestselling lines. Earlier, Ikea had refused a recall and instead opted to send out the free restraint kits to attach dressers to walls.

The tip-over statistics are shocking. The CPSC says someone in our country is injured every seventeen minutes by some sort of tip-over, be it dressers, TVs, or refrigerators. In fact, they estimate that falling TVs or tipped furniture sends a child to the emergency room every thirty minutes. These accidents cause an average of one child's death every two weeks. Since 2000, tip-overs of dressers and bureaus have caused at least 206 deaths. That is shocking.

It's not only Ikea dressers at issue. They are just in the spotlight now because of the massive recall and settlements. There are other dressers that cause the same tragedies. Making it all feel so much worse is the fact that it is so easily avoidable.

How do you keep your home safe from these all-too-common disasters? Read on.

TIPS TO TACKLE TIP-OVERS

- Look for shorter dressers.
- Check for industry standards and make sure they are met.
- Do not leave toddlers alone in their rooms. Nearly half of all tip-overs occur in a bedroom. Patterns indicate many tip-overs occur when children climb on the dressers, pulling up on open drawers.
- Check for tip-over weights of at least sixty pounds hanging off a drawer.
- Do not place a television on a dresser.
- Keep drawers closed.
- Attach safety straps to drawers so they can't be easily opened and used to climb.
- Remove temptation. Remove items such as toys, stuffed animals, games, remote controls, candy or snack dishes, and any other thing children love from the tops of TVs and large furniture like dressers and armoires. Think like a kid.
- Anchor all your top-heavy furniture to the wall with anti-tip devices like braces, wall straps, or brackets. They are inexpensive and easy to install.
- Think beyond just armoires and dressers. Anchor bookcases,

shelving units, changing tables, and appliances—anything heavy. Just because you can't imagine climbing on it doesn't mean a child won't.

- Keep furniture away from doors that could possibly knock it forward. I made this mistake with a tall, slender mirror that sat upright on an attached easel. It was out of place by a few feet one day, and when the door opened, it bumped the mirror and it fell forward. Neither of the twins was in the room. Imagine what all that sharp glass could have done to them. I screwed the next mirror to the wall.
- Secure your televisions. If they aren't mounted up on the wall or on a wall hinge, anchor them to the wall or a stand with an anti-tip device like a strap.
- Mount all flat-screen TVs to the wall or furniture. Position old-style CRT TVs on low, stable furniture. It is best to use furniture designed specifically to support a TV, like media centers or TV stands.
- If you aren't using your old CRT TV, get rid of it. It's a real danger.
- Push your TV as far back on the piece of furniture as you can.
- Keep all of your TV and cable cords away from your child's reach.
- New furniture is often sold with anti-tip devices. Install them as soon as the furniture is placed in the home.
- Follow manufacturers' instructions to install anti-tip devices correctly.
- Check points of attachment to ensure your anti-tip devices are secure.
- Install stops on cabinet and dresser drawers to keep them from being pulled out entirely. Why? Several drawers open at the same time can shift the weight and make the piece tip over.
- Do your best to secure glass-topped coffee and side tables that are toddler height. Get clamps to keep the glass from sliding off.
- For more information, go to the website devoted to this topic launched in 2015 by the CPSC: anchorit.gov.

CELL PHONE BATHTUB DEATHS

When I got the news a fourteen-year-old girl from Lubbock, Texas, had been electrocuted in the bathtub, I assumed she'd dropped a hair dryer, radio, or curling iron in the tub. I couldn't really grasp how she could be in the tub taking a bath and drop the appliance in the tub at the same time. We all know that electrical plugs have to be, by code, a certain number of feet away from a tub to preclude this exact scenario. Then I learned the truth. It wasn't a hair dryer, curling iron, or radio. It was a tween's best friend: a cell phone.

MADISON COE

Madison Coe, a fourteen-year-old from Lubbock, Texas, had just graduated from middle school. Visiting with her dad in New Mexico, she headed to take a bath at her dad's house on July 9, 2017, a quiet Sunday afternoon. Just like every other tween and teen, Madison loved texting and talking to friends on her cell phone. In fact, she loved it so much, she posted a photo showing an extension cord connected to her phone and charger all bundled up on a bath towel next to the bathtub. The caption said, "When you use [an] extension cord so you can plug your phone in while you're in the bath."

What was meant to be a joke turned into a tragedy. When Madison was found, there was a burn mark on the hand she would have used to reach for her cell phone. At first, many thought Madison accidentally dropped her cell phone, a Samsung Edge Plus, into the tub while she was taking a bath, but later it became clear Madison's phone was never immersed in the tub with her. She had touched the frayed but plugged-in extension cord while sitting in the tub.

IRINA RYBNIKOVA

But sadly, Madison's death was not a one-off. Fifteen-year-old Russian martial arts champ Irina Rybnikova was killed on December 8, 2018, when her charging iPhone fell into her bath. Irina was found dead in the tub at home in Bratsk. Reports revealed that Irina was texting friends in the tub when her phone slipped. The teen girl was electrocuted and died of heart failure before her parents found her.

In a similar, but subtly different, incident, another death occurred by smartphone electrocution. On July 11, 2016, twenty-three-year-old Chinese flight attendant Ma Ailun, who was set to be married in August of that year, was in the tub and using a smartphone charger, but she may have been using an uncertified counterfeit charger that could have caused the problem. Warnings had circulated regarding a flood of uncertified chargers, likening them to pocket grenades. Her sister's blog indicated she may have taken the jolt when she tried to answer a call while her iPhone was charging. Police noticed her neck had an obvious electronic injury.

Counterfeit chargers may present hazards because they don't have to meet safety standards, including overheating, which could have been a factor in Ma's death.

Research shows cell phones on their own are not powerful enough to deliver a harmful, much less fatal, shock. But when the phone is charging, a fatal shock is in fact possible.

TIPS: WATER AND ELECTRICITY DO NOT MIX

- It is never safe to have an electrical extension cord or power cord of any kind near the bathtub.
- This rule applies to other items like hair straighteners, hair dryers, curling irons, and similar items and all electronic devices and games.
- If you use electrical appliances like hair dryers or razors in the bathroom, take thirty extra seconds to unplug and store them in a cabinet with a safety latch or lock when you aren't using them.
- Even better? Use them in a different room (like your bedroom) where there's no water.
- Get an electrician to install special ground-fault circuit interrupter outlets in the bathroom and kitchen, which reduce the chance of an electrical injury if an appliance ends up in the tub or sink.

APPLIANCE DEATHS

We take many modern technological conveniences for granted—as well we should, for most of the time these tools just help us get things done quickly and efficiently. But any powerful appliance must be respected and used properly or the results can be catastrophic.

PARIS TALLEY

Even at this moment as I am typing away, I remember the news of a baby girl's death by microwave. I felt like a robot as I forced my way through the program that night, all the time wondering, how did this happen? Read on.

On August 30, 2005, China Arnold and her boyfriend, Terrel Talley, were drinking and arguing over the paternity of Arnold's twenty-eight-day-old baby girl, Paris. The following morning the boyfriend discovered the baby cold, stiff, and lifeless. Arnold was infuriated by her boyfriend's recent infidelity, took it out on her daughter, and said as much to Talley. At the emergency room, Arnold feigned ignorance and said, "My baby's burned?" But the attending physician was skeptical because the injuries were obvious.

After several trials and mistrials, Arnold was convicted of aggravated manslaughter and given a life sentence in May 2011.

Poor Paris's story is horrific to contemplate to this day. It is a chilling reminder of how dangerous and powerful microwave ovens are. But what, if anything, can we learn?

MICROWAVE SAFETY TIPS

- Keep microwaves up at least as high as a countertop, making it less easy for a child to maneuver an infant into it.
- Keep your eyes on the glass window in the door. It is see-through for a reason.
- Warn children about the dangers of microwaves.
- Purchase smaller-sized microwaves, which make it nearly impossible to stuff a child or pet inside.
- If you have small children, put a safety latch on the microwave. You can remove it later.
- Most microwave injuries are heat-related burns from hot utensils, containers, food, or drinks that have been overheated, and liquid explosions.
- Most injuries do not relate to radiation. That said, there have been very rare instances of radiation injury due to unusual circumstances or improper servicing.

- People fear that microwaves interfere with pacemakers, but modern pacemakers are microwave safe. That said, your pacemaker or the one used by your loved one may not be. Ask your doctor and the pacemaker manufacturer. Better safe than sorry applies here.
- Read and follow directions in your microwave's manual on use and safety.
- Use cookware made for microwaves or labeled microwavable to avoid a microwave fire.
- No aluminum in the microwave (including plates and foil).
- No metal, plastic, or paper in the microwave, either.
- Use only glass and ceramics.
- Never heat food that's sealed or in packaging.
- Do not heat water past the boiling point. It can explode with the slightest movement and cause serious burns. (Add sugar, coffee, milk, or a tea bag *before* heating so there will be no hot water explosion.)
- Watch for damaged doors, hinges, seals, and latches. Make sure the door isn't bent or damaged. These issues lead to microwave radiation leakage.
- Never use your microwave when the door is open.
- If the light or fan turns on by itself, have your microwave repaired immediately.
- If possible, position your microwave away from other kitchen heat sources. For instance, don't have it near the oven or beneath an appliance that heats up. Doing so can make your microwave overheat.
- Never cover the vent of a microwave at the top when you are using it.
- If an item in your microwave catches fire, unplug the microwave immediately. Keep the microwave door closed.
- Let the item cool before you take it out. Microwave temperatures soar quickly. Wait at least a minute before touching it.
- No oversized food containers in a microwave. They could cause electric shock or fire.
- Don't use your microwave as a storage unit.
- Don't place other items like utensils or plates in the microwave. Doing so sends the wrong message to children about what is acceptable to place in the microwave.

FRIDGE AND FREEZER FRIGHTS

I recently visited with the mom and sister of a teen girl, Kenneka Jenkins. Their questions about Kenneka's death are still unanswered. Security video from September 9, 2017, shows Kenneka wandering the halls of the Chicago O'Hare Crowne Plaza hotel in Rosemont, Illinois. Kenneka was found facedown inside a walk-in freezer in a kitchen that was not in use at the time. The cause of death was hypothermia. She had been drinking at a party inside the hotel earlier in the evening.

Kenneka's family has filed a lawsuit against the Crowne Plaza, its security contractor, and the restaurant that was renting the kitchen space. They say all three were negligent for failing to secure the walk-in freezer or thoroughly searching the premises when the teen girl first went missing. Her body was discovered twenty-one hours after she went missing. Much has been made of the facts surrounding the case and many theories have emerged, but one thing is not in dispute: the teen died from being locked in a freezer, unable to get out.

Typically, the victims of fridge and freezer deaths are much younger.

DAWLTON LEE DELBRIDGE, KAYLEIGH MAE MEEKS, BROOK'LYN LEIGH JACKSON

Refrigerator dangers were driven home to the residents of the small town of Live Oak, Florida, in Suwannee County on January 13, 2019. Three little children, six-year-old Dawlton Lee DelBridge, nineteen-month-old Kayleigh Mae Meeks, and four-year-old Brook'Lyn Leigh Jackson, were playing outside in their own yard when they all decided to explore a freezer that had not yet been brought into the home.

The mom of the four-year-old had been outside watching them jump on a trampoline. She went inside momentarily to use the restroom and says that when she came back out, she couldn't find the kids. She immediately woke another mom inside and the two started searching the property, including a vacant home next door, for the next thirty to forty minutes. All the while, the children were struggling for air inside the freezer. In the horrible moment they opened the chest-type freezer, they found the children, none of them breathing. The moms frantically tried to resuscitate the tots and called 911. EMTs rushed the children to the nearest hospital. They couldn't be saved.

When Suwanee County sheriffs inspected the freezer, they saw a metal plate had been installed on the freezer so that a padlock could be added. They believe that when the three tots climbed in, the lid closed and the hasp plate fell shut, so even if the three were capable of opening the door, the metal plate held the lid shut in place.

Refrigerators, freezers, and coolers are meant to be airtight. When the door is closed, a child shut inside will have very little air. Older fridges could only be opened from the outside and became death traps for children inside. More advanced designs using a magnetic mechanism decrease the danger dramatically because the fridge can open from the inside unless a hinge, hasp, or lock is placed on the appliance.

Fridge and freezer deaths became less common after the Refrigerator Safety Act of 1956, which changed the way refrigerator doors stay shut and led to the creation of magnetic mechanisms instead of fridge latches. Many states enacted laws to prohibit abandoning appliances with airtight lids that a child could get into. The problem is still present, though, when someone tosses out an old fridge and doesn't do it properly.

FRIDGE AND FREEZER SAFETY TIPS

- Identify all appliances that could potentially lock someone in with no way out.
- Childproof older fridges and any other appliances that are abandoned or not in use. The most effective way to do that is to take the door off the appliance with a screwdriver. In fact, in many jurisdictions, it is illegal to get rid of an old refrigerator without removing its door beforehand.
- Obviously, keep children away from older refrigerators, dryers, coolers, and freezers, even if they are still being used.
- Install door locks on the garage, laundry room, or storage area where these appliances are stored. Make sure you place the lock high up on the door so children can't reach it.
- Teach your children not to play with or inside appliances.
- Report any unsafe or abandoned appliances.

TRAPPED IN THE COOLER

I never thought of a simple ice chest or drink cooler as a mortal threat. That is until I saw gut-wrenching home surveillance video out of Pompano Beach, Florida. The surveillance system was set up in the Wanes family home to protect it and them from burglars, but it caught something very different and very dangerous. On the video, captured March 2, 2019, the camera is trained on a back patio. It's a dream patio, with a built-in barbecue grill, floor-to-ceiling glass doors, and a beautiful terra cotta inlaid tile floor. And there's a big white Igloo ice chest on that floor.

As I watched the home security video, out of the doors blasted five-year-old Nicholas Wanes. He is in the middle of a game of hide-and-seek, and after frantically looking around, he heads straight for the cooler, hops in, and closes the door. My mouth got dry as I watched.

Moments later, I see his dad, desperate, run out onto the porch, searching. Then came his mom. They are literally running in every direction looking for their son. They pass the cooler over and over, looking. Then, as a seeming afterthought, the dad lifts the cooler lid, and before he can pick up his son, Mom is all over it and grabs him in a hug and lifts him out...alive. If you look carefully, you can actually see his little fingers through the gap of the lid just before the cooler automatically closes and locks and Nicholas can no longer push it open from inside.

The little boy later said he'd wanted to play hide-and-seek but found a "not good" spot in the cooler and was really scared.

The family is now speaking out about the cooler, an Igloo seventy-two-quart Marine Elite. They have also removed the lock so the life-threatening event can never happen again. Igloo, one of the country's favorite cooler companies, apologized and has recalled four coolers in the Marine Elite line. But the Wanes got it right. Remove locks from coolers. Period.

DRYER DISASTERS

Three-year-old Brantley Lloyd had a wonderful party for his birthday. The happiness turned to sorrow and shock just one day later. Apparently, sometime during that next day, August 7, 2019, baby Brantley crawled out of his crib and wandered into the laundry room. Chet Lloyd found his son in the dryer in the Chic's Beach, Virginia, townhome laundry room. Chet was clearly devastated and described Lloyd as extremely hot and covered in sweat. Brantley's asthma was likely exacerbated due to heat and panic, poor little angel. His dad tried to resuscitate him and called 911, but to no avail.

WASHING MACHINE TRAPS: KAYLEY ISHII

On February 2, 2009, a four-year-old girl from Mission Viejo, California, Kayley Ishii, somehow managed to climb into the family's front-load washer on an ordinary Monday morning. Her fifteen-month-old brother joined the fun and unwittingly pressed the button, so inviting to little ones, that turned the machine on. The washer was a Kenmore 417 with an "easy start" button, and its control panel was just twenty inches from the floor. It was noted by a local sheriff that once the machine starts, it's extremely difficult to open the door. It is estimated that the four-year-old was in the machine, full of water, for only about two short minutes before her mother found her. Kayley passed away that very night at the local hospital. It was determined she died accidentally of blunt force trauma in the washer.

KLOE MCIVER

When Lindsey McIver's four-year-old son came running to her early on a July morning, he was crying so hard she couldn't make out exactly what he was saying. The Conifer, Colorado, mom tried her best to interpret, but suddenly three words hit home: "Kloe inside washer." Can you imagine the shock that overcame her?

Lindsey and Alan McIver rushed down to the family's basement, where the new washer was, and there they saw Kloe, locked inside the machine, which was tumbling and filling with water. She was screaming, but the machine was airtight, so no one could hear. Alan yanked the machine door so hard, it pulled the machine from the wall, but it was locked and wouldn't open. They then managed to stop the new machine mid-cycle and rescue Kloe. The beautiful baby only suffered scrapes and bruises, on the outside anyway, but I imagine the incident will always haunt her.

The McIvers had just gotten the new front-loading washer one day before Kloe was trapped. In fact, they hadn't read the manual yet. Now they have upped the safety by adding a child safety lock to the washer door, and they also activated the child lock feature on the washer settings. They have spoken out to alert others about washer dangers, sharing Kloe's scary story and her miracle rescue.

LAUNDRY ROOM SAFETY TIPS

- Find and activate the built-in child lock feature on your washer's electronic control panel. Many models feature this in order to block somcone from changing the washing cycle mid-operation. It also can prevent the door being opened by your child. Tots love the colorful flashing lights that are found on the electronic control panel and, of course, try to reach them and press the buttons. That could easily stop the washer and allow the child to open the door and get inside.
- Don't keep hampers or stools around your washer or dryer that could allow your tot to crawl on top and get into top-loaders.
- It is so simple to install an exterior washer safety lock. The lock stops the washer door from opening.
- Look for washer models that have locks that alert you when someone tries to open the door mid-cycle.
- Push your washer as far back and tightly against the wall as possible, keeping with manufacturer's guidelines.
- Reduce any space on either side of your washer. Get the sides as close to the dryer or wall as you can. A tot can get beside or behind the washer or even pull out the power cord or water or drainage hose. Imagine that awful hot water on a tot!
- Make sure your washer is sitting level on the floor, which will prevent it from rocking back and forth while in churning mode. Use a bubble level to do that. If you aren't installing it, make sure the installers check the level. You can get a bubble level online or at the hardware store.

- Place your front-load washer on a pedestal.
- Keep the door to the laundry room or closet closed. Lock it if possible, even if it's just a hinge lock placed high up on the door so a child can't reach it. Mine could open that type of lock before age two.
- I know that moisture and heat can build up in the laundry area, but it's not worth the risk to leave the door open. Use a dehumidifier.
- Use washer locking straps. You can get them on Amazon. While a tot may still be able to slightly open the door to your washer or dryer, it will be almost impossible for them to climb in. I believe these straps should be included on the appliances when sold. This is how they work: One end of the strap snaps onto the door, the other onto the drum container. They use a peel-and-stick attach method. It's easy for you to unsnap, but not for your little one. These straps can be used with washers, dryers, freezers, refrigerators, dishwashers, microwaves, and ovens. Some may claim that's overdoing it. If you agree, ask the parents of the children I've mentioned above.

DISHWASHERS

Good news: there have been no known child deaths in dishwashers. But while researching the topic, I learned that dishwashers have been responsible for thousands of home fires. Also, their door gaskets can become contaminated with black mold and fungus, so regular maintenance and cleaning are required.

Knives should always be loaded pointed down to avoid cutting tiny hands. Also, make sure that your dishwasher is always turned off when you finish using it.

PART TWO

Protecting Yourself

CHAPTER EIGHT

Safe While Exercising

IT COULD NEVER HAPPEN TO ME

It's so much easier, so much more pleasant to go about our days with blinders on, at least to some degree. When we hear of a violent crime, many of us, including me, immediately begin to rationalize why it would never happen to us. It's easier to reason "She was out so late!" "Why was she jogging all alone?" "Why was she walking to her car in a lonely parking deck all by herself?" The "why-it-won't-happen-to-me" list in our heads is endless, and I believe there is a reason for that. In our imaginations, it won't happen to us because we don't *want* it to happen to us. Even subconsciously, we differentiate ourselves and our daily routines from "her," the victim.

The reality is, we aren't different from "her." Violent crime can enter our lives the same way it enters the lives of other people going about their everyday routines. It's scary and sobering...and true. Instead of cowering or being paralyzed with fear, I want to do something about it.

MISSY BEVERS

At the time of her death, Terri "Missy" Bevers was an instructor for a high-energy aerobics workout class. That morning, she was prepping to lead a five a.m. fitness class at Creekside Church in Midlothian, Texas. The forty-five-year-old married mom of three was clearly super fit. She often wore a T-shirt that said CAMP GLADIATOR across the front and had sculpted muscles and a vibrant demeanor: *gladiator* was the perfect word to describe Missy.

That morning, just minutes before class was to start, one of her students came upon Missy, covered in blood and lying unresponsive on the floor. Missy had been murdered at five a.m. in a church in rural Midlothian, Texas. It doesn't make sense.

When security footage from the church that morning was reviewed, cops were stunned to see Missy's killer sauntering into view...and I do mean sauntering. With a unique stride, Missy's killer was decked out in a full SWAT uniform, complete with black pants, black top with POLICE emblazoned on it, black tactical boots, and a motorcycle helmet hiding both face and neck. How odd. And why? There was no sexual assault and no robbery to speak of. Despite incredible efforts by local police and beyond as well as intense media scrutiny, as of this writing, Missy's case remains unsolved.

This thug who murdered Missy was in full protective gear and had a tool that was likely used to enter the building. Was that the murder weapon? The killer was able to subdue and murder a woman who was incredibly fit, awake, and aware. But was she aware of her surroundings? Did the killer surprise her in some manner? Was the killer lying in wait before she got there? If this could happen to a woman like Missy Bevers in a church, of all places, in a beautiful rural setting where most people can't even remember the last serious crime, what does that mean for the rest of us?

What about walking or jogging in parks, on roads, and on biking trails? None of these scream out "Danger!" Right? But danger doesn't scream a warning or sound a little ping ahead of time, like our Apple Watches or smartphones. It just happens.

KARINA VETRANO

When I heard about the case of Karina Vetrano, I thought of my dad. Whenever we were together, he would race-walk and I would jog along beside him. We all did everything together as a family: exercise, suppers, vacations...everything. Karina had a similar relationship with her dad, Phil, and they jogged together nearly every day. Phil had recently retired from the New York Fire Department.

Photos of Karina show she's absolutely stunning, with long dark hair and a perfect smile. She was brainy as well, with a master's degree in speech pathology and aspirations to write. Karina headed out for a run on the afternoon of August 2, 2016. While she usually ran with her dad, that particular day Phil's back was hurting and he didn't join her.

I've talked with Phil many times about that afternoon. He remembers Karina going out the door, her earbuds and a big smile in place, headed toward Spring Creek Park, less than a block from their home in Queens, New York. Phil tells me that within fifteen minutes, a horrible feeling came over him, and he started calling Karina's cell. It went straight to voice mail. He tried texting her over and over and got no response. Even now, when he tells his story, I can hear the same urgency still creeping into his voice. He says he felt her calling, "Daddy, I need you."

And he was right.

Phil Vetrano began the search for Karina. Local police came to help. Hours later, it was her own dad who passed a single stalk of tall grass that was bent over and broken. He stopped. Something inside told him to go back to the spot, and when he did, he saw another stalk bent down. He followed a procession of bent stalks and found his daughter several feet off the trail they had run a hundred times and more.

Phil saw his daughter facedown and only partially clothed with her jogging shorts around her ankles. Her body was covered with bruises, scratches, and cuts, and she was beaten so badly that her teeth actually broke. The medical examiner confirms Karina died from strangulation.

The *one* time he didn't run with her, she was murdered.

Over years of interviewing literally thousands of victims, I've learned from so many of them and their families that very often, a strong sense of foreboding takes over just before tragedy strikes. I always ask when investigating crimes, "Did you have an intuition or any warning something was wrong?" Based on all their answers, I'm sure these feelings have to be acknowledged, taken seriously, and acted upon immediately. Check your own safety and the safety of your family.

That hot August so many years ago, before cell phones and when I had never even contemplated crime, much less prosecuting crime, I had that foreboding the moment I was told to call Keith's family. I know that feeling that washed over Phil Vetrano.

Months passed and no arrests were made. But then a cop remembered the name of a loiterer written in a notebook months before. That name was Chanel Lewis. Lewis was totally unconnected to Karina, which made the police's task much more difficult. But after DNA from Karina's body matched Lewis, he gave a rambling confession. Believe it or not, even with DNA and a confession, the first jury mistried. The Vetranos were devastated, but they didn't give up. The second time around, the jury convicted. The perp bragged from behind jailhouse walls that he made the front page of the two most popular New York City papers. That's his mindset to this day.

I couldn't help but notice that, all the way through the investigation and leading up to the trial, the campaign to attack the victim raged full-force. It's an age-old technique used in everything from murders to rapes to child molestations and arsons. The idea is to sully the victim and make the jury care less about them and much less likely to hand down a guilty verdict.

Sometimes I think we, the public, feel more secure in blaming a victim than confronting the truth that horrible crimes happen to wonderful people every day. It puts you in the safe zone.

Take, for instance, the Natalee Holloway case. She was a lovely girl, received straight A's in high school, was a member of the National Honor Society, and had gotten a full scholarship to the University of Alabama, where she planned to study pre-med. She was just a high schooler.

But people still twisted her story from the beginning: *She was bright, but she was at a bar drinking shots with guys she didn't know? She got in a car and left with them? She left all her friends late at night at a bar to go be with some guy she just met?*

That's not what happened at all. Natalee went out with her high school friends the night before they were heading home from their senior trip to Aruba. They went to where they perceived the fun was, a crowded hot spot restaurant and bar on the Aruba waterfront across from where the ships dock, Carlos'n Charlie's. It was just a fun night out, and she had no reason to fear for her safety. Many other people that night did the same thing Natalee did.

There was nothing to attack, but people did anyway, because casting Natalee in a bad light meant it would not happen to them: *I would never go off with some guy I don't know from a bar.*

I firmly believe Joran van der Sloot slipped Natalee GHB, the "date rape" drug. Can you imagine the pain Natalee's parents have suffered from the time they got the call that Natalee was missing, flying down ASAP, searching for their daughter in an unfamiliar milieu, and to this day, not knowing what has happened to her? Aruban officials botched the case, Natalee has not been found, and as I predicted, judge's son Joran van der Sloot, unapprehended, went on to commit another heinous crime. In 2012, van der Sloot pled guilty to the murder of another beautiful young girl, Stephany Flores Ramírez, in Peru. He's serving a twenty-eight-year prison sentence, reportedly has access to drugs and alcohol, and has even impregnated a woman, all behind bars. Still, no justice for Natalee.

It concerns me that the cold attitude toward victims can possibly infiltrate jury deliberations. But I get it: distancing ourselves from crime victims insulates us from the fact that, yes, this *could* happen to us. This leads me to Vanessa Marcotte.

VANESSA MARCOTTE

Less than a week after Karina Vetrano's murder, another successful and accomplished young woman was attacked and killed while out running. On August 7, 2016, Google account exec Vanessa Marcotte was assaulted in a deadly attack in a quiet, rural area in New England. Vanessa lived in Manhattan and regularly visited her mother, who lived in the small town of Princeton, Massachusetts, population under four thousand. It's hard to fault her for thinking she was safe on a Sunday jog before hopping the Peter Pan bus back to Manhattan.

Hours passed, and when Vanessa didn't return, police were called in. That evening, Vanessa's body was found less than a half mile from her mother's home. She was on a heavily wooded trail, completely naked, with burns to her face, feet, and hands in a poorly devised plan to hide her identity. Vanessa had a broken nose and crushing injuries to her throat. All of her clothes, her cell phone, and her earbuds were gone.

The search was on, but several times it appeared the trail had gone cold. Vanessa's murder was ultimately cracked by a utility worker who spotted a man on a path near where Vanessa's body was found and a patrol officer who happened to see a car that matched one near the Marcotte murder scene with a hood up.

Thirty-one-year-old Angelo Colon-Ortiz, a married father of three who lived in the nearby town of Worcester, was arrested. He was a third-party contract worker for FedEx and routinely made deliveries throughout Princeton and the surrounding area, making him intimately familiar with all the local neighborhoods. His neighbors describe him as often making unwanted sexual comments to women who lived nearby.

Vanessa's case reminded me of how often I would travel on weekends to visit my parents in rural Bibb County, Georgia. Sundays there are quiet, slow, and peaceful...the perfect time for a run before heading back to the airport and a heavy workweek. I can just imagine her setting out that afternoon with no inkling of what was to come.

The two cases, Vetrano's and Marcotte's, are different yet similar. Vanessa, like Karina, was very accomplished. She'd attended private school and Boston University. She was on the rise in her career in digital marketing. Both Vanessa and Karina were near family in familiar settings. And they both fought valiantly to live. And they both, in death, had their characters questioned for simply exercising and crossing paths with a random killer.

What is the lesson, then? That it *can* happen to you, to us.

ALLY BRUEGER

There are other precautions to take when it comes to exercising out in public. The case of Ally Brueger reminds us to vary exercise routes, patterns, and times of day. Ally lived with her parents in Rose Township, Michigan. She was a nurse but also a poet who was pursuing a master's degree in creative writing. She was in great shape and exercised routinely.

On the afternoon of July 20, 2016, Ally went out for her daily ten-mile run along the same course. She never returned. Her parents were distraught when they learned their Ally had been found dead. Then, to add to their pain, they learned she died of a gunshot wound along her usual path. As of this writing, Ally's case remains unsolved, although her mom tells me she has very strong suspicions about what happened that afternoon.

Ten miles is a long way, and anyone wishing to do you harm has a lot of opportunity. It's a perfect setting for a stalker. The fact that there was no sexual assault indicates it might not have been random, just a creep with a specific grudge. There were four shotgun shells at the scene, but only one hit Ally, in the back, so she was likely running away. These facts don't preclude a rape motive, actually. That might have been the intention, and she was simply shot as she fled.

Unfortunately, her long and predictable route made it easier for her assailant.

MOLLIE TIBBETTS

On July 18, 2018, University of Iowa student Mollie Tibbetts went for a run at seven thirty p.m. and, very simply, just never came home. The search for her grabbed headlines across the country and became the topic of conversation everywhere. Theory after theory was espoused, and everyone in her life was scrutinized. None of the facts surrounding her case seemed to add up, including a text from home that evening while she was doing homework. Her text indicated she was in fact home, but the pet dog was found locked in the basement as if she had left.

Finally, through use of various home surveillance systems that spotted her along the road jogging, a break in the case came. A car with "noticeable patterns" on its side drove repeatedly in and out of the surveillance footage where Mollie was running. It was deduced the car had approached Mollie.

A search for that particular make and model with those particular markings was run. And that is how twenty-four-year-old Cristhian Bahena Rivera, an agricultural worker who knew the area, was busted. He confessed he followed Mollie in his car and then parked, got out, and ran alongside Tibbetts, who was wearing earbuds. According to his own account, Tibbetts showed him her phone and said she was going to call police. Enraged, the attacker beat her to death and put her in his trunk. He then drove away. He claims his anger caused him to block her brutal murder from his memory. Sitting at an intersection, he says he looked down and saw Mollie's earbuds in his lap and realized she was in his trunk. He then drove to a cornfield and covered her battered body with cornstalks.

The killer was caught, but Mollie's parents and boyfriend face a lifetime without her. What can we learn?

JENNIFER EWING

Any discussion of safety while exercising outside must include mention of bicycling. For some reason, people feel they are safer on a bike. Not true.

On July 25, 2006, Jennifer Ewing, a married mom of three who was beloved in her community of Sandy Springs, Georgia, went biking on the Silver Comet Trail, which runs from Smyrna, Georgia, into Alabama. She did this same ride several times a week, each time without incident. The Silver Comet Trail was a busy and public route, but there had been several disturbing incidents there. Jennifer, as her family told me, was beautiful and brave. I wonder if she, like we all do at times, felt invincible the day she set out for her usual fifty-mile ride.

But that day was different from all others because Jennifer met convicted rapist Michael Ledford. Ledford knocked her from her bike at mile 32, dragged her seventy feet off the trail, and tried to force her to perform an oral sex act. When she bit him instead, he stomped her dozens of times and left her to die on a mound of green kudzu. When blood on Jennifer's bike matched Ledford's DNA, he was convicted for murder, rape, aggravated sodomy, aggravated battery, and aggravated assault.

JOGGING AND EXERCISE SAFETY TIPS

"You better stop that running. Your uterus is going to fall out."

I remember distinctly when my maternal grandmother, Lucy Minerva Fulwood Stokes, warned me that the running had to stop if I ever hoped to have a family. The fact that I did it while wearing shorts and a sports bra in the early evening was just gas on the fire.

I loved her so much that I named my only daughter after her, but I did not take her advice on running. I run to this day, and I sometimes bring Lucy and John David with me.

After covering the cases of Ally Brueger, Karina Vetrano, Vanessa Marcotte, and so many others, I reflected on my grandmother's stern warning. Why should women have to worry about running alone? Men would never be warned to run in packs or, better yet, to just stay inside. Why us?

The harsh reality is that in a perfect world, we women would not have to worry about being outdoors alone, but that perfect world does not exist, and I know it firsthand. So, on this point, I must disagree with the cadre of those who claim safety tips for women exercising outdoors are misogynistic and outdated.

If you don't believe me, ask Ally's or Karina's parents or all the others whose daughters, wives, or sisters were attacked while jogging. Women running outdoors and alone are not the problem; the problem is that there are humans who think like predators, like lions on the Serengeti. And we women are their prey.

I know you have heard it all before: don't run alone, carry pepper spray, be aware, and on and on. Still, don't scoff. Heeding any one of the following tips may someday save your life. With that in mind, here is a comprehensive list of runners' safety must-dos.

- Let's start with an obvious one: don't run alone. Part of me screams, *"Why not?"* Advising women to wrangle a group run every time they go outdoors is advice that sounds ridiculous and inconvenient. No man is told to gather with the others like sheep. We are not sheep either, but the research says that women are more likely to be attacked while exercising than men. There is no doubting the cold, hard statistics, and cold they are. So how about just a buddy? Don't have or want a human buddy? How about a dog?

- For those of us who may not have a running buddy or who have a dog that won't cooperate, there are alternatives. As I said, part of me screams in frustration at safety tips, but the rest of me thinks of Ally, Karina, Vanessa, and so many others before them and, sadly, yet to come. That side wins out. Their voices ring in chorus as I hit the trail.

- If you can't arrange a running or walking partner, get another protector...in a can. Take the plunge and buy pepper spray or mace. Then carry it.

- Remember, pepper spray and mace are not legal in every state, so check first with a Google search. Defense sprays come in a variety of styles and are super simple and convenient. Try a small canister with a Velcro strap around your wrist. You can nail an attacker up to twelve feet away. What's not to love?

- Also consider pepper gel, which I like better than pepper spray because if it's windy or even if there's a slight breeze, regular pepper spray can backfire and spray back toward you. We don't want that. Pepper gel doesn't present that problem. There are plenty of choices on Amazon. Take a look at the ones that are police strength and include a flip top and a quick-release key ring.

- Keep pepper gel or spray, a super-loud whistle, and a mini flashlight on your keychain. I made room on my keychain for all three with plenty of room to spare for photos of the twins. It doesn't feel completely right when I tell women and not men to take protection with them, yet I still say it. It's not fair, but I'd rather be alive and politically incorrect than the reverse. You never know when you will encounter danger along the way, be it animal or human, and I'm not sure which is worse.

- Another great alternative is to run with another kind of personal safety device: a noise alarm. These things scream like a siren. If you're in trouble, someone is bound to hear this sound and you'll likely convince your attacker to back off. I have a few favorites. You wear Run Angel like a bracelet, so your hands are free. I learned while tromping through the most crime-saturated areas of inner-city Atlanta to keep my hands free at all times. No exceptions. An added bonus is that "guardians" you select and add into its app are alerted by email and SMS and shown the time, date, and location by coordinates and map links whenever Run Angel is activated. It can also connect with your smartphone so you can reap safety benefits via cell phone. Awesome. Also consider bSafe, an app that, with a single punch of a button, becomes a siren, contacts law enforcement and tells them your GPS location, and records video. Another alternative is the LifeLine Response app. LifeLine harnesses GPS to help emergency personnel locate you. Even simply dropping the phone can cause the app to connect with local police.

- You can always amp up the safety by simply turning on the tracking device on your phone before you head out, allowing tracking via iPad. Your "guardians" should note if the dot (you) doesn't move for an extended period of time.

- Sorry to be the one to break it to you, but the music has to go while you are outside running, jogging, or walking. I love to work out to music, because it makes me go faster, which means I keep my heart rate up and burn more calories. But knowing what I know, I save it for the elliptical indoors. What I know is that Ally Brueger and Karina Vetrano were wearing earbuds at the time they were last known to be running. Video surveillance captures a glimpse of Karina jogging by ostensibly with earbuds still in her ears just before the fatal attack. Stop and consider this idea: there are obvious times you absolutely must have all your faculties turned completely on. If you are alone, especially at night, when your vision is not 100 percent, you need all your Spidey senses to tell you what is around you. That includes not only what's in front of you as you run, but what may be behind you or beside you. Think bushes, trees, shrubs, telephone poles, or anywhere a perp could lurk. Plus, can't we ever just disconnect and be quiet? Your answer may be no, but please listen to me.

- Don't run at night. This really cuts me to the core—not only is that my favorite time to run because I'm slammed all day long with work and the twins, but I also enjoy running alone at night, especially just at dusk as it turns dark, more than any other time. The workday is done, I don't feel like I need to be doing something else (like work or the twins), and I'm more at peace so I can actually enjoy running. But running at night, unless I have no alternative, is now a never-never.
- If you absolutely must run at night, there are ways to minimize your risk. Stick to a route you've run before so you will know the pitfalls and danger zones. Also, it's easier to get back to safety if you know the route.
- I also advise running in a neighborhood of houses, if possible, preferably your own. Why? Because, most likely, people are home, which means that when confronted with danger, you have a reasonable chance of getting to someone's home and a safe area. And unlike running among apartments or businesses, you can run right up to the front door. There have actually been a few times when I've been out running at night and became concerned about a car that was lurking the few times I looked back. Both times, I ran straight up to a home that had lights on. Before I could even knock, the car was gone. Both times. It was probably just a coincidence, but what if it wasn't?
- If long work hours make it impossible to run during daytime hours, think about a home or gym treadmill. I broke down and got a gym membership in Manhattan for this very reason. That particular gym had facilities near both my office and my home.
- If you don't want an extra bill each month, try high-intensity interval

workouts in bursts of ten minutes here and there on the stairs or around the building during the day if forty uninterrupted minutes is a no-go. Strength training during the workweek and running outside on weekends or days off could work and ensure that your runs can happen in the daylight.

- Here's my last word on running at night: I want to be here to raise my twins. There's no way I want David to do it alone. They would live on their iPads, make all F's, and have no table manners. I know this. Running at night? Never again.

- Take your cell phone when you run. Not only can you call for help, but cell phones can easily be traced through a locator app, and it doesn't take a court order or a subpoena to get the info. When danger lurks, time is critical. There have been times when I was running and suddenly sensed danger. I whipped out my cell and pretended to be talking to give the appearance that I wasn't "alone" and that someone was nearby that could show up pronto.

- Change it up! Vary your running direction and time of day. Stay in a known neighborhood, but don't run the same route all the time. In Mollie Tibbetts's case and others, I firmly believe her killer knew her route. Evidence suggests he drove along her running path on his way home from work in the early evenings in the days before the assault. I wonder how many times he had seen her jogging happily along? The thought of it is chilling: Mollie jogging on an open highway in rural Brooklyn, Iowa, never suspecting she was being stalked and targeted for assault and death. Believe me, I get it. If you exercise outdoors frequently, you have a favorite route for whatever reason. I do. I always start to the right, and I have certain hills or inclines I like to take on and certain places I check for time. But don't do that anymore. Do not run the same route over and over or even at the same time of day. A regular routine makes it easy for predators. They don't even have to think. They know exactly where you'll be at what time, how often, and for how long. Even simple changes matter. Run at varied times of the morning or afternoon. If you always go on Tuesdays, pick another day of the week. If you start to the right, running counterclockwise every day like me, go clockwise. Seek out new paths or trails in daylight hours or with a buddy.

- When you're working out on a road, run facing the traffic. While it remains to be seen, reports have emerged that Mollie Tibbetts's killer first approached her from behind, maintaining somewhat of an element of surprise. Other reports state he drove past her several times, back and forth, first from behind. Whichever theory is proven true, common sense dictates that you can't fight or run from a threat if you can't see the threat.

- Do not leave home without letting someone know you're heading out, whether it's day or night. Text, call, or send an email to someone you trust. Let somebody somewhere know you're running and a general location. The most critical hours in any search are those immediately following the disappearance. After a crime victim has been gone seventy-two hours, the likelihood they will live drops dramatically. That clock starts ticking whether anyone knows it or not. As I always say, minutes count. Someone must sound the alarm, and that someone is the person you told you were out running. Hear me.
- Take your ID. Whether it's your driver's license, your library card, or a scrap of paper stuffed down your sports bra with your name, address, and number on it, they all work. When you need help, it helps first responders if they know who you are.
- I tie my single apartment key onto my shoe and wedge it into the laces, keeping my hands free. If you carry a key, carry it between your fingers as a weapon.

SAFETY AND YOUR GYM

Let's face it: Gyms and workout places are magnets for creeps who like to watch women exercise and sweat. I took an aerobics class when I first started practicing law in Atlanta. The studio was sandwiched between a bar and a restaurant. Inevitably, within fifteen minutes we had to pull down the blinds because there would be ten or fifteen men ogling us. It was irritating. Those guys remind me of the pedophiles who hang around at hotels that are hosting beauty pageants or cheers and dance events for kids. You just know there's a pervert or two in the bunch.

So, given the proximity of those pervs, you need to be on your game when the workout's over and you head to your car. Many of our schedules put gym time at the end of the day and into the night. That's all the more reason to be cautious. Be smart. Be all business about it.

Forget your phone. Be focused in your stride over to your car. The call can wait.

Have your bag under your arm and your keys out. Finish your sports drink or water before you leave or wait until you get home. Leave your laptop or purse at home, at work, or at least in the trunk. There should be no distractions, no fumbling around with three or four things in your hands.

Please ignore the idiotic suggestion to park at the end of the lot so you can get in some extra steps. That is horrible advice. Park as close as you can and under a light if possible. Try not to park in between two big SUVs or trucks. Those big vehicles provide cover for someone looking to do you harm. You're like a sheep surrounded by mountain lions.

Many gyms offer swipe cards that grant you twenty-four-hour access—we value that round-the-clock dedication to fitness. *Hey, look at her! Working out at midnight. That's dedication!* Well, I'll be blunt: It's plain crazy to be walking in a dark, empty parking lot to go work out in an empty gym, and then walking back to your car in that still dark, still empty parking lot at one a.m. or later. Don't be crazy. Keep your workout hours sane.

Last but not least, take a self-defense class, preferably in person. These classes are offered year-round from organizations like the YMCA, police department, schools, universities, and women's groups. Some are even free. Get up and get moving. It may sound far-fetched, but it makes a huge difference and actually changes the way you think and fight. Just like law school forever changed the way I think, self-defense classes change the way your body will respond to a threat.

Did you ever see one of my favorite movies, *Miss Congeniality*? I love Sandra Bullock. I actually showed it to Lucy on a plane. We both love the part where Bullock's character, while undercover on the runway at a beauty pageant, improvises a "talent" with self-defense moves. Her mantra is SING: attack the solar plexus, instep, nose, and groin. SING. Go online, do some research, and find a class. Too bad Sandra isn't teaching them.

Sandra Bullock aside, be ready to fight—maybe for your life. Don't be a target. Stay alert, be prepared, and listen to your gut. If you get a feeling something is wrong, act on it. Be ready to run, call for help, or, if you have to, stand and fight.

I am.

CHAPTER NINE

Safe Shopping on Your Own

Shopping can be lots of fun, but like so many other activities, it should be approached with a watchful eye. Predators are always out there lurking, looking for opportunities to rob you and worse. When we go to the mall, we are busy and distracted trying to get things done. We might also have money on us and on the way home might have valuable items in our bags. Crooks know this and are ready to pounce if you give them the slightest opening.

CHRISTINA MORRIS

The story of Jonni McElroy and what she has endured since her daughter's murder really made me think twice about a simple trip to the mall. Jonni's daughter, Christina Morris, was just twenty-three when she was last seen on grainy surveillance film walking into a parking garage at the high-end Shops at Legacy in Plano, Texas. A male companion seemed to be walking near her that August day. She was never seen alive again.

After much legwork, police identified the man in the tape as Enrique Arochi, an acquaintance of Morris's. But though the investigation was extremely detailed, with cell phone records, DNA, surveillance tapes, statements, and witnesses, no one could find Christina.

Jonni became obsessed with finding her daughter and, frankly, what mom wouldn't? Jonni moved from Tulsa, Oklahoma, to Plano, Texas, to devote herself full-time to the cause, leaving behind her husband and stepchildren. Dr. Phil even tried to save their marriage but couldn't. I saw Jonni on TV many times, and her heartbreak was visible as she pled with anyone to come forward with clues to help find her daughter. She even visited Arochi in jail, begging him to reveal Christina's whereabouts.

He refused. Years later, word came that Christina's remains had been discovered when workers were clearing away brush about forty-five miles from Plano in Anna, Texas. At long last and at great cost, Jonni had peace.

Christina spent part of her last evening in and around the Legacy Shops, and that is why she parked there. So often, we feel safe and secure in so-called upscale surroundings. The Shops at Legacy include Angelika Film Center, Capital Grille, Del Frisco's, Bluemercury, Francesca's, and Urban Outfitters. This is where the "beautiful people" go to stay beautiful, an oasis of luxury and privilege.

You are lulled into a sense of complacency because you're surrounded by other women shopping and everything looks like an airbrushed version of reality. You know that there is security, cameras, and other people like you. You can see Porsches and Jaguars and BMWs parked in a line at the valet. Who would associate that with violent crime? That's the mistake. Her guard was likely down because the eye tricks the mind.

It was just before four a.m. that Christina and Arochi are seen on the tape. Did she want someone to walk her to her car in the dark? Or did she believe that in those surroundings she was free of danger?

You'd think that there would be a security guard and surveillance cameras working. But it doesn't take a lot of brainpower to beat a security camera at a shopping center. They are often not robotic or motion-sensitive. They are fixed in specific areas, and criminals simply find their victims elsewhere.

Luckily, the cameras captured enough to point toward Arochi, but whatever he did to subdue Christina, he did off-camera. Arochi's dumb luck is just one reason you cannot always count on surveillance video cameras for protection.

NIGHTTIME STEALTH ATTACK

There was an attack at the Staunton Mall in Staunton, Virginia, in December 2017 that would make anyone uneasy. Around eight p.m., just as the mall was beginning to close, a sixty-three-year-old woman was walking to her car in the parking deck when she was brutally bashed on the back of her head and knocked down. She was robbed of everything she had—all her cash, credit cards, ID...everything. The perp then took off on foot and got away. It happened right in front of the Belk department store, but no one saw a thing and certainly no one came to her rescue. Even surveillance cameras couldn't help. She had been carrying several bags, looking for her keys and trying to locate her car. I have no doubt the thief was hiding between a couple of SUVs or trucks and jumped her out of nowhere.

"UPSCALE" DOES NOT MEAN SAFE

Believe me, many of these attacks are preventable. Still, a person intent on crime will not be stopped by much, not even a mother with her child. There were two horrific attacks at the ultra-upscale Town Center in Boca Raton, Florida. How upscale? Some of the tenants are Neiman Marcus, Louis Vuitton, Cartier, and Tesla. But price tags didn't matter.

In August 2007, a woman, who wished to remain anonymous, was leaving the mall with her two-year-old son. After she secured him in his seat, she went to get behind the wheel, looked back, and saw a man in the car pointing a gun at her son. He forced her to go to an ATM and withdraw money. Sometime during this nightmare, the kidnapper bound the woman with zip ties and handcuffs. He also made her put on goggles with a sponge inside to obscure her sight. After driving around for a while, the assailant left the woman and her son in their SUV in the mall parking lot and then fled the scene. Even though the attacker zip-tied her neck to the SUV's headrest, she broke free, got help, and reported the crime.

Just months later, in December that same year, single mom Nancy Bochicchio was at the same mall with her daughter, Joey. The time of year was hectic and the mall was packed with last-minute Christmas shoppers. But amidst Christmas decorations and carols being pumped into posh stores, a predator lurked. A man attacked Nancy, forcing her to an ATM to withdraw money and return to the mall. There, he bound and gagged mother and daughter and shot each in the back of the head as they sat in their black Chrysler Aspen. Who would shoot a seven-year-old little girl for five hundred dollars?

These cases and others much like them are especially disturbing because the mall predators knew these ladies had their children with them, but it didn't make a difference. The malls in question are some of the most luxurious in the area, with guards, security, video surveillance, and plenty of people around.

TIPS FOR COMING AND GOING AT THE MALL

The first thing you do when you get to the mall is park your vehicle. And that's when your safety-first thinking should kick in. Treat the whole event seriously and get these ideas into your standard operating procedure. Always give off the vibe of being in control and focused. That itself will repel many criminals. In most situations, being safe has a lot to do with being smart. And if some of these tips seem obvious, bear with me. You can't repeat good advice often enough.

- Park as close to the entrance as you can. Get your "hidden steps" elsewhere.
- Lock your windows and doors. Every time. Make it a habit for your whole family.
- If you have not memorized your license plate number, take a picture and have it available. You'll be glad when you see about thirty vehicles in the general area that look like yours and are the same color.
- Park in well-lit areas. Park right under the lights if you can. Park near easy-to-remember landmarks, like the handicapped parking spots.
- Snap a picture of the area where you park, noting the row or section, if you are deep in a sea of cars. That way, you can easily find where you parked and walk purposefully rather than wandering aimlessly. If you're in a parking garage, write your level, row, and section on the ticket.
- Don't leave valuable things in your car in plain sight. Put all presents, bags, backpacks, briefcases, laptops, or tablets in the trunk *before* you reach your destination.
- Carry your key in your hand with the key pointing out like a gun.
- Do not linger in the parking lot, on arrival or on departure. Don't

start a phone conversation and lean up against the car to finish it. Keep moving.

- When you are in your car, you are not completely safe. Never roll the windows down. If someone approaches you, get away from them. People approach all the time, acting like they're asking for directions, or they say they want to borrow five dollars or that you dropped your purse or phone to get you to roll down your window. Do not do it! I'm always tempted when people want money to hang my arm out and give them a few bills, but that's all it takes. And it's a hard lesson to teach your children too. Be generous but in a safer setting.

- Do not park between two tall SUVs or trucks. It provides cover for a potential attacker. This tip applies to parking anywhere. Don't do it.

- In a valet situation, never leave the key in the ignition. Give it to the attendant. And hand over only the ignition key, not all of your keys.

- If you are at the mall and have car trouble, stay in the car and use your cell phone. Or go into the mall and get help from security, but don't get out and try to fix your car.

- Once inside the mall or on your way out, you may need to use the bathroom. If it's down a darkened hallway or in some back area, just hold it, especially if it's near closing time. Those bathrooms are not monitored or supervised. Any guy can walk in the bathroom and sit in the stall next to you and wait for you to come in. If you can help it, never use the bathrooms that are near the big exit doors—they're a perfect spot for a kidnapping. Try to find a bathroom that is near the food court or another busy, crowded area.

- If at any time you don't feel right, approach a security guard and express your concern. Trust your gut if something seems off or out of place. I know you've heard it before, but I can't stress it enough: trust your instincts.

- Stay off the phone inside the mall too. Maintain that aware and focused demeanor. This is not the time for multitasking, because you only have one task: to get your shopping and errands done. The distracted shopper is a sitting duck for a predator.

- Always, always, always stay with your children when they go to the bathroom.

- Don't carry a purse. I keep my ID stuck down in my bra. If anything, I may have a cell phone, which I can give up easily or use as a weapon. Keep your cell phone and all money in your front pockets. Don't put your wallet in your back pocket.
- If you have to have a purse, get a crossbody bag with a strap that you wear over your shoulder like a guitar. Those are not worth the effort for a purse snatcher. Carry it with the opening facing you, and if you are walking with someone, have the bag between you. If they don't have an easy shot at your bag, they'll leave you alone.
- In any event, don't go down over a bag or a credit card or a cell phone. Hand it over. Don't fight about it. If they want your bag, give it to them. If they want your ring, give it to them. Don't resist. Get the moment over with and don't let it escalate.
- Keep an eye out for the nearest exit as you walk the mall. You never know when you might want out. Look for emergency call boxes in the parking lot.
- When you get to your car after shopping, look under it, around it, and in the back seat before you get in it. If you left it locked and it is not locked, don't get in. It needs to be your standard operating procedure that you lock it, just like you lock your door at home. It needs to be something you do automatically, a part of your muscle memory.
- If you come out and see that your tire's gone flat or you see your window bashed in, go back inside. Don't stand there and make all your phone calls. It could be a ploy. A perp could let the air out of your tires, get between the cars, and wait for you to come back.
- Do not use revolving doors, especially those automatic ones. Somebody with really good timing can grab your purse or your package and get away while you're still going around in a circle.
- When you have a lot of bags, consolidate. Put everything in one or two large shopping bags so you're not fumbling with fifty different bags.
- Don't leave your bags anywhere, even for just a few moments. In the bathroom at the mall, don't put your bags on the sink counter and go into the stall. Don't do that. They will not be there when you come back. If you're shopping alone or have an inkling of fear, find the security guard. They're there to help you.
- Always put whatever you've purchased in your trunk. If you don't go straight home, you don't want those bags attracting the attention of potential thieves.

- If you can do it, save your most expensive purchases for last so you can go straight home with them.
- Try not to use an ATM at a mall, especially after dark. If you must, try not to take out a lot of money. If you see somebody loitering near the ATM at the mall, keep walking. It's not worth it. Also try not to use one if it's close in proximity to a door. It's a perfect setup for a kidnapping or worse.
- If you have to use the ATM, look around the area before you approach. If anything bugs you, leave. And once there, don't linger. Be that serious person again. Have everything ready, walk up, use it, and get out quickly. Don't stand there and count the money after it comes out. Who are you going to complain to? There's no banker there.

Changing and Dressing Rooms

- Don't leave belongings unattended. Take all that you have with you into the room. When you go out to look in the mirror, don't stray far.
- Pay attention to people watching you. Be aware.
- Tell a salesperson you're going in to try on clothes. He or she will be aware of you and pay attention to the area.
- Look at the dressing room to see how many stalls are being used. Pick one with no one nearby, if you can.
- Try to shop with other people. It's not always possible because we're all so busy, but it's worth the effort to coordinate. If you're in a group, even just two people, you're much less of a target.
- Pay attention to any slats in the door in the changing room. If the door slats angle down into the room, anyone can look in on you when they're just walking by. Some retailers do it intentionally so they can monitor what's going on. But so can creeps and thieves, so beware!

DANGER IN PARKING LOTS AND DECKS

We drive everywhere in America these days, especially when on a shopping trip, which means we have to park. This setting can also be fraught with danger unless you're prepared and have your wits about you.

DRU SJODIN

One night I was sitting in a perfectly dark studio guesting on *Larry King Live*. Joining us that night were the parents of an absolutely stunning girl from Grand Forks, North Dakota, Dru Sjodin. She was leaving her job at the local mall in Grand Forks, talking to her boyfriend on her cell phone as she walked through the parking lot to her car. The boyfriend heard her say something like "Okay, okay..." and she was gone. The line went dead. He tried to call back over and over with no luck. Hours later, he got a call from her mobile, but when he answered, he only heard a beeping sound and static.

In the end, it was discovered that paroled rapist Alfonso Rodriguez Jr. had kidnapped Dru at knifepoint, molested her, and murdered her on November 22, 2003. That night, in the dark of the studio, I broke down and cried as I listened to Dru's heartbroken parents.

KELSEY SMITH

I remember reporting on Kelsey's disappearance like it was yesterday, trying to hold it together while processing the heartbreaking news, pulling out facts and details that maybe, just maybe, could help find and save Kelsey Smith. I was pregnant at the time and was creating a Target registry. I remember being so sick, my sister-in-law ended up doing a lot of it. But I had gone to work that evening, and I saw Kelsey's face and heard the words "Target store parking lot."

It was only about seven p.m. on June 2, 2007, in the Target parking lot in Overland Park, Kansas. It was probably not even dark yet when Kelsey was taken. I was prepared to do all I could do to help find her, even travel there to join the search. I had just come back from traveling to California and to the Virginia Tech shootings. I was prepared to do it again.

Then we learned there was Target surveillance video. I've long said that even NASA could get a few tips from the Target and Walmart surveillance teams. What we saw was Kelsey getting a gift for her boyfriend. It was their six-month dating anniversary. I briefly remembered doing things like that at her young age. She called her mom from inside the store, bought the gift, and left. She was never seen alive again.

But about four hours later, her old Ford Crown Victoria was discovered empty and abandoned outside in the Macy's parking lot at the "nice" Oak Park Mall directly across the street from the Target where she shopped. Inside the car, cops found Kelsey's purse and wallet and the Target purchases still there, untouched.

A closer look at the enhanced Target video showed Kelsey parking her car in the Target lot, then going inside. The video even pinpointed the spot where she was calling her mom and buying the anniversary gift. She never spoke to anyone else in the store, and nothing odd happened inside Target. At first, it showed nothing more than a flash in the direction of Kelsey and her car, consistent with someone running at a distance in that direction. But the grainy surveillance video, once enhanced, showed what looked to be a man forcing Kelsey into her car in the parking lot. Reportedly, the Macy's video showed that Kelsey's car was dumped there about two hours later, at 9:17 p.m., when it was only barely dark.

Combing through more of the Target video, cops realized that a single white man in his twenties appeared somewhere in practically every part of the footage where Kelsey did. He never spoke to Kelsey but hung around her, then left for the parking lot as she went to the cashier. Meanwhile, unidentified fingerprints were discovered on a seat belt in Kelsey's car.

It was a faint cell phone ping that cracked the case. It had taken Verizon four long days to hand over cell phone records despite requests from local law enforcement and the FBI. But finally, a Verizon tech identified a cell ping, and in less than an hour, Kelsey's body was found in a wooded area about eighteen miles from the Target. Kelsey was sexually assaulted and choked dead with her own belt.

After the Target video was disseminated, police acting on a tip closed in on twenty-six-year-old Edwin Roy "Jack" Hall, arresting him just as he was trying to skip town with his wife and four-year-old son. Hall claimed they were leaving on a "family vacation." His fingerprint matched the print on Kelsey's seat belt. Cops learned that Hall first saw Kelsey as she drove into the Target parking lot, noted she was alone, and followed her throughout the store. Then he waited outside near her car. As she approached her car, juggling her keys, bags, and purse, he pounced.

The memory of her parents begging for her to come home in those first few days still plays out in my mind. I also recall a sense of futility about Dru and Kelsey. What could have been done to save them and to keep this from ever happening to anyone? Now, with a daughter and son of my own, I have some ideas. Boy do I.

TIPS FOR STAYING SAFE IN PARKING LOTS AND DECKS

So, who exactly do predators target?

A woman loaded down with packages in both arms, a purse, and/or a child.

Someone distracted and wearing earphones or yakking into their cell phone.

Someone staring down at their iPhone.

Someone fumbling in their purse instead of looking around them.

Someone who looks timid, lost, or confused.

Someone who looks intoxicated.

Someone who looks friendly and gives off nonverbal signals that say, "Approach me!"

Someone who never thinks to look around and notice she's being followed.

Someone parking close to or between larger vehicles like trucks or SUVs. These large vehicles provide a predator the cover they need and prevent witnesses that may be in the parking lot or driving by from seeing them.

Someone with their back turned, loading bags into a trunk or back seat.

Someone seated in the car with the car door open, stretched into the back of the car.

Don't be *any* of those people—ever.

- Walk with your pepper spray at the ready, and don't be afraid to display it, especially at night. No pepper spray? Keep your finger on that panic button, mace, or screaming sound alarm.
- Do not let someone get close enough to your car to pull off a carjacking. If they are that close to your open window, they are close enough to unlock the back door or reach the inside driver's door handle and whip open the door—then, it's over.

- Always have an escape plan. On a plane, they tell you before takeoff to check for the closest exit. When you are in a car, know your best exit strategy.
- If anyone you don't know approaches your car, lay on the horn and drive away fast. If you have no choice, give up your belongings, bags, or car without fighting back. It's not worth it. You can get a new purse, but we can't replace *you*.
- Did you know that cars built since the late 1990s usually have an emergency button on the remote lock/unlock device? It's usually a red button and makes your car horn blow to help you find it. Remember, the bad guys hate noise, because it makes people look. Be ready to use it if you must.
- Mega parking lots and parking garages are a predator's playground.
- If at all possible, don't use the parking deck elevators or stairs. They are both traps predators use to their advantage to isolate you from the sight and sound of others while cutting off your escape routes at the same time.
- No one outside the stairwell or elevator can hear your cry for help through thick concrete or an iron-supported elevator shaft. I walk with the twins straight up or down the parking aisles while staying out of the way of drivers.
- When parking, always pick a central spot that is well lit once it gets dark outside. The same goes for when you park on the street. Park under a light.
- If possible, park where there are passersby or attendants, even if you, like me, do not want to spring for valet fees. Try to park near the valet or valet stand.
- Always note where you park in a deck or lot. Write it down, take a photo, text a note to yourself. After a busy shopping trip, you'll be glad you did.
- Try your best to park your car in the direction that allows you to return directly approaching the driver's side of the car. You are the most at risk getting in or out of cars.
- When you are coming back to your car, if you believe a car next to yours or near yours is suspicious or if you notice someone or a team sitting in a car and watching women exit the store, don't go to your car.
- If you must go, find others, even if it's just one other shopper or store

employee walking in that direction. and go in a group. Blend in. If that's impossible, wait until security can walk you.

- Don't unlock or start the car by remote the very moment you leave the store. Wait until you are closer to the car before starting it. If your make and model allows, unlock only the driver's door. In a crowded shopping mall parking lot, you don't know who may be watching and waiting among parked cars, waiting to hop a ride in your back seat.
- Have your keys ready before you head out of the building, so you're not fumbling or looking down into your purse or bags.
- Once in the car, shut the door and lock it.
- Don't futz with your purse or your bags or stretch way back into the back seat to grab or place something, turning your back on what's happening immediately outside your car.
- Start the car and leave. You can rearrange your possessions all you want to when you're safe at home.
- When you are visibly distracted, especially leaning into the back seat, is just the moment an attacker might hitch an unwanted ride and more.
- If you have a child with you while you are loading things into your car, place your body in a position so the cart and the car door, swung open, make a barrier of sorts surrounding you.
- Keep your child in the cart until after you load the groceries.
- Buy a convex mirror at a car wash or AutoZone-type store. Attach it to your trunk lid or the rear of your minivan. It's just as easy to use as a rearview mirror in your car and makes it so easy to glance up and scan behind you.
- Now, let's load your baby. Remember, load your baby last, and don't stand with your back to the parking lot, begging to be bonked on the head from behind. A mom with a baby means nothing to a predator except that you are more vulnerable than another lady who may not be carrying a baby and therefore more quick on her feet.
- Never turn your back to the parking lot while you lean through the open door. Slide into the seat beside your baby. Then immediately lock the doors to focus on buckling the baby in. You should have your keys with your mace, pepper spray, or screaming sound alarm on it. Hop out, slide into the driver's seat, relock those doors, and skedaddle.

- Yes, I'm one of those people who would always push the cart back to a cart corral or to the grocery store itself. But you know what? They pay people to do that, and unless you are getting a check every week for straightening parking lots, let them do their job while you do yours—keeping yourself and your child alive. If you still don't feel good about it, ask a male clerk to walk with you and stay until you drive away.
- Obviously, look into the back seat before you get in the car.
- Make sure you have the loudest car alarm at the mall. Place stickers on your car windows warning perps they will be noticed. Car alarms are really tricked out now, with 120 dB sirens, tilt sensors, glass break sensors, and all sorts of features. But what do I look for in a car alarm? A panic button and sheer volume.
- Always position your body to use your shopping cart as a shield or even a weapon. Laugh now and thank me later.
- As you approach your car, take a quick look at your tires. An old trick is to place a sharp object under a tire or to let the air out. If this has happened, go back into the store and get assistance or call for help.
- And yes, I'm sure you can change your tire all on your own, but at least alert someone and ask security to stand by. This is not a plug, but ever since the twins were born, I've always belonged to AAA for this very reason.

CHAPTER TEN

Elevator Assaults

When people hear the words *elevator attack*, many immediately think of the infamous fight between Beyoncé's little sister, Solange Knowles, and Beyoncé's famous husband, Jay-Z, which was caught on an elevator security camera, leaked, and played on a loop around the world. That tussle was after the fanciest party in the world, the Met Gala. When I hear the words *elevator attack*, I think of very different scenarios.

Most recently, I was jarred after I saw a brutal and deadly elevator attack caught on CCTV. In this elevator attack a woman ended up dead.

Her name was Tatiane Spitzner. In August 2018 in São Paulo, Brazil, she was assaulted on tape by her husband. He is shown physically restraining her and then roughly pushing her out of the elevator. Soon after, she plummeted to her death from their fifth-floor apartment. The video also shows the assailant, Luís Felipe Manvailer, later trying his best to clean the elevator walls and doors, revealing a kind of violence we know exists but rarely see. This case caused an uproar in Brazil about domestic violence and how society must intervene more effectively. And it started in an elevator.

Even early-morning elevator trips to your bus or car in order to get to work on time require you to be on your toes. At eight a.m. on October 8, 2018, in the East Village of Manhattan, thirty-six-year-old Melvin Collins followed an unsuspecting woman into a residential apartment building. He got in by "piggybacking" a resident who had used a required keycard to enter before the door shut him out. He then followed the woman onto the elevator and began groping and kissing her. She got out of the elevator, but he pursued her into a stairwell and continued his assault by attempting to strangle her. Only her screams sent him running. Thanks to surveillance cameras, he was identified and arrested the next day. Now a sign is posted in the building, warning residents to stay alert.

Be alert for an assault? At eight in the morning? Yes!

I also think of the elevator bank I rode so many times in the old Fulton County Superior Courthouse in downtown Atlanta. For more than ten years I rode in those elevators, never imagining a vicious attack would ever occur inside. But one did recently.

On May 8, 2018, a legal assistant entered an elevator on the fourth floor of the courthouse and Ruben Washington followed her in. He immediately began choking her. She started to scream but was able to punch a bunch of buttons inside the elevator, which stopped at the eighth floor. When the doors opened, a district attorney and another man pulled Washington off the victim and detained him until the police arrived. That could have been me, a thousand times over.

ELEVATOR SAFETY TIPS

We use elevators every single day and think nothing of it, right? Think again. Why are elevators such potentially dangerous places? Let's start with the space. It's a perfect place for a violent offender to confine or trap a victim, a small space with the only way out—a huge metal door—sealed shut. Just those facts should keep you alert to what is happening around you if you enter an elevator alone.

And you are alone. Most elevator security cameras do not work, and even if they do, there is not likely to be a security guard monitoring the feed. Remember Chandra Levy? She was romantically linked to Congressman Gary Condit, though he denied it. When she disappeared on May 1, 2001, she was living in an apartment building that had security cameras in the elevator, but the tapes were regularly recycled. When investigators began to look for her comings and goings near the time of her disappearance, the tapes for the days in question had been taped over, hindering the attempt to reconstruct her last days.

For precautions when riding an elevator, read on.

- If possible, ride an elevator with someone you know, a co-worker or neighbor.
- Take the time to look inside the elevator before you step in. If someone's inside who appears unsafe, behaves oddly, or simply gives you a bad vibe, don't get on. Use another elevator, or wait for it to return again.
- If the lights aren't working, do not get in.
- While you wait for an elevator, make sure you stand off to the side so you have the chance to get a look at who is inside before you step on.
- As you are waiting, if someone you don't know approaches or is already there and things don't feel right, wait for the next elevator. You must trust your gut.
- If someone darts in just as the doors close, stay alert.
- If someone gets on and doesn't punch a button, get off.
- Once you are already on, if someone raises your hackles, get off at the very next floor.
- Don't chitchat with people you don't know.
- If someone becomes aggressive while the elevator is moving, get to the button panel and push all the buttons you can—except for the Stop button. The Stop button may get you stuck between floors—just what the attacker wants.
- Once on the elevator, stand immediately beside the control panel. Stay near the door. Keep your back to the elevator wall. Never turn your back on another person, male or female, if you can help it, unless the elevator is jam-packed.
- Pay attention to what's happening around you, even in an elevator. Don't just zone out and listen to the piped-in Muzak or fiddle with your cell phone.
- Do not be distracted by looking down into your purse or briefcase.
- Pay attention to what is around you; don't just stare directly ahead. Keep a 360-degree watch. It's easy to do with your back against the elevator wall near the control panel.
- Even if you don't feel it, act confident.
- Keep your keys (with pepper spray or noise alarm attached) in your hand to use as a weapon if you must.
- Keep purses and briefcases closed, wrapped diagonally across your

body. Remember, sometimes thieves will cut your shoulder strap from behind, so try to keep your back to the wall.

- If you are attacked, be ready to fight. Statistics prove that women who fight back have a much higher survival rate than those who don't.

I know; simply riding an elevator seems so harmless, doesn't it? I wish that were true.

CHAPTER ELEVEN

Safe in Your Home

Attacked in your own home? It sounds so foreign, so improbable, so fantastical. It could never happen to me, to us, in *our* neighborhood.

That's what I thought until I covered a home invasion murder in an upscale Indianapolis neighborhood on a cul-de-sac full of upper-class families whose garages were snug with Mercedes, BMWs, and Infinitis.

This is what I learned: home invasion fears are real.

AMANDA BLACKBURN

On the morning of November 10, 2015, Davey Blackburn left his house on Sunnyfield Court at six in the morning to go to the gym. Home alone with their baby boy, Weston, was twenty-eight-year-old Amanda Blackburn, who was twelve weeks pregnant. Less than an hour later, neighbors heard gunshots.

Around eight thirty, Davey, who was a pastor at a local church, came home to find his wife nude on the floor, dead from shotgun blasts. She had also been raped.

In the weeks that followed, I went over and over the facts in my mind, twisting and turning them like a Rubik's Cube. Sifting through documents, I noticed that in the police affidavit Davey stated he left the door to the home unlocked. This is not to say what occurred was his fault. He couldn't know who was lurking in their neighborhood, their heaven on earth.

Then the facts unfolded. Another burglary occurred just two homes from the Blackburns' house at five thirty that morning. Those thieves had to spot Davey Blackburn leaving his house half an hour later. Neighborhood security cams spotted Amanda's killers fleeing the scene in a dark-colored SUV packed with loot…but it didn't matter. Amanda was gone and the family's dreams were shattered.

Murder suspects Larry Taylor Jr., Jalen Watson, and Diano Gordon, all with long rap sheets, called themselves the Kill Gang. Police believe they committed not one but two other burglaries in the Blackburns' neighborhood before murdering Amanda. Police also investigated their involvement in an earlier robbery and rape in the Westlake Apartments complex, where they were living, just one week before Amanda was killed. In that case, thugs entered the home through a patio door. They were also investigated for a third burglary and a car theft.

Gordon pled guilty to felony robbery resulting in serious bodily injury and two counts of burglary. Watson pled guilty to one count of robbery and two counts of burglary. Both had other charges dismissed, including murder, upon acceptance of the pleas. Gordon and Watson have agreed to cooperate in the prosecution of Taylor Jr., the man accused of firing the gun. Taylor was awaiting trial at the time of this writing.

The beautiful, love-filled future the Blackburns seemed headed for was never to be, destroyed by a home invasion just after six a.m. in one of the "safest" suburbs in Indianapolis.

What, if anything, could have changed the outcome?

Often in these cases, there is some laxity. Guards were let down. These invaders showed Amanda no mercy. Here is a young pregnant mom trying to defend her one-year-old child. It did not matter. That's reason enough to make your home as safe as possible all the time. There are people you want to keep out, who you don't want anywhere near anyone you love.

TERESA SIEVERS

Amanda's story leads me to the investigation into the murder of a Bonita Springs, Florida, doctor. Teresa Sievers had spent the weekend in Connecticut with her husband and two girls, visiting family. On the night of June 29, 2015, Sievers flew home to Florida early in order to see patients the following morning, leaving her husband and girls with relatives. But at some point after she got home from the airport, someone invaded her home. Sievers was brutally bludgeoned seventeen times with a hammer and left dead on her kitchen floor, still wearing the same clothes she wore on the plane, according to airport surveillance video. One in particular of the many facts didn't sit right with me: somehow, the night of her murder, Teresa Sievers's home security system failed to work.

As it turned out, the investigation revealed that the alarm system was manipulated by someone very close to the family, Curtis Wayne Wright, a computer wiz and tech geek who happened to be the boyhood friend of Teresa's husband, Mark.

Wright and another man, Jimmy Rodgers, were later arrested when a mountain of evidence led police to them. The pair, who met in jail, had driven to Florida from Missouri, turned off the Sieverses' alarm system, bought the items they'd need for the murder at Walmart, killed time at the beach, and then went to the Sievers home to lie in wait for Teresa. They killed her, taking turns swinging the hammer, when she walked in the door. Later in his plea deal, Wright told police that Mark Sievers was the mastermind of his wife's murder.

The Sievers marriage was not in good shape, and they had consistent money problems. There are a lot of salacious details I will leave out. But Teresa Sievers, a doctor and mother of two, died because her home security system had been breached. Yes, it was an inside job.

MURDER ON THE PANHANDLE

But what about Melanie and Byrd Billings? Unlike Amanda and Teresa, Melanie was not home alone at the time of their deadly home invasion. I've seen the video of home invaders dressed in ninja garb, creeping through Melanie and Byrd Billings's backyard and, ultimately, invading the home.

Their home was big and spacious—it had to be, because the Billings family numbered eighteen, including sixteen children both blended and adopted, many of them with disabilities. In fact, Byrd and Melanie were well known in their community for taking in children with Down syndrome, autism, and other disabilities. The local sheriff referred to Melanie as "an angel."

They had been married for eighteen years, and each came into the marriage with two children from earlier marriages. Then, believing they had plenty of love to go around, they began adopting children with nowhere else to go. They designed their home to suit the children and all their needs. Byrd and Melanie clearly had big hearts to go with their big family. One after the other, the children were adopted, and they all lived happily ever after. Almost.

At seven thirty in the evening on July 9, 2009, one of their daughters, Adrianna Billings, showed up at a neighbor's door pounding and screaming that her mom and dad were dead. At the Billings home, cops found their laundry room door kicked in and Byrd Billings dead on his bedroom floor. Melanie was found dead in a nearby hallway. Both had been shot repeatedly with a 9mm handgun.

Deciphering the events of that evening was extremely difficult. Reportedly, nine of the children were home and asleep the night of the murders. According to police reports, the children indicated their dad was sleeping and was woken up by a knock at the door. The children said that "bad men" were wearing masks over their faces and that their mom got "shot in the shirt."

The police investigation revealed that two suspects ran toward the Billings home through the backyard, two others invaded by kicking in the laundry room door, and three men entered through the front door. Byrd and Melanie were shot immediately. But why? What possible motive was there to break down a door, invade the home, and gun down a mom and dad whose children needed them so desperately?

Melanie and Byrd owned a used car lot and a loan company by the name of Worldco Financial Services. The burglars imagined there were millions of dollars to be found in the Billings home. After gunning down Byrd and Melanie and leaving a family of disabled children to find their parents dead, they took the home safe and a briefcase. But the safe didn't contain millions—it held only some family papers and jewelry along with prescription meds stored safely away from the children.

Traced through tips and home surveillance video that captured shots of the getaway car, eight men were tracked down and brought to justice. Seven were charged with murder one, home invasion, and robbery. One was charged with accessory after the fact. But even though they received some justice, the Billings children will never have their parents back again.

Why? Home invaders clearly are not deterred by the fact the whole family is home.

Over the course of my legal career, I have prosecuted, investigated, and covered many, many felony cases, usually violent personal attacks, that started with a home intrusion.

Just don't call any one of them a "burglary gone wrong."

I never liked that term. The burglar has already broken into someone's home. How does it go "wronger" than that?

Burglars will often tell you, "Oh, I was just going in to get the television," as if their initial criminal intent lessens the impact of what they ended up doing.

I'll never forget what one defendant said: "Well, my little nature got up."

That was how he explained how his erection led to a rape.

So, a "burglary gone wrong" is just an offensive euphemism, an attempt to airbrush over what really happens when a thief morphs into a sexual predator or, worse, a killer.

What really happens is you are violently attacked in your home, possibly your children are taken or hurt, or you are sexually assaulted and/or murdered. That's what we're talking about, and that is how we should refer to it and think about it. It isn't one crime that went wrong. It is a horrible crime on its own and should never be reduced to some kind of collateral event.

THE RED RAPIST

There was a case in Atlanta that went unsolved for a long time. The perp gained notoriety after going unapprehended for so many months, stalking the city. He became known as the Red Rapist.

He would typically enter women's homes all over Atlanta, usually through an unlocked or open window. He would always wear red while committing his atrocities and then, in a horrible gesture, leave a red rose with the victim, displaying a level of gruesome premeditation and twisted taunting, as if they had been on a date.

At the time, DNA technology was in its infancy. We couldn't get it from the crime scene or the victim's body. We could recover semen and blood type, and that was it.

I found one woman who could identify him by sight. His attacks were always between two and six a.m., and she got a good look at him in the early-morning light. I knew an eyewitness could be torn apart on the stand under cross-examination, but there was another victim who felt she could identify his voice. And, of course, we had the relentless and strikingly similar routine of his attacks. We eventually put together enough evidence, including fingerprints at one crime scene, two pretrial line-ups, and copycat modus operandi, to put him behind bars on charges of rape, aggravated sodomy, kidnapping, and burglary.

But that case, along with so many others, hammered one idea into my brain. Which brings us to today.

I am no longer in the courtroom. The Red Rapist is still behind bars, but I'm here to raise the warning his case represents: You absolutely must lock your windows and doors. And it's something you should not cheat on.

I know there are times when you go into the backyard.

There are times when you go back and forth from the house to your car.

There are times when you run down the hallway in your apartment building, like mine in New York, and you use a shoe or something to wedge the door open. I have done it myself. And it's a mistake.

We all do it. My mother, who lives with me, loves to leave her windows open at night. She wants the fresh air. I wait for her to fall asleep, and then I go in and shut and lock them. I have to look at "being home" in a different way.

And that's how I want you to look at it. I want you safe in your home. I want to share what I have learned. I do not want history to repeat itself in your lives. I want to learn from history and give some measure of redemption and meaning to the lives of victims of home assaults that I have studied in my work.

THE SAVOPOULOS FAMILY AND VERALICIA FIGUEROA

One such case concerns the family of Savvas and Amy Savopoulos of Washington, DC. In May 2015, they, their ten-year-old son, Philip, and Veralicia Figueroa, their housekeeper, were brutally murdered in a home invasion.

I have a theory about how it all happened, and there is a lot we can learn from this case. Based on what I know, the villain, Daron Wint, recently fired from a company owned by Savopoulos, ordered a pizza to be delivered to the Savopouloses' house. He intercepted the pizza, posed as the delivery boy, and approached the door.

Despite being an accomplished and shrewd businessman, Savvas seems to have been extremely relaxed about security. The home had no security system, and it seems they would just open their door to anyone who knocked.

Wint knocked, and they opened their door to him. Over the next nineteen hours, he destroyed their lives. He tortured Philip to get a $40,000 ransom delivered to the house by an associate of Savopoulos's. He then beat and stabbed his captives to death. He set the house on fire and drove away in the family's Porsche.

His DNA was found on a pizza crust that was discovered on the porch. Cops got a match because Wint had a long rap sheet and his DNA was already in the DNA databank. On October 25, 2018, Wint was found guilty on twenty counts of kidnapping, extortion, and murder. He was sentenced to life in prison with no possibility of parole.

This case illustrates some harsh facts about home security we all need to remember: a home security system with panic buttons in multiple locations is essential. They could have tripped the alarm and had help on the scene before it got out of hand. And beware of delivery men at the door with something you didn't order. I wish they had never opened that door.

THE PETIT FAMILY

One of the more outrageous crimes in recent memory also involved a home without an alarm system: the assault and murder of Jennifer Hawke-Petit and her daughters, Michaela and Hayley, on Monday July 23, 2007, in Cheshire, Connecticut. The night before, Jennifer and Michaela were seen at a grocery store by one of the perps, Joshua Komisarjevsky, who followed them home. He and his accomplice, Steven Hayes, intended to rob the house and leave the family alone, but there was a change in plans.

Early in the morning they arrived at the house to find Jennifer's husband, William Petit, asleep on the porch. They hit him in the head and tied him up in the basement. Then the mom and the daughters were tied up and locked in their bedrooms. Hayes later said that they were not happy with what they could take from the house but saw a bankbook that indicated they could get some cash. This is the change of plans I mentioned earlier. Who's to say what these killers were planning?

After getting some gasoline in cans taken from the Petits, the men drove Jennifer to a bank and had her withdraw $15,000. She was able to communicate her situation to the teller, who called 911.

The Cheshire police went to the scene but stayed hidden on the perimeter. Unfortunately, during that time Komisarjevsky sexually assaulted Michaela, and Hayes did the same to Jennifer. Cops soon realized that the intruders had strangled Jennifer, doused Jennifer and the girls with gasoline, and actually escaped in the family's car. The girls, tied to their beds, died of asphyxiation. The monsters were apprehended a block away. Both men were found guilty of a host of heinous crimes and sentenced to life in prison without parole.

The telling of the Savopoulos and Petit family stories is painful for me. But we can learn from them while we pray for them. Both cases show the importance of an active alarm system. We tend to think of alarm systems as being important when we are away. But these tragedies show the value of a security system when you are home. The Petit family attack lasted seven hours. Could there have been a chance to trip an alarm before the evil took over?

TIPS FOR STAYING SAFE AT HOME

Personal safety is an ongoing concern even when you are tucked away in your home. Predators not only detect weakness in how you get around town, shop, or exercise, but they can tell if you are careless once you get back home.

But what can you do to fight back? Over my years of investigating, prosecuting, and covering home invasions, burglaries, and personal assaults in the home, I've amassed the following suggestions that I consider golden rules.

Come on Over!

- When you are at home alone, if possible, don't schedule repairs, exterminators, cable repair, or any other kind of service or inspection. When you do have a worker in your home, make sure you have company. If family is not available, try your best to have a friend or two stop by.
- If you're single, keep up the appearance that you have a roommate so as not to reveal to a stranger, no matter what uniform they may be wearing, that you live alone. If you are asked outright, lie through your teeth.

Turn on the Lights

Do your children ever say, "Mom, I'm afraid of the dark"? Mine do. And there's a reason for that. We fear what we don't know and what we can't see. And there is a reason to fear the darkness. But I say don't be afraid, be prepared.

Lights are one of the easiest ways to keep the bad guys away from you, your children, and your home. When interviewed, admitted burglars say lights do stop them from breaking into homes. Of course they do! Common sense dictates that stealthy crimes are easier to pull off under cover of darkness, so let there be light!

- Have more than enough lighting around your doors, entry points, driveway, garage, and paths to or around your home. While you are installing those bright lights, add motion sensors.
- Motion sensor lights are fantastic. When a burglar walks near your back door or around the corner of your home, the lights suddenly turn on and reveal their presence. They'll wonder if you saw them through the window and if you are calling the police. It's a good reason for them to run.
- Now there's even smart lighting that you can control remotely with any device you can connect to the internet. Use it to turn lights on and off unpredictably, giving the impression that you're home even when you aren't. I've done it, even from a plane.

Shut Door, Turn Lock

Let's talk about doors and windows.

- It's so obvious, I almost hate to say it, but keep your doors and windows shut and locked even when you are home. It's just ingrained with me now; the twins do it, too, thank goodness. When I shut the door, I turn the lock. Tell your children to do the same. Every time. I also turn on the burglar alarm even when we are there—especially when we are there.
- With all the sensational crimes we are constantly hearing about, it's hard to believe, but many, many burglaries and home invasions start with the perp walking right through an unlocked door. Don't let that be your door. Locking your doors and windows is one of the simplest and easiest things you can do to safeguard your family and your home.
- Of course, you are going to open windows or go out into the yard or onto your porch. But, for the most part, learn from the past, don't repeat it. Lock your doors and windows and switch on that alarm when you are home.
- Always double-check the locks and outdoor lights before you go to bed.
- But do not nail your windows shut. If you must get out in a hurry, it could cost you and your children a lot more than inconvenience.

No Keys under Mats

- Do not leave your spare key under the doormat or flowerpot. Put it in a convenient place only you and your family know about. Some suggest leaving the key with a neighbor. I do not. What if they're not around when you need the key? Then you're really in a mess. But the flowerpot? The mat? Don't be a cliché.

Don't Let It Slide

- Always wedge a metal pipe or wooden bar in the floor track of sliding doors and windows. The pipe should be the same length as the door's track with no wiggle room. Yes, the intruder may be so determined to get in that they will find another way or even

break the glass, but they'll likely realize it would be a lot easier
to just leave.

- Speaking of sliding doors and sliding *glass* doors, consider additional
  alarm measures like a glass-break sensor that will alert you if glass
  windows, panes, or doors are shattered. Even if you don't have sliding glass doors in your home, if you have numerous windows, large
  windows, or decorative glass panes, glass sensors are very useful.
  Glass-break detectors work simply: They use a microphone to monitor noise or vibrations coming from the glass. If those vibrations
  reach the frequency of breaking glass, they set off an alarm.
- Glass break and motion detectors are worth using. We all know that
  door and window alarms alert us to intruders, but they activate only
  if the door or window is opened. What if the thief shatters the glass
  window or sliding glass door and then climbs in? That guy would be
  in your home in seconds and roaming about inside, possibly waiting
  for you, and all without ever tripping your alarm system. Think
  about that.
- Motion detectors can also help when a crook enters your home
  through the attic or crawl space, which happens more than you
  think and is another example of an intruder getting in your home
  without accessing the doors or windows or tripping alarms. Motion
  sensors don't rely on how the robber got in. As soon as motion is
  detected, the alarm sounds. If you have pets, your alarm company
  may be able to offer a motion sensor that your pet won't trigger but
  a burglar will.

Doors

- External doors should be solid core. As much as I love those beautiful little windowpanes, remember that the door serves a practical
  purpose: to keep people out. If you absolutely must have a gorgeous
  glass-paned door or glass panels around your door, please make sure
  the glass is strengthened with security window film. It looks great
  and prevents intruders from breaking the glass and waltzing right in
  the front door. If possible, go a step further and fit security screens on
  your entry doors. Better to overdo it than regret not doing it later.
- External doors all need deadbolts. The deadbolts should be at least
  one inch long: the longer the bolt and higher the grade (grade 1

deadbolts being the strongest), the more force they can withstand, such as kicking or battering. But don't install deadbolts that require an inside key to unlock them in the event you need to get out fast. You don't have time to fumble looking for a door key. Imagine if you were trying to escape with your children. Seconds count.

- If you change apartments or move into a new house, change the door locks yourself or verify with your landlord that this step has been taken. You don't want a stranger walking around with keys to your home.

Look Before You Open That Door

- Peek out before you open your door. Make it a habit. If you can't see who is at your door, install a peephole. This is even more important if your front or back porch cannot be seen from the inside of your home. It's quick and easy and can make a world of difference. You do not want any surprises when you open that door.
- Home security systems often come with a wireless keychain. Keep one near your door or take it with you when a stranger knocks. Have it there and do not hesitate to press it if you need to call for help in a split second. Better safe than sorry. You'll thank me later. On second thought, let's hope you don't have to thank me.

Occupied

Do all you can to maintain the illusion you are home. Make your home look lived in at all times of the day or night.

- Keep the TV or radio on when you leave. If possible, have the TV or radio sound positioned near the front door and other entry points like back or side doors to make sure it can be heard outside or upon entry. Set them to a channel where there is talking—a shopping network, talk show, or news gabfest—so voices can be heard.
- Remember to keep your landline telephone ringer on the lowest volume setting. A phone ringing off the hook inside is music to a burglar's ears and sends the message you're not home.
- Get timers for your lights and radios so they come on and off during the evening. Make sure you stagger the timers as to when they turn

on and off so burglars can't spot their use pattern. And this isn't just for when you are out of town; this is all the time, especially when you're simply out for the evening or working late.

- Leave shoes by the front door, including men's, if you have any.
- Ask a neighbor or friend to collect your newspaper and mail while you're away.
- When you travel, don't let the bad guys know it. If you can, have someone take care of your place while you are gone. Burglars regularly case neighborhoods looking for any clue you are gone.
- Don't leave trash at the edge of the street days in a row.
- Don't let an overstuffed mailbox give your travel schedule away. Take care of business. Now.

Remember what I mentioned about burglaries "gone wrong," the sugarcoating of rapes, robberies, and murders in the home? When perps think you're gone and break in, what happens when they find out you're there? Don't ever let your place look as if you are not there, whether you are home or not. But while you are gone, keep the following additional tips in mind.

- Keep the grass cut and debris off your yard.
- Cut back tree branches that act as a natural ladder to second-story windows.
- Keep trees and bushes in your yard trimmed and pruned, whether next to the house or farther away. I know that's a tall order, but don't give a prowler a place to hide or give the appearance of an unkempt, empty home.
- On that note, the FBI tells us to think twice about tree houses, sheds, playhouses, swing sets, slides, and so forth being in your backyard at all. If you must have them, think about their placement. They need to be positioned so you can easily see them and so they do not provide a hideout for the potential intruders scoping your home.
- Don't leave notes on the door when you're not there. If you need to get a message to your family, the babysitter, the mailman, the delivery guy, or any other service person or vendor, do it by text, phone, or email.
- Do not leave your garage door open, showing that cars are gone. It's the single most common entry into your home. Controls are available that allow you to close and open your garage door remotely. All you

need is internet access from your phone, PC, or tablet to remedy the safety threat presented by somebody in your family leaving the most common home-entry point wide open.

- Also, garage doors typically lead straight into your home. Even when you are home, an open garage door is an invitation to burglars to come on in. In addition to keeping those garage doors closed, make sure that if you have a garage door opening pad with a code, don't pick something easily guessable, like 1-2-3-4 or your street address numbers. Reprogram that touch pad.

- Add a garage door contact to your door and window contacts. That way, if the garage door opens while the security system is armed and the code is not entered, the alarm goes off nice and loud. Just hearing it usually makes burglars tuck their tails and run, not just away from your TV and laptop, but also away from you and your children. Make sure you leave enough time for you to get in and out but not so much that it's unsafe. If you don't add a garage door contact, then secure the garage door leading into your home.

- And while we are on garage doors, there are other doors of concern. Pet doors (yes, I'm serious—see below) and basement doors are often used by intruders. Remember that these criminals are on a mission, and they'll do whatever they can to get in. Don't make it easy for them.

- Know your neighbors. I'm not saying you have to be best friends, but know them. They, like you, do not want crime in their neighborhood, much less in their own home. They can be on the lookout for anything out of the ordinary on your property and call your cell phone if necessary. Maybe they'll even roll in the trash bins for you when you're away. I always move newspapers and flyers from driveways, even for neighbors I don't know, when I'm jogging.

- For Pete's sake, don't post your vacation or work trip photos online while you're gone and your home is unattended. Anyone can go online and find your address.

- Get rid of geotagging on all your photos. All a bad guy has to do is check you out online, find out you're vacationing at the Grand Canyon (or wherever), then check out your other geotagged photos to find out where you live. Don't give away the farm online.

- Close curtains and blinds, at least partially. Your family and friends may know you are there alone, but intruders don't need to. They *will* know if they can look straight in and see for themselves, and if a bad guy is already peeking in, he doesn't need much egging on. Don't tempt him with a view of a room full of expensive goods, electronics equipment, laptops, money, a purse, an iPad, or jewelry in plain sight that he can grab. Consider stashing jewelry, cash, and other things of monetary or sentimental value (like my grandmother Lucy's engagement ring) in a safety deposit box, a home safe, or super-secret spot only you and your family know.

Remember, the bad guys are lurking, waiting to pounce. It's not just in the movies, I promise you. The crooks don't need to see your belongings or know whether someone is home, much less look at you or your children. It's your home and your stuff, not the Grab-and-Go!

Diversion Can Safes

Can't stand the thought of being away from that beloved sentimental possession? I've got an answer for you: diversion can safes. They look exactly like a can or jar of an everyday product, like beverages, peanut butter, or household cleaner. You could probably use the real thing, too—after a nice washing, that is. No need to get my grandmother Lucy's engagement ring crusted with peanut butter.

Smart Doorbells

Speaking of looking before you open that door, have you heard about the Ring smart doorbell? It and similar devices send an alert to your cell phone when someone's at the door. They allow you to see exactly who's at your door without ever opening it.

Smart doorbells can be wireless or connect to existing doorbell wiring. Using your current wiring has the advantage that the doorbell gets its power from the wire and connects to your existing buzzer, chime, or ring. Wireless doorbells require you to check and charge or replace the batteries.

When a visitor, delivery person, or crook rings your doorbell, the bell rings as normal but the doorbell sends an alert via Wi-Fi to one or more smartphones. When that alert occurs, you then use your cell phone to stream the doorbell cam live with up to a 180-degree panoramic field of view. Only an owl could get a better view. Some come with a motion detector and will send you an alert if something is moving near the door. Others feature infrared night vision as well, so bad guys can't shroud themselves in darkness and beat your high-tech doorbell. That's *smart*—literally.

These incredible smart doorbells can also work hand-in-hand with your virtual assistants like Alexa or Siri. You can launch them with your voice in real time, hear and speak to visitors from your phone or tablet, and check your door or porch anytime with or without the doorbell ringing.

Get a Dog

Big or small, it doesn't matter, as long as they can bark like mad whenever somebody comes to the door or into the yard. Police advise that having a dog, no matter the breed, is a major deterrent to break-ins and attacks. No can do? Get an automated sound device that has a dog barking option that can be heard from outside. Go all the way and get BEWARE OF DOG signs and plant them in the most visible spots possible.

Personal Security Apps

Download a personal security app to your cell phone. Many of them are free. They feature super-loud alarms you can activate if you perceive a threat. If you've set the app to tracking mode and you don't make it to your preselected destination, your hand-picked emergency contacts are immediately alerted with your GPS location. If you already carry your cell phone everywhere, why not turn on the app?

They are obviously great for joggers, bikers, and hikers, but consider a personal security app for everyday use. It can come in handy when you're walking to your vehicle, emptying trash at your apartment, headed to the gym, or whenever and wherever you may need it.

Get a Home Security System

You don't have to break the bank to get a home security system; some are as reasonable as $14.99 a month for 24/7 monitoring with no long-term contract. You can install many of them yourself and take them with you if you relocate to another house, condo, or apartment.

When questioned, confessed burglars admit that if they spot a home security system, they walk away and look for another target. I worry less and sleep better knowing I have an alarm system complete with cameras that are turned on and activated not only when I'm gone but when I am home with the twins.

Do not place the alarm keypad directly beside the door. The control pad or keypad is the core of your alarm system and is used to control the security in your home, as you arm and disarm it. Why place it in plain view for thieves to try to disarm it as soon as they get in? At least make the burglar use as much time as possible getting to it and trying to disarm it. That gives the alarm more time to get the cops there.

Some homes have a single pad, while others have multiple pads placed near the doors used most often and in the bedroom for panic button use. The security code typically must be activated within thirty or sixty seconds of you entering the home before the alarm goes off and police are alerted. Some activate immediately.

Many homes have the keypad at the front door or garage door, which may not be the most strategic choices. Why? According to a *Washington Post* study, about 10 percent of burglars enter through the garage and nearly 35 percent invade right through the front door. If you are home at the time of an invasion and your alarm isn't on, how do you get to the keypad? I have an extra keypad in the bedroom between me and the twins. I want to be ready if I have to be.

Speaking of being ready, go through a plan with your children about what to do if someone breaks in while the family is home. We've had the plan in place from the get-go, and I remind them of it frequently. They also need to know how to work the keypad to arm and disarm the system and, heaven forbid, to push the panic button. I don't want to scare them, but it's more important that they be ready.

It's not all about the robbers, either. Home alarms help in so many ways. They can help save you from multiple other threats like carbon monoxide, fire, smoke, and flooding. They can even help in medical emergencies. They really are crime stoppers and so much more.

Still convinced you can't afford an alarm system? Okay. Get burglar alarm yard signs and window decals and place them in plain view on your property, mailbox, front door, gate—anywhere you can think of. Criminals don't want to stick around and find out if your sign is a fake.

Stay on Alert

- Report all suspicious or odd activity in your neighborhood, especially if you live alone or have children in your care. You must trust your instincts and be acutely aware of everything around you in your own neighborhood or apartment complex.
- Call the police if you encounter someone who gives you the creeps and makes you feel uncomfortable or if you witness a disturbing or suspicious activity or situation.
- Carry it further and tell your neighbors and notify your landlord. For all you know, this may not be the first time the creepy dude has been reported. When it comes to protecting my twins, better safe than sorry.

Don't Make Me Squint

Be sure your street address is visibly posted so police can find your home in an emergency. What good is an alarm system if the cops can't find you? Clearly display your home's address on your mailbox and on your home itself. Help first responders find you as quickly as they possibly can.

Be your own best protector.

DOGGIE DOOR DANGERS

I have a doggie door. Do you?

I actually have two, one down low for our dachshund-mix that only allows him to go out, and one up high installed in the garage door for the cat, Cinnamon, to come and go as she wants. After covering the following stories and others, I'm rethinking my plan.

It broke the heart of friends and family in 2014 when they were called and told their daughter, sister, and friend Monique Williams, a beloved twenty-nine-year-old nurse at Kedlac Regional Medical Center, was found dead, shot once in the head and laid across the bed in the master bedroom of her nice, neat little home.

How did it happen?

Aaron Newport, Monique's former beau, without a key to the home, broke in through her doggie door and killed her and then himself. A tearful vigil was held by the entire Kedlac medical staff and many more friends, all in pain and shock over her passing. But Monique's story is not an isolated event.

Sadly, there are other similar stories. In 2008, I covered a more high-profile case, the murder of Anne Pressly, a twenty-six-year-old anchor at a Little Rock, Arkansas, TV station. Over several months, the investigation revealed the tragic story.

Anne lived in a small house in a very nice section of Little Rock called the Heights, a peaceful, quiet, family-oriented neighborhood. Crime is almost nonexistent in the Heights.

Pressly worked hard to obtain her BA in political science from Rhodes College in Memphis before she got her first big break and was hired at KATV in Little Rock to produce and report for three TV programs: *Good Morning Arkansas*, *Midday Arkansas*, and *Saturday Daybreak*. It wasn't long until she worked her way up to a full-time on-air reporter position. While out working on a story, she landed another role, as Candice Black in the film *W* directed by Oliver Stone.

Anne's case made me think back to all the early mornings and late nights I spent investigating, working the streets of Atlanta, researching the law and writing questions and arguments for jury trials in inner-city Atlanta. I recall that for years, my mom, Elizabeth, would call me long-distance from her desk at work at seven a.m. sharp every weekday to make sure I was up and on my way to work at the courthouse. It hurt my heart when I discovered that Anne's mom did the same. Every morning, she would call her daughter in the dark wee hours to make sure she was up and getting ready for her TV morning shift.

On the day Anne died, her mom, Patti Cannady, placed her customary early-morning call to wake Anne for the *Daybreak* program. When the phone just rang and rang, Patti knew immediately that something was very wrong. Patti went right over to Anne's bungalow only to find her daughter in bed, bludgeoned to death. Her face was unrecognizable. There was so much blood that initially police thought she must have been attacked with a knife, but that was not the case.

Amid her parents' heartbreak, the investigation and the search for her killer began. Rewards up to $50,000 were offered, and still there was no suspect.

It was only a month later when Curtis Lavelle Vance was arrested not only for the attack on Anne but for a burglary and rape seven months earlier in nearby Marianna, Arkansas, where he lived. The two police forces worked together to find Vance because DNA from Anne's case matched DNA from the earlier attack.

Vance pled not guilty and the case went to a jury trial. During final arguments, the prosecutor held up Anne's KATV headshot and, at the same time, held up another photo for comparison. The second photo was from Anne's autopsy. Her face was so brutally beaten, the prosecutor said her face "looked like an egg," with her nose pushed completely over to one side.

Jurors broke into tears. They then were reminded of several statements and confessions Vance had made, including one in which he stated that he went to Anne's neighborhood to steal laptops and zeroed in on her little cottage. He entered through a Dutch door she had devised and left open for her two cocker spaniels. He found a computer and Anne.

When Anne woke to find Vance standing over her in the dark, she began to fight him. In one of his many rambling statements, Vance said that when Anne fought back, it enraged him, and he began to hit her over and over with a gardening tool. Anne's left hand was broken in the attack in addition to the other savagery.

Vance was convicted at trial, and when the jury verdicts were opened and read in open court, Cannady raised one hand to heaven, called out "Praise God," and broke down sobbing.

At first, Little Rock police had been convinced Anne was targeted by a TV stalker, some viewer full of rage over unrequited love, possibly imagining a relationship with Anne. That was not the case. Anne's killer was just a petty criminal on the prowl for anything he could steal and any woman he could victimize. The improvised doggie door made it possible.

Anne's case reminded me of the tragic murder of Kathryn Dettman, also a television reporter, who was stalked and eventually killed by a neighbor in 1998 in Waco, Texas. Police were called around eight thirty in the morning by a neighbor who had heard loud, disruptive noises coming from Dettman's place. When they were let in by the building manager, they found Dettman's killer standing in the apartment, covered in blood. The investigation revealed that Anne often left her door open in the early-morning hours so her cats could come and go while she got ready for work. That's how her killer got in that fateful day.

In these last two cases, the victims' safety was greatly compromised by their efforts to accommodate their pets. Their too-relaxed approach proved fatal.

If you have an indoor-outdoor pet, what's the answer?

First, don't even *think* of getting rid of your number one intruder deterrent: your dog. Remember that and read on.

BEING SMART ABOUT YOUR DOGGIE DOOR

If your pet door is large enough that a Great Dane or Labrador can wriggle inside, so can a human. Believe it or not, a full-grown man can make his way in through pet doors built for even smaller dogs. But they're not coming inside for a treat or a nap on the doggie cushion. If you do have a pet door, lock it with an old-school lock and key just like you would your back door.

Get a pet door that has security measures built in, like metal security sheets or locking devices, or one whose flaps open just enough to let a lap-sized creature in and out. I've done a lot of investigation on this and learned that newly designed pet doors can include a metal panel and metal flaps and feature aluminum tunnels as opposed to plastic.

Lock your doggie door at night and whenever you are away. Use a deadbolt lock. Several pet door styles come with a sliding metal plate that you can lock into place.

Consider something different, too: don't put your doggie door in a door. Installing that pet door in a wall is a great idea if you can do it. This placement stops potential burglars from being able to use the doggie door flap to reach up to the inside locks on the door itself. Also, wall-installed doors are much more secure than those installed into a door and are shown to be much harder to crawl through.

Make sure you get the correct size door for your particular pet and install it in the right position. The door should be only the width of your doggie's shoulders and placed at the height of your doggie's back. The opening should barely accommodate your dog. If someone does try to gain access through the pet door, you want it to be difficult, time-consuming, uncomfortable, and noticeable to neighbors or passersby.

Get your tech on. Now pet doors come with electronic locks that only unlock when a chip on your pet's collar gets near the door. The door then automatically unlocks. These doors cost more, but they work.

Speaking of getting your tech on, now pet doors can be alarmed. You first estimate your pet's weight, then install easy-to-use sensors that trip if anything meaningfully over that weight moves through the door.

Install motion sensor lights pointed at the doggie door. When someone tries to stick his head through, *bingo*. He's lit up like a Christmas tree. Good idea, right?

In addition to a motion-activated light, try a motion detector just above the pet door that buzzes, rings, or makes some sort of sound whenever anything gets near the door. Some even flash an alarm light, sort of like the hazard lights on your car.

Install a timer in the room your pet door leads into for lights to go on and off in that room throughout the day and night.

I know that's a lot to digest on the seemingly simple and nonthreatening issue of doggie doors. But most important is that you and your children are safe, that your children have parents to raise them. Don't let Anne's mom be your mom. Don't let Anne be you. Love your pets for sure, but please, secure your doggie door.

CHAPTER TWELVE

Driving Dangers

I can't tell you how many times I have covered a story like this one. Sometimes I felt there were more copycat stories than I could possibly cover...it was as if they were in our show rundown every other night. The questions in the studio became an eerie echo of themselves.

"What kind of car is it?"

"What?"

"I said, what kind of car? What kind of car was she driving?"

"We have thirty seconds left. Somebody find out now."

I would hear the music intro, then a sound on tape (SOT) of the distraught mother. She's begging the public to help find her daughter. She breaks down in tears and the camera is so close to her face I have to look away from the raw emotion.

The SOT is ending, the mom's voice melts into a reporter track, and I hear my line producer counting seconds. Three, two, one...

"Welcome back. I'm Nancy Grace. Thank you for being with us."

From my peripheral vision, I can see my own face talking onscreen, and just at that moment I hear it. The executive producer comes in my ear, inaudible to the viewer, and quickly says, "Blue Toyota Camry."

"We are looking tonight for a blue Toyota Camry..." Then he says the tag number in my ear, and I repeat it almost as fast as he says it. She was last seen in her car. But now, where is she?

It got to be standard operating procedure, every time there was a missing woman—be it a young mom, a college student, a high schooler, or a grandma—the show staff knew to have the year, make, model, and tag number associated with the missing or murdered victim. It matters. That information may be the only way to save the victim's life.

How many hundreds of nights did that or a very similar scenario take place? I can't even count them all. But what does that true story mean right now, right here? Let me tell you.

Here are just a few examples of the many cases I have covered while on CNN-HLN in which a woman was taken from her car or assaulted in her car and ended up dead. I can't tell you how often I led a show with the kind of story I just described:

Breaking news tonight, live, Fredericksburg. A twenty-one-year-old beauty found dead in her silver Kia about thirty minutes from her own home. When local homeowners come to inquire, thinking she's asleep at the wheel, they realize the girl is dead. We learn that in the days leading up to her death, Heather Ciccone had complained about a female stalker.

* * *

Breaking news tonight. Authorities have just identified a body found in a Hays County cornfield, a white Toyota Camry found abandoned nearby. We've confirmed the ID of twenty-six-year-old Brittany Parker. Tonight, her family is begging for help to solve this case.

* * *

Texas police are desperately searching for a nineteen-year-old missing mom, Shonda Townsend. Shonda was driving home from a day of boating and grilling out at a friend's house and sent a text message to her mother saying she was on her way. She never made it. Authorities found her ransacked car a few hours later in front of a residential home, the keys reportedly thrown across the street into a field. Cops searched the home and interviewed everyone in the area, but there has been no sign of the young mom. As Shonda's two-year-old son waits at home, hoping for his mother's return, cops continue to search for Shonda, admitting foul play is likely involved.

* * *

The variety is endless: young, old, night, day, strangers, family members, out with friends, home with family. But the end result is the same: a woman is separated from her car and ends up dead. How many more? I can't count them all, but what I can do is think and analyze the thousands of similar cases and come up with answers. With millions of cars on the road, they all blend together. The only thing that sets them apart from the rest is the make, model, and tag number... and the fact the person last driving that particular car has vanished.

MELANIE URIBE

But there's one more story I want to tell you.

I was filling in as guest host for Larry King one night in New York City, beaming out by satellite from Penn Station. The program that night was about psychic detectives. At the time, I was a dyed-in-the-wool nonbeliever.

Why?

Because my world was made of hard facts and evidence, evidence that could be admitted into court. Not psychics, whose testimony would likely not be admitted and, even if it was, could make some jurors skeptical of the legitimate facts and evidence I brought before them.

Why taint a case? Right?

That night, after the show, I walked out onto the dark, chilly streets around Madison Square Garden to get a ride home, and my head was swimming with all I had just learned about so-called psychic detectives solving cases and a woman named Etta Smith, who told me she had had a vision about Melanie Uribe.

On December 15, 1980, Melanie, a recently divorced mother of an eight-year-old boy, was driving to her night shift nursing job at Pacoima Hospital in Burbank, California. Melanie was last seen at a red light near the hospital. She never made it to work. She was known to never miss work or even be late, so her supervisor called her home and, when no one picked up, sounded the alarm and called police.

The next morning, police found her abandoned pickup, but there was no sign of Melanie. Her truck had been set on fire and was completely burned out. Also found at the scene of the truck fire was Melanie's white nurse's uniform.

The rest of Melanie's story is what made the headlines. A little over a week later, Etta Smith, a thirty-two-year-old employee at Lockheed Aerospace, had a vision, which she told me on *Larry King* that night was like a movie. In the "movie," she saw very clearly a canyon, a curving road, and something white that she thought was Melanie's nurse uniform and body. Not thinking of herself as a psychic, she went to police and described the area she had seen, an obscure portion of Lopez Canyon. Sensing no one believed her, Etta took her family members with her to the canyon and sure enough, "feeling" Melanie's trauma, she saw a body in the brush and white nurse's shoes. It was Melanie, and the autopsy showed that she had been robbed, stripped, raped, and beaten to death.

Police naturally suspected Etta and arrested her. She spent four days in jail before a man confessed to killing Melanie with two other men. In 1987, a jury awarded Etta roughly a year's pay ($26,000) for false arrest. For many people the story started and ended with Etta's vision. For me, it all started with a single mom in her nurse's uniform stopped at a lonely red light.

Three men, complete strangers, happened to pull up at the same red light. They spotted her like a lion spots a gazelle. Approaching Melanie's truck, they somehow got her door open and abducted her right there on the spot. A trio of thugs jumped Melanie, carjacked her, raped her, and beat her dead with a rock as she literally begged for her life…or so they bragged afterward. Melanie suffered a horrific death, and her little boy was raised without a mom.

We can also learn from stories with good endings. I'm thinking of Dorothy Baker, who managed to fight off an armed attacker to save her little boys. Her story amazed me. I'll start my tips there.

Dorothy's van had been having problems with its locking mechanisms and very likely didn't lock on June 14, 2013. Unbeknownst to Dorothy, a man had been stalking her in the local Kroger, then followed her to the CVS. Now hiding in her unlocked van, he had no idea what was coming.

When Dorothy and her boys returned to the van, he jumped into the front seat and demanded she drive to an ATM for money. She refused, and he pulled a knife. But, willing to endure anything to save her children, including being slashed across the chest by her attacker while her two little boys screamed in the back seat, Dorothy grabbed the knife and punched him, then drove her van into a pole, hoping to knock him through the windshield! While struggling with him, she managed to call 911 and for help. Eventually, the thug jumped out of the van and tried to run away, but Dorothy told me she ran him over with the vehicle and immobilized him. Speaking to reporters after the incident, Dorothy said she told the attacker, "You messed with the wrong witch!"

Dorothy Baker fought back and won. I pray you never have to.

CAR SAFETY TIPS

- Make sure your doors are locked!
- Some repairs have to wait. I understand. But not the locks on your car doors.
- Whenever you find yourself stopped in traffic, be it at a red light or a stop sign or waiting for the driver in front of you to turn, always leave plenty of space to pull out from behind the car in front of you so you can't get blocked in.
- Keep all your doors locked and the windows rolled up while you are driving near others. I know it gets hot, but if you need air, just crack the window.
- Always lock your doors and keep your windows rolled up when you leave your car, even if it's just for a quick errand. How hard is it to press the remote lock button on your keychain when you leave your car? Not hard at all. For me, now it's second nature.
- Be super cautious when you enter crowded intersections. Squeegee-wielding guys washing your windshield, street vendors, corner preachers, "charities" raising money, people selling water or T-shirts, newspaper sellers, panhandlers—you don't know them. While we typically don't fear kids or teens, I learned the hard way as a prosecutor that youths are often tricked into working for an adult as part of a scheme, whether it's selling dope or hoodwinking a lady at an intersection. They don't care if your children are in the back seat.
- Keep everything of value—your purse, cell phone, laptop, handbag—out of sight. Don't get hijacked over your cell phone. It happens.
- Be alert. Thugs often work in pairs. Don't be distracted at your own

window by one perp only to be robbed by his accomplice on the passenger's side.

- If you absolutely must speak to or interact with someone outside your vehicle, only crack the window a tiny bit.
- *Never* give a ride to a hitchhiker or any stranger. I've actually done it, and I look back on that moment and wonder, *What was I thinking?*
- Don't fall for a "good Samaritan" trying to signal you something's "wrong" with your car. Only stop if you know that they are correct and that it is more dangerous to keep driving than to stop and isolate yourself, thus making you and your car a sitting target.
- If you suspect someone is following you, drive to the nearest police station or find a safe and busy public place for help. Better safe than sorry. And you don't have to drive like the opening scene in a James Bond movie. Take a few different turns or circle the block to make sure they're gone before you go home. Do not go directly home if you think someone is following you.
- Stick to well-traveled streets so you don't end up at some dead end because of the stress of feeling you are being followed. Don't make it worse by getting lost. Make a mental note of your turns.
- If you don't feel safe getting out of your car to make it to safety, stay in the car with your doors locked and lay on the horn. In fact, lay on the horn in even remotely dangerous situations. Better to be wrong and thought of as just another "crazy woman driver" than to be right and do nothing.
- Avoid distractions while driving. Keep the volume low on the podcast, news, or music you're playing so that you can maintain a level of high awareness of all your surroundings. As tempting as it may be to check phone messages, don't.
- In that same vein, do not check or update your Instagram, Facebook, Twitter, or Snapchat while at a stop sign or red light. Criminals can't wait for you to do that. All they need is one single opening, that moment you aren't paying attention, to smash your window and grab whatever is in your passenger or back seat, or worse.
- Make sure your car insurance covers roadside assistance. I love AAA. I've called on them several times.
- Do not interact with other drivers on the road: no waving, thumbs-up,

lights blinking, nothing. You never know who is driving alongside or behind you.

- If a stranger continues to try to get your attention, continue driving or turn off at the next exit or intersection, wait, then resume your trip.
- Never run out of gas. Don't wait for the warning light, as I have done way too many times.
- If you can help it, do not drive in dark and unfamiliar areas. It makes it easier for you to get lost.
- Drive with GPS and tell someone where you are going.
- Be very careful about asking strangers for directions. Rely on your intuition. If you sense anything wrong, stay quiet and wait for someone else.
- Charge your phone and keep a charger in the car. Make sure you have emergency numbers already programmed into your phone (AAA, family, insurance).
- Don't accept rides from strangers no matter how friendly they seem. Ted Bundy was friendly before he murdered his victims one by one. I've talked to some who survived.
- Don't give rides to strangers. Ted Bundy again.
- Don't follow a stranger who claims to know the way to where you are going. Please. He may lead you straight to the end of a dark road.
- If you have a flat, drive extremely carefully and slowly to the next service station or somewhere in public that is crowded and busy. You may ruin your tire, but you may have saved your life. I did it on the interstate. I put on my hazards and drove the next twenty minutes at about fifteen miles per hour. I never thought twice about it. Even if you ruin the tire, you will not have risked your life.
- Do not ignore car maintenance.
- Breakdowns on the side of the road sound like the beginning of a tired and predictable horror movie, but believe it or not, it still happens. Lessen the chances of this happening by taking care of your car and its upkeep.

The other day, I took the twins to play in front of our local church. Safe, right? But one of them left the car door open, and when I tried to crank up to leave, the battery was dead. I looked up at the sky and said, "Oh Lord, I will be late for work. What am I going to do?" Believe it or not, right then I thought I actually saw an angel in the air, just over the roof of the church.

Actually, it was a person, the church custodian, Stan. He was up there sweeping off leaves. He got down in a jiffy and jumped the car with the cables I keep in the trunk, and I got the twins home for baths and supper and me on my way to work on time.

But what if Stan hadn't been there? What if it had been me and the twins on the side of the interstate or a back country road?

During that incident, I couldn't help but remember what happened to a coed on the very first day of spring semester at Pierce College in Woodland Hills, California. She went to her car in a lot near the Performing Arts Building around eight p.m. and found her battery had died. In covering the story, I learned from the L.A. County sheriff that she did the right thing and called for a jump service. Soon after, a guy showed up in a white four-door Prius with a towing company logo prominently displayed on the side of the door. He got her car started and then attacked her.

After the assault, she managed to get into her car, lock the doors, and race away. She at least got away with her life. Many others haven't been so lucky. Keep your battery in shape.

Ever heard the phrase "Where the rubber meets the road"? It refers to a moment or location where things get real and serious. It's a great metaphor, because the less tread you've got on those four tires, the more at risk you are for flats and blowouts, both of which are very serious situations. I remember being so broke in law school and college that I'd go looking for the cheapest retreads. I did it then. But I don't anymore.

- Change your oil. I know it's elementary, but I actually broke down on the interstate once because I hadn't changed the oil in so long. I was stretched too thin, working a couple of jobs plus school plus law review. I got a tow and a huge bill, but I was lucky.
- Upgrade that flip phone to a smartphone. Oh, how I loved my flip phone, but it had to go. I use GPS at all times, especially now that I have the twins.
- Don't get lost or disoriented, and remember to keep an old-fashioned map in case you can't get a cell signal or your phone won't charge and you have to go old-school.

- Be aware of police impersonators as well as the fake roadside assistance threat. Don't forget that Pierce College student I told you about. Ask for ID at the get-go. Real officers shouldn't be offended.
- Ask the towing or roadside assistance service for a vehicle description and driver name. If you are suspicious when help arrives, stay in your car with the doors locked and call dispatch again. If they act irritated, that's their problem. Follow your instincts. Same for "police" in unmarked cars.
- Just as when you are jogging, keep mace or pepper spray as well as a loud noise alarm in your car. Remember, your car likely has an automatic alarm as well. Don't be afraid to trigger it.
- In the event you do break down, you become a predator's dream. You must stay in your car to call for help. Do not give any indication to passing motorists that there is a problem. Remember, a good Samaritan can easily be a wolf in sheep's clothing. If someone comes to your window, crack it only slightly if at all. Do not, under any circumstance, accept a ride.
- If you are worried about another car crashing into you—which is unlikely—hide near the car until a person you know, roadside assistance, or a cop comes to help. When a cop or roadside assistance does come, remember to get ID first.
- If possible, avoid highway rest stops. I'm sure you've heard stories about crimes at rest stops. They're not just creepy campfire stories to scare you over popcorn. They're true. Roadside rest stops are notorious for crimes on women.
- If you need a restroom, go to a restaurant, gas station, or mini-mart. Pass the rest stop by.
- Never nap at a rest stop. When I see "rest stop," I think "rest in peace." Don't add to the lore by becoming another statistic.
- Before you turn off your engine and get out of your car, anywhere, wait until you *know* it's safe to do so. Look around, look in your rearview mirror, and always park as close as possible to your destination. Get out of your car and go straight in, and go straight to your car and leave when you come out.
- Last but not least, be ready to fight if the person approaching you means to do you harm.

ROAD RAGE

Do not chase down drivers who have slighted you on the road. This one is especially important when I think of seventh grader Alexis Wiley. On March 5, 2010, Alexis and her mom, Sonya Randle, a Texas Southern University police officer, were driving along, minding their own business, when a twenty-four-year-old later identified as Richard Calderon bumped his Cadillac into Sonya's Nissan Altima from behind and took off. Sonya took off after him to get his tag number. After she got the tag number, she kept driving. To Sonya's surprise, her daughter Alexis told her the Cadillac was now weaving through traffic, following them. He did more than follow them. Suddenly, gunshots rang out. A single bullet broke through the rear of Sonya's Nissan and struck Alexis in her head as she was looking back as the perp chased them. Later, the shooter, Calderon, claimed he was just defending himself because he thought someone was attacking him to get his "fancy" car and its expensive rims. Alexis played cello in the school band and loved volleyball and softball. Her mother will never see her alive again.

Over what?

We've all heard about road rage. Do not get into a verbal exchange with other drivers, even when they are wrong and you are right. Is that what you want on your gravestone?

"I was right"?

I don't.

So, remember, no fist shaking, gesticulations, cutting the wrongdoer off to teach them a lesson, slamming on brakes to get revenge on a tailgater—nothing. It's not worth it.

ROAD RAGE DON'TS

- Don't assume everybody around you on the road is normal. They're not. There are lots of wingnuts out there, and many of them, sadly, have guns. Accept that reality.
- You want to drive slowly in the fast lane and someone wants to pass you? Move over and let them.
- Don't try to make a citizen's arrest.
- Don't chase someone to reprimand them for bad driving.

- Don't give the hairy eyeball to bad drivers, even when they deserve it.
- Don't text while driving. It's dangerous, and it drives road ragers crazy. Accept without question that they could be wingnuts with guns, so don't antagonize them.

If you are the road rager and you can't stop shooting birds, shaking your fist, honking your horn, and doing all those other antagonizing roadway shenanigans, ask yourself, *Is this who I want my children to see and become?*

I don't.

Don't end up on one of my TV shows.

CHAPTER THIRTEEN

Crimes at Concerts
and Live Events

A name still runs through my mind over and over, and I've never forgotten it: Morgan Dana Harrington.

I recall the first night I covered Morgan's disappearance and spoke with her father, Dan Harrington. He told me it all started with a group of twenty-somethings planning for months to go to a concert. Morgan's parents told me she had the concert tickets taped to the fridge for six months before the event, that's how much she and her friends were looking forward to their big, fun night out on the town. And why not?

Morgan was an intelligent, artistic twenty-year-old, excelling at Virginia Tech University. On October 17, 2009, Harrington and three of her friends headed out to the John Paul Jones Arena at the University of Virginia for the long-awaited Metallica concert. During the concert, she left her seat to go to the bathroom. When she didn't come back, her friends called her cell phone. She answered and explained she got locked out of the arena because of the concert's strict no reentry policy and told them not to worry. That call was at 8:48 p.m. Morgan was never heard from or definitively seen alive again.

When I spoke with Morgan's dad, he was desperate for answers. How could Morgan go out for a night of music with her friends and then seemingly vanish into thin air?

After the concert, her purse and cell phone, with its battery removed, were found in the nearby parking lot of UVA's Lannigan Field. Someone matching her description was seen near the field and the Copley Street Bridge, about a quarter of a mile from the arena, between nine and nine thirty p.m. It was the last confirmed sighting of anyone matching her description. That night her father sensed she was abducted, as she wasn't the type of person who would have gone off on foot from the arena or to hitchhike or anything like that. There was no surveillance video, but authorities believed many of the reported sightings were credible, so the police quickly moved their attention away from the arena and focused on the spot where she was last seen.

More tips and purported sightings came in as the weeks passed, but they didn't pan out.

The search for Morgan ended, but not the way we had hoped. The following January, Morgan's remains were found by a local farmer just ten miles from the John Paul Jones Arena. Her body had been disposed of in a remote seven-hundred-plus-acre tract of land, nearly two miles off the closest road. Several of Morgan's bones had been broken, and she had been raped.

When another young woman, Hannah Graham, went missing and was found murdered in September 2014, the name Jesse Matthew emerged. Matthew was already suspected in sexual attacks at two colleges he attended, Liberty University and Christopher Newport University. On September 15, 2015, Matthew was charged with Morgan's kidnapping and murder on the basis of forensic evidence. He pled guilty to the murders of Hannah Graham and Morgan Harrington on March 2, 2016, and is now serving four consecutive life sentences.

He's off the street, which is a relief, but where does that leave the parents of Morgan and Hannah? And us? The parents still mourn the loss of their daughters. As for us, what can we learn? I racked my mind and spoke to dozens of experts, police, and survivors. This is what we've come up with.

CONCERT AND LIVE EVENT SAFETY TIPS

While we should not fear a night out for a concert, show, or sporting event, a penny's worth of safety is worth a pound of cure. Make these tips a part of your planning.

- First, know where you are going: the event venue and its location. The layouts of so many concert and event venues are confusing. Finding a bathroom, exit, or smoker's area can get you all twisted around and make it hard to find your way back to your seat and to your group. You need to know your section and row, maybe more, in order to find your seat. You do not want to get lost inside a venue.

- Go with friends or co-workers. This is a *major* safety tip. There truly is safety in numbers. If you can't carpool or travel to the venue together, then meet up at an agreed-upon spot. Always go with a friend or date, and once you get there, adopt the buddy system. Do not dive into that crowd alone.
- Let your family or friends know where you are going. A text or email will do.
- If possible, try to get to the venue early, before it's completely packed and disorienting. That way, you can get a look around for exits, security guards, bathrooms, concessions, and pay phones if you need them.
- Once you and your friends get there, take a moment to agree on a meeting spot in case you get separated. My family and I always do it at airports. There was once a "statue" at the Atlanta airport that looked like a penguin carrying a suitcase. "The penguin" was about twelve feet tall and made from luggage and airplane engine pieces. The penguin is long gone, but we still meet up at "the penguin" aka baggage check. At other airports, our standard meeting spot is baggage claim. Concerts and live events get crowded and loud, so it's easy to lose someone. Don't let that happen to you. Remember, have a plan and keep it simple so friends can remember it and act on it even if they've been drinking or are panicked.
- As soon as you get there, scope out the security guards and where they are positioned. Almost always, they are your friends.
- Be aware of the people around you, not just the ones you came with.
- Keep your money hidden. A concert or live event provides easy prey for muggers. They know you have money, credit cards, and a cell phone. Don't flash it or count it in pubic. Keep it hidden where you can get to it easily, like a pocket.
- Don't carry a purse; they can be snatched or pulled by thieves, often with you still holding on.
- Do not accept alcohol, drinks, drugs, or cigarettes from anyone. You have no idea what any of it might be laced with.

- Bring your cell phone and make sure it's fully charged. Do not try to record video of the whole concert or event and end up with a dead cell phone.
- Bring a portable charger or a backup battery like a Mophie. It fits right onto your phone, so you don't need to plug in anywhere for a supercharged boost of power. Mophies give you basically a whole extra day of backup power, doubling the amount of charge you have on the cell phone alone.
- Have important numbers memorized. This is critical. If everything goes wrong and you end up separated from your friends and your cell phone is dead, borrow another concertgoer's—a woman's—and call a friend or family member to meet.
- I've spoken with so many crime victims, and I can't tell you how many times they saw or came in contact in some minor way with the person who harmed them. Almost always, they got a bad feeling. If you get that bad feeling or sense that someone is menacing or stalking or just rubs you the wrong way, act on those feelings. Especially note if someone keeps popping up wherever you are. They are following you. Tell a security guard pronto. These gut instincts are almost always worth your attention. Obey your instincts and don't worry about what somebody else may think of you. How many times in your life have you said out loud or to yourself, *I wish I had followed my first instinct and [broken up/quit the job/taken the job/picked a different route/whatever]*?
- Guard whatever you're drinking. I ask for drinks with lids and straws. How many true stories do we have to hear about GHB, the date rape drug, being slipped into drinks? Or Quaaludes, ecstasy, ketamine—you name it. Don't let it happen to you.
- If you get the sense something is off-kilter, or if things get out of hand or are simply not going the way you like, leave. No one wins a medal for staying until the bitter end.
- Outside the venue, security may no longer be as visible and may be much sparser. Parking lots are prime hunting grounds for predators: there is less security and lots of drunk and high people out wandering in a darkened parking lot. It's a predator's playground.
- Avoid chokepoints, tight spaces eventgoers must pass through. Exits and entrances are chokepoints and are often a chosen target for

evildoers. If you can't avoid them, pass through them as quickly as you can.

- Important: before you leave for the event, have a plan in place to get home—whether it's by car, bus, train, subway, or carpool! Don't just try to catch a ride home or figure it out later.

- At the end of the event or show, do not deviate from your plan. Even if you've had a fuss or disagreement with your friends or your ride, stick with the plan and get home with them. Sort it out the next day. Arrive alive.

- Even if you think it's safe to walk the one block to the bus, don't. Try to catch the very closest bus and then connect to get home. Crooks are like hyenas: they are watching the obvious spots for easy targets, the watering hole on the savannah or the walk to the bus stop. If you must walk to the public bus or train, walk with your friends or pause when leaving and blend in with a group. It's not hard. Just walk a short distance behind them; you don't have to become best friends. Repeat: do not go alone.

- When you do get to the bus, subway, or train, sit in the front. Try your best to be near the operator. It matters. I do it so much in NYC that I know many of the operators by face and some by name. I talk to them about my dad, who was with the railroad for many years, and guess what? They remember.

- Always consider the weather outside the venue, and dress with that in mind.

- Of course, have a great time, but keep your eyes open and notice what's happening around you.

TIPS FOR STAYING SAFE DURING MASS SHOOTINGS

When I first envisioned writing this book, I never dreamed I'd include the following. Dispensing advice when it's you against a mass shooter may seem like just empty words. It's not. Considering the horrific shooting on October 1, 2017, at the country music concert outside the Mandalay Bay hotel in Las Vegas and after speaking first-hand to so many of the victims, I know I must include tips on how to stay safe in the event of a public shooting spree. So, in addition to the tips above, please note the following, which apply to shootings at live events such as concerts and shows but also to movie theater and mall shootings.

- Don't go through life with blinders on, including at concerts and events. Think clearly and notice anything that seems odd or out of place, such as a person acting angry or aggressive or someone who comes across as not being there to have a good time.
- Unattended bags or backpacks should raise a red flag. Alert security immediately if you see one.
- Go online beforehand. Do some homework; it doesn't take long. Pull up the event venue and check out the layout and the location of your seat and the exits. What exits are near? Is it close to a staircase or an elevator? Better yet, download the venue layout on your phone so you will have it with you.
- While you are online, google the performers or event you plan to see. Is either one the target of hate talk or threats? Have they gotten a reputation for violence at their performances?
- If you notice something that raises your hackles, tell someone, such as a security guard.
- Avoid the worst of the crowds. Arrive early and leave early or late in order to circumvent getting stuck in the surges in and out of the venue.
- Don't block your ears with earbuds or headphones.
- Stay on the outskirts of a massive crowd to be closer to exits. It's easier to navigate around a big crowd than to cut through it. If a stampede begins, get to the outside of the crowd and hold on to anything you can: a column, supports under a stairwell, anything that won't move.
- If, God forbid, a shooting or similar incident occurs, get out. Get to that exit.
- Try to determine the direction of the threat. If you can't see the source, try to discern the direction based on crowd reaction.
- If you can't leave, try to find a safe room, such as a closet that locks.
- Take cover, remain silent, and listen for police or rescue.
- Try to stay with your group in order to help each other.
- If you can't leave, experts say that, as difficult as it will be, you must stay down and still on the floor, and under no circumstance should you bring attention to yourself.

- Put your group plan into action, meet, and leave.
- If exits are blocked, break windows to get out.
- What would you do if someone in your group was shot or hurt? Do you know how to make a tourniquet? Do you know how to apply pressure to quell bleeding? Because of the world we now live in, get trained in first aid. I have.

CHAPTER FOURTEEN

Parties Gone Wild: Staying Safe at Bars and Restaurants

I t's not complicated: parties out of control equal danger.

Going with your gut instincts is a common refrain for me, and here's another example: don't go to gatherings or parties that have a chance of getting out of hand. You can probably discern the difference between a quiet cocktail or dinner party and a hastily thrown together rave that will likely feature police sirens before it's over.

"Wanna go to a party?"

It sounds like fun...it usually *is* fun. But how many times have the cases I've investigated that ended in murders, armed robberies, or sexual attacks started with those very words? I can't count them all. What could be more fun than a Halloween party and a Poison Ivy costume inspired by the iconic evil villainess in *Batman and Robin*? Read on.

CHELSEA BRUCK

In 2014, Chelsea Bruck was a twenty-two-year-old resident of Maybee, Michigan. She attended a Halloween party on October 26, 2014, in rural French Township, Michigan, dressed up as Poison Ivy. Around three a.m., Bruck left the party. A fellow partygoer, Daniel Clay, also left the party and, according to his later testimony, offered Bruck a ride. She got in his car, and she was never seen alive again.

A heavily publicized six-month search that involved me covering it repeatedly and begging the public for help along with the distribution of over 1 million leaflets eventually led investigators to Bruck's body, which was found in April 2015 in a wooded area about ten miles from the location of the party.

In September 2015, Bruck's red shoe and green leggings were found near where her body was found, and Clay's DNA was present on them. Clay claimed that Bruck died accidentally of asphyxiation during consensual sex, but the medical examiner determined the cause of death to be blunt force trauma to the face and head. In 2017, Clay was convicted of first-degree murder and sentenced to life imprisonment.

The party went out of control because word of it spread quickly and virally on Facebook and Twitter. A party planned for about two hundred people ballooned into a huge gathering of more than twice that size. When I covered the case, we showed video from the party, and it was a raging, chaotic scene.

Another issue was that Chelsea, dressed as Poison Ivy, could not be identified as herself by other people at this crowded, hectic gathering. They saw Poison Ivy with red hair, not Chelsea with her blue eyes and long blond hair. When she left the party with someone, that person was equally hard to identify for the same reason.

I eventually learned that Chelsea was a sheltered young lady who lived with her parents, and they often drove her to work. Once she got to the party, Chelsea left her phone in a friend's car, and though she tried, the friend never got that phone back to Chelsea before she left the party—not surprising in a sea of five hundred people. That mistake hampered the early investigation, because the phone might have allowed Chelsea to call for help, and the GPS on the phone would have helped to locate her.

The press, social media, and pundits make much of parties out of control, like the one Chelsea attended, that, thanks to social media, mushroom into a menacing giant of a party, with nearly a thousand people showing up. For instance, there's the Keene Pumpkin Festival, which had been held for twenty-five years without incident and drew thousands to the tiny town of Keene, New Hampshire. The festival features hundreds of colorful gourds and a tower made of jack-o'-lanterns. In its first decade, the festival appeared in the *Guinness Book of World Records* for most lit jack-o'-lanterns in one setting (28,953!). It sounds lovely, right? Think again.

In 2014, this fall festival turned ugly, with thousands of revelers tearing down street signs and starting fires. College students from nearby Keene State College and other schools were the main instigators. Police showed up in riot gear as the out-of-control attendees threw rocks and bottles. It wasn't about pumpkins anymore; it was about anger and booze. Since that year, the festival has been dramatically scaled back. It moved to Laconia, New Hampshire, and was renamed the New Hampshire Pumpkin Festival. A nice tradition was lost to out-of-control drunks.

Then there is spring break.

On the gorgeous Florida Panhandle, Panama City Beach authorities were once thrilled to open their city to spring breakers in exchange for the flood of tourism dollars that came along with them. The harbinger of things to come arrived on March 27, 2005, when Robert J. Bailey and two of his buddies drove all the way from Milwaukee, Wisconsin, to Panama City Beach to "look for women," and they ended up shooting a local police officer. After checking in to the Sugar Sands Motel, the three headed to a bar and then went out on the prowl for girls. Driving down a road slowed with spring breakers, they stopped to talk to women walking by. Their white Dodge Durango blocked traffic, and when Sergeant Kevin Kight pulled up to move them along, Bailey stated he didn't have a license and had a parole violation and then gunned down Kight with a Taurus 9mm. Robert Bailey murdered Kevin Kight in cold blood—on Easter Sunday, no less. What would have happened to an unsuspecting woman if he had gotten her alone?

Social media has added fuel to the spring break flame. Now it only takes thirty seconds to a minute for a bar, restaurant, group, or individual to post a party online and round up a herd of five to six hundred partiers in no time—people with no connection to each other and thus a cloak of anonymity. Violence returned to Panama City Beach in 2015 when a gang rape occurred on the beach. Video showed partiers oblivious to the violence occurring just yards away. A nineteen-year-old woman was intoxicated and assaulted by three men in plain sight, but no one intervened. Local police say that video was hardly the first one they've seen with footage that alarming.

The partying got so out of control that the local government had to pass ordinances to ban drinking on the beach during March and April to dampen the wild scenes unfolding right under their noses.

Who wants to be invited to that "party"? I don't.

Of course, parties can get out of control in the dead of winter, too.

On December 31, 2017, in Seven Hills, Ohio, cops showed up to a house party thrown at an Airbnb location where literally hundreds of people "showed up" for a New Year's "banger" after it was advertised on Twitter. Drunk adults were so packed into the house that they were vomiting standing up. Police say attendees paid a $5 cover charge for the mob party and that they found the homeowner had locked himself in a bedroom to get away from the drunken throng. The home was completely trashed, TV screens were shattered, and windows were broken out.

Some party!

Before you head out to a party that could easily become dangerous, answer the following questions:

Did you hear about the party strictly through social media?

Are you familiar with anyone who is throwing the party or doing the inviting?

If you say yes to the first and no to the second, I don't want to be a party pooper, but don't go!

Is social media to blame? Or the partiers themselves? Calling them *partiers* is certainly putting lipstick on the pig, because in the eyes of the law, they are perps. True, the parties are advertised on social media, but it's not an anonymous network that makes parties get out of control—it's the people who attend the parties. I don't want *you* to be one of the people harmed or who go missing at a so-called party.

But think about it: Are out-of-control parties glamorized in movies and online? While you may have never actually attended a party that ends up as a headline—and not in a good way—certainly you've read or heard about them. For instance, who hasn't heard of the "party boy" who ended up trashing his family home and neighborhood while his parents were away on vacation?

I know it sounds like a "fun" movie, but it happened in 2008 when the real-life party boy, Corey Delaney from Melbourne, Australia, advertised his party via text and social media and more than five hundred people showed up. After damaging police cars, smashing mailboxes, and throwing rocks, glass, and bricks, the tab for the damage and police services, including a helicopter, surpassed $20,000. Delaney's night of expensive infamy was rumored to be the inspiration for the 2012 movie *Project X*, which in turn inspired several other social media–driven parties that caused more damage than anything else. One of these parties in Houston resulted in the death of an attendee when a gun came out as police tried to stop the revelry.

Would you want to be plastered up against a wall in that scenario? I wouldn't.

GETTING HOME FROM A NIGHT OUT: SAMANTHA JOSEPHSON AND UBER SAFETY

Many nights on the town involve drinking, and there are ways to plan for getting home safely: a designated driver, calling a cab, or a ride-hailing service like Uber or Lyft.

These services are relatively new, however, and you must be smart about them. As I was finishing this book, a tragic story was in the news. Around two a.m. on Friday March 29, 2019, college senior Samantha Josephson ordered an Uber after a night out in Columbia, South Carolina. Surveillance video shows her standing on the sidewalk using her phone. A black car pulled up and she got in. Fourteen hours later and seventy miles away, her body was found by two hunters. The killer is in custody, but the Josephsons have had their world upended permanently.

These services are generally reliable, but you must make sure the car you enter is in fact the one sent by the service. The app will show you the driver's name and the car's make, model, color, and plate number. Don't get in any car but that one.

The driver will have your first name from the app, too. Without giving the answer first, ask the driver who they're picking up before you put one toe in a car.

TIPS BEFORE YOU HEAD OFF TO A PARTY

- First, don't go to a party unless you have direct knowledge of who's throwing it.
- Before you leave for the party, make sure you have the Uber or Lyft app on your cell phone and know how to use it. For areas that don't have those services, have a local cab service in your contacts and make sure they take credit cards.
- Make sure your GPS and Google Maps apps are working before you leave. Program the party location into your device.
- Once you get there, if it's getting rowdy and you look around and realize you know no one, or you can't find the handful of people you

do know, you really must leave. If you can't drive, call a ride service. Do not hitch a ride. If you're worried about getting to your car, get someone to walk with you or watch you as you walk. As a last resort, call a friend or family to talk to you on the phone as you get safely to your car.

- If someone tries to start a disagreement with you, don't try to talk it out. Walk away. Leave the area quickly and quietly.

- If you are attending a party where there is security and are being bothered, get their attention. No security? Try the staff manning the bar. If it doesn't get better, leave. Do not hesitate to call police.

- Do not wander off on your own. Stay around others you are comfortable with even if you just met them. But remember this warning: you don't really know the people you just met at a party. Your "relationship" is tenuous and a matter of happenstance. They might be fine people, but you don't know that yet. Act like it.

- Do not explore the area around the party alone or with someone you just met. Stay inside the venue.

- If a fight breaks out, don't stand around and watch. You can get hurt. Leave.

- Beware of drink spiking. It's so easy for a bad guy to slip drugs or alcohol into your drink if you leave it unattended or simply look away. Never allow someone you don't really know to bring you a drink, even when it's toward the end of a party and it's someone you've been talking to for a while. You don't really know the person, and they could be setting you up. Always get your own drink so you will always know what you are drinking.

- If you're not sure whether your beverage has been spiked, leave it. Get another drink.

- If your drink has been spiked, you will likely feel dizzy, sleepy, or as if you are going to be sick or faint. You will likely lose consciousness quickly. You *must* tell someone, be it friends, bar staff, or security. If no one you know can help you, you *must* call 911. Do not trust a stranger, even another woman, to help you. This is extremely serious and can end up with you in the hospital or worse.

- Try not to drink premixed cocktails or punches when you don't know the ingredients. Avoid the punch bowl unless it's a family gathering. Stick with liquid straight out of a bottle that you either hold yourself (beer) or watch being poured directly from a bottle.

- Try to get a drink with a lid and a straw or just a lid. If you can't, cover your drink with a napkin or your other palm.
- Eat before and while you're drinking.
- Go to parties with a group. Have a plan to get home. Leave with the people you came with. No one should be left behind, and no one should leave alone. Have a conversation about it before you go.
- Have a designated sober driver. If it's you, honor the deal.
- Count the number of drinks you have. Set a limit and stick to it. You know how much alcohol you can or can't handle.
- If your friends are really your friends, you will watch after them and they will watch after you.
- *Remember, no friend gets left behind.* Do not let anyone in your group leave alone with a guy she just met. Tell her to settle for giving him her phone number. If the intentions are sincere, he will call.
- Absolutely no drinking "games." They should really call them what they are: get-women-drunk-and-assault-them games.
- If your designated sober driver drinks or does drugs, call a ride service.
- Don't be afraid to say no. If you don't want to drink or continue drinking, say no, or if you feel that's just going to bring unwanted attention, carry a cup full of soda or water. And a word to the wise: if your friends mock you for not drinking, you have the wrong "friends." Trust me, I've been there.
- If you wake up in a strange place, call the police pronto.

PART THREE

Travel Safe!
Don't Become a Statistic

CHAPTER FIFTEEN

South of the Border, Abroad, and Domestic Travel

Growing up on a red-dirt road in rural Georgia, I knew I wanted to go *somewhere*. But I didn't know enough about the world to even know where. Then over time, through books and the single TV station signal that filtered its way down the giant antenna on the back of our roof, I found out there was a whole world out there waiting to be explored.

I can still remember my first plane trip; it was shortly after my fiancé was murdered. I flew to Philadelphia to stay awhile with my sister, who taught at the Wharton School. At the time, I was overcome with grief and not in a tourist state of mind. But I do distinctly remember looking out the window at the clouds and wondering if Keith was in them.

After that one plane ticket, I really couldn't afford any more plane trips. But I had another chance at travel. My dad, Mac, was a railroad man for over forty years, and with that came a pass for free travel for his wife and children. I couldn't believe I was so lucky! Just fourteen or fifteen hours and I could be in Philly. So, I'd take the train back and forth to Philadelphia from the old Amtrak train station in Atlanta.

Later, I learned to dive and traveled from one dive spot to the next, but I spent most of my time underwater. I only came up, exhausted, to have a quick dinner and crash, never exploring beyond the ocean floor.

After each dive trip, I realized a little more of what I had been longing for on that red-dirt road where there was nothing but soybean fields and tall pine trees as far as the eye could see. Looking through my dive mask, it became clearer to me: I wanted to see what was beyond the pine trees, beyond the edges of Bibb County, Georgia.

Looking back, I guess I was bitten by the travel bug before I even knew I had the fever. Now, all these years later, I want to take our twins, John David and Lucy, to see the world. And I want to see it with them.

I want to take them to all the wonderful places whose names I didn't know as a child. But now, I have to say, whenever I consider traveling with them, I also consider the downside of travel.

Frankly, I almost wish I didn't. I wonder sometimes if it's better to merely dream of something beautiful rather than discover that it's not exactly what you think it is at all. But knowledge is power and, when you leave your own red-dirt road, I want you wearing all the armor possible.

We'll start our discussion of travel safety where Americans travel most frequently, Mexico and the Caribbean.

TRAVELING SAFELY SOUTH OF THE BORDER

AMERICAN WOMAN KILLED IN MEXICO AFTER U.S. ISSUES TRAVEL WARNINGS
The headline leapt off the page at me when I read it in the summer of 2018. Travel advisory? What travel advisory? I dived all over Mexico for years with my dive buddies and never heard of any travel warnings. I remember those sugar-white beaches and the bright turquoise blue water of Cozumel. How could it be that bad? But I read on.

Mexican police were investigating a murder. The victim was a twenty-seven-year-old traveling in Mexico with her husband and celebrating their first wedding anniversary. Raised in Chicago, Tatiana Mirutenko had moved to San Francisco for a job with a pharmaceutical company. She had visited Mexico over thirty times, said her heartbroken dad, and she loved the country—the number one tourist destination for Americans crossing US borders.

One of Tatiana's fun dreams was, as I like to say, to fly in and eat my way out. She wanted to try out all the best dishes in Mexico on her anniversary.

On the trip, she and her husband dined at two of the top-rated restaurants in the world, Pujol and Quintonil, in one of Mexico City's upscale neighborhoods, Lomas de Chapultepec. Tatiana loved the dining. She even texted her mom and dad photos of the food. How many of us have done the very same thing?

While walking after dinner in Lomas de Chapultepec, Tatiana was struck and killed instantly by a stray bullet from a shooter passing by on a motorcycle. The intended target was a bouncer, who was wounded but survived.

Tatiana came home to her parents not in a first-class seat next to her husband but in the cargo bay, her body cooled in a casket for burial. That's the harsh truth. Tatiana Mirutenko became a statistic, one of over twenty-five thousand murders in Mexico in 2018, according to Mexican police.

How many homicides have there *really* been? Think about it.

Tatiana's dad says that just one year earlier, they were choosing flowers for his daughter's wedding. And now, they had to pick flowers for her funeral.

Reality check: the US State Department has in the past issued a level 4 "Do Not Travel" advisory for major parts of Mexico. This is the same level travel warning set for incendiary states like Iraq, Syria, and Afghanistan.

Translation?

Before you travel to Mexico, check for State Department advisories and do not put a single toe in any region of Mexico with strong advisories in place and, according to the US State Department, exercise increased caution if traveling to any part of Mexico at all. While there are often US State Department travel advisories regarding Mexico, apparently nobody's listening, because last year alone, 35 million tourists threw caution to the wind to travel there. And that number is growing. After Tatiana's murder, homicides have only risen in the tropical "paradise," especially in the US tourist magnet Acapulco, which is often one of the top murder spots in the world each year.

It's not just a matter of armed criminals, pickpockets, and swindlers. It's not just dopers and gangbangers fighting drug wars over turf and money. We know well that Americans risk shootings, gang wars, assault, and sexual attacks across the border. But now we are learning that tainted alcohol flows like water at luxury resorts and that death is a distinct possibility while relaxing in a major US tourist haven.

ABBEY CONNER

I will never forget meeting the dad of a brilliant young American girl on the television studio set belonging to my friend Dr. Oz. I had studied the case carefully, but when I met Abbey Conner's dad, Bill, I learned so much more, especially about what else is happening south of the border.

In January 2017, the Conner family traveled from Wisconsin for a dream vacation to Playa del Carmen, Mexico. They settled into a fancy, five-star resort, but two hours after checking in, Abbey, just twenty years old, was found floating facedown in a hotel pool at the Iberostar Paraiso del Mar resort. Nearby was her brother, twenty-three-year-old Austin, also facedown in the pool. As their dad told me in detail what happened, his voice cracked.

Other guests realized something was horribly wrong when they spotted both siblings floating facedown in the pool. Abbey had a broken collarbone and was most likely already brain-dead. Austin was out cold with a concussion and a huge lump the size of a golf ball on his head.

When Abbey and Austin didn't show up for dinner, their mom, Ginny, tried to call them. Around that time, an Iberostar employee rushed over to Ginny with a manager, who said there had been an "accident." By that point, the siblings had already been fished out of the pool and taken to a local hospital, but Ginny says she and her husband weren't notified. Abbey's dad told me that once they realized the local hospital there in Mexico was not equipped to help, they had Abbey air-lifted to a Florida hospital, but to no avail. Abbey passed away a few days later.

Even now, brother Austin insists there was no accident. He vividly recalls the two of them going to the pool, swimming, and then getting a seat at the poolside bar. There was a group of people there that the two didn't know, but they joined them and started talking. Austin says the bartender poured a line of shots and everyone there took one. The last thing he remembers was sitting there talking. And then he woke up in an ambulance.

But how do two people end up facedown in waist-deep water in the pool with a blow to the head and a broken collarbone? And no one, especially resort employees, saw a thing?

It's no surprise that local Mexican officials declared Abbey's death accidental, but Bill told me local police refused to investigate. Even when they hired an interpreter and went to the local police department in person, they say police refused to make a report.

Iberostar Paraiso del Mar Resort insists they acted appropriately and with urgency, but Abbey's family disagrees. They are adamant Abbey was served tainted alcohol rising to the level of poisonous and have filed a lawsuit against the resort and the US booking website. Their suit says that the alcohol confiscated from the resort contained toxic methanol, there were no lifeguards on duty as there should have been, and there was no surveillance. To top it all off, they say the resort refused to let their investigators on the property.

As a matter of fact, supporting these claims, Mexican law enforcement reportedly conducted raids and seized over 1.4 million gallons of tainted alcohol from Mexican resorts, bars, clubs, and businesses. The family's wrongful death filing says Abbey's death was "entirely avoidable" and that Iberostar hotels knew tainted alcohol was being served.

After Abbey's completely unnecessary death, Mexican authorities swarmed more than thirty establishments to seize even more alcohol being stored in unsanitary conditions. According to reports, hundreds of gallons in one seized stash of alcohol contained extremely dangerous levels of methanol, a dangerous chemical found in windshield washer fluid. Another American woman, Kathy Daley, stated she too is convinced she drank tainted alcohol at a Mexican Iberostar hotel in 2017. She says she couldn't get out of the pool or stand up and was vomiting.

In fact, the *Milwaukee Journal Sentinel* began an intensive investigation and amassed over two hundred US tourist reports of like incidents at luxury resorts all over Mexico. The fact that you may be staying in a five-star resort may mean nothing. Iberostar refutes the report, but the State Department has now clearly warned Americans traveling to Mexico to consume alcohol in moderation and immediately seek medical attention if they feel sick. Sadly, as grateful as I am for the advisories, no warning, investigation, or exposé will bring Abbey back.

My concern only deepened after I had a chance to leave the *Dr. Oz* set and talk with Abbey's dad one on one. I started wondering how many other innocent American travelers were losing their lives on dream vacations. With crime rates in Mexico skyrocketing, I discovered that even the resort island of Cancún, one of my old dive spots, is setting new records for murders. I had no idea what was happening around me when I was there. Just recently, three trash bags of human remains from more than one victim were found dumped in western Cancún early one weekday morning. Even in 2017, tiny, once peaceful Cancún had a whopping 227 murders. In 2018, it more than doubled to a record 540.

The overall crime rates in Mexico are even more disturbing. *There were 16,339 homicides reported in Mexico in just the first seven months of 2017,* including 953 murders in Acapulco alone. American tourists like Tatiana have been shot by stray bullets and gunned down at restaurants and nightclubs, and bodies riddled with bullets have been found on beaches and in trash bags. And there is no sign of improvement. As a matter of fact, as we go to print, Mexico's interior ministry announced that murders increased by 33 percent in 2018. In raw numbers that means 33,341 murder investigations versus 25,036 in 2017.

I keep thinking about Tatiana. I think about what her parents and husband have gone through. A feeling of helplessness washes over me when my work brings me to these kinds of stories. Studying the research, I wondered, could it be that more Americans are reported homicide victims in Mexico than in all other foreign destinations put together?

I went to the State Department website and read the travel advisories. This is what I found:

We want you to know the danger of traveling to high-risk places and to strongly consider not going to them at all. Traveling to high-risk locations puts your life, and possibly the lives of others, in jeopardy. Traveling to high-risk areas puts you at increased risk for kidnapping, hostage-taking, theft, and serious injury.

They specifically warn:

Exercise increased caution in Mexico due to crime and kidnapping. Some areas have increased risk.

Here is more from the travel advisory:

Violent crime, such as homicide, kidnapping, carjacking, and robbery, is widespread. The U.S. government has limited ability to provide emergency services to U.S. citizens in many areas of Mexico as travel by U.S. government employees to these areas is prohibited or significantly restricted.

U.S. government employees may not travel between cities after dark, may not hail taxis on the street, and must rely on dispatched vehicles, including from app-based services like Uber, or those from regulated taxi stands. U.S. government employees may not drive from the U.S.-Mexico border to or from the interior parts of Mexico with the exception of daytime travel within Baja, California, and between Nogales and Hermosillo on Mexican Federal Highway 15D.

If the US government places all these restrictions on its own employees while they are in Mexico, what does that mean for the rest of us? Think about it. They go on to insist that we do not travel to Colima state due to crime, Guerrero state due to crime, Michoacán state due to crime, Sinaloa state due to crime, and the Tamaulipas state due to crime and kidnapping. All these regions in Mexico include tourist spots.

IF YOU DO TRAVEL TO MEXICO

The State Department provides the following tips for those traveling in Mexico:

- Use toll roads when possible and avoid driving alone or at night. In many states, police presence and emergency services are extremely limited outside the state capital or major cities.
- Exercise increased caution when visiting local bars, nightclubs, and casinos.
- Do not display signs of wealth, such as wearing expensive watches or jewelry.
- Be extra vigilant when visiting banks or ATMs.
- Enroll in the Smart Traveler Enrollment Program (STEP) to receive alerts and make it easier to locate you in an emergency.
- Follow the Department of State on Facebook and Twitter.
- Review the Crime and Safety Reports for Mexico.
- U.S. citizens who travel abroad should always have a contingency plan for emergency situations. Review the Traveler's Checklist.

Bottom line: when the US issues a travel warning, *listen*.

According to my research and backed up by *Forbes Magazine* in 2016, more Americans are killed in Mexico than in all other countries combined.

After discovering these harsh realities about travel to Mexico, I asked, *What else am I missing?*

BELIZE, JAMAICA, ARUBA

I began to research other travel victims. The statistics were surprising and spread beyond the borders of Mexico. I researched the case of an American, Drew DeVoursney, and his girlfriend, Francesca Matus, who went missing in Belize. My sister-in-law and her husband traveled to Belize for their honeymoon and loved it. They tell me they didn't spot a thing that seemed dangerous. Just a few short years later, that sadly wasn't true for Drew and Francesca.

It all started in May 2017 when a friend went to pick the couple up and drive them to the airport in Belize. Francesca was headed for Toronto, and Drew was flying home to Atlanta. Drew had attended Montreat College in North Carolina but left to join the Marines after September 11 and did multiple tours in Iraq. Francesca was a beloved mom of two and was looking forward to coming home. But when their friend Michael arrived, the gate was closed and no one was home. Their cars were both gone, but Drew's bicycle was still parked in the driveway. Another friend, Joseph, says he had just seen them that Tuesday night at a local hangout, Scotty's Bar and Grill, in the coastal tourist town of Corozal, near the Mexican border.

Realizing their absence was totally out of character, he immediately reported the two missing. The mystery only deepened when Francesca's Isuzu Rodeo was found hidden among tall stalks in a remote sugarcane field ten miles from Scotty's. Police brought in scent dogs, and it was only one day later that the bodies of Francesca and Drew were discovered in Corozal. Investigators determined they were victims of a double homicide. Autopsies revealed they were strangled to death. They were already in advanced decomposition, but the coroner observed that both had had their wrists taped.

Strangled dead and wrists taped? Bodies dumped? Car abandoned in a sugarcane field? What?

You'd never suspect it if you look at touristy descriptions of Belize, a "sleepy, seaside" country on the bay of the Caribbean Sea whose coastal waters are "milky-blue." No one would ever believe what is happening there. On the northern border of Belize are attractions like the old English Fort Barley and ancient Mayan ruins. Corozal claims to be a perfect base for fishing in the bay and tourist shopping trips to Chetumal and is even host to bird and wildlife at Shipstern Nature

Reserve. The serene picture is ruined when we learn about strangled Americans with their wrists taped.

The risk level in Belize is not to be ignored. In 2019, it had the world's fourth-highest murder rate, 44.7 per 100,000, said the United Nations Office on Drugs and Crime. Keep in mind that figure is per capita for a small population. It also has an extremely high general crime rate, according to the Overseas Security Advisory Council, although burglaries and theft make up most of those crimes.

Belize is not the only paradise with problems. If the name Desiree Gibbon doesn't ring a bell, it soon will. Twenty-six-year-old Desiree, from Hollis, New York, absolutely loved Jamaican culture and had visited there with her mom and family many times. Her happy times there came to an end on her last trip to the American tourist haven when her body, with her clothes soaked in blood, was discovered in bushes along a local road in St. James Parish, Jamaica, in January 2017. Her throat had been slit, and her torso, legs, and wrists were covered in bruises. Desiree, a model and aspiring documentary filmmaker, was last seen three nights before her body was found.

Hotel surveillance video spotted her dressed in a favorite T-shirt, shorts, sandals, and a bandana. She's seen calmly walking from her hotel that evening with her cell phone and turning left. She was never seen alive again. Her mom, Andrea Cali-Gibbon, has watched the video repeatedly, hoping for clues. None have come.

Local police showed no interest in the surveillance video, which was brought to their attention by Desiree's family. Desiree's murder, just four miles from the famed Montego Bay, only highlights the soaring murder rate in Jamaica as the tourist industry tries its best to downplay it.

The only update? Her parents flew down to Jamaica to identify and claim their daughter's body. Her mom ended up clutching a crucifix beside Desiree's coffin inside the same Queens church where Desiree was baptized and received First Communion. No future, no film school. It was all cut short in the tourist hotspot of Jamaica.

Of course, the island of Aruba became world famous when American high school beauty and honor student Natalee Holloway went missing there on her senior trip. Natalee's body has never been found. I have spent hours with Natalee's mom, Beth; her dad, Dave Holloway; and her then stepdad, George "Jug" Twitty. Their pain of losing Natalee will never go away.

But Natalee isn't the only American girl to disappear in Aruba. I also investigated the case of American Robyn Gardner. Another stunner, Robyn was in Aruba vacationing when the Maryland native seemingly disappeared into thin air in 2011.

Both women went missing from the same tourist town, Oranjestad, known for its resorts and casinos. Reports are that Gardner must have simply been "swept away" while snorkeling in tranquil waters off Baby Beach. Again, as in the Natalee Holloway case, it seems Aruban police have done everything possible to thwart the investigations. Is it because of a potential black eye on the Aruban tourist machine? Neither body has ever been found, and to this day, no arrests have been made in their disappearances. Natalee and Robyn are just two of many Americans who've gone missing in Aruba and whose cases have never been solved.

Why?

GIRLS' GETAWAY TRIP TURNS DEADLY

How many times have I been asked by friends to go on a girls' getaway? So far, I've never gone on such a trip because of work and family, but another female lawyer managed to make it happen. In October 2018, Marie Kuhnla, a respected lawyer with Suffolk County Legal Aid, went on a girls-only vacation with some friends and one of their daughters. Marie never came back.

The ladies headed to an exclusive Club Med resort in Turks and Caicos. They had a great time snorkeling, doing water aerobics, and singing karaoke. In fact, Marie declared over and over it was the best vacation she'd ever taken. One Sunday afternoon, Marie went to her room for a nap. No one saw her that night but everyone assumed she was still sleeping. The next morning, when Marie didn't answer her door, her group knew instinctively something was very wrong. They say the resort wouldn't help at first, so they started searching on their own. The friend's daughter found Marie, strangled dead, in some bushes and tall grass at the edge of the resort. She was described as a "gentle soul," and her family is still searching for answers.

How did an educated woman, familiar with criminal activity as a defense lawyer and not one to drink, drug, or party, end up going from a Sunday afternoon nap to strangled dead in the bushes of an expensive Club Med resort?

What, if anything, could have changed the course of these events? I'm not quite sure, but foreign travel has a set of concerns that you should take to heart so that your dream trip doesn't end up a nightmare.

DOMINICAN REPUBLIC

More than two million Americans visit the Dominican Republic each year. The island is an attractive island paradise. However, a word of caution is appropriate. In 2018 and 2019, a total of six American tourists died at resorts in the Dominican Republic. Tainted alcohol appears to be involved, but until toxicology reports are released, it is impossible to assign a cause of death. It is frustrating that these reports are not available, as the earliest cases are more than a year old. If you plan to go there, try to get the latest information on these deaths and factor it into your decision.

TIPS FOR INTERNATIONAL TRAVEL

- The first rule of travel abroad is be prepared. It's not just for Boy Scouts. Safe travel starts before you leave.
- Research your destination. Read traveler reviews, and once you arrive, ask people you meet on location for the safest areas, restaurants, sightseeing spots, hotels, and events. Set off with knowledge of your surroundings, attitudes toward Americans, social mores, local practices, as well as local crimes and scams. Be informed about where you are headed. Learn which areas are safe and which are dangerous, and specifically for you as an American. You are easily recognizable abroad as an American. As you travel, know you have a bull's-eye on your jacket.
- Before you leave home, look at the US State Department website and find travel tips and country updates. The State Department also has a Smart Traveler Enrollment Program. It's brilliant.
- Arrive in daylight hours. This will allow you to get your bearings

and see where you are staying, judge the neighborhood for safety, and see how to get around there. You may also see the local transit system and how to use it.

- Study a map before you leave to get a general understanding of where you are headed, including landmarks. It could be a lifesaver.

- Learn the language. Definitely learn important phrases in that language, such as "Call police," "I'm in trouble," "Where's my hotel?" It could be critical if you become the victim of a crime or are afraid. You'll be in much better shape if you can speak at all on your own to police, doctors, or dentists. There are many online courses to help you grasp a basic-level understanding of any language. As a fallback, my eleven-year-old twins told me how to learn phrases on my cell phone. They love it. You type or say the word into the app, and it speaks and writes the same phrase in whatever language you choose—pretty great.

- Get travel insurance. Some plans guarantee emergency evacuation assistance and emergency medical care around the clock every day of the year.

- Mark your luggage with something distinctive in addition to just tags. This move protects you from a con man trying to switch your loaded bags for empty lookalikes.

- Be vigilant at transfer points, when you are going from one place to the next, such as airplane to baggage pickup, baggage pickup to cab, cab to lobby, check-in to room, hotel to next hotel. Traveling from one place to another with all your things is a perfect time for thieves to strike. Huge airports and train stations are the perfect hunting ground for bad actors.

- Watch your things carefully. Intended thefts or robberies can turn into something much more serious. Keep an eye on your belongings and safeguard them within your hotel as well. That may very well stop a life-threatening incident before it happens.

- Don't make it easy for pickpockets: Tie the two zipper tags of your backpack or handbag together with a black shoelace or sturdy string. It won't prevent an aggressive thief from trying to rob you, but it may buy you time to react. It will also keep those zippers reliably closed as you run through an airport.

- Stay together at airports. Don't get separated from your party.

Make Plans

- Plan out your day before you leave the hotel and have a clear idea of your route, be it by foot, car, or public transit.
- Most hotels hand you your keys in a small folded piece of cardstock paper. It's nice, but it also has all of your pertinent information in one place: your hotel and your room number. If someone gets that from you while you're out and about, they'll also know you're not in that room. Throw the paper away or leave it behind.
- Use a tour guide who is experienced and has a good reputation, especially when you head for a remote or isolated area, such as archeological sites, ruins, or the countryside.
- Never accept beverages, cigarettes, gum, or snacks of any sort from people you first meet while traveling. Many drugs have no smell or taste.
- Steer clear of protests that may turn violent.
- Try not to drive after dark, and always keep a full tank of gas. Other countries may not have twenty-four-hour roadside assistance.
- Safety isn't a negotiable item: You must be smart about it. And being smart includes wearing a seat belt in any vehicle in which you travel. Buckle up. Always. Everywhere.

Money Matters and Skimming

Only get cash from inside a bank or from the staff at the front desk of the hotel (which is a distant second choice, but often happens outside bankers' hours).

Beware of skimming. ATMs anywhere in the world can be used to copy your bank card data completely, remotely, and automatically. You won't even know it's happening. ATMs are usually skimmed in public spots at common areas in malls, gas stations, and stores with lots of foot traffic.

Skimmers are practically undetectable. Victims are totally blindsided and only find out they've been robbed when fraud shows up on their accounts even though their debit or credit card never left their possession.

Here's how it works. Thieves attach a small device to the ATM so that when your card is swiped, the device grabs and keeps all the information stored in the thin magnetic strip on the back of your card, including your name, the card number, and the expiration date. Then the crook takes all that data to use your card online or create a fake credit card containing very real credit information... yours.

Sometimes the crook can also place a tiny and unnoticed camera near the ATM that records you entering your PIN. With the PIN, the fraudster can make cash withdrawals from your ATM. When you use an ATM, lean forward and shield the keypad the moment you enter your password. And for Pete's sake, don't blurt it out to a family member or anyone else who may be doing the transaction for you.

Be aware that some shopkeepers and restaurant workers work with skimmer rings. When you hand over your card, that's their chance to simply swipe it through a skimmer. You won't find out until your card gets declined somewhere, usually at a very inopportune moment, or you look at your account online and find charges and withdrawals you never made. By then, the damage is done. As I often say, go with your gut. If the place feels shady, use cash or shop or eat elsewhere.

Use a credit or debit card that gives you support 24/7/365. My card does, and quite often they call me when they spot an odd charge. (It's American Express and I hate the yearly fee, but the company is great regarding fraud protection.)

Know the phone numbers to block your cards if they are stolen, including the international ones. It's in the fine print on the back of your credit card, but you need to have it stored elsewhere in case you lose the physical card.

Leave the Jewelry at Home

Don't flash your cash or your valuables. Why travel with expensive or sentimental jewelry? I've done it, and it drives me crazy the whole trip. It wasn't anything expensive or extravagant; just my grandmother Lucy's engagement ring. I wore or carried it for decades. Then I didn't know what to do with it when all jewelry started to inflame a rash on my hands. I was afraid to leave it in hotel rooms when I dived, so I'd wrap it in tissue and stick it down my bra. Ridiculous. But I did that for years because I didn't want to be apart from her ring.

There were many, many near catastrophes with Mamaa's ring, but I finally decided to stop traveling with it when I had a major scare during my stint on *Dancing with the Stars*.

I was with David and the twins at the Santa Monica Pier, enjoying the rides and playing games. I threw a ball and my actual wedding band flew off my finger because I had lost so much weight dancing! After we spent forever digging through a ball pit to find the ring, I stopped traveling with both. It took a near catastrophe for me. Don't let that be you. Leave treasured, irreplaceable items safely at home.

Parading expensive jewelry is crazy. Your designer shoes, your watch, even your camera could be many times more valuable than the monthly or even annual local income of everyday people in your destination. People will do anything to survive. Don't be their victim.

Don't travel with valuables or wads of cash. If you must, use the lobby safe to store them. If you travel with them and can't use the lobby safe, at the very least use an anti-theft daypack or backpack. Still, even that adds on a whole host of problems, because in many venues backpacks and daypacks are not allowed in for security reasons.

Keep your passport with you or in the lobby safe. Keep it close to your body, for instance, in a money belt under your clothes, zipped inside an interior pocket, or in a bra holder.

There is an entire industry devoted to anti-theft travel clothing, from anti-slash fabrics for purses and clothes to hidden zippers, protective passport pockets, and even RFID (radio-frequency identification) protective wallets and passport sleeves. (Not only are credit, debit, and ID cards identity theft targets, but so are all your wireless devices like laptops, phones, tablets, and car key fobs. This is because each of these send wireless signals that can be intercepted and used by crooks.)

For those of us who are less techy, we can still go old-school with the commonsense approaches I outlined above. I do, however, really like the anti-theft clothing, and it comes in every type you can imagine. From long pants to shorts, shirts, hoodies, coats—they make it all now. These clothes, purses, and backpacks look like regular brands but there's a difference: cell phone pockets, secure wallet compartments, secret passport pockets, expandable pockets to hold maps or guidebooks, and even hidey-holes for items you carry along with you, all sewn into your clothing. They are usually lightweight and water resistant, which I really like. It's all easy to find online.

Don't Get Scammed

I'm more concerned about your life and safety than I am about your possessions, but so often we hear of scams aiming to get money or stuff that suddenly "go bad," and the victim ends up assaulted or dead. Travel guidebooks can detail all the local scams, but here are a few.

In the mustard scam, someone "accidentally" sprays mustard, ketchup, or other liquid onto your jacket or shirt. When someone offers to "help," they pick your pocket, stealing your valuables while wiping off or cleaning your shirt or jacket.

The classic taxi scam is prevalent. Either the meter runs superfast or the cabbie claims the meter is broken. Avoid this by knowing how much the ride should cost. Ask at the front desk before you head out. If the driver tries to work a deal for the rate, offer the correct amount. If he refuses, get out. Routinely try to get the driver's ID number when you first get in.

Never get in a gypsy cab, ghost cab, or dark cab. They're unlicensed no matter what you call them. Don't do it no matter how honest the guy seems and no matter what great deal he offers you. Registered radio taxis are the safest choice. You can ask for them at your hotel or call them yourself. You can also have someone at a restaurant or bar call them. When using a registered radio taxi (which you order by phone), there is a record of who picked you up, their registration number, your pickup location, and your destination. That leaves much less room for perps to hijack you or your money as opposed to unregistered gypsy cabs, which are essentially undetectable when reporting an incident.

Also, use your cell when riding in a cab. It gives you the ability to find the best route for yourself via Google Maps, MapQuest, Waze, or whichever app you pick. I do it loud and proud in the back seat of cabs and Ubers. I don't mean to suggest their directions are wrong, but it makes me feel more secure, so I do it anyway.

Walk away from any street game you come across, like three-card monte or shell games. Why do people still fall for these? When traveling, you see people playing games on the streets of tourist areas and suddenly, you decide you can beat the con. You *will* lose. It's not a legitimate game; it's a con.

Refuse "free" items like rosary beads, a cross, a rose, or really anything. The con man or woman insists on giving you something and then wants money. It's happened to me with a red rose. I had little Lucy with me, and I gave it back.

In the bike and scooter scam, you rent a bicycle, scooter, or motorcycle. You have fun, then bring it back. Then the owner suddenly claims there are additional charges or even that there are necessary "repairs" because of damage you caused. How to beat it? Take cell phone photos of the bike before you head out with it. The photo will show the true condition of the bike before you used it. Walk around the rental before you use it with the owner, so they know you are taking the photos. Be careful with the bike. Some scams include the owner sending someone to "steal" the bike, so you have to pay for it in full. Act like you own it until you return it.

The big flirt happens when you travel overseas and suddenly you are a magnet for the opposite gender. Locals love you. You have the greatest conversations with this local you just met.

Could it be love?

No. It could not be love. It's a scam. Con artists prey on people traveling alone or without a bestie there to warn them. Don't wake up after a native slips you a roofie (GHB) to find your money and valuables gone or worse. Look for love when you get back home.

Oops, someone gave you the wrong change. But it's no accident. Currency overseas can look similar and difficult to compute. Scammers intentionally give you the wrong change and short you. They hope you won't notice. Take the time to get familiar with the currency. And count your change.

I could list scams all day. You can find more of them and ones specific to where you are traveling online. I don't want you to lose your money, but more so, I don't want a scam to blow up and you to get hurt.

More Commonsense Travel Tips

- Only carry the cash you will need for that day, and use cash first if you can. Use credit cards sparingly if possible.
- Copy your passport. Leave a few copies at home before you go.
- Travel lightly. It's easier to keep eyes on your belongings, they're easier to handle, and it allows you to be hands-free more often when walking about.

- Going out at night? Try to go in a group.
- Don't get drunk or high. Bad things happen. You become a very easy target. And there's nobody to call because you are in a foreign country, away from home, family, and friends. Staying alert means staying sober. You can't make good decisions if your judgment is clouded by drugs or alcohol.
- When you are out, guard your drink. It's so easy for anyone to slip a roofie into your drink.
- After going out at night, either return to your hotel with a group or take a cab, Uber, or Lyft. Don't walk home alone.
- Never change money on the street or out in public places such as flea markets or street fairs. Use small bills. This approach reduces the chance you will fall prey to the wrong-change scam or someone mugging you for all the money you're flashing.
- Keep a list of emergency numbers on paper that you carry with you. Include numbers for your hotel, other local contact numbers such as friends or tour guides, local emergency services like ambulance, police, and fire, as well as the US embassy. Keep the list on you as well as having an electronic backup stored on your cell phone. Keep a copy elsewhere in case you lose your phone or it gets damaged, such as in your email's inbox or in the cloud. Program the numbers into your phone as well.
- Don't keep your wallet, cash, credit cards, ID, passport, and checks in one wallet or place. Lock anything you are not using that day in the hotel lobby safe. If you carry more than one of these items on your person, place them in different spots or pockets.
- Don't carry things like your wallet, keys, passport, cash, or cell phone in your back pocket. That's a pickpocket's dream.
- If you must carry any of those items with you, keep them to your front as well as in different locations on your body, including multiple pockets. If you insist on carrying a purse, wear it across your body with your hand resting on it in front of you. Never, ever let it dangle from one shoulder or wear it cross-shoulder to the back. Likewise, when you sit down, keep your bags in front of you at the table in your lap or on the floor where your ankles or feet can feel them. Wrap the strap around your ankle or chair.
- Always look back to check your table or seat for forgotten items when you leave, be it your airplane seat or your seat at the dinner table.

- If they're a stranger, they're a danger. Don't strike up conversations or get sucked into yakking with strangers. Do not blurt out personal information. Strangers do not need to hear your life story. If they ask for it, there's a reason, and it may not be a nice one.
- Never become careless or be lulled into a false sense of safety. You are not on home turf.
- Beware of panhandlers and beggars wherever you are. I know it hurts to see those less fortunate than we are. In 2018, police in Pelham, New York, issued a be-on-the-lookout announcement after a brutal assault on the local subway platform. Police were on the hunt for two suspects, a woman and a man, who savagely beat a commuter after he brushed by them when they insisted he fork over money to them at the station. Around five a.m. on a Monday, the sixty-one-year-old victim walked past the panhandler and kept walking toward the platform. The male panhandler followed him, punched him in the face several times, and then dragged him downstairs into the street, where the beating continued and the perp tried to rip his bag from his shoulders. It was all caught on video, including the female accomplice circling the victim like a wolf before joining in the beating. That was right here in America. Abroad, where begging is often well beyond what we see in the states, many criminals pose as beggars. You are the mark. Be careful.
- Don't use your credit card at internet cafés. There's a fox in the henhouse. Perps use key-logging software on the computers in trendy internet cafés. You get a cup of overpriced coffee and gab to friends back home; the thief gets your credit card info.
- Actually, stay away from public Wi-Fi in general. Why? Because public Wi-Fi makes it so easy for crooks to hack into your cell phone or laptop. Try a portable router to easily set up your own Wi-Fi hotspot in your room. All you need is a SIM card, which is sold at airports and kiosks. You could set up a virtual private network (VPN) through a simple app or use your own cell phone hotspot (with a security code).

Blend In

Once you get to your destination, blend. Merge into your surroundings. Try to become invisible. The clothes you pick matter. Muted, plain and simple clothing is nearly always best when traveling. Wearing an Atlanta Braves baseball cap or an "I love NY" T-shirt, no matter how awesome we think they are, will send a message loud and clear. That message is "I'm a tourist; take advantage of me."

Blending means not sticking out with your expensive American designer clothes, dripping in jewelry and sporting two-hundred-dollar running shoes or the equivalent.

Don't look at maps out in the open, and be super careful when you approach someone to ask for help. Displaying lots of jewelry and wearing your Louis Vuitton jogging suit with a map hanging out of your Gucci purse is not a good look. The cons will see you coming a mile away.

Stay Connected but Keep It Private

- Check in back home regularly. Let them know where you are and how to reach you. I will never forget my mom and dad raising the alarm when I was on a dive trip. They were right. I had a dive mishap and had one toe in a decompression chamber when I got through to them. When I missed my regular call, they were on alert. They, thousands of miles away, knew when they hadn't heard from me that something was terribly wrong. My call calmed them, but had they not heard from me, they might have begun efforts to locate me, and if my situation were worse, their actions would have saved valuable time.

- Enable location tracking and install remote wipe software onto your smartphone. If your cell phone is lost or stolen, you can track it down. The remote wipe software can destroy or remove all data on your phone, ensuring that a perp can't get access to private information about your identity, children, travel plans, credit, and finances.

- Password protect your cell with a strong and uncommon password.

- Don't post your activities on social media. Con men have Facebook and Twitter just like you. Don't advertise your trip, your hotel, your day trips, or any place you go where you don't want uninvited company. And deactivate geotagging on your photos.

- Guard views of your hands when you type in your PIN, codes, passwords, and user IDs. High-res cameras can catch every stroke so that thieves can reproduce them. If you don't thoughtfully protect this information, you might as well blare out your PIN over a loudspeaker at the local flea market.

- Don't bring your Social Security card or birth certificate with you. You don't need either.
- Don't take all your credit cards with you. One or two will suffice.
- Try your best to stay in public view when alone. Avoid remote or isolated areas, such as lonely beaches or hiking trails—even more so at night.
- Look at maps inside a shop or restaurant, not out on the street like a confused, bewildered tourist—that is, an easy mark. Maps are a great aid if you don't know the language. You can simply point to where you want to go.
- Beware of all strangers, male or female. When out and about, do not just be wary of men on the take. Do not assume that the women you meet on vacation are safer than men. This is not correct. In some situations, yes, women or groups of women can provide a haven from danger. But not always. Be careful and don't assume all women are not threats.

Identity Theft

Predators come in all shapes and sizes. I've been covering the case of Lois Riess, a mom who went missing from her home in Blooming Prairie, Minnesota, since it first started. My blood ran cold when video of her emerged at a Florida seafood restaurant chatting up another woman, Pamela Hutchinson, at the bar. Why? Because at that time I knew there was a multi-state manhunt for Riess, wanted for murdering her husband. And why was she chatting up another blonde at a bar over a thousand miles away from home? Because she was looking for a female look-alike so Riess could kill her and assume her identity. Which is what she did to Pamela.

After the scene at the restaurant, Riess then left her second victim's dead body cooling in her Florida condo, driving off in Pamela's car with her identity and credit cards while wearing Pamela's straw hat. Assuming Pamela's identity, Riess headed for the Mexican border. She was finally apprehended at a luxury resort chatting up yet another female döppelganger. I guess Riess needed another lookalike's identity to assume in order to get across the border.

Translation? Don't trust a woman any more than you would a man.

For more on preventing identity theft, especially online, see the tips in chapters 18 and 19. All of the security precautions I offer have an overwhelming message of protecting your personal information and identity. You must make every effort to be safe and secure, online and in everyday life.

Be as Smart as Your Phone

Be vigilant when you get inbound calls to your hotel or cell phone. Don't hand over sensitive information on inbound calls.

Let's say you get a call from your credit card company or bank, reporting fraud. Hang up. Call the number on the back of your card. Under no circumstances do you divulge your card number, passcodes, or any other sensitive information unless and until you can confirm that caller. Similarly, do not trust a call from inside your hotel. If someone calls about a repair, the AC or heat, a delivery, or packages, hang up and call the front desk. Someone physically in the hotel may be trying to get access to you or your room.

Outsiders can call the main desk and then get transferred several times so that by the time their call gets to your room, it appears as though the call is coming from inside the hotel. And never, never carry on a conversation with a so-called wrong number.

HOTEL SAFETY IN THE UNITED STATES

"Dad, I'm naked all over the internet!"

Those were the words of Erin Andrews as she described how she was victimized in a Marriott hotel right here in the US, in Nashville, Tennessee, in 2008. The superstar sportscaster broke down in tears on the witness stand when she described the moment she learned footage of her naked was, in her own words, "all over the internet." And she was right.

At first, Erin didn't believe it, thinking the naked images were of someone else, someone that possibly looked like her. But it *was* her. In 2009, a year after the crime took place, she got a call from a friend who broke the news while Erin was in Los Angeles. She screamed into the phone, "No, there's not! I don't do that!" Erin hung up and called her parents, testifying, "I was just screaming…I said, 'Dad! I'm naked all over the internet.'" In fact, she was screaming so loudly, the L.A. hotel where she was staying called to check on her.

She calls the following months her "glazed-over time," when she moved home with her parents and was so traumatized that she put her mom's quilts over the windows. I feel awful for her, even now as I'm writing this. To make matters worse, haters gossiped that she had planted the nude video of herself as a publicity stunt. This is a woman who was a rising star, gaining more momentum every day. The last thing she or her career needed was more publicity, especially this kind. But the haters wouldn't let up.

It turns out that Erin Andrews's stalker was David Barrett, an insurance executive from Chicago. After cops busted him dead to rights, he revealed how he did it. He smugly explained that when he first went to register and check in, he was told the room he wanted wasn't available. So he waited in the Marriott's restaurant. From the restaurant's house phone, he called the hotel operator and asked to be put through to Andrews's room. When the operator connected him, the house phone displayed Andrews's room number. He then knew exactly where she was. He spied on the maid cleaning the room next to hers and, realizing it was now vacant, asked for that room. He got it. Stage one was complete.

Entering his room, Barrett could hear Erin talking on the phone next door. He waited and listened until he heard her leave her room, then got to work. He had learned to alter hotel door peepholes by quickly pulling the peephole device out of its door and cutting off a piece of it with a small hacksaw. This gave him a clear view into her room from the hallway. He then slid the peephole back into place. He lay in wait, listening for her return. When Andrews eventually came back, ear to the wall, he listened for the sound of her shower running.

When he could hear the shower stop, he sneaked back into the hallway, removed the peephole, held his cell phone up to the peephole, and began filming Andrews in the hopes she'd be walking around her hotel room naked. She was.

Motive? Money. Idiot that he is, he'd made a string of "bad investments" and needed cash. But when no one would publish his surreptitious video of the TV star, he posted it online. No one knows why he did such a horrible thing to a young lady he didn't even know. He says he picked Erin Andrews for no other reason than because she was popular and trending online. Barrett admits to taping Andrews in Columbus, Ohio, and Milwaukee, Wisconsin, as well. He also admits to surreptitiously filming at least ten other women.

Barrett got a slap on the wrist and was sentenced to just two and a half years behind bars. Andrews filed a $75 million lawsuit against Barrett as well as both the owner and the operator of the Nashville Vanderbilt Marriott. In 2016, Andrews was awarded $55 million in damages from Barrett and the hotel's owner. Barrett will not likely ever be able to pay much of his share, but Andrews later reached an undisclosed settlement with the hotel owner.

Erin Andrews's story was shocking, to say the least, and extremely upsetting to women all over. What she lived through was awful, and yes, she did live through it. But the toll her travel nightmare took on her still isn't over. While it hasn't tainted her on-air charisma, she's still taunted and mocked and even has flashbacks. She just doesn't show it.

How can you avoid a similar creep spying on you?

Peephole Hack Warnings and Tips

An uncovered peephole is a privacy risk. Anyone can saunter by and tamper with it.

Remember, when you look through your peephole from inside your hotel room out into the hallway, you should be able to see clearly. Peephole lenses manipulate light by using concave and convex lenses, allowing you to see out while outsiders cannot see in. But if even only one lens is removed, peepholes are nothing more than a little round hole in your door.

When you look through your peephole from inside your hotel room, you should have a clear view outside. If your view is obscured or cloudy, the peephole may have been altered.

When you first enter your room and throughout your stay, check around the door for anything like a rolled-up piece of paper or a small ball of paper on the carpet. It may have fallen out of the peephole. Once the Peeping Tom removes the outer glass of the peephole, they often place rolled-up paper into the hole to look straight into your room or a balled-up piece of paper to fill in the hole.

Did you know there is an openly sold device called a peephole reverser? It allows a Peeping Tom to view what's going on behind a closed door through a peephole in real time. A peephole reverser fits in a coat pocket and gives a stalker a clear view into your room. It works on all major brands of standard peepholes and can be used at any hotel, apartment, or home door. A perv can look at least ten feet into your room. They even have a special lens that negates any distortion and lets them see directly into your room as you come out of the bathroom or get dressed.

The moment you check in, place a piece of duct tape or a Band-Aid over your peephole on the inside of your door.

If you suspect your peephole has been altered, you must ask to be moved to another room immediately. Some experts advise that you can simply cover the hole, but I disagree. Once you know your peephole has been altered, who knows what else may be going on with that particular room? Get out!

OTHER US TRAVEL DANGERS

There are many other safety considerations to note while traveling in the US.

HOTEL SAFETY, PART 2

Growing up in rural Georgia, I only *dreamed* of ever staying in a wonderful hotel. What I knew about luxury hotels was only what I read about or saw in movies. They were always magical and fantastic, with beautiful grand staircases, rich carpets, and incredible music playing on a grand piano in the lobby, and handsome bellmen were at your beck and call. That's what I thought they were all like.

When my life took a U-turn following my fiancé's murder, I abandoned the idea of teaching Shakespearean literature. Instead, I went to law school with the hope of becoming a felony prosecutor. At the time I finally made it into the district attorney's office in inner-city Atlanta in 1987, a case made the headlines and rocked the city.

MARGARET RAGLAND

A young woman from Birmingham, Alabama, had traveled with friends and family to Atlanta in November 1987. She was to be the maid of honor in her best friend's wedding. The afternoon of the evening wedding, most of the ladies went on a shopping trip to what was then the height of big-city shopping in the South, the Lenox Square mall right on Peachtree Street. It was across the street from the elegant hotel where the bridesmaids were staying, the Terrace Garden Inn, in prestigious Buckhead, just a stone's throw from the governor's mansion.

While her mom and friends shopped across the street, Margaret Ragland, twenty-five years old, decided to forgo the shopping jaunt, rest up, and take a nap in order to be fresh as a daisy for the wedding. It was not meant to be. Ragland, from a prominent Birmingham family, was brutally stabbed to death in her hotel room at the Terrace Garden Inn. To this day, her murder remains unsolved.

I remember it like it was yesterday. All the cops and investigators in the know kept inexplicably tight-lipped. Every clue evaporated, and no matter what they did, they came up empty-handed. How could a young woman be brutally murdered with no motive whatsoever and her killer vanish into thin air without a trace? Well, it happened. And it forever changed my vision of the "grand hotel."

But what went wrong?

Was someone hiding in Margaret's room when she returned for a nap?

Did someone pose as room service or delivery and force their way in?

Did she open the door for her killer?

Did someone jimmy the door while she slept?

Did she leave her door unlocked and unwittingly pave the way to her own death?

Did someone have an extra key to her room?

Was there a homicidal hotel employee?

What happened to Margaret Ragland?

We'll likely not ever know. But there are precautions you can take to keep you and your loved ones safe when staying overnight in hotels.

What can we do in a world where doors mean nothing? Let's think this through. There *are* ways to fight back!

STAYING SAFE IN HOTELS

Be wary of everyone. For the most part, hotel staff are like us, trying to do their best and make a living for their families. But low pay and long hours, compounded by a never-ending flow of demanding or rude tourists, only magnifies the temptation to dupe travelers.

We also know that thieves are often never caught, which means they don't have a rap sheet. No rap sheet means they can get jobs with unsuspecting hotels and inns, and that means they have access to your spare key or key card.

Some crooks are known to wait until they hear you in the shower. That is what happened to me and my now husband, David, on one of our very first trips. We had been out swimming on the Florida Panhandle and rushed in just in time to take a shower and head to dinner. I still remember the moment we came out of the bathroom, just in time to hear our room door shut. You got it: both our wallets were gone. The good news is that we were both safe and made it home. I got a new driver's license, but I could never replace the wallet photo tucked behind the license. It was of my fiancé, Keith, and I had carried it everywhere...until then.

As always, don't be flashy about money or possessions in the hotel restaurant, bar, or lobby. Don't leave your valuables in plain sight in your hotel room, either. My old suitcase is so beaten up, any hotel staff in their right mind would take one look and run the other way. Keep it tucked in the back of your mind that hotel staff are there to help you but also have the keys to your room and the codes to your safe. Be discreet always and do nothing to tempt anyone to invade your privacy and rob you.

How Safe Is the Safe?

Modern hotels, or those that have been updated, have in-room safes that allow you to set your own combination code. These are much more reliable than safes with a general code or safes that, believe it or not, still use a key.

However, most hotel room safes have a code known to hotel staffers so they can open it in case you forget the one you set. Many hotels never change the default room safe code, which can be easily found online. If an employee were to raid your safe, he wouldn't leave a trace. You'd have no proof you were ever robbed and thus no proof for your insurance claim. And what if the items stolen were irreplaceable, like your grandmother's engagement ring or your laptop full of work or family photos and videos? *Eek!*

Don't travel with irreplaceable items. If you must bring them, don't trust a room safe if you did not set the code yourself or the default code has not been changed. Test it: try creating your own password, then attempt to open it with the default code found for that model online. If it works, that safe is no good. So make sure it *is* safe before putting anything valuable in it.

Get Creative

Never leave your passport behind in your room. But if you must do so, remember that some items like papers or passports can be hidden elsewhere in the room, such as taping it to the bottom of a table or chair or behind a mirror. As for bigger items like your laptop, definitely don't leave it sitting out or charging in your room. With so much information and so many photos on my laptop, I usually leave it at the front desk when leaving the hotel at any time. I ask them specifically to look after it, and I get the name of the person who takes custody of it. I ask them to put it into the registration safe, and I stand there and watch while they do it. While the computer itself isn't worth much, all my work product and thousands of stored family photos and videos mean the world to me.

Lost Key?

If you lose your hotel room key (and I don't mean you just left it behind), insist on a new room. No exceptions. If for some reason you lose control of your key, you must change rooms. I know it's a pain, but you really must not be lulled into believing you simply lost or misplaced it. It may very well have been swiped, either planned or as a crime of simple opportunity. But how can you know the motive of someone who took your key? To steal your money? Or worse?

Stow All Valuables

Do not leave anything of worth laying out in your room. First, it could be stolen. Second and more important, it might be spotted by a perp who may come back for your stuff while you're in the room.

Insist on Privacy Regarding Your Room Number

When you check in, ask the front desk staff person to write down your room number, not announce it out loud for anyone standing nearby to hear it. Most hotels don't blurt out the number now, but if they do say it out loud, ask for a different room and for the number to be relayed in writing.

Book Secure Hotels Only

First and foremost, chose the right hotel. The *right hotel* means a *secure hotel*. Go online and study the neighborhood, read consumer reviews, and look up your chosen hotel. Yelp or TripAdvisor.com offer reviews of hotels and include specific information if safety is an issue there.

Keep Your Bags Close

Stay close to your luggage while you check in. Do not get separated from your bags when you get out of your car, bus, or taxi. Keep them with you or in your sight. Lobbies are busy and noisy, and that's a perfect cover for thieves.

All Business at Check-In

At registration, don't get sucked into chitchat and let a thief take your things. Don't turn your back on your bags; lean your luggage against the counter between you and the agent. After a few times, it becomes second nature.

Always Be Smart About Your Cards

At check-in, do not place your credit card up on the counter, much less leave it there. Any novice thief can snap a photo of the card's numbers with a cell phone or camera. A good camera can snap the numbers at a distance. When the clerk hands the card back to you, give it a hard look. Make sure that it's not a fake.

Chain of Fools

Do not trust the hotel room door chain or bar lock that you swing into place. They are very easily disabled with items so simple you'd never believe it, including the do-not-disturb sign hanging on your door. Burglars only need a credit card or piece of wire to get into your hotel room. Door chains and bars are so flimsy they could never withstand significant force from outside.

Most thieves also know about lock bumping or will use a bump key that can easily open a locked door. These keys are available online, and there are videos that show how to make the simple tools that open what you thought was a secured door.

Luckily, there are alternatives to these flimsy deadbolts and chains. I discovered a device called the Lock Locker. It has one long flat section that fits around the door handle and a second piece that fits over the deadbolt. The device makes it virtually impossible to open the door from the outside, even if the intruder has a key. It slides over the deadbolt, keeping it in place and stopping lock picks, copied keys, maintenance, hotel staff, stolen keys, even 3-D printed keys. And bump keys. It works with strong magnets that hold the device together. If you don't like the Lock Locker, there are many, many different devices online, and they are inexpensive. They are not a bad idea for home use, either.

Be an Alarmist

Travel door alarms are inexpensive but effective. Of course, an alarm won't stop an intruder, but it will almost certainly scare one off. There are many styles, but the most common one hangs from the door handle and has two prongs that you push in between the door and its frame. If the door opens, the prongs loosen and come apart and the alarm goes off. It's so simple, and it works on every door.

If you are concerned about other entry points to your room, travel motion detectors are also effective. They are simple infrared sensors that sound an alarm when they detect movement. When aimed toward a hotel window or door, they serve as a great security measure. Just make sure you don't have them near an open window, as even a simple curtain flutter will set one off. Don't point it at your bed if you toss and turn at night. You will need a model that senses movement at least ten feet away so you have plenty of leeway to position it in your room.

As an extra safety measure, keep your keychain car fob on your bedside table. Many fobs have panic buttons that can be used as an alarm if there's an emergency. When you press the button, your car will flash its lights and blow the horn repeatedly. If the car is near your room, it draws attention to your location.

Safety buffs keep their key fobs wrapped in aluminum foil for a good reason. Cars can be burgled if a crook scrambles the key fob signal and unlocks your car. Folding foil around the fob thwarts the scrambler.

Be Exclusive

Always use hotels that block access to floors unless the guest has an elevator key card for that floor.

The easiest way to keep it secret you are a woman traveling alone is to use your first initial rather than your full first name when you make the reservation, or use "Mr. and Mrs."

Police That Front Desk

Once you're checked in, use your cell phone and call the front desk. Ask to speak to *you*. The operator should offer to connect you, but if they relay your room number, you've got trouble. They could give that number to anybody.

24/7 Staffing

Book hotels with twenty-four-hour front desk staff in case of an emergency. Even less expensive hotels have them. AAA knows a lot about hotel amenities like twenty-four-hour staff, even at bargain prices.

Maintain the Illusion You Are Present

Hang the do-not-disturb sign on your room door and leave the TV or clock radio going loud enough to hear in the hallway but not so loud as to cause neighbors to call management on you. I advise cable talk channels; from the outside, they sound like conversation. I also leave the bathroom door closed but the light on inside, so that if someone does come in, they may believe I'm in the tub.

Stay Anonymous

Never, ever put your name on a doorhanger, whether for room service, overnight breakfast orders, shoe shining, a newspaper, or laundry request. A room number will suffice. Adding your name is equivalent to screaming out your hotel window, "Hey! I'm all alone in room 301! Come and get me!"

In the same vein, instead of leaving an order selection card for a single meal on your door, just go old-school and pick up the phone and call room service before you retire. Do not advertise for anyone lurking in the hall that you are in your room alone. The hotel can take a breakfast order from you the night before over the phone.

Review the Reviews

Read guest reviews of hotels and their neighborhoods just as you would read reviews of restaurants. Especially peruse safety concerns. You can read frank consumer reviews and not just the glossy pamphlets in the hotel lobby.

Always Be Discreet

Keep your voice down when you're checking in or even discussing your hotel on your cell phone. The world is full of bad guys, and they can pop up in the most unsuspecting places, like at the table beside you at brunch or in your hotel lobby. Loose lips sink ships. Pipe down.

Be Streetwise

Ask that your room be as far from the street as possible and on a higher floor. This lessens the chances of a host of safety issues, from Peeping Toms to burglars or worse.

Fire Concerns

If fire is your fear, request a room closest to a concrete or reinforced stairwell. Keep in mind that, generally speaking, the highest a fire ladder can reach is to the seventh or eighth floor.

Evaluate Your Room Immediately

When making your way to your room, pause as you get off the elevator so others don't see in which direction you're headed. Glance behind you as you walk to make sure no one is following. As soon as you make it to your room, check it out thoroughly. Look behind doors, in the closet, in the bathroom, behind the bathroom door, behind the shower curtain, under the bed, on the balcony, and in the armoire. While you are checking the room, leave your door cracked in case you get a surprise. You can crack it open with the door bolt or even a shoe. A full check includes testing the door's lock to make sure it's working as well as confirming it also has a working deadbolt. Close and bolt the door. Keep the deadbolt locked whenever you are in the room, even if briefly.

After you inspect your room, find the nearest fire exit. Fire exits come in handy for any number of reasons. Make time to count your steps to the exit in case the halls are dark or smoky and you become disoriented. There's usually a map on the back of your door or in the desk. Take a look at it or snap a shot of it on your cell phone. Make it a habit, just like snapping a shot of where you park your car.

The Wedge Issue

For extra security, put a chair or some item that's noisy against the door. If your door is opened during the night, at least you will hear it clang up against the object. Most likely, whoever is opening the door will skedaddle once the door hits a barricade. Little doorstops are easy to find online and take up practically zero space in your suitcase. I like one called the DoorJammer. The harder someone pushes against your door from the hallway, the harder the DoorJammer pushes down into the floor inside your room. It's tiny but mighty and easy to use. There are countless others that work, and they are all pretty cheap. Remember, wedges work best on wood or tile. They do work on carpet but work even better on carpet if you get the type with a Velcro strip to prevent sliding. Some even come with an alarm that alerts when the wedge is moved during the night. The door must open inward for the wedge to work, but most hotel doors do so.

Get Locked In

Lock your room windows. If you have a balcony, lock your balcony doors. If your room is hot and you're above the second floor, it's likely safe to sleep with the windows open. If your room is on the second floor or below, change rooms, put the AC on, or prepare yourself to, sadly, swelter through.

Stranger Danger

Never, ever open your door to a stranger. Once they're in, it's very difficult to get them out. If someone claims to be from maintenance or room service or have a delivery, they will certainly wait on the other side of your closed and locked door while you double-check their story with the front desk. Sometimes I ask room service to just leave my food outside and I get it a few minutes later.

When maintenance or room service or a delivery person *does* come to your room, prop your room door open so you can make a quick exit or scream if necessary. When you open the door for hotel staff, or anyone for that matter, keep that door chain secured until you are sure who's knocking. Only disengage the chain once you've confirmed the visitor's identity. The chain lock isn't much, but it's something that can buy you precious time.

Be a Lobbyist

Enter and leave your hotel through the main lobby, ensuring that witnesses see you. It should be well lit, thus making it more unlikely a perp is lurking just outside the door. That can't be said for side or back doors and parking garage passages.

Get Your Group On

If you can, enter and leave the hotel with a group, even if it's not really *your* group. Wait for a few people and simply walk along with them. Don't confirm suspicions that you are traveling alone by being seen over and over by yourself. Avoid solitary situations when you can. Yes, you can travel alone, but use your head.

Car Smarts

If you sense danger, call a staffer to walk you to or from your car. Reduce time spent in unsecure environments, like hotel parking decks and lots. When you are waiting at the hotel for a taxi, Uber, or Lyft, wait inside the lobby, not outside alone. I'm a firm believer in self-parking and walking to wherever I'm going. But when traveling in unfamiliar surroundings, I spend the extra money and use valet parking. Walking through an isolated deck or dark parking lot out of town isn't worth the valet savings. Don't be penny wise and pound foolish.

Be Flashy!

Sleep with a flashlight next to your bed so you can find it in the dark. I have a mini flashlight I always carry on trips.

No Candid Cameras

Also check your room for peepholes or pinpoint cameras in walls, around doors, heating and air-conditioning units, ceiling squares, and connecting doors that open into adjoining rooms, even if they seem securely closed. And yes, it happens. There are a lot of freaky dudes out there. Don't be their next victim.

Tell a Friend and Leave a Note, Too

When you go out, send a quick text to someone who knows you're traveling and let them know your plan. Leave a note in your room as to your plans, too. That note may save your life. It's best to do both, because a contact would be the first to miss you if they can't reach you and the physical note in your room would be for purposes of police, hotel staff, or investigators. Let's hope they never need it.

It's Curtains

Whenever you leave, pull your curtains closed. Anyone from the outside looking in can't tell your room is empty.

Keep Checking

Check the locks on your windows, doors, and balcony each time you enter or exit your room.

Be a Card Carrier

Whenever you venture out from your hotel, make sure to carry a hotel card from the front desk or at least scribble down the address. This may save the day if you get lost when you're out jogging or sightseeing. In case you are in a location where you don't speak the language fluently or at all, at least you will have your hotel name and number. Cards are usually sitting out by check-in, or you may have to ask—take two. Place the second card beside your room phone and leave it. If you need to relay your address over the phone for any reason, you will have it there and handy.

Trust Yourself

If a hotel doesn't feel right, leave. I refer to the gut instinct a lot in this book, and there's a reason: it's usually right. There are always other options available when you get the wrong vibe. Don't ignore it.

All these travel safety tips may seem like a huge data dump when, in your mind, you just want to go and have some fun and relaxation. That's what Drew, Francesca, Natalee, Abbey, Desiree, Tatiana, and so many others had in mind.

I can't help them now, but I can help you. I want you and your family to have all the fun in the world, to see everything, do everything, eat and drink everything. I want you to come home with a lifetime of memories. But after you make those memories, I want you and your family to come home...safely.

CHAPTER SIXTEEN

Cruise Ship Catastrophes

Cruise ships summon up visions of a vast, endless swath of crazy-blue ocean only ending when it meets the sky, beautiful dining on fancy food with thick tablecloths and all the right forks and spoons placed in all the right places, awesome pools and hot tubs, endless on-board entertainment, and daily jaunts on land for unforgettable port experiences. Right?

That's what I had in mind, too, until I heard the name of George Smith and then met his grieving family in their lovely New England home.

GEORGE SMITH

Twenty-six-year-old George Smith, from upscale Cos Cob, Connecticut, married his dream girl, Jennifer Hagel, a soon-to-be third-grade teacher. The wedding was gorgeous, and after dancing at their reception, the two set out on a once-in-a-lifetime honeymoon cruise across the Mediterranean, including Spain, Greece, Italy, and Turkey. It sounds like a dream. It turned into a nightmare.

On the evening of July 5, 2005, the new groom just disappeared. *Just disappeared?* How does a newlywed "just disappear" on his honeymoon? His disappearance sent waves of panic throughout the cruise ship industry and shocked Smith's community and the wider world. The mystery gained momentum and shed a harsh light on a major tourist trade.

Bloodstains were discovered inside George's cabin and, worse, down the side of the ship. Suicide was immediately ruled out; he was on top of the world with his new bride and the life they were just beginning.

An accident was highly unlikely, as the guardrails around the ship, including the one on the honeymoon cabin perched on deck nine, were so high you'd have to be an Olympic gymnast to just "fall" overboard. All of which led detectives to ask a horrible question: Was the missing groom thrown overboard?

What had happened leading up to the bloodstain down the canopy outside the honeymoon suite? The evening before, July 4, the *Brilliance of the Seas* cruise ship pulled anchor and set sail from the Greek island of Mykonos for the Turkish port of Kusadasi. Onboard were 2,300 passengers, most of them from the US. After touring the town and playing on its sun-drenched beaches, the honeymooners headed back to the *Brilliance* for dinner, then the casino and disco onboard.

The couple were seen that evening in the disco with a group of friends they'd made on board, drinking and laughing well into the night. Specifically, the group was taking shots from a bottle of absinthe, a highly potent liquor not sold on the ship and obviously smuggled on board. But in the hours just before sunrise, George vanished.

Some accounts claim George and Jennifer had a brief argument over a cruise employee flirting with the bride. The story goes that Jennifer got angry, kicked George, and in a haze of alcohol, stomped out of the disco. At the time, Jennifer remembered nothing after leaving the group. Around three a.m., the disco closed and three of the friends helped George, by then totally inebriated, to his cabin only to discover that Jennifer wasn't inside. George insisted they find her immediately, but at 4:02 a.m., the groom came back to his cabin having had no success.

George Smith, the groom with the world before him, was never seen alive again. His body has never been found. The only clue? A deep-red bloodstain on the life raft canopy just beneath their cabin's balcony.

Spending time with George's family was heartbreaking. They tried to smile and tell me funny and poignant stories about George, but just beneath their recollections was a deep sorrow that he was gone from their lives, exacerbated by not knowing what happened to him. His disappearance brought about major changes in the cruise ship industry, including the Cruise Industry Passenger Bill of Rights and the Cruise Passenger Protection Act, supported by George's parents. The act calls for more transparency regarding crimes on board as well as more protection when it comes to passengers' rights.

While I'm all for transparency in reporting cruise ship crimes and gathering statistics to inform passengers, what's really important is stopping those crimes before they happen and not just reporting them afterward.

The most effective way to stop cruise ship crime is by gaining knowledge and then using it—wielding that knowledge like a sword. A cruise ship is like a floating city in the middle of the ocean with bottomless drinks and zero police.

First, statistics show the most common crime aboard cruise ships across the world is sexual assault. Sexual assaults on the high seas outnumber all other crimes on board combined. Then there is the reality that sex crimes are vastly underreported. Also, there's the disturbing fact that it's up to the cruise line security to classify the assault, and we believe that many incidents are misreported as lesser crimes, such as simple battery or simple assault. That means that since sexual assaults are the number one crime on cruise ships, the "problem" is more like an epidemic and much more serious than is shown in the data.

It seems that the cruise ship mentality enables sexual assaults. Everyone is relaxing on vacation and lulled into being much less vigilant under the mistaken belief they are going to be protected and nothing can go wrong on board a self-contained, floating island of revelry. The booze flows freely, and nobody has to worry about driving home. Teens and even tweens can explore the ship on their own and end up in very dangerous positions.

TEEN CRUISE NIGHTMARE

In 2015, a Florida mom set sail with her fifteen-year-old girl aboard the *Carnival Breeze*. During the last leg of the trip, the teen visited the ship's alcohol-free teen hangout. While there, she saw a group being kicked out because they were too old for the club. When the teen girl left the club to go for free ice cream on another deck, she reports she was raped by the same guys forced out of the kids' club. The lawsuit filed by the girl's mom says the five men pushed her daughter onto an elevator, dragged her to one of the men's rooms, and violently molested her.

The lawsuit claims that Carnival failed to provide a safe environment for teen guests and protect them from predators. She argues that had there been better monitoring by ship surveillance cameras, ship security could have stopped the adult men from lurking around the teen club. Carnival denies the claims.

The whole scenario really strikes home with me. I have taken the twins on not one, but two cruise trips. Both trips were with Disney, and both were wonderful—in fact, they were everything I thought they'd be and more. But there was this one incident involving my son, John David. Believe it or not, I have been accused of being a "helicopter mom," one of those moms who can't bear to let her children out of her sight. And you know what? Maybe it's true, and I accept that. After my fiancé's murder, I live in a world where I believe bad things do happen to innocent people and something tragic may very well happen to someone I love. That threat is very real to me.

By the time we went on the second cruise, the twins were nearly eleven years old. My son, John David, loves foosball, board games, video games, any games. So, after two days of him begging, I agreed he could go to the ship's tween fun spot. Of course, I went and inspected it, and it seemed wonderful and had all sorts of safeguards to protect the tweens. I left John David and Lucy there armed with walkie-talkies to summon me from anywhere on the ship to come get them when they were ready. Lucy called first, and I fetched her. I left John David there with a playmate from school and stern instructions to the staff they were not to leave the kids' club without Mom being called.

Well, as it turned out, the staff did call Mom—the friend's mom!

At ten p.m., after calling and calling his radio, I discovered John David was gone. He had left on his own. At first, I sent David and stayed behind with Lucy in case he made it to the cabin without David. I frantically radioed him over and over on his walkie-talkie. I imagined pervy dudes loitering outside the kids' club, waiting to follow my son and pounce on him. Would he be dragged into a room? Would he be attacked? Would he be thrown overboard like George Smith? Years after Smith went missing, he was all I could think about aside from John David.

I lasted about three minutes before I burst out into the narrow hall in my pajamas, dragging Lucy behind me, calling out his name. To this day, I remember the moment I saw him come around a corner in the distance. I ran to him. He was safe in my arms. I had him. He had simply left the tween club on his own after staff had called "a mom" and took his time getting back to our cabin.

After they fell asleep, I stared at the two of them in the dark all night. My story had a happy ending. No one was at fault, and no one was hurt. I wish that were true for other cruise ship victims. In fact, most cruise ship travelers don't encounter crime, but serious crimes do take place on cruise ships. It seems to be even more shocking than crimes on land, I think, because we let our guard down on vacation and especially on cruise ships because we believe we are in a contained environment surrounded by other vacationers like ourselves who just want to have fun with their families. It is not a threatening atmosphere.

Another enabling factor is there is no immediate police presence. In the George Smith case and others like it, witnesses scattered far and wide without police detectives to fully question them first, copy their passports, or, at the very least, find out where they live. Cruise investigators are simply cruise ship personnel, guards hired by the cruise line itself. Wouldn't a cruise line investigator want to save his employer from possible civil liability and a round of nasty PR? How would it look if a cruise ship employee turned out to be the wrongdoer, just like the investigator?

JACKIE KASTRINELIS

Recently, I spoke to heartbroken parents still searching for the truth about what happened to their daughter. I wanted to help. Twenty-four-year-old Jackie Kastrinelis from Massachusetts was an incredible talent and dreamed of heading to Broadway. But unlike many performers, Jackie was a blend of talent, smarts, and beauty and actually had a shot at making her dream come true. On her path to Broadway, in February 2013 she took a gig performing on the *Seven Seas Voyager* off the Australian coast. After her set one evening, Jackie disappeared.

Hours later, Jackie was found dead in her cabin. Oddly, cruise officials determined she died of an extremely rare "adult sudden unexplained death syndrome." Ship authorities also stated she "hit her head" while singing at rehearsal and was "given meds" by ship doctors. Her parents are absolutely convinced she was murdered, largely because of alleged errors and cover-ups by police and forensics at the time of her death.

There is also the glaring issue of semen from an unknown male in her underwear. Authorities did not collect enough DNA samples aboard the ship, meaning they had little chance to find out much about the unknown male. Apparently, enough samples were not taken from males onboard to determine the "donor," and the pool of suspects have now scattered to the four corners of the earth. Jackie's parents, Kathleen and Mike Kastrinelis, cannot get answers no matter how hard they try. Imagine their pain and frustration.

MERRIAN CARVER

Another dad, Kendall Carver, has devoted his life to cruise ship reform after his daughter, Merrian Carver, boarded the Celebrity cruise ship *Mercury*, on August 27, 2004. The ship set sail from Seattle to Alaska, and Merrian, a young investment banker, was seen by a cruise employee the next day. That was the last sighting of her alive.

The ship made port in Prince Rupert, British Columbia, as well as Juneau, Skagway, and Ketchikan, Alaska, but it seems Merrian never went ashore. When she missed her flight back home to Massachusetts, her family immediately reported her missing. Eventually, it was discovered that all of her belongings had been left in her cabin. To make matters worse, the ship had donated most of her property to charity. Records show she never bought a single drink onboard or ordered room service. Her parents sued, but her death remains unsolved. Carver insists that cruise lines operate with practically no regulation regarding crimes.

Are there answers? We know cruise ship passengers already have certain rights, says the Code of Federal Regulations. Those rights include receiving a security guard from the ship to help you if you are a crime victim on board, the right to a sexual assault forensic exam, the right to confidentiality, the right to information as to how to contact your embassy if you find yourself in a foreign land, and the right to report the crime to the FBI and US Coast Guard or the Department of Transportation.

Another ongoing plan is to assign sea marshals to all cruise ships, much like air marshals on planes. But your best protector is, of course, you. That goes for protecting your children, too. Even if there were sea marshals in place, cruise liners are huge vessels that carry thousands of people. A sea marshal couldn't always be around to protect you.

PORT ADVENTURES TURN DEADLY

Typically, at every stop along the cruise, the ship arranges port excursions. We've done it and loved it, from rain forest hikes to driving through a monkey preserve and touring a banana farm. But now, I really study before I pick a port adventure. I want you to think long and hard before you pick your day trip. We've picked several for the twins, and I consider them very carefully. Why? Because of the following story.

EGAEL TISHMAN

I was struck when I first learned a newlywed groom was killed and his new bride was in critical condition in the hospital after a seemingly innocent shore excursion.

Twenty-four-year-old Egael Tishman and twenty-seven-year-old Shif Fanken were thrilled when they chose a dream vacation cruise immediately following their July 2018 wedding. The Israeli couple boarded the Royal Caribbean's *Allure of the Seas* in Fort Lauderdale, Florida, just after their wedding ceremony. The *Allure* got them to Roatán, Honduras, five days later without incident. In fact, they were having a great time on board the luxury liner. Excited to try all things new, they decided to try a zipline experience they found on the Royal Caribbean's website billed as the "Extreme Caribe Zip Line Tour" on Roatán.

The bride was buckled up and sent down the zipline first, but about halfway down the line, Shif became stuck. Egael was already buckled up and sent off behind her, and the two collided in midair, rescue workers said. Apparently having fractured a rib, Egael was struggling to breathe. He was given oxygen in the ambulance but passed away on his honeymoon.

You must pick your port adventures with the same care and discernment you would use at home—even more so, in fact, because you may not be familiar with the basic information abroad, such as where the hospital is and the quickest route there. Are there urgent care clinics? Are there buses or cabs to get you there? How do you call an ambulance? These are health emergency considerations we know how to manage quickly at home. Overseas, not as much, or maybe not at all.

Remember that just because the cruise staff protects you to a degree on board, your cruise status doesn't give you a cloak of invincibility on land. Keep close track of your possessions. Stay mindful.

And don't forget, when on your port excursions, follow the earlier tips for travel abroad.

PIRATES? NOT SO MUCH

While no pirate attacks on cruise liners have occurred for at least the last five years, cruise liners still take safety measures to guard against them. Specifically, precautions are taken in regions in or around the Gulf of Aden near Somalia and Yemen. There have been at least six pirate incidents in that region and one ship was hijacked. In one 2009 case regarding the MSC *Melody*, passengers fought off modern-day pirates by hurling deck chairs and tables at the pirates as they tried to board. Guess what? It worked!

But I can tell you this: if a cruise ship must dim exterior lights and tell passengers to keep cabin lights on low so they can sneak past pirates, I think I would take my family on a different cruise. Luckily, in most of the world, *Pirates of the Caribbean* is a movie franchise and a ride at Disney, not a legitimate concern for you.

WORST WORDS ON A CRUISE SHIP? "MAN OVERBOARD!" AND "FIRE!"

For some perspective, know that passengers going overboard and fires at sea are very rare occurrences. Most cruises from the US are extremely safe, and that is why we have taken the twins on two of them and plan on many more.

A fire is a cruise liner's worst nightmare, as the ships are constructed with combustible materials. Fires usually occur and are contained within the engine room, and most cruise liners go overboard (pardon the pun) with fire suppression systems. They cover the ships with both CO_2 and mist devices. Crew are highly trained in fire suppression and have specific instructions on how to handle the danger to ensure passenger safety. As far as what you can do individually, follow instructions, for Pete's sake!

Know how to swim and make sure your children do as well. By all means, attend and participate in the safety drill that takes place on every American cruise ship before you head to sea.

As to man overboard fears, it's simple: no horseplay around guardrails, and don't get drunk and go for a walk on the deck. That covers it.

CRUISE SHIP TRAVEL TIPS

- Don't get drunk. I've given this tip more than once, but it bears repeating. Think back to the missing groom, George Smith. While we are not sure exactly what happened, we know that every witness account included heavy drinking that night, specifically the absinthe. Man overboard incidents usually involve horseplay near a deck rail and booze. On board, it's so easy for people to get carried away because the atmosphere is fun and festive, and the drinks are unlimited. Know your limits, and stay aware of how much you've had.
- This is always true but bears repeating: be careful who buys or brings you drinks. Never take drinks from strangers. Always get your drink directly from the bartender. Guard your drink at all times. Never agree to be walked to your room by someone you've just met, especially after you've been drinking. Please, keep your wits about you. Write your deck and cabin number on a piece of paper and keep it in your pocket just in case your drinks impair your memory.
- Don't make it obvious you're alone. If you are traveling alone, make a friend early on the trip, a friend who would notice if you are not around or don't answer phone calls or texts. It's the law of the jungle. Predators try to isolate their prey from the herd, then attack. There is safety in numbers or, in certain cases, the appearance of numbers.
- Don't wander around isolated or hidden areas of the ship by yourself. One thing I loved about our Disney cruises is that when I was jogging or walking around the deck path, I noticed the enclosed or more isolated areas were well-covered by security cameras. I also noticed phones on the wall you could use if you needed assistance.
- Double your safety measures when walking about at night.
- Just because you retire to your cabin doesn't mean you're safe—yet. Not all room doors shut completely on their own or automatically.

Make sure you pull the door closed and slide the bolt over. Same for when you leave—make sure you hear the click.

- Ask your steward for a doorstopper.
- Review the hotel room safety tips noted earlier. Those rules apply on cruise ships, too.
- If you order room service, call. Don't leave the order on your door handle to advertise that one person—you—is in the room.
- Use your peephole! All the doors on a cruise look alike. You don't want to let your drunk neighbor into your cabin, do you?
- Don't broadcast your cabin number when you are out and about.
- Don't give your cabin number to anyone unless you must.
- Practice balcony safety. George Smith either fell or was hoisted off his balcony. Accidents around cruise ship balconies are so easily avoidable. Yes, I love the sound of the ocean just like everybody, but keep your balcony door locked at night and check it before you go to sleep. Keep it closed and locked when you leave and check it again when you return just as you would in a hotel room. Window cleaners and maintenance workers can easily get into your room if your balcony door is wide open or unlocked. It's possible a neighbor with a balcony could get access to yours, and presto, he's in.
- Use your in-room safe. It's not there just to hog your closet space. Better yet, if you are that concerned about a possession, leave it at home.
- Don't leave things lying about. Judging by our cruise experiences, most stewards are honest and hardworking. But why tempt those who aren't? Don't leave valuables lying about your room.
- Speaking of your cabin steward, get to know yours. Ours have always been delightful and super nice to the twins. That meant a lot to me. Make their acquaintance on the very first day and be genuinely friendly. They always seem to be about, and I guarantee your steward is the one most likely to notice someone different trying to gain access to your room. Don't be shy with a tip.
- While you're at it, befriend the staff at your ship's front desk. They know all and see all. Meet them and tip them as well. The best time to meet them is sometime other than check-in or lunchtime; those times are the most chaotic for them.
- Don't flash cash. Most things on the ship, such as food, drinks, and activities, are either paid for in advance or charged to your cruise

ID card. Keep enough for incidentals like tipping, but otherwise, put away the green.

- Never go to crew cabins or quarters. No good will come of that. At best, they may get found out and fired and you may get bounced off the cruise at the next port. At worst, you end up a victim. Don't risk it.
- Don't duck out and hide during the onboard safety drill that takes place before the ship departs. It's part of the experience. Suck it up and be a good sport.
- When you head to land for your port fun, take a card from the ship with you. Also, follow the same drill as when you park in a parking deck. Your ship is "parked," too. Take a quick cell phone snap and, if you can, write down or text someone the name of the port and its location. Believe me, when you are on the other side of a foreign city trying to explain to a cab driver who doesn't speak English where you want to go, it's lot easier to whip out that photo or show that note.
- Write down the all-aboard time, or snap a photo of the announcement board showing it. It's easy to forget and almost impossible to catch up to your cruise once it sets sail.
- Carry an emergency phone.
- Carry an emergency number for several ship officials or cruise directors when you leave the ship.
- Take an onboard class or go to a fun activity if you can and get to know a few of your cruise mates.
- Never be rude to the bartender—or any cruise staff, for that matter. You want them on your side, and you don't want the reputation of being a pain in the backside.
- If your cruise involves exploring outside the US, register with the Smart Traveler Enrollment Program (STEP) for notifications about safety conditions within the region, alerts, and emergency notifications.
- Hear and heed your inner voice. Don't lapse into a false sense of safety because you are now part of one big happy cruise family. Even blood relatives can turn out to be thugs with rap sheets.
- Remember those safety phrases in local languages? You need them for cruise destinations as well, not just when you travel by land or air to a new country.
- Before you leave, follow the earlier tips on passport copies, driver's

license, travel docs like tickets and itinerary, emergency numbers and credit cards.

- When you first go onboard and find your cabin, check the room for safety. That includes bathrooms, balcony and cabin doors, under beds, and in closets, just as you would in a hotel.
- Try to stay in public areas. It's a cruise ship...not a cruise family.
- Use commonsense rules with your children. Don't let them run wild across the ship. Know where they are and how they are getting back to you. Reread my drama with my son, John David. The best-laid plans can and do go afoul.
- Remember, many cruise ships do not have lifeguards at the pools. Luckily, ours did. Find out if yours does.
- In the event of a catastrophe like a fire or capsizing, follow your instincts and the advice of ship personnel.
- Most cruise ships have sinks, water, soap, and instant hand sanitizer at every meal entrance. *Use it!* Don't get waylaid by somebody else's germs.
- P.S. Have fun!

CHAPTER SEVENTEEN

Camping and RV Trips

There was a time I thought nothing at all about camping under the stars or hiking by myself. After prosecuting felonies for ten years in inner-city Atlanta, I became keenly attuned to all sorts of felonies, but not necessarily those crimes occurring off the grid. But when the twins came into my life, it changed the way I see the world.

SAMANTHA KOENIG

When a young barista disappeared in 2012, I was riveted. Samantha Koenig went missing from her coffee stand job in Anchorage, Alaska. I couldn't compute the facts of her disappearance. Police cleared her boyfriend, exes, and co-workers. One night she was at work, and the next day she had vanished. But where? All that was left behind was a cafe Americano on the counter.

Enter Israel Keyes.

Keyes said his first crime was a sexual attack on a teenager. Shortly after that attack in 2001, he began killing his victims. At that time, he was working as a carpenter in Washington State and would choose his victims very carefully, all strangers and all adults. He revealed he especially loved targeting people camping or hiking alone and was drawn to remote areas where there was very little chance there would be witnesses. Police now suspect Keyes committed at least twelve murders across the US and, like many other serial killers, preferred wilderness areas as a favorite hunting ground...for people.

Keyes, who had no connection whatsoever to Samantha, was apprehended for her kidnapping, rape, and murder when his rental car was caught on camera at a Texas ATM after using her stolen debit card to make withdrawals of ransom money deposited by her father. That proved to be one of his only mistakes after years of stalking his victims across the country.

During forty horrific hours of videotaped conversations, I heard Keyes lay out many of his "favorite" murders. He also revealed he enjoyed killing, admitting he targeted lone victims he could overpower. He especially chose women with no pets or children in tow, making their murders easier and simpler. We know that Keyes kept "body disposal kits" hidden in Washington State, Wyoming, Upstate New York, Arizona, and Texas. But since Keyes refused to disclose many of his victims' identities, investigators now have the extremely difficult task of creating a timeline of his movements, then comparing them to unsolved homicides and missing persons.

I've never been able to get Samantha out of my mind. Samantha was kidnapped at gunpoint from Common Grounds Espresso in Anchorage. Keyes forced her to a shed, then raped and strangled her to death. He blasted music inside the shed while he was assaulting and murdering her so no one would hear her screams. One chilling detail: he went on a cruise before coming back to begin his play for ransom. He sewed her eyes open, applied makeup, braided her long hair, and then took a blurry photo of her to use as proof of life in order to get ransom money. He then dismembered her body and, pretending he was ice-fishing, cut a hole in a frozen lake near Palmer, Alaska, and dumped her remains in the cold waters beneath the ice. I spoke at length to FBI special agent Bobby Chacon, who was in charge of the freezing cold-water dive to locate Samantha's remains. Over the course of several hours, Chacon detailed to me how her remains were ultimately retrieved by an FBI cold-water dive team. Samantha was just one of the victims Keyes would seek out in remote places. If he hadn't confessed to these details after his apprehension, we still wouldn't know what happened to Samantha and many others.

TRISTAN BEAUDETTE

Not long ago, David and I were deciding between two choices for our son's Boy Scout trip. One was camping out in the wilderness, and the other was heading to another state for a NASA weekend. The camping trip was much closer, and the NASA weekend involved a very long drive. It was while we were weighing these options that I first heard the name Tristan Beaudette.

It may not ring a bell at first, but Tristan Beaudette was a research scientist with a PhD in chemistry from the University of California at Berkeley. He was also a husband, married to his high school sweetheart, Erica Wu, and a devoted father of two little girls. According to those closest to him, he was "happiest out in nature, and spent every chance he could hiking, biking, snowboarding, and camping with his family."

In June 2018, Erica, an OB-GYN resident at the University of California, was digging in for a long weekend of studying for exams. Tristan had the idea to take his two little girls for a camping trip to Malibu Creek State Park. It's a beautiful area that provided the backdrop for movies and TV shows like *M*A*S*H*. Early that evening, while the three of them were tucked away inside their tent, shots rang out. Those shots were aimed directly at Tristan's tent and hit their mark. Tristan bled to death in front of his two- and four-year-old daughters.

Time passed with no resolution. But then, seemingly out of the blue, police arrested parolee Anthony Rauda, charging him with not only the murder of Tristan Beaudette but ten other shootings targeting unsuspecting campers, some of them sleeping.

Some of the remembrances of Tristan's wife, Erica, struck me. In an official statement, she said that Tristan "rejoiced in sharing his love of the outdoors with the girls and believed that campgrounds were the definition of a sanctuary where people could feel safe and secure." She described him as a "devoted husband and father whose life revolved around our family, our happiness, and his hopes and dreams for our future."

Some of the photos are heartbreaking. One shows him holding hands with his two daughters, gazing out at nature. Another shows him with his family roasting s'mores, his arms around Erica and one of his daughters sitting in a kid-size teal-and-purple camp chair. That same minicamp chair was later found at the scene of his murder.

After I covered the Tristan Beaudette case, my family and I headed out for a seven-hour ride in the minivan to the Boy Scout NASA event. I didn't feel like going camping after studying Rauda.

Here are tips I've formulated over years of investigating and covering wilderness and camping attacks. All of these tips apply to camping and campers, whether you're in a group or on your own.

CAMPING AND RV SAFETY TIPS

- Be prepared. Don't leave home without prepping. Have your maps, camping locations, and trail plans ready to go. Don't just store them in your cell phone, but have a hard copy, too. In remote areas you may not get a signal strong enough to pull up your data, or your battery may go dead. If possible, keep hard copies of all the information not only with you in your backpack or gear but also in your car as a safety backup in case of water damage to your primary copy. I put mine in watertight plastic storage bags like oversized sandwich bags.
- Use reliable and up-to-date maps. I remember when we took the twins on an RV trip and, after much planning, found out certain roads in California had been closed due to flooding. We had to reroute, which caused a lot of drama, but luckily, we found out ahead of time through our local AAA.
- Get familiar with new equipment before you go. Don't discover you can't pitch your new tent, light your camping lantern, or make your water purifier work at ten o'clock at night in the middle of nowhere.

OFF THE GRID? SURE! MIA? NO WAY!

- Let someone know where you are by text, email, or note. Don't just casually mention it in a phone call or leave a verbal message that can be forgotten or accidentally erased with no way to undelete. Include details about your estimated time of departure and arrival, where you are headed, your campsite, and the location of trailhead (where you start your hike). If you can, leave a tag number on your car or rental.
- Get to camp during daylight hours. I've made this mistake several times. I get so entranced with seeing the country, I want to see it all. But the consequences outweigh the extra sightseeing. If you don't

get off the road before nightfall, the campgrounds may be full and you may be out of luck. Arrive in the afternoon at the latest.

- Also, selecting a pitch site and setting up camp in the dark is a big no-no. It's harder to gauge what you are walking into, and while setting up, you will be less able to be aware of what is happening on the edges of your campsite.
- No drinking while out camping. Keep a clear head so you can be keenly aware of all things surrounding you. You need all of your senses working at their height.
- Never overestimate your skills. Don't try a thirty-mile hike on your own and plan to get back safely to your campsite if the most you've done so far is a five-miler. Don't set up a scenario where you will end up stranded on a trail, exhausted and staring into the dark.
- Remember, hiking with a backpack loaded with gear is a lot different than strolling around your neighborhood or local lake gabbing on the cell phone. Especially if you are a beginning camper, try a few nights with friends before you go solo, if possible.
- Always bring an emergency device. They work like personal locators because they send out distress signals. Keep it on you. Some campgrounds have hosts. If you camp near one, you are positioned near radio contact with park authorities.
- Camp near a host or a family. When you arrive, find out the name and number of the host on call. Enter the number into your cell phone.
- Bring your dog. No intruder wants to meet up with teeth and claws.
- Visit camping forums online to find out about your desired campground.
- Keep your cell phone with you at all times and keep it fully charged.
- Bring a Mophie, extra batteries, or a power bank.
- Do not go out walking alone at night.
- Plan with family or friends back home to check in with them within a certain time period. It doesn't have to be on the dot; it can be mornings before work or sometime after dinner. Make it daily or every other day. It's just two minutes of your time. Regular check-ins are especially important if you decide to head to a more remote area.
- Determine how long it will take you to get to your designated goal each day and let family or friends know that.

- Drive for shorter time segments during the days so you can stay alert.
- Consider a personal security alarm. It frees your hands, and an attacker is not likely to pursue a very loud and moving target.
- If you wear a safety whistle around your neck, thread it onto a beaded-metal chain that can't be used as a ligature. Consider a bracelet whistle.
- Know how to signal SOS. SOS, the international distress signal, is simply three short bursts, three long sounds, then three short bursts again. This is easily achievable with your RV or car horn, whistle, or noisemaker. Three short blasts, three long sounds, then three short bursts. Pause, then repeat.
- Check for car repairs before each and every trip.
- Pick campgrounds with 24/7 security, no weekends or evenings off. I've made that mistake before.
- Park close to other RVs.
- Keep a dummy or a blow-up figure that will pass as a man or fellow traveler easily spotted through your RV window.
- Consider signing up for an RV group online or in real life. There are dozens of groups for solo RV lovers that all have one thing in common: they want to see the world from an RV.
- Never, ever allow a stranger inside your RV.
- Some RVers carry stun guns in the glove compartment, a gun in the oatmeal box, or even a hammer behind the driver's seat and under the commode.
- Don't flash money or jewelry when you get to the camp. People are watching more closely than you think.
- Keep phones, iPads, and laptops charged. Get a booster to find and keep a signal when you are out of range.
- Get a cell plan that includes the best coverage nationwide.
- Some suggest carrying a satellite phone or emergency tracker.
- If you hear someone outside your RV at night, do not wait! Hit the horn, crank up, and drive! If you're hooked up, make sure you live to fix it later.
- Plan routes and check for park availability one or two days ahead. Even if a website says there is availability, call and make sure.
- Read the online reviews from other campers. Learn from them.
- Keep your keys with you. Keep a second pair hidden within the RV. Make the hiding spot easily accessible in case of an emergency.

- Keep your cell phone within arm's length at night.
- Know your GPS coordinates at all times.
- Place tools or items that could be used as a weapon in various spots around your RV so you can grab something no matter where you are inside. Do not leave them outside the RV under any circumstance—they can be used against you.
- Many RVers keep a baseball bat beside the bed or in the bathroom.
- Use your car or RV horn as an emergency signal or sound the alarm from your key fob.
- Get a loud horn, like a bullhorn or megaphone, or even a siren. It will wake up the other campers in the night, and that's just what you want in an emergency.
- It may sound cliché, but stay aware of the surroundings. Stay away from rest stops. They are a predator's paradise.
- Do not stop at places that are empty or vacant.
- When you park and hook up, select a spot near lights that shine at night and activity.
- Try to park your RV in a lot with surveillance cameras.
- Research can help you find apps that keep you safe, including locations and routes. Many of the apps have comments from other travelers who have been to spots you will visit. Learn from their wisdom... and their mistakes!
- You must have a flashlight.
- Keeping a pair of men's boots or tennis shoes outside your RV is a great way to ward off intruders.
- Keep up the illusion you are not alone. For instance, set out two folding or camp chairs outside the RV.
- Even if you don't carry a gun, slap pro-gun stickers on the RV to scare off unwanted guests. I'm sure they'd rather target a victim they believe is unarmed.
- Place "beware of dog" placards in your RV windows.
- Carry pepper spray, wasp spray, or bear spray near the driver's seat or hidden within your RV. You may end up using it on the two-legged menace, not a bear or a wasp.
- Travel with a group of friends for a couple of trips before you strike out on your own.
- Make friends with other female campers at camps where you are staying. There are tons of groups to help you find like-minded

women travelers as well (check out Solo-Net, RVing Women, or Roadtrek SoloTrekkers).

- Choose a trusty RV you can handle and have it checked over by a mechanic. Learn to drive it confidently before you take off on a trip, including parking and hooking up to water and other amenities.
- Keep your RV maintained to avoid surprise breakdowns. You do not want to end up stranded on the side of the road. Follow a maintenance schedule. If you are renting the RV, make sure it's checked out thoroughly before you hit the road.
- This may be my most common tip: follow your instincts. If you get a weird vibe, leave. There will be another spot down the road.
- Always park your RV "Batman style," so you can drive straight out. Backing up can be a difficult and lengthy process, so get it out of the way up front if you can't pull straight through. If there's an emergency, you'll be able to get out quickly.
- Obviously, make sure your RV doors and windows are locked and closed while you are inside the RV, both day and night. Keep those RV doors and windows locked while you are out of the RV as well. Always double-check locks.
- Copy important documents like insurance papers and emergency numbers and keep them in a safe spot.
- Before you take off, create a checklist for setting up and breaking down camp with your RV. Keep it handy.
- Make sure you have GPS navigation and know how to use it. Have hard-copy map backups in case you run into bad reception.
- Never broadcast that you are traveling alone.
- Call out "hello" when you return and "goodbye" when you leave the RV. This may require acting skills if you do not actually have a partner inside.
- If boondocking or "dry camping"—parking your RV in a place without amenities like water hook-ups, such as a parking lot—try to park where there are other RVers.
- If you've let darkness creep up on you and you can't find an RV park, try a Walmart. They've been known to let an RV park for one night only.
- Avoid boondocking in spots that look fine by day but have potential to turn dangerous at night.
- Rest stops can be located in remote or deserted areas. This is the

perfect place for predators. If you must stop at a rest stop, which I advise against, know the mile marker and name in case you need to report it.

- If you must go to the bathroom, head to a gas station or restaurant as opposed to a rest stop.
- If you have to take a nap, try an RV site instead of a rest stop. It may cost a few bucks, but you will live to travel the next leg.
- Never let your children go into a rest stop bathroom by themselves. Keep them with you at all times.

PART FOUR

Cybercrimes and Security: When Technology Turns Dirty or Even Deadly

CHAPTER EIGHTEEN

Cybercrimes and Threats

All the conveniences of modern technologies like Wi-Fi make our lives easier. But they also make it easier for people to sneak into our lives and wreak havoc.

Where to start?

Do you know that feeling of waking up suddenly in the middle of the night, convinced you heard something...something wrong? I do.

BABY MONITOR HACKING

On the night of December 17, 2018, Ellen and Nathan Rigney of Houston, Texas, heard something, but it wasn't a tree limb against the side of the house or the wind chimes on the back patio.

It was a man talking to them in the dark, every other word a sexual expletive.

When they flicked on the lights, he ordered them to turn them off. His rant ended with words that left them cold: "I'm in your baby's room. I'm going to kidnap him."

Nathan Rigney flew up the stairs to find four-month-old Topper sleeping like a...baby. No one else was in the home. Standing there in Topper's room, Nathan realized that some perv had hacked their Nest baby monitor. How long had he been watching? How many times before? Who was he?

All these were questions that would never be answered.

Ellen Rigney told her story on Facebook and said she'd never forget that voice as long as she lived.

Technology has taken baby monitoring way past old-school walkie-talkies. It's connected to Wi-Fi now and a whole new ball game. Yet, with all the positives of Wi-Fi baby monitors come drawbacks such as hacking vulnerability.

In South Carolina, when twenty-four-year-old Jamie Summit woke up one morning in May 2018, she noticed the baby video monitor was turned directly to where she was sleeping. She thought nothing of it. That evening, though, while she and husband Kevin were having dinner, Jamie's smartphone alerted her that the monitor's camera was moving, but everyone that had access to move it was right there at the table.

They ran to baby Noah's room in time to see the baby camera panning around the room. It turned to stare at Jamie's bed, where she slept and breastfed, then quickly back to the bassinet. They grabbed the camera and disabled it.

The stories go on and on, but the premise is the same: cyberpervs are hacking baby monitors all over the country, and the sobering part is that it's like taking candy from... well, a baby.

Once connected to your baby monitor, a hacker will have full access to the same controls that you do when logged in remotely. If you have a talk-back feature or the ability to pan and zoom the camera, the hacker will as well. It makes a burglar's job so simple; all he has to do is sit back and take in the audio and video in your home to determine a perfect time to come over and break in.

It's not just burglars who may benefit. Identity thieves can try to peek at personal documents or your computer screen or listen as you talk on the phone to the bank or credit card company.

While Nest cameras and similar technologies are being targeted, any home device connected to the internet is vulnerable to hacking—anything you interact with via Wi-Fi, from your printer to your thermostat to your phone and tablet.

If your baby monitor gets hacked, you risk not just an invasion of your privacy but the theft of vital information from home computers and mobile devices. There go your bank accounts and credit cards. Simple vulnerabilities that have already been addressed and corrected in mainstream products like your PC, laptop, and mobile devices have not come to baby monitor security.

And it isn't always the creepy scenario of some perv spying on you through the baby monitor. There are people who spend time sweeping the internet just to find unsecured cameras and cameras that are still set to the factory setting for user code and password. It's not about you specifically.

It was serious enough that the Federal Trade Commission acted. The FTC made waves in the baby monitor market when it went after TRENDnet for lax security in designing and testing software, including the settings for the cameras' password requirement. The FTC said that because of that weakness, consumers' private camera feeds were made public on the internet.

When I found out about this strong consumer advocacy, I was so proud I once worked with them. According to the FTC, hackers took advantage of this major flaw and then posted links to the live feeds of hundreds of cameras. The private video, streaming online, showed infants asleep in cribs, tots playing, and moms and dads walking around all through the home in various states of dress. To their credit, TREND-net then uploaded a software patch to its website to warn customers. And remember: all these invasive attacks start with baby monitors.

How to fight back?

One option is to go for a less sophisticated monitor that doesn't connect to the internet but instead uses old-fashioned radio technology. That, too, can be hacked, though, and the quality has been compared to two cans connected by string. The other problem with radio technology is you can't check in on your baby or babysitter with your smartphone or while away. So, even though Nest has had its problems, it's still a good choice if you change the username and factory password.

When you are considering getting a digital or analog signal, remember that digital monitors are usually more secure than analog.

BABY MONITOR TIPS

- Update your baby monitor password, not only changing it from the factory set password when you first get it but regularly thereafter. (See below for my overall advice on all of the passwords for all of your devices, accounts, and programs.)
- Stay current on updates to your baby monitor software. Tech companies are always shoring up cracks in security and trying to stay one step in front of the hackers.
- Watch for factory reset overrides, though. Some baby monitors can

reset to factory defaults without warning, even allowing the passcode authentication to be skipped. That's like logging on to your laptop or cell phone without using the security code.

- The Nest or monitor device should be unplugged when not in use.
- Two-factor authentication (TFA) sounds complicated, but it's not. TFA gives an extra layer of security to online accounts beyond just a password. Instead of just one piece of proof—your password— to show you truly are the authorized user, TFA asks for a second verifier, such as your cell phone number. This procedure helps make sure nobody can hack into your account just by knowing your user name and passcode.
- To change your password, you need to have the cell phone that's connected to the account so you can get a text and then enter it as proof that you are really you. That's what TFA is all about, having another bit of information a hacker wouldn't have. It's available on Apple products, Facebook, Gmail, Yahoo, Instagram, Twitter, and others. Look for help on these sites, or just do a Google search for "two-factor authentication." It's so easy.
- In addition to TFA, you could also activate the WPA2 encryption codes on your routers or subscribe to a virtual private network (VPN).
- Turn off your baby monitor when not using it. It may be just for parts of the day or night or while you are on vacation. But you will stop hacking in those time periods and perhaps thwart future hacking attempts.
- Put a Post-it over your baby monitor's lens when you aren't using it.
- Remove old default login credentials that may fill in automatically.
- Check logs for odd access entries, such as times you aren't there or weren't using it.
- Update the firmware in your camera.

HOME WIRELESS SAFETY TIPS

Home is where the heart is…and the internet, too. You must secure your home wireless network. Do not be lulled into a false sense of complacency. Never get sucked into believing "Hackers would never target *me!*" They can and they will. No bank account is too big or too small for hackers to at least try to infiltrate. You have to protect your internet and wireless access. But how?

Going wireless means you have connected internet access to a wireless router, which allows multiple devices to connect from different places around your home without being tethered to the wall. They all go through your router. If you don't secure your router, anyone can hack in and use your internet service for free and worse.

- Change your home's Wi-Fi password regularly, and give some thought to making it stronger and truly hard to decipher. This idea works for all the vital passwords in your life, and it will come up again. Change your passwords.
- Do not let me find out your code is 1-2-3-4! That goes for any device or service for which you have a password or code. Take this seriously.
- Change the name of your router. A default ID is assigned by the manufacturer. Change your router name to something unique others can't guess and therefore easily hack.
- The manufacturer also presets your router password. Hackers compile lists of common manufacturer passwords and can crack them if they're not changed. Change your password to something strong, at least twelve characters long, as you should do for all passwords. (See below for more password tips and ideas.)
- Select your router's security level. WPA2 or WPA are more secure than WEP.
- You can also turn on WPA2 encryption. It makes it even harder for hackers.
- Use a firewall. Your security software and your operating system come with a firewall already installed. You must turn it on.
- Make sure you install antivirus protection in addition to the basic protections provided by both Windows and Mac systems. There are paid and free versions.
- Install router software updates. I keep mine set to receive automatic updates. This is important because updates include security enhancements.
- Don't use outmoded security software to combat advanced hacking techniques. Hackers are always looking for the newest, sneakiest way to hack your system. Stay up to date.

BE SMART ABOUT YOUR SMART DEVICES

- Do not leave your devices alone. Their physical security is equally important as their digital security. If devices must be left unattended, lock them so no one else can use them.
- Keep your desktop computer shut down or at least lock its screen when you're not using it. Same thing with your tablet or smartphone.
- Try to keep sensitive data like Social Security numbers and bank account numbers off your devices.
- Never plug in a USB whose source you are not sure of. It could be loaded with malware.
- Make sure you have a password or PIN on your mobile device, be it phone or tablet.

DON'T FALL FOR THE BAIT OF "PHISHERS"

Don't get phished. Phishing is a type of hacking that tries to obtain your credit card info, Social Security number, secret codes, user names, and other data about you through legitimate-looking emails and other communications.

Why?

To steal from you.

Malicious emails can pretend to be from credible sources. I've gotten them from phishers purporting to be the US Postal Service, Verizon, American Express, and even the US government. One even masqueraded as the IRS. My sister-in-law even got a fake summons to appear in US federal district court.

There are so many deceptively "innocent" phish titles, such as "Gmail attachment," "College Football," "Holiday e-Card Alert," "Thanksgiving Day Recipes," "Flash Update Required"—the list is endless! All of these and many more are just clever attempts to get you to share your data.

If you give a phisher information like your cell phone or landline number, you've given them a way into your life.

How?

Cross-directories can connect that phone number to an address or an account. Next thing you know, you've had your direct deposit information used to siphon your bank account, charge your credit cards, or open new accounts.

The bad guy accomplishes this by tricking you into clicking on their website link, and when you do, they get your IP address and possibly other info. Their email may sound urgent and direct you to "update your account information." When you click that link and enter your information, you unwittingly send your username and possibly your password and other information directly to the perp. Phishing is a danger via email, text, and phone. Beware.

How can you avoid phishing?

Check the sender's email address. If you look carefully, you will see a discrepancy between the phish and the real thing. It happened to me when I got a very "phishy" email from American Express. I called AmEx and found out the email was a fake. Call the real entity (credit card or utility company, bank, Social Security office) using a phone number you look up yourself, not one given in the email. Verify that email! Never give anyone your Social Security number or any personal information when you did not contact the company first.

Authentic websites never display your email address in the header or subject line.

If you want to verify a specific link, go to www.virustotal.com. This site will let you know if you should click on or share a link you don't immediately trust. You may come across information about small, legitimate companies whose names you don't recognize. You may also come across harmful sites that look benign. VirusTotal will show you the difference.

Bottom line: a lot of phishers look like the real thing. Verify before you click, especially if the communication varies from the way you usually interact with that company.

PASSWORD SMARTS

- Develop a unique, strong, and long password for each of your important devices and accounts. Experts recommend twelve to twenty characters or more. Use a mix of characters, letters, and numbers. *Do not use 12345!*
- Do not take easy shortcuts like reusing the same password over and

over. If hackers get it, they have the key to not one but all your accounts, from Netflix, to savings and checking, to your retirement and college funds. Use a password management program to help you create strong passwords; that way, you only have to remember one strong password. Some can also alert you of potentially compromised passwords, and they can be set to send reminders to update them.

- Never write down your passwords, especially anywhere near your computer.
- Never use the "show password" feature on your screen and shield view of your hands if anyone is near when you must type in a password, such as in a public place or on a plane or train. You never know who's looking over your shoulder, getting an eyeful of what you're typing.
- Don't share passwords.

BACK UP REGULARLY

Protect your data, work, photos, and contacts. Consider backup storage in "the cloud"—connected computer sources—not just within your device. Cloud backup is just copying files, apps, or whatever you have stored in your tablet, laptop, PC, or device, and storing it all on a remote network you can access through the internet. That way all your data is kept separate from a possible device failure (your computer self-destructs), malware attacks, or some other disaster (you drop it in the neighborhood pool or bath, your child pours chocolate milk into the keyboard, etc.).

Back up everything, including files, folders, photos, videos, documents, and disks. Leave nothing unprotected. Save your data.

I have a special redundant backup system for photos. In addition to Carbonite, I have automatic backup on my phone and devices, and I use a setting in Dropbox to automatically back up photos. There are lots of alternatives, too. Google Photos is free. Find one that works for you.

You can also keep copies on external drives. My husband talked me into that, and two years later, it paid off. When I left my laptop on a plane, mistakenly thinking the flight attendant had stuck it into my backpack, I was devastated. Then, I remembered that external drive.

Some experts advise you to encrypt photos before copying them onto an external drive, in case someone else gets hold of it. I'll say it again: back up important data and files.

RANSOMWARE

Be on the lookout for ransomware, a huge cyberthreat. Ransomware encrypts your data, locks you out of your computer or device, and demands a fee in exchange for the decryption code. Avoid ransomware by using an antivirus program and not clicking on suspicious links in emails or on the internet. Never negotiate with or pay someone using ransomware. You are dealing with criminals, and there is no guarantee you'll ever get your data back. If ransomware does strike your computer, rely on your own backup copies of your data that you store in the cloud or on thumb or other kinds of drives.

PUBLIC WI-FI WISDOM

Think twice about joining free Wi-Fi hotspots. Whenever I'm out and about, the temptation is strong. When you are in a hotel, nail salon, coffee shop, airport, or any public place that you believe offers free Wi-Fi, confirm the name of the network with staff before you get on. It's super easy for a perp to set up a free Wi-Fi spot using some version of the venue name to rope you in, like a poisonous spider spinning its web waiting for you, the gnat, to fly by. Starbucks offers Wi-Fi via Google. Get to that level of security before you sign on.

Make sure you turn off file sharing when on a public network. Look in your device's settings to find the place where you can do that.

Some experts even advise setting up a virtual private network (VPN) for browsing as opposed to using public Wi-Fi. It's worth looking into if you find yourself often using the internet in public.

Turn off Wi-Fi when you aren't using it.

Never use or log on to your accounts using someone else's computer. You have no idea if the device has a malware infection such as a key logger that copies everything you type.

SAFE ONLINE SHOPPING

- Never shop from a device that isn't yours.
- Never store your credit card information with a site or on a device.
- Shop only with trusted and known websites.
- Make sure any shopping site connection is encrypted. Look for a lock icon in the address bar. Check to see if the shopping address begins with "https" and not just "http." That *s* indicates the shopping site has a Secure Sockets Layer (SSL) certificate.
- Some experts advise that you use a designated card only for shopping online. Using one account for your online shopping makes staying on of top things much easier.
- If you shop on an unknown site, use caution. Red flags for shopping sites are misspellings, poor grammar, low-resolution or stock photos, or repeated reboots.
- Check your credit card statements at least once a week to make sure no one has used them without your knowledge.
- Do not use identical passwords on all your shopping accounts.
- Do not click for automatic fill-in for home address or credit card details.
- Do not agree to conditions and terms before reading them.
- Do not click on social media offers without reading them first.
- Never hand over confidential data online unless it is a trusted site like your bank, credit card, or large vendor that you have contacted directly.

DOWN WITH FAKERS

Do you hate fakers? I sure do, and I've met plenty of them in the TV industry as well as in the courthouse. If you agree, I'm sure you feel the same about fake social media profiles.

But how do you know when a social profile is fake?

When you first spot a profile picture, do an image search on Google or www.tineye.com. Like a reverse phone directory that matches an address or name to a number, these searches will show you everywhere that photo shows up online. By doing an image search, you can find out if the profile photo is a stock photo or if a different person is using it. If a ton of results show up, it's a fake.

Never accept friend requests from people you don't know. Fake profiles can trick you. Of course cybercriminals want to be your "friend," but they're not interested in you. They're interested in your data.

Beware of LinkedIn fakers. Hackers love to come at you through LinkedIn to get your info. They'll use a fake or sometimes real company name from your industry, hoping you'll think you're expanding your network. But you're not.

Beware of pretenders who claim to be with your credit card company, airline, bank, or other trusted entities who ask for your password, date of birth, or other critical data. Always guard that kind of information with great care.

BAD SOCIAL MEDIA HABITS TO BREAK

Do not overshare on social media. It affects your cybersecurity. Information like your home address, date of birth, zodiac sign, and names of pets can all be used against you. Somewhere out there is a hacker collecting the information you share on social media in order to get into your accounts and drain them or create a fake identity, a fake *you*.

Do not check in on social media! Here's the deal. Facebook Places, Foursquare Swarm, Snapchat, and other apps encourage you to use the GPS on your cell phone to alert friends to exactly where you are. When you tap the Check In button, you see a list of nearby places and pick a place matching where you are. By checking in on Facebook, you plant a story in your friends' news feeds. You are supposed to write down what you do there and basically create a trail for friends to follow and see what you did at that spot days, or even years, before. It may be part of a giant "location war" between the giants Facebook and Foursquare, but it's a nightmare for you.

Think about it: Is there a better way to tip off the bad guys that you are not home?

Don't check in from the airport. Those shots of you and your kids in beach shirts or snow gear while juggling the luggage are super cute, but hold it! Don't check in with Instagram posts loaded with your awesome vacation photos. Remember, more data about you online gives cyber-criminals more data to gather and use against you. You might as well lease a billboard on Fifth Avenue with giant letters declaring, "I'm on vacation...Rob my house!"

Protect yourself and your children. I strongly advise you wait to post until you are back home.

Some experts even warn not to check in when you're at home, so bad guys never know your exact location. And yes, they can hack into your check-ins. Your friends aren't the only ones looking to see where you are.

Smart geotagging is no geotagging. Don't do it. Ask others not to tag you, too, and configure your social media settings so you have to approve it anytime someone tries to tag you.

If you have a history of check-ins with geotagging from local spots you visit often, home, or work, you can still go back and delete your prior history locations. It's not that hard. For Instagram, simply go to "edit location." For Facebook, you must manually edit each post and delete the location. Then make sure you click off location information for all your future posts.

When you are on social media, hide your full email address or account. You can do this in your privacy settings.

GET RID OF SPAM

Spam is a hacker's best friend, so block it. Empty the spam folder regularly, too.

- Unsubscribe to emails or newsletters you no longer want. Take the time to scroll to the bottom and click on "unsubscribe."
- Be super careful about whom you give your email address to.
- Mark unwanted email as spam.
- Disable automatic HTML graphics downloads from emails. It's in your settings.
- Never click links or open zip attachments from unknown senders.
- Remember, anyone can be hacked. No one is safe from these threats.

WATCH YOUR APPS

- Avoid unsecure sources when downloading apps. Rogue apps can attack your data.
- Do not install apps on your tablet, PC, or phone from a source you cannot verify.
- Beware when you see a big sign on your screen that urges you to "install" an app. Check it out before you hit that button, or suffer the malware consequences.
- It is best to use only the official websites and app stores associated with your device to download your apps.
- Don't be a digital hoarder. Get rid of old apps you no longer use. Keeping them around makes it that much easier for hackers to use them to invade.
- Revoke permissions for apps that ask to access sensitive information like messages or any other data.
- Disable your phone's ability to install third-party apps. Don't download or install apps from ads, blogs, or online contacts. They may, even unintentionally, infect you with malware. Know that sometimes even app store apps may be infected, although it is less likely.
- Examples of dangerous apps include those that claim they can change your Facebook profile, apps presenting as a virus protection or removal, and apps to "clean" your computer.
- Enable the "Find My..." app or its equivalent on your smartphone and tablet.
- Keep your apps updated. They'll run better, and many updates include patches for better security.

BROWSE SAFELY

First and foremost, keep your browsers up to date. Install updates on browsers as they become available.

There's one super-easy way to safeguard your browsing, and it only takes a couple of minutes to set up. Install the HTTPS Everywhere browser extension on Chrome, Opera, Firefox, and Firefox for Android. When this extension is active, data you receive and send from major websites is encrypted, so cybercriminals can't observe your keystrokes and steal data like passwords, email addresses, Social Security numbers, addresses, or credit card info. This one simple and free extension encrypts all your communications with tons of the major websites. Find it at https://www.eff.org/https-everywhere.

TROJAN HORSE ADS

Believe it or not, even on credible websites, "mal-ads" can be found. These are seemingly innocent ads that, once opened by you, release malware. Once malware is injected into your computer or device, your data can be stolen or destroyed. As I say so often, trust your gut. If the ad doesn't look right, scroll past it.

You *will be* infected with malware on naughty sites—and some other not-so-naughty sites as well. When you spot an "interesting" photo of, for example, a bikini shot, be careful. Cyberperps infect those photos or even their banner ads with malware. The rest of the website may or not be malware-free, but many times you don't even have to click to be infected. These thieves love to infect eye-catching banners or photos with malware, even if the rest of the website is safe. Even worse, you don't even have to click on the banner or photo to catch the infection.

Beware of "fileless malware." This type of malware does not use any particular file to infect you. Usually, an antivirus program can protect you by spotting an infection on your hard drive and then removing or quarantining it to safeguard your computer. But with fileless attacks, no file is ever dropped into your system, so usual antivirus techniques don't work.

Absorb this statistic: about 90 percent of all web attacks on data are funneled through advertising. What's the answer? Ad blockers.

Ad blockers are browser extensions or apps you download and install. They block incoming pre-roll ads in videos, pop-ups, and over-lays, to name a few. Aside from the irritation ads and pop-ups cause, ad blockers also stop malicious advertising loaded with malware.

FILE SHARING

Another unwitting culprit can be peer-to-peer (P2P) file sharing. It all starts so innocently. P2P is simply when you share digital media like music, movies, books, or games with other anonymous users. You access digital files on software that searches on a P2P network like BitTorrent. Even Microsoft uses P2P for playing games online and their update distributions. Be cautious.

BY EXTENSION

It's time for an extension check! Cyberperps seek outdated plug-ins and browser extensions because it's easy to forget them or let them get out of date. Go to your browsers and uninstall or delete those old browser plug-ins. Make sure all the ones you currently use are updated.

Many browsers like Firefox and Chrome get regular updates and keep plug-ins like Flash current, which helps performance. And, as you know by now, updates often increase security.

CHAIN, CHAIN, CHAIN

Chain letter email messages grab your attention in several ways, such as sharing alarming (fake) "news" that gets you to click and share, touting sensational (fake) celebrity news, asking you to donate to a cause with upsetting stories about children or families in peril, or using celebrities' names without their permission to get you to click or donate. Once you click, download, or send, the virus grows. Learn to spot this stuff and delete it immediately.

NO SHORT LINKS

Beware of short links from unknown sources. Don't succumb to temptation and click to find out what it is. I can tell you right here what it is: it's a malware infection that will then spread to all your contacts even if you haven't contacted them recently. If you are that curious about a short link that pops up out of nowhere, go to a link extender like CheckShortURL.com to find out what the link really is.

SPOT SCAMS

If it sounds too good to be true, *it is*.

If it appears to be "free," *it's not*.

You have *not* won some wonderful prize out of the blue.

It's a scam and it's all about getting into your money. But to this very day, offers of "free" goods and services still work. People fall for it. Please, don't be one of them.

When you spot an offer for a free trip, gift cards, iPhones, or coupons, stop what you're doing and back away from the keypad. Do not click.

Don't be fooled by a scam using a popular name like Starbucks, Outback Steakhouse, or Cheesecake Factory.

Here's a confession: My husband fell for fake online tickets for "cut the line" entry for the four of us at the Metropolitan Museum of Art in New York. He lost $100. And he should have known better. The Met wouldn't let you cut the line if Santa Claus dropped you straight off his sleigh onto the museum's front steps. Luckily, he charged it on American Express, so he disputed the charge. My husband fell for an online scam! Believe me, he knows better.

Beware of "urgent" messages that require your immediate action directing you to "download this" or "respond immediately" or "click now." These are very often fraudulent.

Be leery of hard-luck stories and their senders who need you to send them money so they can send you an even bigger sum as a "reward." The "Nigerian Gentleman in Trouble Needs Money" scam has stolen millions.

Social media scams have made their way to the big leagues; you can find them on Twitter, Facebook, and Instagram, just to name a few. No social media, no matter how trusted, is immune. So, *you* have to be ready.

Scammers are scheming 24/7/365. Watch out for any unknown entity trying to get you to "like" a page, comment, share, or tag them or their photo or blurb. If you do, it guarantees the action will show up in your feed and give them a way to reach more people: your contacts.

WEBCAM DANGER

Everyone is susceptible, even the rich, famous, and powerful. I remember when Miss Teen USA Cassidy Wolf broke down when describing the moment she opened an email. In it were photos of her naked. Those photos were surreptitiously taken through her own webcam. To make matters worse, she then got a blackmail demand: create better photos, a video, and a sex show, or the images would be made public. Her beauty pageant career would be ruined.

As it turned out, a high school "friend," Jared James Abrahams, managed to install Blackshades malware on her laptop as well as hacking up to 150 other women. He had been secretly watching Cody in her bedroom through her webcam for over a year. Abrahams's arrest coincided with an investigation involving the FBI and police in nineteen countries as part of a global operation. Abrahams was sentenced to eighteen months in prison after pleading guilty to one count of computer hacking and three counts of extortion. He hacked into over a hundred accounts and demanded nude photos or nude Skype sessions with his victims.

After living through her webcam hacking nightmare, Cody advises changing passwords often, deleting browsing history regularly, and putting a sticker over the webcam when not in use.

Miss Teen USA isn't the only one advocating webcam safety. Even the former director of the FBI, James Comey, puts tape or a Post-it over his laptop or PC webcam. Think about it: the FBI and Miss Teen USA can't both be wrong.

DIFFERENT ACCOUNTS, DIFFERENT EMAILS

Many experts advise setting up different emails and passwords for different purposes. That means separate emails for shopping, Facebook, Uber or Lyft, personal emailing, and business. If one is hacked, the others are not affected—yet.

TAKE NOTE OF UNSUPPORTED SOFTWARE

Have you ever seen a notice that a company has discontinued support for a particular software program? This is big. Ending support means that it's no longer implementing or updating security, which opens that software up to countless security threats. It also means no more technical support for that software. Bottom line: don't use unsupported software, including your browsers.

WHEN THE ANTIVIRUS IS A VIRUS

I nearly fell out of my chair when I saw the alert pop up on my screen: "You have been infected. We have detected 96 potential risks. Download Antivirus XYZ now!" I'd like to add that the warning was framed in bright green neon with red "click" spots. Needless to say, it got my attention, and I actually started reading it. It even had audio. Luckily, I simply got distracted by having to literally rush out the door to get the twins somewhere, basketball or choir or something. That something may have saved literally thousands of photos and videos of the twins, and many years of work.

I nearly fell victim to one of the most tried-and-true plays in the cyberperp's bag of tricks: the old "fake antivirus" scam. Reliable antivirus companies never disseminate information like that. But the fakes look so real, so legit!

What's the danger of the fake antivirus? If you activate it, you think you are downloading an antivirus program that is actually malware. You are literally doing the opposite of what you think you are doing. It hits cell phones, too. Bottom line: only download antivirus from sources you trust.

SECURE YOUR CELL PHONE

All the above advice regarding ads, browsers, links, phishing, apps, extensions, and scams apply to your mobile devices too. Here are some additional tips.

- Never leave your mobile phone physically on its own anywhere.
- Always have a security password set for your mobile. You may lose your phone, leave it behind, or leave it unattended on a tabletop, and then it's all over.
- Four-digit passwords are easier to break, so make your password as strong as it can be.
- Draw a pattern on the keyboard instead of a numeric code if your phone allows it.
- Activate fingerprint ID if it's available on your phone, which is the hardest to hack.
- Use facial recognition if your device has it.
- Make sure the auto lock is activated to lock your screen after a very short period of inactivity. Fifteen seconds is perfect.
- Back up your smartphone data, just in case. Specifically, set up automatic backup in the cloud.
- Turn on encryption if your device has it. Enable it.
- Install an antivirus program on your cell phone. A mobile antivirus program won't be as powerful as one for a desktop or laptop, but it's better than nothing. If you plug your phone into an infected laptop or PC, the infection spreads to your phone.
- Don't connect your phone to an unknown computer.
- As with your laptop or tablet, do not connect your cell phone to public Wi-Fi, especially when viewing or typing sensitive data, unless you can verify that it's a legitimate hot spot. Sorry. You will have to use your mobile data. It costs you money, but you and your data will be much safer.
- Keep Bluetooth turned off when you're not using it. Only enable Bluetooth when needed.

FACTORY DATA RESET

If you plan to get a new phone, make sure you wipe your old phone clean before handing it over. Otherwise, you are handing over not only an old cell phone but years of sensitive data. Execute a factory data reset to wipe all your data so its next owner won't be able to access your contacts, credit cards, bank accounts, and, basically, your life. Remember, *back up all that data first*.

Cybercrime is one of the fastest-growing categories of crime throughout the world. Don't fall victim to crimes and scams that endanger so much and so many. Educate yourself and implement these safeguards consistently across your digital life. Make sure you can enjoy all the wonderful advances and conveniences of the tech revolution while staying safe from the predators that lurk all around.

CHAPTER NINETEEN

Internet Dating and Online Ads

I know so many couples who have met online and ended up in happy relationships and marriages. It works! But is internet dating safe? And what about posting or responding to online ads for goods or services? There are so many success stories, but on the other hand...judge for yourself.

JENNIFER ST. CLAIR

In December 2018, a young Fort Lauderdale woman, thirty-three-year-old Jennifer St. Clair, was thrilled to go out on her first date with a handsome guy, Miles McChesney. They met on Tinder, and from what appeared online, McChesney, thirty-four, had it all: looks, personality, and smarts. The two planned a triple date, meeting up with two other couples to go for a night out. It started out well when Miles showed up looking handsome, riding an expensive black Harley-Davidson motorcycle, and wearing the same million-dollar smile he had online. According to Jennifer's family, the group went to several restaurants and bars and, at the end of the evening, were heading home. That's when something went horribly wrong.

Jennifer was thrown off the Harley and into oncoming traffic on Florida's busy interstate I-95. But, according to witnesses, instead of helping her or even bothering to call 911, McChesney gunned his motor and fled the scene. Due to the state of her body, even the medical examiner couldn't determine whether Jennifer died on impact or sometime immediately afterward when she was run over by nine other cars.

So far, McChesney—who has not been charged with any crime and is not cooperating with authorities—hasn't publicly explained why he reportedly left Jennifer there to die on the highway. Maybe it had to do with his rap sheet and the times he'd been in halfway houses and prison. Whatever the case, Jennifer's family has now filed a wrongful death case against him that states McChesney is accused of "carelessly and negligently" operating the motorcycle, causing St. Clair "to be expelled from said motorcycle into oncoming traffic" on Interstate 95.

I bet McChesney's Tinder profile didn't mention a thing about his rap sheet. Or that he'd gotten out of jail only nine days before Jennifer died.

MAEGAN TAPLEY

Maegan Tapley was known for handing out cookies in her neighborhood at Christmastime. A real sweetheart, she must have thought she hit the jackpot when she met Erich Stelzer online in December 2018. A twenty-five-year-old bodybuilder who posted weightlifting and diet advice videos to YouTube and Instagram, Stelzer stood six foot eight and weighed in at nearly three hundred pounds of pure muscle. With big brown eyes and a perfect smile, he made a great first impression online.

After meeting on Tinder, Maegan and Stelzer went out a few times. Then on December 27, Stelzer showed up at Maegan's home in Saugus, Massachusetts, looking for a ride to his place in Cohasset. Maegan agreed to take him home.

Soon after, police responded to a domestic disturbance call and said they found Stelzer "actively assaulting" a woman identified as Maegan Tapley with a knife. In order to save her, officers had to shock Stelzer with a stun gun, said the Cohasset Police Department. The family of the Massachusetts bodybuilder said he had been undergoing mental health treatment. Stelzer got medical treatment after the tasing but became unresponsive on the way to the hospital and died. Maegan was also rushed to the hospital with multiple stab and slash wounds but managed to survive. A GoFundMe page for Tapley announced that Maegan would need "many surgeries" and revealed that not only was she stabbed and slashed, but most of her hair was ripped from her head in the attack as well. Maegan's mom, Susan Tapley, said Maegan would require extensive plastic surgery and needed an eye specialist. She told a reporter at NBC Boston, "I feel for [Stelzer's] mother. She just lost her son. My daughter almost died because of his lunacy."

SYDNEY LOOFE

Twenty-four-year-old Sydney Loofe from Lincoln, Nebraska, was looking forward to her date on November 15, 2017, with Bailey Boswell after they met on Tinder. Loofe was so excited about the date that she posted giddy Snapchat photos of herself after primping, including the caption "Ready for my date."

But the very next day, when Sydney didn't show up for her job at Menard's, a home improvement retail chain, her family and friends became concerned. A search party set out and the FBI was called in.

It was three weeks before Sydney's body was found, dismembered and stuffed in garbage bags out in the middle of a marshy field. A pair of alleged online-dating grifters, Aubrey Trail, fifty-two and male, and Sydney's date that night, Bailey Boswell, twenty-four and female, were charged with first-degree murder and improper disposal of human skeletal remains. Court documents say Trail confessed to using an extension cord to strangle Sydney while her date, Boswell, cleaned the crime scene. The two posted Facebook videos declaring their innocence onto "Finding Sydney Loofe," a site created by Sydney's family during their desperate attempt to find her. Trail was convicted of murdering and dismembering Sydney but is now demanding a new trial and complaining about prison conditions. Boswell, also charged with first-degree murder, is awaiting trial at the time of this writing.

TORONTO SERIAL KILLER

Outdoorsy landscaper Bruce McArthur met plenty of dates online through Grindr, Scruff, and SilverDaddies. From 1998 to 2017, he preyed on men in Toronto's Church and Wellesley neighborhood, known as Gay Village. It wasn't until eight of them went missing that cops finally realized they had a serial killer on their hands. After a nine-day excavation of property and materials belonging to McArthur in January

2018, it was revealed that human remains were found "every day." Sometimes, it was just a tooth or a bone fragment, but ultimately a total of eight dismembered bodies were hidden in flower pots, plastic planters, and a compost pile in a ravine behind a house to which McArthur had access. The carnage and violence would seem to be more than enough to turn anyone off dating apps forever. The victims were Abdulbasir Faizi, Skandaraj Navaratnam, Majeed Kayhan, Soroush Mahmudi, Dean Lisowick, Selim Esen, Andrew Kinsman, and Kirushna Kanagaratnam. Many of their families had no idea they were even on a dating app or had ever met anyone online.

I could go on, but each story has a similar end. It's enough to turn you off online dating or dating apps forever. But don't throw the baby out with the bathwater. Read on.

ONLINE DATING SAFETY TIPS

- Don't offer too much information on your dating profile. Experts recommend not giving your full name until after your first date and after you have a chance to make an educated assessment of your date. Why? Giving your full name, thus making your name too easy to research online, gives your prospective date access to you and your background. Why hand that over to someone you can evaluate only by what they trickle out online? Be genuine, but hold back.
- Create a free Google Voice number to share before your first date rather than giving out your cell, home, or work number to some-one you don't know. Google Voice is a service that gives you a separate and distinct number to give prospective dates. Download the Google Voice app. Your phone will work the same. Try it. If things go sideways, just block unwanted calls and move on to the next prospect.
- Don't reveal where you work. What if things don't go as you'd like and your date shows up at your job? Describe what your education is and what you do for a living and why you love it, but leave specifics for later—if there is a later.
- Meet up for the first time in a public place. It's so obvious, but for your safety, you must have all your first dates in public. No hiking

up in the hills, no long drives with the top down, no walking along a secluded park path at night—no, no, and no! If it all works out, you'll have plenty of alone time—until you have kids, that is.

- Don't let your new online friend pick you up or drive you home. Drive yourself or take a bus or an Uber or Lyft. You don't want them to know where you live or work quite yet, nor do you want to be driven off in a car with a stranger. You might as well hitchhike on the highway for Pete's sake. Get there yourself, and then, when the romance is in full bloom, feel free to let him pick you up in his Bentley.
- Be careful of what your online photo reveals. No shots of you in front of your car or front door at home or in front of your office, or even standing in front of diplomas or other identifying information.
- Go one step further and use a photo of yourself that you will use only on dating sites. Why? A Google image search on a photo you have posted elsewhere may reveal all sorts of information you should only share later in the game.
- Don't rush that first date. Have several conversations and get to know the other person as well as you can before you meet. Fight the temptation to meet ASAP. Give them a chance to reveal their personality and look for inconsistencies in what they say.
- Don't drink too much or get high. You don't know this person, and anything could happen. Plus, it's a bad look. Think of your future children seeing snaps of Mommy drunk on her first date with Daddy.
- As gallant as you may think it is, don't let him walk you home. Why? The same reason I told you not to let him pick you up or take you home on date one. Better safe than sorry.
- If you get a weird vibe, leave. Don't worry about being rude. Make excuses and get out of there. Or just get out of there. That's why there's a ladies' restroom, which you can use as a ruse to leave the table and scram.
- Tell someone the details of your meet-up. A simple text or email will do, but do put it in writing in case it's needed later. Briefly include the location, time you're meeting, and when you expect to be back home. Text again when you get home. As an extra precaution, send your contact the link to your date's online profile.
- Carry pepper spray. You probably won't need it, but if you do, use

it. You can laugh about it on your tenth wedding anniversary—with someone else.

- Be your own private eye. Google every date's name, phone number, and photos. Check them out on LinkedIn, Facebook, Twitter, and other social media, and do a reverse image search on Google. The works. Don't get too stalkerish; just investigate. It's a fine line; don't cross it.
- Never set up a date by text chain. Talk to the person, many times, before you meet.
- Ask questions (nicely).

The right one is out there. Make sure you live to find them.

ONLINE AD DANGERS

Crime and commerce have found a whole new arena: the internet ad marketplace. Online personal and classified ads are disrupting our economy and our lives. Newspapers across the country have gone out of business after losing this enormous source of revenue. But responding to an ad on a website for goods and services seems like a promising idea—cut out the middleman. But there are hidden dangers in this way of doing business with strangers.

THE CRAIGSLIST KILLER

Just the name Craigslist Killer should send a chill down your spine. The story all started on April 14, 2009, when Philip Markoff, a second-year med student at Boston University, answered a Craigslist ad for massage services. Markoff met the masseuse, Julissa Brisman, in his Boston hotel room, zip-tied her, and killed her. At the time, he was engaged to Megan McAllister, who had been a med student as well. Markoff was then connected to two other robberies of defenseless victims, both of whom he found through Craigslist, the source of his grisly nickname.

On August 15, 2010, Markoff committed suicide in his Boston jail cell. It was one day after what would have been the year anniversary of his canceled wedding.

Julissa's tragic story started with her online ad for goods and services. And online ad crime is much more common than you may think.

A Missouri family was robbed and shot at when trying to buy their teen son his first car from a Craigslist seller.

Feds busted a robbery ring set up behind bars using Craigslist.

There are literally thousands of similar stories, and they all have one thing in common: people responding to online ads. You can find trouble whether you placed the ad or if you responded to it.

STAYING SAFE WHEN DEALING WITH AN ONLINE AD TRANSACTION

The following tips apply whether you are selling or buying.

- Insist on meeting in a public place.
- Never go to the other party's home.
- Never invite the other party to your home.
- Take someone with you.
- Take your cell phone with you.
- Let others know where you are going.
- Leave the details with someone about where you are going and what you know about the person with whom you are meeting.
- Never meet someone for this kind of deal in a random parking lot. Use a food court in a mall or meet in front of the police station. Many police departments have set up designated and monitored exchange spots; ask yours if it has one.
- Understand that you may be dealing with anyone, from a little old lady to a violent felon. The internet doesn't vet who buys and sells online.
- Google the other party's email to find out if it shows up in relation to anything bad.
- Exercise extreme caution when buying or selling something expensive.
- Never wire funds.
- Do not take cashier's checks.
- Do not take money orders.
- Do not give financial data like your bank account number, PayPal info, credit card, or Social Security info.

- Do not purchase anything sight unseen.
- Do not meet with anyone making vague inquiries.
- Remember, you owe the other party nothing. If you pick up on an odd vibe or notice anything at all out of the ordinary, burn rubber and leave.

CHAPTER TWENTY

Burglar Alarm Backfires

How many people have your home alarm code?
Think about it.

The one-off babysitter whose name you got from a friend or co-worker?

The refrigerator repair guy?

The bug guy?

The guy who installed the ceiling fan last year?

Your old friend from school who came to town to visit you last Christmas?

I bet the number of people who have your code has grown without you really intending it to or even thinking about it. But now, you have to think about it. You may totally trust your friends. But what about your friends' friends whom you have never met? Or their friends or teen children or grandchildren? And what about those handymen listed above or other people in and out of your home whom you don't really know? And what about the handyman's friends who could get their mitts on your alarm code?

The only way to avoid big problems is to change your codes often.

I have emphasized the importance of handling passwords and codes properly in other sections of this book. And it's important enough to review again here.

Never use 1234.

Believe it or not, there are statistics to show that nearly 30 percent of all four-digit codes in the US are the same twenty codes. I found this out when I read a study by Nick Barry, founder of DataGenetics. I was shocked at what I learned. He reviewed over three million passcodes starting with 0000 all the way to 9999 and discovered that almost 11 percent of the 3.4 million passwords were 1234! The first runner-up was 1111, and third place went to 0000. I looked the rest over: they include 1111, 2222, 3333, 4444, all the way to 9999, plenty of James Bond variations like 0007, and, of course, 6969 (no comment).

Alarms come with a preset code. You need to change it immediately when the system is installed. After you change it, make sure the old one no longer works. Many alarm systems allow multiple codes to work simultaneously. That could include your old code or the factory preset code.

Think beyond your own birthday or your children's birthdays. Your family's birthdates are online. Anyone who knows you can figure out all of your birthdates and plug them right into your burglar alarm keypad.

That goes for your anniversary, too.

Set up guest codes. Give out different codes to guests, babysitters, or handymen. That way, if one of them quits or has a falling out, you can just delete that particular code without affecting your family at all.

Reset your codes to different numbers at least twice a year. Directions are in your alarm's user manual or just call the manufacturer and ask for tech help. Change it up.

Power outages for any extended time could disable your alarms.

Alarm systems run on electricity. If a breaker flips or the electricity goes down, the alarm system could be disabled. Make sure your system's backup batteries are working. Your alarm system depends on them. They are usually found in the keypad or panel.

Here's the issue with batteries: they have a short life. They can go dead after about twelve hours of use. And if they're not placed properly, they won't work even if they're brand-new. So, if your home alarm system is running on batteries for any length of time, check the batteries.

Think about Hurricane Katrina, flooding, or wildfires. The bad guys are just waiting for some natural disaster to use to their benefit to thwart your alarm system. They are. I know. They are the human equivalent of the jackal in the wild. They may intend to just come in and loot. But what if you're actually home when they break in? Keep them out by being smart about your batteries. And hope for calm, sunny days.

If your home is in an area prone to power outages, get a generator. I did.

We've all heard of the bad guys cutting your phone signal by yanking or cutting the cord outside the home. You are then isolated, and worse, your home alarm system has been compromised because it uses the phone line to call your alarm company, police, fire, or EMTs.

What's the answer? A cell or radio backup.

They are not as reliable as a landline, but this is plan B. There are even alarm systems now that immediately send a signal if your landline is tampered with, so when it reverts to cell or radio, you know it's happening. Your noise alarm should still work even if the phone line is cut and the alarm company isn't notified. This means you will know there has been a breach and hopefully can call 911 yourself.

Test your system regularly.

Warning: VOiP (voice over internet protocol) phone lines may not work with your alarm system. If you change phone service, retest your system pronto. VOiP is much more economical but not as reliable, as it doesn't have a traditional landline.

Get to know your neighborhood watch captain and group. If your alarm sounds, they may be able to get there even before police, as they are already in your neighborhood.

Make sure your alarm company has your gate code and related information the police will need to get in when the alarm company calls them. Very often, cops just do a drive-by; if they can't get in or don't see anything amiss, they assume it was a false alarm, which it often is.

ANN BARTLETT

This reminds me of a very upsetting case that touched me personally. Ann Bartlett of Dekalb County, Georgia, dialed 911 just a few minutes after one a.m. Ann was distraught because she had "set the house on fire" with the oxygen concentrator she used to sleep. During the call, Ann's phone went dead. You'd think that would be a tip-off, right? But the dispatcher couldn't get back through...because the phone had gone dead. It was a portable phone, powered by battery and outlet.

Firefighters arrived but didn't see a blaze. So they left. Five hours later, Ann's home was consumed by a roaring blaze. Ann was found lying beside the garage door, burned beyond recognition. The garage door and the portable phone needed electricity, which the fire had disrupted. She couldn't see in the dark to manually open the garage door, and seeing nothing amiss, no one had helped.

Point? Make sure cops and firefighters can get through your gate, get all required information from your alarm company and also have a plan B for when electricity fails.

PART FIVE

Protecting Our Elderly

CHAPTER TWENTY-ONE

Our Seniors in Danger

As a brand-new prosecutor I, like all other practicing lawyers, had to take continuing legal education classes every year. Many of the prosecutors in my office at the district attorney's in inner-city Atlanta were traveling a few hours away to the Prosecuting Attorneys' Council for their annual classes. I decided to go see what it was all about.

When I arrived, one of the sessions on forensics had just started. I walked in silently and closed the door so as not to interrupt the speaker. I turned around and faced the podium and immediately saw an image I will never forget.

The large room held about two hundred prosecutors from various jurisdictions, but you could have heard a pin drop. In the darkness of the slide show, I saw the naked body of an elderly woman lying splayed across a bed in a ransacked bedroom. She was dead. It was one of the first dead bodies I had ever seen outside of a funeral. Even now, after all the crime scenes I've processed, autopsies I've attended, homicide photos I've analyzed, and cause of death reports I've read, I'm still gripped with a wave of revulsion at the cruelty depicted in that one photo in a darkened room over twenty years ago.

Since that powerful day, I've learned and seen firsthand that our seniors fall victim to violent crimes, murder, rape, and burglary, often in their own homes. We must do all we can to protect them.

THE COLUMBUS STOCKING STRANGLER

On a warm May evening in 1970, elderly Marion Brewer was robbed and attacked in her hotel room in Albany, New York. Two months later, also in Albany, eighty-five-year-old Nellie Farmer was raped, beaten, and robbed in her own apartment before being found strangled dead. Farmer's body was found covered with items from the home. A third elderly female was attacked, but lived.

Fast-forward five years to Syracuse, New York. Another string of attacks on elderly women begins when two more little old ladies are beaten, raped, and strangled with a scarf inside what they and their families believed to be their own safe homes. Jean Frost was raped and strangled nearly to death in her home in Syracuse, and a watch was stolen from her home. Then, Marion Fisher was found raped and strangled just outside Syracuse. When her body was found, her face was covered. As in Albany, all the Syracuse attacks took place in a flurry of just a few days.

Fast-forward two years, far south of Syracuse and Albany to the sleepy town of Columbus, Georgia. Sixty-year-old Mary Willis Ferne Jackson was alone in her home when she was attacked, brutally beaten, raped, and strangled dead with a nylon stocking. Jackson had been the director of public health education in Columbus for the previous twenty-six years, and when she didn't show up for work, everyone knew something horrible had happened. Police found her home strewn with papers and other articles, including a pillow and an opened suitcase. Drawers had been flung open and their contents were left hanging out, but diamonds and other valuables were never touched.

Jackson's body was found on her bed. Her killer had tied a nylon stocking and a dressing gown cord together to make a deadly ligature and then wrapped it around Jackson's neck over and over, leaving deep crevasses. Her left eye was full of blood from a massive blow, her sternum was fractured, and her vagina was torn and bloody. Postmortem, her killer covered her face and body.

Days later, seventy-one-year-old Jean Dimenstein was beaten, raped, and murdered with a stocking. Dimenstein, unmarried and originally from Philadelphia, owned a department store in Columbus and had been out the night before to a steakhouse with two friends who watched her walk into her house safely after dinner. To get in, the killer removed the hinges on the door leading from her garage into her kitchen. The MO was the same, and Dimenstein's body was found buried under a pile of sheets and pillows.

Then came several more rapes and murders. Eighty-nine-year-old

Florence Scheible was murdered on October 21. Scheible was nearly blind and needed a walker to move about. A few days later, Martha Thurmond was killed with a nylon stocking. Two months passed before seventy-four-year-old Kathleen Woodruff met her end. Woodruff had been the widow of University of Georgia football coach George C. Woodruff and the close friend of the famous American novelist Carson McCullers. Woodruff was strangled with a football scarf.

Several weeks later, elderly Ruth Schwob, who ran a textile business founded by her late husband, woke in the middle of the night. A man in a mask was straddling her in bed and trying to strangle her with a pair of tights. He certainly didn't expect Schwob to be trained in judo. She fought him off and had just one brief moment to press a bedside alarm, causing her attacker to run from her home. Local police found Schwob sitting on the edge of her bed. A knotted stocking was tied around her neck, and she was still gasping for air.

Schwob's bedside alarm saved her life, but when the attacker fled, he only went two blocks from her home to find his next victim, seventy-eight-year-old Mildred Borom, who was raped, beaten, and strangled to death with a cord from her venetian blinds. Borom's body was covered with garments from her home.

A couple of months and a few blocks away, schoolteacher Janet Cofer met the same fate in her own home as well. Cofer was raped, strangled with a stocking, and left dead with a pillow pulled over her to cover her face.

But why the intervals between the spates of rapes and murders? And why cross the country from Albany to Syracuse to Columbus, Georgia? Simple. Because as soon as the so-called Stocking Strangler first moved to Albany, elderly women suddenly began to be raped and murdered one after the next. Carlton Gary's fingerprints were found at the scene of the last attempted assault in Albany, but he was charged only with robbery. He served a light sentence and was paroled from the Onondaga County Correctional Institution. He moved to Syracuse, and immediately elderly women were targeted for rape, brutal beatings, and murders. One survivor described Gary to a tee.

Again, Carlton Gary escaped true justice and was never charged for any of the Syracuse crimes but, instead, got his parole revoked for selling coins stolen from one of his victims. Then, to rub salt in the wound of injustice, Gary sawed through bars in his cell and jumped from a third-floor prison window to escape. He then headed to Albany, Georgia, and settled into a home two blocks from his victim Gertrude Miller's home. One month after his escape, the first of the Columbus murders occurred. After seven more murders of elderly women, Carlton Gary was caught, thanks to a single fingerprint in a victim's home.

Carlton Gary went to trial professing his innocence, but his fingerprints at four of the Columbus crime scenes, DNA, and eyewitness accounts landed Gary on Georgia's death row. The condemned Stocking Strangler did not accept a final prayer or make a final statement.

HELL IN THEIR OWN HOME

Greensboro, North Carolina, is beautiful, and the countryside around it is stunning. What I really like, though, is the low crime rate. With that in mind, Mary and Lloyd Cox have lived south of Greensboro for over sixty years and have always loved it. But one Saturday night, the peace and security of living in a rural setting was destroyed for them forever.

On December 28, 2018, the two were snuggled in at home when, before they even realized what was happening, a twenty-three-year-old man crashed through their back door, screaming out, "I am Ryan Christopher Mendenhall!" He appeared out of his mind with anger, booze, belligerence, and hate. Mendenhall began trashing the home they worked so hard to perfect in their golden years, destroying furniture, throwing items to the floor and breaking them, and then attacking the two seniors in their own home. Lloyd Cox was beaten so badly that he couldn't see out of one eye, and bruises covered his face and body.

With the intruder's foot wedged into their door, the two seniors barricaded themselves in their back bedroom, throwing all their weight against the door as best they could. They tried desperately to keep the bedroom door closed even as the door was being battered and rammed against them on the other side. Police arrived in the nick of time to stop the perp and save their lives. The Coxes were rushed to the hospital, and Mendenhall was booked on assault, battery, assault on a female, breaking and entering to terrorize and injure, and vandalism. Shockingly, he made bail and is awaiting trial at the time of this writing.

While thankful to the deputies and EMTs that saved their lives, their peace is shattered, and they wonder what could have happened to them—and even more disturbing, they wonder, will it happen again?

HOME SECURITY TIPS FOR SENIORS

In addition to the home safety tips you can find in chapter 11, here are added tips especially for seniors. Read on.

- Install emergency alert buttons near the senior's bed, bathroom, kitchen, and doors.
- A home security system is a must.
- Install a security device to enter the garage as well as doors to the home.
- Install a deadbolt on your senior's bedroom door.
- Set all electronic devices on high volume—doorbells, alarms, phones, everything—to ensure your senior hears them well.
- Install chime devices on all doors so your senior hears if someone comes in and out. Keep the volume on high.
- Use big-button cell phones that are easily readable and illuminated so your senior doesn't have to fumble to call emergency services.
- Use big-button landline phones as well.
- Extra lights are needed inside and out for seniors as eyesight dims. This includes walkway, garage, security, and motion sensor lighting.
- Install a cordless phone. Seniors need to keep a phone with them inside the home. Make sure the cordless range extends throughout the home. If it doesn't, get a second phone to make sure the home is completely covered for phone service throughout.
- Install a solid metal or wood door.
- Replace those lovely but risky decorative glass doors, as noted earlier.
- If your senior insists on keeping them, the decorative glass in doors should at the very least be safety glass and covered with privacy film.
- Seniors, take your phone with you to the door. Remember, you don't have to open the door or even answer it. You can speak through the door and tell the unwanted visitor you are not expecting company and to go away or you will call police.
- I advise seniors to have the Ring system installed so they can see

immediately on their cell phone exactly who is at the door. Then, make sure your senior's phone is a larger one so they can plainly see the face on the screen. Practice it with them several times.

- Know who you are letting in.
- If it is a repairman or some other representative, ask for ID before you let them in. Keep your door chained while you inspect the ID. If you have a doubt, call the business before you open the door. The guy can wait.
- Have routine checks deposited electronically to avoid mailbox or home theft. Burglars and thieves know seniors get checks on a schedule.
- Ask your local police to perform a home security check to give ideas to beef up your home security.
- Use a medical alert system to get help immediately. One push of a button summons help when the senior can't reach a phone. Consider home automation for thermostat, security lights, and locking doors in case a senior forgets or is traveling.
- Consider enabling remote control access for a trusted person to access your senior's alarm and automated systems. Children or caregivers can manage the system for the senior and get an alert if there's a window or door left open.
- Get a "granny-cam" to watch out for your senior.
- Invest in water detection sensors and carbon monoxide, smoke, and fire alarms.

THE KNOCKOUT GAME AND OTHER ATTACKS ON ELDERS

The rules of the game are simple and savage. A group chooses a lead attacker, finds a vulnerable victim such as a senior, and the leader punches the victim, knocking the victim out. If the victim goes down on the first punch, the gang scatters. If the victim doesn't go down, the others join in the "fun," kicking and punching the unsuspecting victim. That's the "game."

In February 2016, all eyes turned to Paterson, New Jersey, when a teen threw a monster punch at an unsuspecting man crossing Rosa Parks Boulevard. Not only did the punch knock the unwitting victim flat, the seventeen-year-old thug, Kristian Gonzalez, ended up with his face and his felony knockout punch pinged around the world almost instantly when it was posted on Facebook. The person videoing the attack is heard cheering on Gonzalez as the victim lay in the street unconscious.

During court hearings, Gonzalez admitted under oath he neither knew his victim nor acted in self-defense. In fact, he admitted in sworn testimony he knew his punch left his target, a street cleaner, completely unconscious. Gonzalez said his intent was to cause serious bodily injury. The sixteen-year-old who cops say cheered Gonzalez on from the sidelines and also recorded the brutal attack is charged with aggravated assault and endangerment.

Afterward, the thirty-seven-year-old street cleaner suffered from pain in the back of his head. He said he required stitches because of the assault, and his mouth was hurt.

YVONNE SMALL

A seventy-six-year-old Canarsie woman, Yvonne Small, was going about her business at the corner of Alabama and Wortman in East New York. It was broad daylight, almost lunchtime that Friday, when out of nowhere, she felt a crushing blow to her head. She'd become the latest victim of the knockout game, sucker-punched by an unknown, anonymous brute who targeted her because she looked vulnerable and unaware. Small fell to the sidewalk, landing first on her head, and was rushed to Brookdale Hospital. Witnesses state the punk was spotted lurking in the area, waiting for the right victim, just before the attack. Ironically, Small was attacked just hours after an "anti-knockout-game" rally nearby.

ROY COLEMAN

The knockout game, fed by social media when attackers brag and post videos of their attacks online, goes on. Twenty-nine-year-old Conrad Alvin Barrett recorded himself in November 2013 punching seventy-nine-year-old Roy Coleman. Barrett even narrated the video, laughing out loud and speculating whether his knockout punch would get him national coverage. As he's laughing, he yells out "knockout" and runs to his car to drive away, leaving Coleman on the ground with two jaw fractures.

How much that must have hurt. Now Coleman has difficulty even speaking. He can no longer live on his own. The video is so graphic I can hardly watch it, but as I do, I think of my eighty-seven-year-old mom. Barrett is behind bars serving a seventy-one-month prison sentence. That sentence is too good for him.

RODOLFO RODRIGUEZ

So often when I am out walking or jogging, I run into a ninety-one-year-old neighbor puttering along with her walker. She always has a smile on her face and really inspires me. I couldn't help but think about her and her beautiful smile and the little hats she wears when it's chilly when I heard about Rodolfo Rodriguez.

Rodriguez, ninety-two, was out alone for an evening stroll on July 4, 2018, in unincorporated Willowbrook, west of Los Angeles County. But what started as a pleasant walk after supper ended with Rodriguez beaten, bewildered, bloody, and bruised. He was found alone and disoriented, sitting on a sidewalk stained with his blood. I've never had the privilege of meeting Rodriguez, but when I investigated the facts, I kept getting a mental image of my ninety-one-year-old neighbor in her little hat bobbing along the street. My blood boils.

Rodriguez says that during the walk he took every evening, he passed a woman walking along with a child. It was then that the woman began beating him about the face and head with a concrete block. A group of men joined the attack, viciously kicking him after he had already fallen to the ground.

Rodriguez sustained a broken jaw, two broken ribs, broken cheekbones, and bruises and lacerations to his back, abdomen, and face. The unprovoked attack on a feeble old man sent shockwaves through the neighborhood. The woman, thirty-year-old Laquisha Jones, was sentenced to fifteen years in prison after a no-contest plea to felony elder abuse.

DON'T BE A KNOCKOUT OR STREET CRIME VICTIM

- Stay aware. Do not walk with your head down. Keep your eyes level to see what's around you and who is approaching you. With your head down, you seem unaware, and that's just what attackers want.
- Travel in a group. Groups or couples have not been targeted in the knockout game.
- If you are coming from an assisted-living home, stay with the group from your vehicle.
- Let someone know where you are.
- These attacks are happening outside on city streets. If possible, do your shopping in a mall or strip center. If in a strip center, stay on the walkway hugging the stores, not out in the parking lot.
- Look around before you head in any particular direction.
- Keep in mind that perps are looking for an unsuspecting target.
- Try to stay in well-lit areas. Don't talk on your cell phone or fumble with belongings.
- Identify hot spots where similar attacks have occurred and stay away.
- Consider carrying a whistle or pepper spray and have it ready to use.
- Be aware of any group approaching. Watch their hands, arms, and body language. Move to the side and get them past you if you can.
- Be aware of a group that just passed you as well, especially if they get abnormally close to you and invade your personal space. That's a tip-off.
- Listen to what the group is saying.
- Hug the building wall. That limits the type of attack that's possible.
- Keep your hands out of your pockets.
- Keep your hands free. Don't carry bags, purses, or items in your hands. Use a backpack or cross-body purse.
- If you have to carry something, do so with your nondominant hand.
- Identify your routine and look for any opportunities you are handing over to a knockout puncher. Change it.
- If you suspect you are in danger, promptly change your direction and make noise. If you're wrong, you're just embarrassed. That's nothing compared to a knockout.

TELEPHONE CONS, ONLINE SCAMS, AND GRIFTER FRAUD ON SENIORS

"Grandma? It's me. I got in a car accident and my head hurts. I need some money. Can you help me, Grandma?"

That tender voice over the phone would break any grandma's heart. Can you imagine if your child or grandchild called begging for help? That's just what happened to my friend Stephanie. When her grandmother heard the female voice, it sounded just like Stephanie. She detailed the "crash" through sniffles and sobs and ended the spiel with a polite but urgent request for money.

Here's the catch: Stephanie never called her grandma "Grandma." Since childhood, she had always called her grandma "Mimi," never "Grandma," "Grams," or "Granny." After listening to the telephone con give her pitch, "Grandma" called her on it and asked her bluntly, "Why don't you call your *real* grandmother to help you, because my grandchildren don't call me Grandma!" She promptly hung up on them, laughing.

But how many grandmas and grandpas out there would fork over a wire transfer through Western Union on the spot? Mine would and did for me. When I was behind on a phone bill, I went straight to my Mamaa Lucy, my maternal grandmother. On a very fixed income, she never thought twice but headed straight to her old change purse and took out a wad of dollar bills. Now you know where I got my sweet daughter's name, Lucy.

Whose grandma wouldn't sacrifice for the apple of her eye? And to think, scammers with their fists in my Mamaa's worn-out old change purse? Online cons, phone scams, and even family members zero in on the vulnerable, our seniors.

PHONE CONS: MARJORIE JONES

A lovely lady from Moss Bluff, Louisiana, eighty-two-year-old Marjorie Jones, had one of her most exciting days ever when a man called to tell her she had finally won something: a sweepstakes prize. She was to get the prize after she paid "taxes and fees." But after Marjorie, who lived all alone, wired the first payment, he kept calling to inform her of additional conditions in order to claim her prize. He also told her to keep the prize a secret so the wolves wouldn't circle to trick her out of all the sweepstakes money she was about to claim.

By the time the "secret" came out, Marjorie, who was legally blind, had gone through her entire savings of several hundred thousand dollars, taken out a reverse mortgage on the two-story home she owned, and even cashed in a long-held life insurance policy. It hurts me to even type this story. Shortly after trying to borrow money, Marjorie committed suicide. All that was left were bags full of wire transfer receipts and dozens of unknown numbers on Marjorie's caller ID. She only had sixty-nine dollars left in her bank account. It just makes me sick.

Why seniors? Because they are most likely to have a nest egg, own their own home, and have great a credit rating—sadly, everything a con artist loves. Cons exploit seniors who have been raised to be "polite" and not hang up on them.

They know many seniors won't report fraud because they are afraid they'll be considered senile or irresponsible. Many seniors may not even know who or how to call and report the fraud.

BEWARE AND DON'T LOSE YOUR SAVINGS

If you hear the following pitch lines, *hang up*!

"Act now! The offer expires soon."

"You can't afford to say no."

"You can't afford to miss this."

"You just won a free gift/prize/sweepstakes/lottery/cruise! But you have to pay for postage and handling, taxes, or other charges in order to claim it."

"You need to send money, provide a bank account or credit card number, or simply have your personal check picked up by our courier."

"You don't need to check us out. We're legit."

"You don't need written information about us. I can tell you whatever you need to know."

"You don't need references."

"This is a high-profit offer."

"This is a no-risk offer."

"Meet us at _____ and we can pick up the check there."

If you hear any the above or any variation, don't waste time. Say no and hang up. Run from the phone as if you had seen a monster.

MORE TIPS FOR BATTLING FRAUD

- Have caller ID and learn to use it. When your "grandchild" calls, you will recognize it's an unknown number.
- Don't purchase anything from an unfamiliar company.
- Legitimate businesses know you may want more information and are happy to provide additional information and references.
- Request written materials about the offer or charity.
- Wait until the material arrives before you commit.
- If the material involves a substantial or costly investment, ask someone with a financial background to look it over. Just because it's written doesn't make it true.
- Investigate. Check out the company with the local consumer protection group or the Better Business Bureau.
- Contact the state attorney general or the National Fraud Information Center to see if the company has ever been reported.
- But remember—not all cons have been reported.
- Get the caller's name, number, and street and mailing addresses before you do the deal.
- Ask the caller for a mailing address, then google it.
- Google details like the company name and the caller's name and see what pops up. It's easy.
- Verify the information. Is it the right address and number? Does it exist?
- Before you donate to charity, ask what percentage of your gift goes to commissions and how much goes to the charity.
- Never pay in advance for services. Pay after the service is rendered in full.
- Never hand over money to a messenger. This is not a "service" to you. It's a way to take your money without a trail.
- Never wire money after a phone pitch.
- Take your time. Secure companies don't pressure you.
- There is no such thing as a fee on a free prize.

- If the caller says a payment is for taxes, that's against the law and they are a con.
- Never give out credit card numbers, expiration dates, bank accounts, Social Security numbers, addresses, or places or dates of birth to someone over the phone.
- If you've been scammed, beware of callers who offer to help you get your money back (for a fee, of course).
- If you have information about a fraud, report it.
- Saying no is not being rude.
- Never enter a deal you don't understand, no matter how exciting it may sound in the moment.

REST HOME NIGHTMARE

In June 2018, instead of helping a woman at the very end of her life, three workers at Bentley Senior Living in Jefferson, Georgia, thought it would be fun to make a Snapchat video titled *The End* behind closed doors in the dying lady's bedroom. The seventy-six-year-old resident had suffered a deadly stroke, and the three bums were to stay with her and monitor her until hospice workers arrived to transport her. Instead, the woman lay there dying as the three ignored her, blurted profanities, made obscene hand motions, laughed out loud, mocked her, and smoked a vape pen. A co-worker reported them, and all three, Jorden Lanah Bruce, Mya Janai Moss, and Lizeth Jocelyn Cervantes Ramirez, were thankfully charged with exploiting an elderly and disabled person. They were awaiting trial at the time of this writing. The patient has since died.

REST HOME STAFF BUT NOT REAL NURSES

At one East Texas nursing home in Hughes Springs, an elderly resident struggling to breathe lurched toward nurses gathered at the closest station. The resident had choked on a cookie, and shortly after, he died. When government regulators launched an investigation, they were alarmed to learn that not one of the staff members was trained for emergencies and, shockingly, did not immediately call 911. Why? Did the resident's family just assume the "nurses" were actually real nurses with credentials to go along with the pastel scrubs they buy at the local medical supply warehouse?

In a similar tragedy, an elderly lady residing at an upscale senior home in Augusta, South Carolina, had pulled out her breathing tube many times during the previous two months. But on this day, even with several warnings, she pulled out her breathing tube and no one noticed, much less reacted. Her life could have been so easily saved, but no one acted and she died in her bed. The home was cited for failing to take actions to keep her from harming herself, but of course, nothing could undo what had been done.

ELDER CARE ATROCITY

Sonja Fischer lived at Walker Methodist Health Center in Minneapolis. It was just before Christmas in the wee morning hours, around four-thirty a.m., when a keen-eyed co-worker spotted a male nursing assistant, George Kpingbah, in Fischer's room. That in itself may not have been cause for alarm, but the co-worker reportedly saw Fischer's adult diaper lying open on the bed and one of her bare legs on either side of Kpginbah's hips.

If she hadn't spotted the assault actually taking place, how many more times would this have occurred, and how many times had it already? Kpingbah ended up pleading guilty to criminal sex conduct with a mentally impaired or helpless victim and got eight years behind bars.

But it wasn't the first time. Records obtained by the state showed that Kpingbah had already been suspended three times while Walker Methodist officials "investigated" accusation after accusation of sexual abuse at work. One allegedly involved a sixty-five-year-old woman with multiple sclerosis. Another was an eighty-three-year-old blind and deaf woman who reported she was raped many times at midnight. None of those allegations were substantiated, and Kpingbah remained on the night shift, as he had been for years.

SUFFERING IN SILENCE

Dean Piercy was a World War II veteran just like my dad. Writing this story makes me miss my dad so much. Every time I try to write another sentence, I imagine this happening to my dad, and it is just tearing me up.

Piercy's daughter, Katherine Ford, had always been extremely devoted and visited him routinely. On one visit, she noticed dust on his electric toothbrush. Piercy was suffering with dementia and had not mentioned anything about it to her. She checked and realized his teeth hadn't been brushed recently, so she made it another of her duties to brush them herself after every one of their lunchtime visits together.

Later Piercy began to complain of an awful headache that just wouldn't stop. It seemed that no matter how often she asked the staff there at the senior home to have him checked, it didn't happen. Finally, when it did, the dentist discovered one of Piercy's teeth had actually broken in two and part of the tooth had lodged itself in the roof of his mouth. Can you imagine the pain?

To make matters worse, his daughter had been there every day asking for help, and her dad even had full dental insurance. There was absolutely no reason for ignoring his pain. As it turns out, thousands of seniors in "rest homes" are suffering with cracked teeth, gum disease, and a whole potpourri of dental maladies, many of them painful...or worse. Most of the ailments are because the residents' mouths are not kept clean by simple brushing. Missing this simple task can cause incredible pain. Piercy suffered a lot. Thank goodness his daughter was there to save him. How many thousands of our nursing home elderly don't have a hero?

WHAT TO LOOK FOR IN SENIOR LIVING HOMES

You must do a visual inspection of the home. What you see online may be very different from what you find in real life.

How does the food look, smell, and taste? Taste it yourself. If you don't like it or find it appetizing, neither will your senior.

Lack of hygiene is a huge red flag. You want a place where the staff helps daily with residents' baths, dressing, nail care, teeth brushing, hair brushing, and more. If residents are neglected, that means the home is not doing a very good job.

Lack of dental care is a major issue as well. Investigate.

Look for unsanitary living conditions, including bedding, clothes, bathrooms, and kitchen. Each state has requirements for safety and security, including living conditions. If the place isn't clean, how can you expect your senior to be fed and get meds correctly?

Caregivers' neglect can easily end in dehydration and malnutrition. My eighty-seven-year-old mom lives with us. Getting her to eat can very often be a challenge. I get it. What if your senior is in a facility where workers are negligent?

Residents should be encouraged to move around. If you spot residents sitting in wheelchairs parked out in the hall or otherwise all sitting or lying in their rooms, there's a problem. Lack of mobility causes loss of muscle tone, circulation, strength, and balance. Classes or individual time with workers to increase mobility is so important. Being left in a bed or chair for long periods of time causes infections, pressure points, and bedsores. This is a pain your senior doesn't need.

Broken bones, lumps on the head, and bruises are indicators of neglect or abuse. These are signs of being left alone and your senior injuring themselves or worse. Neglect and other abuse causes anxiety, fear, and depression. Your senior may be afraid or embarrassed to discuss it.

Conduct a background check. Computerized records shared between jurisdictions around the country mean more accurate background checks. Ask at your senior's home if checks have been completed for every employee from the director all the way down to the parking lot attendant and the groundskeepers.

Also, what about the staff's personnel records? Have any of them been dismissed from their jobs before? Has anyone on the staff ever been disciplined, and if so, why? Remember Kpingbah from above.

You can actually look up a nursing home or facility by name in the federal inspection data at Medicare.gov (select "Find a Nursing Home") to find out if that particular home has been cited for abuse, sexual abuse, or other issues within the last three years. Of course, that source is not all-inclusive because so much abuse goes unreported. You can see ratings on staffing, health inspections, and more.

Check to see if your senior's home uses pre-packaged medications, with all meds needed contained in one sealed packet. This cuts the risk of a life-threatening error.

Also investigate and determine if the home has alert systems that ring staff if a resident at risk gets up unassisted.

Are there cameras in entrances, in hallways, and at all exits? There should be.

Is there a security system in place?

Are visitors that come and go monitored? They have to be. There must be a check-in/check-out system.

Speaking of visitors, are visitors, even unannounced, encouraged? If not, you're at the wrong place.

Do alarms warn staff if someone unauthorized enters or leaves?

Who monitors staff?

Who supervises and monitors night-duty staff?

Residents with dementia or Alzheimer's must be protected from wandering. Secure or coded exits do that. Does your facility have them?

Some homes have cameras in rooms when necessary. Does your senior need that, and is it available?

Do staff have necessary training? Find out. "Fake" nurses don't cut it in life-threatening situations like choking.

Staff needs additional training in areas such as Alzheimer's in order to cope with daily situations. Do they have it?

Are there mandatory neglect and abuse reporting requirements at your senior's home? It's the law.

Your senior should be addressed by name, not "Grandpa" or "Granny."

Is there evidence of overmedicating?

Look for fire exits and gauge ease for your senior getting to them.

Are there multiple doors a resident must exit before reaching outside?

Grade individual room security. Do the windows have adequate locks?

Is the staff overworked and overburdened? If so, this means your senior will not get the attention they should. Ask the supervisor for staff-to-resident ratios.

Will your senior have a roommate? Do they have to? Do they get to choose the roommate? What if the roommate is a danger to your senior?

Are you allowed to have a recording device in your senior's room?

Key warning signs

- Weight loss.
- Changes in personality or mood.
- Lack of appetite.
- Bed sores.
- Bruises, lumps, and bumps.
- Change in sleeping habits.
- Depression.
- Lethargy.

You will only notice these changes, which are sometimes subtle, if you stay in touch. Visits are necessary, and not just to give you a warm and fuzzy feeling. They could save your senior's life.

Observe how residents spend free time. Are there activities for them? If they can't get to the activity, a staff person should be coming to their room with an appropriate activity for them or get them to the correct place.

Rely on your senses. Use your ears, nose, eyes, and wits to judge where your senior will live.

Does the staff seem to get along? You do not want your senior to live in a hostile environment. If they are rude and combative with each other, how will they be with your senior?

How does staff spend time once they've completed duties? Do they yak with each other at the nurses' station or spend time with residents?

If you discover an issue with your senior's care, go first to the floor manager. If that doesn't resolve the issue, you have to go up the chain of command, even to the home administrator if needed. If it remains unaddressed, go the agency regulating nursing homes in your state.

For more information, download the Nursing Home Checklist from Medicare.gov (https://www.medicare.gov/nursing-home-checklist.pdf).

Be involved with your senior. This takes time and energy. Spend both.

AND THEN...

Lessons from a Pandemic

What a difference a year makes. Has it only been a year? It took just one year—a year unlike any other—to turn our world upside down. COVID-19, also known as the coronavirus, tore through all of our lives, including mine and my family's, like a wrecking ball.

We had taken the twins on a trip for spring break, although there was still a winter chill in the air and it didn't feel like spring at all...like a warning of what was to come. We got back home and things *seemed* normal. I took off on a flight the very next morning heading, unbeknownst to me, into the vortex, a so-called hotspot, New York City, to launch a brand-new program, *Crime Stories*, on Fox Nation. I touched down at La Guardia and headed straight into the city toward *Crime Stories* HQ. Nothing seemed to be amiss.

The following morning I was up at five a.m. as usual to head to the studio, and work commenced. As I finished one hit after the next, a murmur began. By the time I was standing in a green room to do a late afternoon hit about the new launch, I looked across the bottom third of the TV screen and in all caps on a blazing red banner, I read the word *pandemic* for the first time. I was, briefly, frozen in place. I quickly walked from the green room, grabbed my beat-up roll-aboard from the linoleumed hallway, and headed for a secret side door where I knew taxis, Ubers, and limos were all on standby.

The cold air hit me in the face as I pushed open a heavy double door to the outside, dragging the roll-aboard behind me with my other hand still full of crime stats and research. Walking as quickly as I could, I rapped the side of a taxi.

The cabbie rolled down the side window, and I said one word: "LaGuardia." I had to get home.

As the taxi wove through traffic, my stomach was actually hurting. What was happening? Where were the twins? Where was David? I tried to read the news on my iPhone, but with the taxi lurching though one red light after the next, trying to get through the tunnel and onto the freeway, I couldn't read. And really, it didn't matter what the headlines said; I knew I had to get home, immediately.

I called David and asked him to go get the twins from school, and he did. I phoned the producers and let them know I had to leave. I could hear a lot of voices in the background, and I knew they were knee-deep in breaking news from all over the world. We agreed to regroup, and the phone clicked off.

When I got to LaGuardia, it was a madhouse. I literally ran to security and then to a gate at the very end of the concourse, trying to get on an earlier flight. Crowds were pushing toward every single gate. I still didn't fully understand why.

And I recall, with a piercing knowledge in hindsight, no one was wearing a mask. No one. Including me. I didn't know any better.

Not then, anyway.

I was the last one to make it on the afternoon flight, and I said a silent prayer when I sank into a middle seat in the back of the plane. We were jammed in like sardines, but I was so thankful when I felt the plane lift up into the air and then, a few moments later, heard the grate of the wheels pulling into the plane.

I was headed home.

I made it through two crowded airports and a packed plane without getting the virus, without transmitting it to the twins or David. I was so lucky...But my luck would eventually run out.

In a matter of hours, we were all plunged into lockdown. The twins began remote learning within days. No one could come in or out of the house. That went for the studio as well, and my fledgling program was in jeopardy. No one could figure out a way to make it work without people actually in the control room.

I watched the news in horror as the body count rose, horrible rumors and dire predictions swirled and then came true, and the Age of Zoom took hold. We hung on every word Dr. Anthony Fauci uttered and then soaked in every point and counterpoint like sponges. Which mask? Which hand sanitizer? Is six feet away enough? Who can be around us? How do we navigate empty grocery shelves?

Days passed. We were running out of practice shows to air, and then, literally in the middle of the night, I had an idea. We could record audio separately on a fixed camera, even though no one was in the control room to operate it, and somehow have editors, hunkered down in their homes and apartments for the duration, marry the two together. It would be tedious and very, very time consuming…but could it be done?

It could! Fox Nation managed to pull it off and save the program we had all worked so hard to create. It all depended on a clap. Yes, a clap— with my hands. To marry the sound with the video, they needed a starting point. So now, to this day I do my own countdown, which, in a previous life, I would have heard in my headset: 3…2…1…*clap*…and "This is *Crime Stories*. Thank you for being with us…"

It was a not-so-minor miracle.

Outside the studio, we buried friends and relatives. On one sunny afternoon, one sweet relative was blowing leaves from the family's front lawn. Ten days later he was dead from COVID-19. Then another and another. We watched as they left us, our family members, our friends, people we felt we knew. Dawn Wells, who played Mary Ann on *Gilligan's Island*. Charley Pride, whom I dragged the twins to the Grand Ole Opry to hear sing on stage a few years ago. Roy Horn of Siegfried and Roy. Astronaut wife Annie Glenn. Jazz star Ellis Marsalis, Captain Sir Tom Moore, actor Nick Cordero, actress Carol Sutton…all gone, along with hundreds of thousands more.

As we watched the news about the virus's origins, the rush on toilet paper and cleaning products, the race for a vaccine or even a treatment, the bodies stacked up in cooler facilities, refrigerated trucks and containers waiting in hospital parking lots, I tried to shield the twins from footage of dead bodies on gurneys in hospital hallways as people, young and old, dropped dead around the world. Tents were set up in Central Park, and morgues across the country were filled to capacity.

And then one day, my mom, who lives with us, seemed lethargic. She wouldn't eat the breakfast or drink the coffee I brought to her at the crack of dawn, as I had for the last five years, since my dad went to heaven. She stood clutching her walker, not moving for literally hours. Something was wrong. I finally got her to sit down, and I spoon-fed her a mush of cheese grits with tiny bits of bacon in them so she wouldn't even have to chew.

I reheated her breakfast four times, and it took me a full two hours to get the grits in her with a few sips of coffee. This was all wrong. I took her temperature and blood pressure; they weren't far off normal. As I was sitting there, feeding and talking to her, face-to-face with her only a foot away, she coughed over and over right into my face. I remember thinking, *Oh dear, I'm catching her cold*... and I kept spooning breakfast into her mouth although she didn't seem aware of what I was saying.

A few hours later, I headed down to the studio after getting her an appointment with our doctor to figure out the lethargy and lack of appetite. That was on a Friday. The weekend proceeded with me feeding her and falling asleep sitting up straight in a rocker in her room. Monday morning came quickly. I was driving the twins to school, literally turning in to open the side doors and let them out when I stopped to pick up the phone. It was David. He hardly ever calls when I'm driving. I remember hearing the word *COVID*.

"What?"

He answered, "Your mom has COVID." The rest is a blur. I got the twins home, got my mom, and headed to the ER. They wanted her ID and insurance. They took her away. I didn't know if I would ever see her alive again.

Racing home, we headed to a drive-through for nasal swabs. My little Lucy was so afraid, and we were all upset about Grandmommy. It seemed like no time before we got the news. I had contracted COVID-19. I had transmitted it to my whole family. My mom would turn eighty-nine in a COVID ward, if she made it, where I couldn't see her or touch her. My twins and my husband were facing the battle of a lifetime because of me.

But we had done everything *right*... We followed all the rules, even when others did not. *How did this happen?*

There were days I thought I couldn't get up, but knowing the twins were in the next room kept me going. I watched them like a hawk. My husband, David, had excruciating migraines for the first time in his life. John David and I both lost our senses of smell. The days passed. I tried to talk to my mom on the phone but couldn't get through, and when I finally did, she talked like she was out of her mind.

My little Lucy got better first. Then, my big boy, John David. Then David. Then me. And then, in a Christmas miracle, my mom came home. She was thin and pale and worse for the wear, but she was home, thank God. We came through. I still can't smell a thing, and we all have exhaustion... but we are alive.

So many others are not.

When I hear talk of conspiracy theories and claims that COVID isn't real, I'm angry. With what my family and so many others have gone through and with the death toll still rising, how could people be so blind?

The vaccines were announced, and we quickly signed up on multiple websites, but couldn't seem to get the shots. Even my now eighty-nine-year-old mom got shut out, three times in all. But over and over we tried. One website after the next, one call after the next, be it early morning or late at night, we always got the same answer: a dead end and vaccine slots full to capacity.

Finally, we drove nearly three hours to an old farmers market they turned into a vaccine center, where she got the Pfizer jab! David and I still kept trying, and weeks passed. One day, we got a call and then an appointment. We ended up headed to an abandoned Stein Mart warehouse. I was skeptical, but when we went in, it was full of nurses and technicians, and we got the vaccine.

Is it all over? No. It's not. It's still running rampant as Europe faces yet another wave of the virus. We here in the US will surely be next. But as I examine the COVID-19 pandemic, an echo goes through my mind. What, if anything, did we learn?

Throughout time, huge happenings, controversies, tragedies, and, yes, viruses have changed the course of history.

When Cain struck Abel, murder was born, eventually leading to the Ten Commandments, the first being "Thou shall not kill."

Onerous taxation led to the Tea Party in Boston Harbor and the American Revolution. The great gold rush in the early 1800s, which sent thousands westward to seek their fortunes, many of whom lost their mining claims, their money, and their lives, led to the General Mining Act of 1872.

A cow kicked a lantern and started a blaze that continued for more than twenty-four hours, known as the Great Chicago Fire, killing hundreds, leaving even more as homeless, and devastating the city. It also led to some of the first comprehensive building and fire codes.

In 1954, a precious little six-year-old girl named Ruby Bridges needed a federal marshal to escort her to elementary school. She was immortalized in a painting by Norman Rockwell, and eventually, after many more sacrifices, the evils of school segregation ended in schools across our great country.

Deadly polio swept our country and resulted in the Polio Vaccine Assistance Act of 1955 to help states advance preventative medicine and one of the first ever nationwide immunization programs. As we all head to emptied stadiums, farmers markets, and abandoned Stein Marts for the vaccine, does any of this sound familiar?

In these treacherous times, COVID crimes have proliferated. From fake cures, door-to-door "vaccines," fraudsters on the phone, and texts tricking people out of their money and information in exchange for quack products to murders over face masks, the trickle has transformed into a torrent. NBA star Charles Barkley announced that pro athletes should get the vaccine first since they pay more taxes. NYC real estate magnates allegedly arranged for their wealthy friends to visit the senior centers they owned to cut the line and literally take the vaccines from the elderly. And they did.

Millionaires chartered jets to fly to Canada and then masqueraded as hotel employees to get the vaccine before the ill and elderly. The young and healthy posed as grannies in wigs and shawls to nab vaccines legitimately assigned to others less strong. Celebrity physical fitness trainer and SoulCycle instructor Stacey Griffith drove an hour to cut the line. Wealthy enclaves held vaccine parties to get the jabs first. It goes on and on...bribes, promises, cheating—all to jump the line. The strong and powerful robbing and exploiting those less cunning than they.

Misinformation and fear led to an increase of hate crime attacks on Asians and murders over masks. A lawyer killed his wife when she contracted the virus from her mother and transmitted it to him. A mom beat her COVID-stricken children. It's almost too much to take in. But it's all real, just like the virus.

What can we do? I thought I had done it all to protect my family, but I still contracted the virus from my mom and gave it to David and the twins. It leaves so many of us feeling helpless, ineffectual, powerless.

But I am not. *We are not.*

It may be COVID right now, today. But what about tomorrow, next year, or even ten years from now?

Looking back, what have we learned? There is a great battle raging even now. And more battles to come. We must be armed with information, using knowledge as our swords and our shields. We can't hide away from life forever. We will wade into the fray with facts as our helmets and lessons learned as our gauntlets. Now more than ever we must fight the fight. Don't be a victim. The pages ahead have a great deal of information to keep you and your family safe.

CORONAVIRUS CRIMES

Imagine this visual: a cool, clear pool of water out on a hot, dry savanna. Graceful gazelles, first one, then two, then nearly thirty of the gorgeous creatures come and bend their necks down to drink. In the distance is a deep rumbling, and the gazelles raise their heads to listen to the distant storm. Then a loud crack of lightning strikes—the storm distant no more—splitting the trunk of a tall tree at the water's edge. In that moment of distraction and chaos, as the gazelles turn to run, the predators emerge from the shadows at the edge of the pool, having been waiting there all along, hidden from their prey. The hyenas give chase, and in those moments of fear and confusion, they rip the throats of their prey, laughing as hyenas do.

In this scenario, the coronavirus cons are the hyenas, laughing after the kill. You, sadly, are the gazelle.

DOOR-TO-DOOR CORONAVIRUS "TESTS"

Let the camel's nose into the tent and his tail will surely follow.

Meet the new generation of door-to-door "salespeople." No, not vacuum cleaners, not encyclopedia sets, but fake coronavirus test kits. Do not open the door. Repeat: *Do not open the door!*

It's been reported that some of the perps present themselves as law enforcement or even the Red Cross. Police departments across the country are sounding the alarm about scammers going door-to-door—to *your door*—pretending to perform in-home tests for the coronavirus. Multiple public health departments in municipalities dotting the map have repeatedly announced they will never, ever go door-to-door or perform in-home COVID-19 tests, but those announcements aren't working. The scams go on, and they *are* working.

Fake door-to-door COVID-19 testing is dangerous on so many levels. First, there is currently no such test, so the test itself is bogus. The premise of door-to-door sales calls is an old tried-and-true distraction robbery scam. In other words, the "salesperson" knocks or rings your doorbell, then distracts you by getting you to answer the door and listen to a sales pitch, thus getting a toe in your door, literally. Next, the "salesperson" manages to get their entire body into your home, further distracts you with some bogus health test, and then robs you or even worse.

Another threat is that you may use a credit card to buy the fictitious test, and the thief steals your credit card information.

Testing for COVID-19 is a serious undertaking. If such a test were genuinely performed, the medical professional conducting the test would be draped head-to-wrist-to-toe in medical garb to protect both you and them from potential contamination. Door-to-door COVID- 19 testing is a no-go simply because of the highly contagious nature of the virus itself.

As of this writing, there is no such thing as legitimate door-to-door coronavirus testing. No one from the Centers for Disease Control (CDC) or municipal departments of health makes house calls to offer tests for a fee. In North Carolina, door-to-door perps were offering not only COVID-19 test kits but cleaning supplies to fight the virus as well. It's happening, and it's happening now. From North Carolina to Arkansas and Palm Beach, door-to-door "testing" has been reported.

US Customs and Border Protection has released a photo showing a package of counterfeit COVID-19 "test kits" that had just arrived from the UK at the Los Angeles airport. The package contained six clear plastic bags, each full of vials of a white liquid labeled CORONA VIRUS 2019NCOV (COVID-19) and VIRUS1 TEST KIT. The package was handed over to the FDA for testing.

Scammers are taking advantage of the global pandemic, smuggling counterfeit test kits and going door-to-door in white suits and face masks, claiming to be from a health agency. The FBI issued a warning advising consumers to beware.

At a time when many of us are quarantined, sheltering at home, or self-isolating, you'd think we would be safe behind closed doors. Not exactly. Con artists see us as being *trapped* in our own homes. For them, it's like shooting fish in a barrel—they can't miss.

For years, I investigated, prosecuted, and covered home invasions, burglaries, and assaults in the home. Here are some of my golden rules:

- Look before you open the door! I grew up in a rural setting, and we always flung our doors open whenever there was a knock or the doorbell rang. With neighbors few and far between, excitement pulsed through the house whenever we had a visitor. In 2021? Not true.
- I recommend peepholes on the front doors of homes and apartments, especially the kind with a little sliding cover on the inside so there's no way anyone on the outside can look in.
- If you do not have a peephole, take a look at who's knocking from a side window or some other vantage point in your home.
- Think about it: With social distancing, curfews, lockdowns, or quarantines in place, how likely is it that someone approaching your home or apartment unexpectedly is who they say they are? That likelihood is low to zero.
- Now we have the awesome Ring video doorbell and its progeny. The Ring connects to your Wi-Fi (you may need a booster), and the moment the doorbell rings, the image of the person who is there pops up on your smartphone. We have them installed at both doors, and I love them. If a fake medical professional comes to our door wearing a doctor's costume, we can see them coming and call 911 pronto.
- Modern home security systems often come with a wireless keychain alarms. Keep one near your door or take it with you when someone knocks. Press it if you need to call for help. An ounce of prevention is worth a pound of cure.
- Home security alarm keypads are often placed in master bedrooms and near doors for a reason: so you can reach them at the most likely places for an emergency or security breach to occur. Be familiar with the pad, including where the emergency button is. When that knock comes at your door, know how to use the emergency button if you need it. Keep your home security alarm on even when you are home. As a matter of fact, keep it turned on *especially* when you are at home. You can get a new TV. But you can't run over to Best Buy and get a replacement for *you*.
- If you do not have a home security system, take your cell phone or cordless phone when you answer the door in case you need to make an emergency call.
- Fortify your doors! The more force a door can withstand, such as kicking or battering, the better. Deadbolts are preferred, but don't install deadbolts that require an inside key, because if you need

to get out quickly, you don't want to be fumbling for that key. Seconds count.

* If for some reason, against my strong advice, you follow your impulse to answer the door, do not—I repeat, *do not*—invite or let the person into your home. If they convince you to use your credit or debit card, you have given them the keys to the kingdom, your life savings. Worse, you have set yourself up for a home robbery or an even more serious felony.

Please, don't do it. Once you turn that knob and open the door, it's too late.

FRAUDSTERS TAKE TO THE AIRWAVES
TO PEDDLE CORONAVIRUS "SNAKE OIL"

As of this writing, there is no cure to eradicate or antidote to stop the virus once contracted. But in a time of fear and chaos, many people will try anything to protect themselves, their children, and their family. And believe me, fraudsters are only too happy to help them out—out of their money!

Among the charlatans bringing coronavirus "cures" to the forefront was none other than the world-famous televangelist Jim Bakker. Bakker took to the airwaves again, amid the panic and fear of the virus.

Long before coronavirus had ever hit the headlines, Bakker ruled a multimillion-dollar business as a televangelist alongside his wife, Tammy Faye. They quickly adopted a lavish lifestyle, including minks and troves of expensive jewelry for Tammy Faye, a fleet of Cadillac limos, a vintage Rolls-Royce worth over $60,000, multiple mansions, and a houseboat. I remember what particularly caught my attention at the time: an air-conditioned doghouse for their animals, and $9,000 worth of truffles the two had allegedly flown in from Brussels for a party.

Jim and Tammy Faye Bakker danced to the music, all right, but who paid the piper? The churchgoers and followers of Bakker's ministry, that's who. After a sixteen-month grand jury investigation, Bakker was indicted in 1989 for defrauding his followers out of millions in donations and, later, was convicted and sentenced to forty-five years in a federal pen and half a million dollars in fines.

Bakker somehow finagled a reduced sentence and walked out of jail in 1994. It didn't take long for people to forget Jim Bakker assuming the fetal position and sobbing on the floor of the courtroom during his trial. You'd think he would've learned his lesson, right? Wrong.

As soon as he could, he went straight back on the airwaves, and when COVID-19 hit the headlines, Bakker took to the stage as well, this time hawking a concoction called Silver Solution as a cure for the virus— at $80 for sixteen ounces. Bakker gazed out at his viewers and then glanced back at a silver-and-blue bottle. Questioning a "natural health expert," Bakker elicited the punchline: This pricey concoction "totally eliminates [coronavirus], kills it, deactivates it." Bakker's guest went on to claim that Silver Solution, simple colloidal silver, "has been proven by the government that it has the ability to kill every pathogen it has ever been tested on, including SARS and HIV." None of that is true.

The state of Missouri has filed a lawsuit claiming that Bakker, along with Morningside Church Productions, violated state law by "falsely promising that Silver Solution can cure, eliminate, kill or deactivate coronavirus and/or boost elderly consumers' immune system and help keep them healthy when there is, in fact, no vaccine, pill, potion or other product available to treat or cure coronavirus disease 2019." Following Missouri, the New York attorney general ordered Bakker to cease and desist making his claims and accused him of defrauding the public.

The FTC and the FDA have both warned Bakker that his Facebook page and website were selling unapproved new drugs in violation of the law.

The FDA also sent warnings to six other companies caught selling colloidal silver essential oils, teas, and treatments. Not only does colloidal silver not cure the deadly coronavirus, but it can actually be dangerous to your health, according to the National Institutes of Health.

Jim Bakker isn't the only one making money off fear and desperation. Straight from big- screen productions like *Iron Man 2*, *Thor*, and *Moneyball*, Hollywood actor Keith Lawrence Middlebrook went public to announce that he had personally developed a "patent-pending cure" for COVID-19. He also claimed NBA superstar Magic Johnson was on his company's board of directors. Not only was Middlebrook conning the public into sending him money for a fake cure, but he was also seeking massive money investments.

But I don't want to paraphrase it; I want you to hear it straight from the horse's mouth. Let me quote Middlebrook directly: "I have developed the cure for the coronavirus COVID-19...[An] LA patient tested positive for coronavirus, got up and walked out fifty-one hours after my injection." But Middlebrook couldn't stop himself and allegedly went on: "Investors who come in at ground level, say $1M, will parachute with $200M–$300M...conservative minimum."

Don't worry: Middlebrook was arrested during a meeting when he delivered a batch of coronavirus "cure" pills to an investor who, of course, turned out to be an undercover FBI agent, according to the feds.

The US attorney for the Central District of California, Nick Hanna, gave a statement after the sting. "During these difficult days, scams like this are using blatant lies to prey upon our fears and weaknesses. While this may be the first federal criminal case in the nation stemming from the pandemic, it certainly will not be the last. I again am urging everyone to be extremely wary of outlandish medical claims and false promises of immense profits. And to those who perpetrate these schemes, know that federal authorities are out in force to protect all Americans, and we will move aggressively against anyone seeking to cheat the public during this critical time."

Middlebrook was charged with felony attempted wire fraud. He's looking at a possible sentence of twenty years in a federal pen. And the final humiliation for the actor-turned-con? Magic Johnson says he's never heard of Middlebrook. Ouch.

Wow. If you can't believe a Hollywood star from *Iron Man* and you can't believe a preacher, who can you believe? Maybe a famous conspiracy nut? Like Alex Jones, who still insists the mass shooting at the Sandy Hook Elementary School didn't happen? But believe it or not, Jones still has a huge audience, and this is what they heard.

Jones's home platform has long been the website Infowars, various "news" blogs, video feeds, an online store, and audio, all founded by Jones. One day after the popular Austin, Texas, festival South by Southwest was called off over coronavirus fears, Jones hyped that the cancellation was really a secret government psychological operation meant to create panic. Jones then stated: "But having antivirals, getting your immune system healthy—that is the answer. And, yes, folks, we sell great antivirals."

Jones's online "health" store hawks products chock full of colloidal silver, with catchy names like Superblue Fluoride Free Toothpaste,

SuperSilver Wound Dressing Gel, and Superblue Silver Immune Gargle. Jones claims the products can protect against or even treat the novel coronavirus. In one live production in mid-March 2020, Jones went so far as to promise that "this stuff kills the whole SARS-corona family at point-blank range...It kills every virus."

The New York State attorney general, Letitia James, brought the hammer down on Jones, stating: "Whenever there's heightened fear and hysteria, we start to see scammers...As the coronavirus continues to pose serious risks to public health, Alex Jones has spewed outright lies and has profited off of New Yorkers' anxieties. Mr. Jones's public platform has not only given him a microphone to shout inflammatory rhetoric, but his latest mistruths are incredibly dangerous and pose a serious threat to the public health of New Yorkers and individuals across the nation." She promptly ordered a cease-and-desist letter be sent to Jones.

And that's not all. According to *Wired*, Google removed the Infowars Android app from its Play Store immediately after video surfaced of Jones arguing against sheltering in place, quarantines, and social distancing in the war against coronavirus. The timing was quite the coincidence.

I say good riddance to Jones. You go ahead and gargle with Superblue, Jones. I plan to stick with the advice of the World Health Organization (WHO).

CORONAVIRUS "PURELL PIRATES" GO PRICE-GOUGING

By now, millions of us have heard the true story of the so-called hoarding bros, a pair of Tennessee brothers who, before now, had an unblemished record and a great reputation.

Just twenty-four hours after the announcement that the coronavirus had claimed its first American victim, two Tennessee brothers, Noah and Matt Colvin, took to the road. Their road trip first took them to one of my favorites, the Dollar Tree. With bags loaded, they then wheeled over to Walmart, Home Depot, and more. At each pit stop they bought every bottle of hand sanitizer in sight.

After three days, having wound their way through Tennessee and Kentucky, they'd packed a U-Haul truck with *thousands* of hand sanitizer bottles and *thousands* of antibacterial wipes, cleaning out supplies for miles and miles. It's believed the two had amassed nearly eighteen thousand bottles of hand sanitizer! The hoarding bros then posted hundreds of bottles of hand sanitizer online *for up to $70 each!* Good business? Or plundering, making money off of despair?

In another case, a forty-three-year-old Brooklyn man, Baruch Feldheim, is now facing charges for assault on FBI agents. Eek. Over hand sanitizer? How did it all start? It started when Feldheim allegedly sold a New Jersey doctor, desperate for medical supplies, a thousand N95 face masks along with other medical and cleaning supplies for a whopping $12,000! That's nearly a 700 percent markup!

But that's not all. Feds say Feldheim sent the doctor to a New Jersey auto repair shop to pick up the supplies. You know there's a problem when you're selling supplies out behind the local car repair shop. The doc reportedly told the feds that Feldheim hoarded enough Clorox wipes, hand sanitizer, face masks, chemical cleaners, and surgical supplies to outfit an entire hospital. Think *eighty thousand* face masks, according to reports.

To make matters worse, when the feds showed up to effect a search warrant for hoarding medical supplies and price gouging, court documents say Feldheim blurted out he was infected with COVID-19 and proceeded to intentionally cough on the agents. Feldheim should've heeded the sage advice from Jim Croce: You don't tug on Superman's cape, and you don't mess around with Jim—or FBI agents searching your garage.

Crossing the country to Phoenix, the local CBS station reports that not only doctors but also firefighters and police are getting ripped off by coronavirus pirates. Two congressmen, Ruben Gallego and Greg Stanton, went to the FTC and the US attorney general and called out, as they described it, shameful and un-American conduct. If they are right, then I, for once, agree with the politicians. They claim a local company had drastically jacked up prices, charging the Phoenix police and fire departments a *500 percent markup* for N95 face masks! Police and firefighters are being gouged.

Oregon has also suffered. In March, when coronavirus fears first struck many of us, store shelves were being picked clean. According to the Salem *Statesman Journal*, Keizer Food Market removed single rolls of toilet paper from commercial packages of multiple rolls, *selling a single roll of TP for $3.99.*

The store manager insisted his employees were trying to "help" customers. After much public shaming, a price-gouging cease-and-desist letter was issued by the Oregon Department of Justice. The store was one of seven Oregon businesses and 7-Elevens that allegedly jacked up prices on toilet paper, surgical face masks, and even bottled water.

Price gouging has been reported on eBay as well, with complaints that disinfectant sprays like Lysol were selling for hundreds of dollars each. The California attorney general blasted the greedy sellers as not only disgraceful but illegal...and he's right!

But how can we fight back?

- Plan ahead. Know what you need before you go empty, so when you see it, make the purchase. Do not hoard...just purchase. I know how it feels: When I saw Clorox wipes being unloaded off a truck in the grocery store parking lot, I considered a car-jacking. I didn't, and I bought only two packages.
- Rely on trusted sellers. Beware, because while shopping online may save you from the crazy crowds at your local grocery store, Target, or Home Depot, you at least know who you're dealing with. I haven't seen a single report that, for instance, Target or Walmart has been accused of price gouging.
- Check customer reviews on the seller before you submit your credit card or PayPal info. Once you click, it's too late!
- Be extra careful if you end up dealing with third-party vendors you don't know or have never heard of.
- Carefully read labels. For instance, in the mad rush for hand sanitizer, lots of people ended up with gel containing a reduced amount of alcohol. Hand sanitizer has to contain at least 60 percent alcohol to work against COVID-19, according to the CDC. I know lots of labels say the product "kills 99.99 percent of illness-causing germs," but that does *not* necessarily guard you against coronavirus.
- Washing your hands with soap and water for twenty seconds (then *not* touching your face or biting your nails) is an important way to help get rid of coronavirus germs.
- As to labels, know that alcohol-free products or those containing less than 60 percent alcohol are not recommended by the CDC. Hand sanitizers that use benzalkonium chloride instead of alcohol may not work as well against the coronavirus, says the CDC, although

they are better than nothing. Bottom line: Read the label before you buy. Study the product image. If an online vendor doesn't display a product image, don't buy it. (PS: Don't make homemade hand sanitizer out of whiskey or vodka. Most alcoholic beverages don't have enough alcohol content to work, no matter how much it burns going down your throat.)

- If you are shopping online and the price doesn't make sense, you may consider price-checking tools. They are free to you and track the product's price history. Two examples are CamelCamelCamel and Keepa. They can also alert you if there is a price drop. Nice.
- If you think you are being price-gouged, take a photo of the price and your receipt, signs, or price tags. Hold on to them. It helps if you have photos or proof of comparative prices as well, such as what another store or vendor is traditionally charging for the same product. Get the name and address of the suspected price-gouger. Then call and send copies of your evidence to local police, your state's attorney general, the state's consumer affairs division, and the Better Business Bureau. If you called the store or talked to a manager, keep a written list of the dates and times and the names of the people you spoke to.

Fight back against the price-gouger pirates! We don't allow blood-thirsty pirates on the high seas, and we shouldn't tolerate them online or at the grocery store either.

CORONAVIRUS ROBOCALLS

What if you, you mother, dad, grandfather, or grandmother got one of the following calls?

The coronavirus has caused the US to declare a national emergency. The Families First Coronavirus Response Act has made corona-virus testing more accessible immediately. If you want to receive a free testing kit delivered overnight to your home, press one.

This is a courtesy call from 3M's safety program to inform you that due to the coronavirus pandemic, the government has authorized our laboratories to offer you the safety and medical kit, which at this moment is sold out in the market. We are giving you the priority to have access to the supplies needed before the states lock down.

Greetings. This is an automated message alert from the Worldwide Health Organization to inform you about the EPA's Emerging Viral Pathogen Program for the coronavirus protection. We offer you the opportunity to obtain the most powerful and secure protection equipment to protect yourself and all of your family members.

Thank you for calling the coronavirus hotline. Because of the limited testing we are first taking Medicare members. Will the free at-home test be just for you or for you and your spouse?

The above are actual examples of robocalls—some even repeated in fluent Chinese—made to unsuspecting consumers on their private numbers, people who, like the rest of us, are watching hospital beds fill up as the world coronavirus death toll rises each day. People just like you and me, who will do anything to keep our families safe.

Robocalls are, very simply, unsolicited calls from scammers to trick you into handing over your credit card information in exchange for either a bogus product or absolutely no product at all. And I'm not talking about some lonely guy in his basement making random calls—this is big business, and their attack plans are calculated and cold, raking in millions. Once you give them your banking info, the con on the other end of the line proceeds to raid your accounts, wreck your credit, and more. You can actually hear the calls above and many more just like them at NoMoRobo, a robocall blocking website.

Fear and panic, fueled by 24/7 news hysteria, have spawned countless robocall scams. From lotteries to get a COVID-19 cure to air-duct sanitizing to fake insurance and virus "cures," the calls are relentless. Some estimates are that, since the pandemic started, 1 million coronavirus calls are made every single day, scaring those who get the call and taking advantage of their fears and lack of real information.

How can you fight back against lowlife coronavirus robocalls? Here's how:

- Hang up! The moment you realize you don't recognize the voice on the phone and that voice mentions the coronavirus in relation to anything—be it insurance, a loan, a vaccine, or a face mask—don't wait to say goodbye. Don't worry about being rude; just hang up. Would you worry about being rude to an armed robber? They may not have a gun, but the caller is using coronavirus as a weapon...against you. Hang up.
- Don't wait to speak to someone to tell them how much you hate unsolicited calls or find out if the product is legit. It's not.
- For Pete's sake, don't buy anything or give out any of your information.
- Don't press any numbers, make any menu selection, or even press a number to "end the call" or "remove you from the call list." While the recording might tell you that pressing a number will direct you to a live operator or some other choice, pressing a digit may very well lead to even more robocalls to your number.
- Consider using an app like RoboKiller, Hiya, YouMail, Mr. Number, or NoMoRobo.
- Don't fall for calls boasting about a coronavirus home vaccination or testing kit. As of this writing, there is no coronavirus vaccine or treatment that can be administered at home, nor any authorized home-testing kit. Go to the FDA website to read more.
- If you are tempted by a phone solicitation, fact-check the information before you hand over your credit card number.
- Never respond to any call about getting money or checks from the government. The government will never call you about coronavirus benefits.
- Don't take calls purportedly from the CDC. Why? Because the Centers for Disease Control and Prevention and its experts aren't cold-calling you. For the very latest coronavirus info, go to the CDC or WHO website.
- Don't fork out for charities, donations, or crowdfunding appeals that cold-call you. It's highly likely they are not who they say they are. If you want to contribute, God bless you. Go to a legitimate charity like UMCOR, UNICEF, or the Red Cross. Make that donation count—don't line the pockets of a con artist or robocall behemoth sites.
- Don't fall for robocalls pitching loans or health insurance for coronavirus treatment expenses or services that claim to sanitize your home and "clean" away COVID-19.

- Know that robocallers can spoof or jigger with the caller ID number that pops up on your phone's screen, making it appear to be a number you may know, such as from your area code or using the first three digits of your neighborhood phones. That's called neighbor spoofing, and it makes you think you recognize the number.
- Your phone itself may actually be able to fight coronavirus robocalls, as many handsets now have built-in robocall blockers. Investigate whether your phone does. Go to Google and find the customer service number for the manufacturer of your phone. Call it and ask!
- Google has a new tool named Call Screen that comes in many of its smartphones. When you get an incoming call, tap "screen call." Google Assistant answers for you and asks the caller to ID themselves and give the purpose of their call. Then a transcript of the response pops up on your phone for you to see it. If it's a robocall, you can block the number from calling you again.
- Rule of thumb? Ignore incoming calls from any number you don't recognize. And never press a number on a call you did not initiate— even if some automated voice tells you to.

PHISHING, EMAIL AND TEXT SCAMS, AND FAKE ONLINE ADS

Phishing... what is it? Well, it's not with a line and pole, I can tell you that! In the criminal "phish tank," the con man has the hook, and you, sadly, are the little guppy swimming in a pool of coronavirus fear.

Simply put, phishing is when a perp impersonates a legitimate business and sends you emails, texts, or ads that entice you to pass on critical personal information such as your credit card number complete with security code and expiration date, debit card info, or banking details, such as an account number. Victims are also tricked into providing log-in information, home or business addresses, and even Social Security numbers.

Yes, I know it sounds outrageous and you think that could never happen to you, but it does. These emails look so perfectly legitimate that even an eagle-eyed consumer could fall for them. And if you do, the perps end up with your information, your location, your money, your credit, and maybe even your identity. Phishing scams can even worm in and gain access to your computer and accounts, such as your email account. They can install ransomware that lock you out of all your data or malware that infects your computer and accounts with destructive bugs.

In the time of coronavirus, it works like this: Cybercriminals email, claiming to be a legitimate entity passing on COVID-19 information. The email may direct you to open an attachment such as a list of safety measures, a coronavirus map, emergency procedures, shortage alerts, or statistics. The attachment could purport to be any number of things.

Once you click on the link or attachment, you unwittingly download malicious software, known as malware. That malware gives the cybercriminal control over your computer to access all your information and even log each and every one of your keystrokes. The download contains a virus that can then monitor all activity on your device, be it a tablet, phone, laptop, or desktop computer. If you log in to your employer's computer system, the perp or malware runs through the company's system as well.

How do they do it? How do they outsmart you? By posing as familiar companies or pretending to be someone you may know. It happened to me when I got an email from someone who purported to be American Express. The email looked almost identical to a real American Express email. It had the same pale blue colors and logo. It looked the same, but it wasn't.

My brother even got a fake court summons about a nonexistent case. That's bold! Now, amid fear, anxiety, and uncertainty, cybercriminals are using coronavirus to their own advantage. Some are even stooping to send missives purportedly from the CDC or the WHO.

Not surprisingly, coronavirus phishing is morphing by the hour, already assuming mew forms. Some phishing scams even include warnings, like "You are immediately advised to go through the cases above for safety hazard." According to Consumer Reports, fake emails apparently from the WHO or the CDC offer new updates about COVID-19, suggest an available vaccine or treatment, even claim to be a coronavirus victims charity. That's low.

Oftentimes, recipients are so concerned about the virus that they don't notice details that may otherwise ring a bell of alarm, like poor grammar or spelling mistakes. Also, right now there is a flood of legitimate coronavirus news and information being disseminated by the media, employers, schools, and vendors. The cyber perps hope to get lost in the jungle of legitimate data and ambush you to get a click.

A new ruse, phishing emails seemingly from your company's HR department, are on the rise. They want you to log on to a website posing as your company's website, and once the perp gets your username and password, it's over.

And now, headed our way is a brand-new scam originating out of the UK. Thousands of Brits got scary coronavirus texts supposedly from the government informing them they'd been fined for going out too much and/or straying too far from home during lockdown. The goal is to trick people who, like many of us, are under government-ordered coronavirus lockdown and acquire their credit card, debit card, or banking information. The texts, of course, are loaded with phishing links. And people fall for them! Why? Because many of us are used to getting caught, say, by a red-light or speeding camera. So when someone gets a fine for breaking curfew or lockdown, it seems real. It's not.

Phishing Ads

Scammers post ads about treatments or cures for coronavirus. The ads are usually scary and urgent, playing on fears for our families and ourselves. There are only two logical outcomes of this scenario. One, click on a fake ad and malware is download onto your device. Two, you buy the product and receive something useless or nothing at all. Regardless of the outcome, you very well may have shared personal information with an unknown entity that you can never get back.

Bottom line? It's smart to avoid any and all ads regarding coronavirus products from toothpaste to gargles, supplements to essential oils, coronavirus cures to respirators, investments in fake coronavirus-fighting ventures to donations to fake charities. Just say no by hitting the Delete button.

The US Cybersecurity and Infrastructure Security Agency has warned us about emails with malicious attachments or links to fraudulent websites. Victims often report the subject line relates to the coronavirus. Here are a few examples.

One scam sends emails offering a coronavirus document from the "Mongolian Health Ministry." Once you click on it, malware creeps into your device. "Official" documents—often purporting to come from China, Japan, or Korea—work as a hook to get your click, and they are especially alluring during the COVID-19 crisis.

Here's another: "New COVID-19 prevention and treatment information!

Attachment contains instructions from the US Department of Health on how to get the vaccine for FREE." Believe me, it's not legitimate. Click on this and it could cost you your whole bank account.

Here's another: "URGENT: COVID-19 ventilators and patient test delivery blocked. Please accept order here to continue with shipment." Don't accept it. It's not real.

There are literally hundreds more examples, but most important, how can you fight back? Here are some ways to recognize and avoid coronavirus phishing.

- BOLO! Be on the lookout for any request for your personal information. An unsolicited coronavirus email asking for personal info like a Social Security number or credit card numbers is no doubt a phishing scam. No legitimate health organization or government entity wants that information from you. Legitimate government agencies won't ask for that information. Don't click and don't respond.
- Look at the link and address. Hold the mouse or button over the URL. What does it say? If in doubt, don't click and immediately delete the email.
- Look for poor grammar, punctuation errors, and misspellings. Bad English is one indicator of a phish. Delete it.
- I love this one: "Recommend sanitizing your docs and air filters to protect your loved ones from the Corona virus. For only $159 our highly trained technicians will do a full air duck cleaning and sanitation to make sure the air you brief is free of bacteria. So don't hesitate. Have your duck system cleaned and sanitize now." Please, don't pay a "technician" to have your "ducks" cleaned.
- Beware of generic greetings like "to whom it may concern" or "Dear sir or madam." That's a red flag, and the missive is likely not legit.
- Urgent directives like "Hurry!" or "Must act now!" say only one thing: "Delete me!"
- Coronavirus home vaccines, cures, and home test kits are not real. Delete. Go to usa.gov/coronavirus to find the latest and most accurate coronavirus information.
- Don't click on messages about coronavirus-related government checks. Those agencies will not contact you out of the blue.
- If you spot a misspelling in the URL itself, such as "COVVID-19," it's phishing.

- Even if the website's URL starts with "https," that doesn't mean it's safe. Look closer.
- Do not open attachments from any unknown sender.
- Turn on all your auto updates, including those on your smart phone, desktop, laptop, and tablet. Make sure they're set to update automatically. The newest software is a must.
- Install an antivirus program. I like Norton.
- If any coronavirus-related claim sounds too good to be true, it probably is.

FAKE MEDICAL SUPPLIES, RESPIRATORS, AND FACE MASKS FLOODING THE MARKET

Fake Supplies and Undelivered Goods

In a mad rush to combat coronavirus, an important part of our armor is face masks and N95 respirators. They first popped up—outside the operating room, that is—in airports and on airplanes, a leftover from the SARS scare. Now they are commonplace at the grocery store, laundry, pharmacy, and even out in the open on public streets. Counterfeit goods have been around for a long time, from money to precious jewels to name-brand shoes, clothes, purses, and perfumes—anything can be faked. But who would ever have considered *counterfeit face masks*?

It's hard to believe, but fake masks aren't just sold on the street corners or by fraudsters online. In a very disturbing twist, Holy Name Medical Center in New Jersey was sent a total of one thousand N95 masks from a known vendor they'd worked with for some time. Holy Name is at the forefront fighting the coronavirus, so it was a shock when the hospital discovered the masks were fakes. According to NJ.com, the hospital's PR director, Jessica Griffin, stated the hospital has a policy of testing medical equipment before using it. She said the masks "did not fit the face area properly" and were not marked with specific Centers for Disease Control and Prevention approval labels.

There are three main categories of face mask: an ordinary face mask, a surgical face mask, and a respirator mask.

Ordinary masks are the thinnest. They are meant for day-to-day activities like cleaning and in no way do they provide proper filtration of particles and microorganisms. Although by far the most comfortable, ordinary masks are the least effective in protecting you from a contagious virus. A surgical face mask covers the mouth and nose. It typically is three-ply and has two loops to stretch behind the ears, holding the mask over the face. Face masks catch larger particles and droplets. A respirator is tighter fitting and creates a seal against the face to filter anything inhaled or exhaled by the wearer. A respirator provides the wearer more protection than an ordinary face mask does. There are three types of respirator masks: the disposable N95, the half face, and the full face.

In the time of coronavirus, face masks and respirator masks are in such demand that a huge black market in counterfeit masks has developed. Fakes do not provide the same level of protection as do the real thing. Far from keeping you safe, they can actually harm you, as many counterfeit face masks are made in highly unsterile conditions with zero quality control. Then you, the innocent consumer, put the fake directly over the noses and mouths of your children and family. Think about it: Face masks made in the same sweatshops and basements alongside fake purses and sneakers. Except you don't inhale and exhale directly through your knockoff designer purse or the soles of your fake name-brand sneakers.

But how do you spot a fake?

- Legitimate face masks are three-ply: a translucent layer, a second white layer, and a third colored or white layer. Cut open your mask. You should very clearly see three layers. If you don't, it's a fake.
- Examine the outer box. Look for a registration certificate number. If none appears, your product is likely a knockoff.
- On the real thing, typically there will be a visible product description including the words "medical surgical mask" or "medical protective mask." If it does not have the words "surgical" or "protective," you most likely have a fake.
- If you have 3M masks, simply check the anticounterfeit code on 3M's public WeChat account.
- Real respirators are form-fitting, made from fibrous material, and, like the N95 name suggests, filter out 95 percent of airborne particles. Fakes are pieced together with cloth and look more like surgical masks.

- Surgical masks protect from coughs and sneezes. Logically, the outer layer is waterproof. Test it: Fold your mask like a taco, then pour water into it. The mask should withstand the water, and the underside of the mask should not be damp. And the middle layer of a surgical mask is actually a filter, not just a layer of paper.

Fake Hand Sanitizer

Like other coronavirus-fighting products, hand sanitizer is in high demand. With stores and online vendors selling out of hand sanitizer, counterfeiters are making the most of public coronavirus fears. What can you do to fight back?

- Use logic. For instance, just as you would not expect to purchase a new widescreen plasma TV on a street corner or at a roadside stand, neither would you expect to find legitimate hand sanitizer at such a spot.
- Be wary of new vendors that have just started offering hand sanitizer. Why are they emerging now, in the midst of a global pandemic? There is no coincidence in criminal law.
- Make sure to read the customer ratings for online vendors. They speak volumes.
- Closely read the description online or at the vendor, including the ingredients. You may end up with simply jellied aloe vera or glycerin.
- Closely examine the photo online and at the vendor. Some brands are being counterfeited.

Home test kits, cures, and treatments, as of this writing, are *fakes*. Beware the burgeoning business of fake coronavirus-fighting products. Use caution!

Undelivered Goods

You go online and order coronavirus-fighting products, pay the bill, and then wait. But the products never arrive. You've either collided with major backorders or you've been scammed.

Vendors are facing high demand for medical supplies and health and cleaning products. But remember, anyone can claim to set up shop as a vendor online using practically any name, even names that sound reliable, such as Harvard Supply Warehouse or Jefferson Public Health Foundation. I just made those up. So can anyone else—including criminal con artists.

So what can you do to ensure your vendor is the real deal?

- Go online and search for the company's or person's name, email address, physical address, and phone number.
- Look for and read the company's customer reviews.
- Check for a history with the Better Business Bureau and with the consumer affairs division of your state's attorney general's office. For a list of state attorneys general, see naag.org.
- Google the company name combined with key words like *complaint*, *fraud*, and *scam.*
- Try your best to always pay by credit card so there is a record of your purchase. If you use cash, check, debit card, or money order, there may be no way to get a refund.
- Be prepared to contest the credit card charge if your items do not arrive within a reasonable period of time. If you used a credit card and you never get the products you wanted, you can at least get your money back.

Fake Charities

In a crisis like the coronavirus pandemic, cons crawl out of the woodwork. They even use your good heart and generosity to steal. Beware of charities springing up around the coronavirus. Fake charities may purport to be raising money for victims or research or otherwise fighting the virus. Be careful. Not only will you lose your heard-earned savings, but the money is diverted from real people in need. How to fight back?

- Some fraudsters create names that sound like a legitimate charity. Read the fine print.
- Research before you write that check. Find out who they are and what they really do to battle the virus and help those affected by it.
- Don't be hurried into a donation. If a charity insists on a cash gift, a money wire, or a gift card, just say no.
- Go to nasconet.org to locate the charity regulator for your state.

- Look for information on the charity in question at BBB Wise Giving Alliance, Charity Navigator, CharityWatch, or GuideStar websites.

LOOTING AND BURGLARIES

Police across the country are struggling to keep the peace during extraordinarily difficult times as looters and burglars take to the streets. With shelter in place, curfew, and lockdown orders in effect, bad guys who usually burgle private homes while residents are at work are now looking elsewhere. Easy targets? The pizza parlor, nail salon, or hardware store. All they need is a brick to break a window and they're in.

Looting is usually a grab-and-go mob activity. Looters seem to believe they are entitled to steal.

Even though South Carolina governor Henry McMaster declared a coronavirus state of emergency, two men apparently thought it would be a great idea to go looting. The *Rock Hill Herald News* says the two were arrested just outside a storage warehouse unit in Lake Wylie with stolen items and a stolen truck as well. Resulting charges included burglary, larceny, conspiracy, and possession of burglary tools. Looting is now a felony since Governor McMaster declared the state of emergency.

Police in Santa Cruz, California, busted five men who allegedly set out to rob and loot businesses even though there is a COVID-19 stay at home order by the governor in effect. To add insult to injury, the looters were reportedly wearing hard-to-find surgical face masks at the time of the crimes. Santa Cruz police, already stretched to the limit, are creating a Burglary Suppression Unit to fight looting.

Boarded-up storefronts are increasing. Retailers, bars, salons, restaurants, and other establishments, with no reopening date in sight, are trying to protect themselves from looters. The *Wall Street Journal* reports that business burglaries have risen sharply during the coronavirus emergency. There has been a 75 percent increase in commercial burglaries.

How to fight back?

- Move the most expensive material off-site for now.
- Install a security system that includes a ringing alarm as well as monitoring. They are now very affordable.

- Consider pooling the cost of a security guard with other businesses or residents in the area.
- As for individuals, stay away from retail and commercial areas as much as possible, especially at night. A would-be burglary can turn deadly in an instant.

IN CONCLUSION

For legitimate information about COVID-19, go to the Centers for Disease Control and Prevention at www.cdc.gov or the World Health Organization at https://www.who.int.

Learn the truth about how the coronavirus spreads, prevention and treatment, known cases in the US, symptoms, and travel restrictions.

As of this writing, there is no cure and no way to gauge the impact coronavirus will have on our families, our communities, our country, and our world. But it is possible to fight back. Protect yourself and the ones you love.

Don't be a victim. Keep the faith.

Conclusion

Writing this has been a labor of love, love for all the crime victims and their families I've met, worked with, counseled, direct examined, visited in their homes, and interviewed. There are thousands of them, but they never run together in my mind. From the little girls with a hundred barrettes in their hair to Ms. Leola and her beautiful, solid white living room where she sat like a queen, knitting. Their voices must be heard. But I truly believe what they have to say is not some melancholy dirge.

Instead, we all join in an effort to do the near-impossible: stop history from repeating itself and save one person, maybe you or your child or your senior or someone you love deeply, from the lifetime of consequences that a violent crime inflicts. Crime is ever-changing and ever-adapting to more cunningly rob victims of their joy and more. But it doesn't have to be that way.

Join us. Don't give in to what seems inevitable. Don't be a victim. Fight back against a crime wave that often seems bigger than us. But it's not. In the words of Saint Timothy, keep the faith, fight the good fight, and stay strong to the finish, friend.

Thank you for spending time with me and the many voices that have contributed to this book.

Acknowledgments

To every victim, family, or witness that inspired me and touched my life, thank you.

To Gretchen Young, "my partner in crime" who made this dream become a reality. Gretchen was the North Star of this project, and I am, yet again, so grateful.

To John Hassan, I can't thank you enough for being there every day to make *Don't Be a Victim* happen. You are talented and dedicated—thank you. I'm so glad I found you.

To Dr. William Suttles and the Honorable Lewis Slaton, you gave me the chance of a lifetime, my big opportunity.

To Dee Emmerson, my friend, thank you for all the love and support.

To my sweet twins, you brought love to my life and sat by my side for all the months I wrote and wrote. You inspire me. You give me a reason to go on.

To David, you changed my life so many years ago and you change my life every day. Thank you.

To my viewers, listeners, and readers, you have been by my side for so long and I never forget. Thank you.

And of course, I thank heaven for turning my life around, giving me purpose and strength to keep the faith.

Index

About the Author

An outspoken, tireless advocate for victims' rights and one of television's most respected legal analysts, Nancy Grace is currently headlining Oxygen's all-new series *Injustice with Nancy Grace* and appears regularly on ABC's *20/20* and *Nightline*. She is the founder and publisher of CrimeOnline.com, a crime-fighting digital platform that investigates breaking crime news, spreads awareness of missing people, and shines a light on cold cases. In addition, *Crime Stories with Nancy Grace*, a daily show hosted by Grace, airs on Sirius XM's Triumph Channel 111 terrestrial radio and is downloadable as a podcast. Previously, she was the powerful force behind CNN Headline News' top-rated *Nancy Grace*.

A former prosecutor with an unparalleled record of success, she has guested on *The Jimmy Kimmel Show*, *The Oprah Winfrey Show*, *The View*, the *Today* show, *The Dr. Oz Show*, *Dr. Phil*, and *Larry King Live*, among others, dispensing her firebrand take on the modern justice system. In addition, she was a highlight and fan favorite of *Dancing with the Stars* season 13, finishing in the competition's coveted top five. All of her earnings from the show went to support the National Center for Missing and Exploited Children. In 2011, Grace was named one of the most impactful and powerful women in entertainment by both leading industry trade magazines, *Variety* and *The Hollywood Reporter*.

Grace's first book, *Objection!*, was published in 2005 and became an instant *New York Times* bestseller. Her two subsequent novels, *The Eleventh Victim* (2009) and *Death on the D-List* (2010), were also *New York Times* bestsellers. Her latest work of fiction, *Murder in the Courthouse*, was released in time to coincide with the first in a series of Hallmark movies based on her popular characters, including crime fighter Hailey Dean.

Nancy is the recipient of a TV Daytime Emmy for her legal

contributions on *Daily Mail TV*, several American Women in Radio & Television Gracie Awards for her "Nancy Grace Investigates" prime time report on Court TV and has been awarded the Individual Achievement/Best Program Host honor. Grace has also been widely recognized by many notable victims' rights organizations.

Grace's life changed forever in 1979 when her fiancé, Keith Griffin, was shot and killed. In the aftermath of that crime, Nancy abandoned plans to become an English professor and turned her focus to criminal justice. She became a Law Review graduate of Mercer Law School, then received her Master of Law degree in constitutional and criminal law from New York University. Additionally, she manned the hotline at an Atlanta battered women's center for nearly ten years.

Nancy Grace initially came to television from the Atlanta Fulton County District Attorney's Office, where she served for a decade as a special prosecutor of felony cases involving murder, rape, child molestation, and arson. Known for her authentic sensibility and for not holding back her opinion on high-profile cases, she was tapped to co-host Court TV's *Cochran and Grace* and, later, the live daily trial coverage program *Closing Arguments*. She also presided over the daytime hit *Swift Justice with Nancy Grace*, for which she received an Emmy Award nomination.

Grace married investment banker David Linch in 2007. Another life milestone followed: the birth of twins John David and Lucy. "These babies are my miracles," she says. Nancy, her husband, her mom, and her twins reside in Atlanta and New York City with their rescue pets: a dog, a cat, and two guinea pigs